GALERIUS AND THE WILL OF DIOCLETIAN

Between Diocletian and Constantine, there was Galerius. *Galerius and the Will of Diocletian* offers a fresh study of this critical period in the transformation of the Roman world. Using the political and personal relationship between the great emperor Diocletian and Galerius, his junior colleague and successor, the book comes to some quite different conclusions about the nature of Diocletian's regime than previously accepted. Drawing from a variety of sources − literary, visual, archaeological; papyri, inscriptions and coins − the author studies the nature of Diocletian's imperial strategy, his wars, his religious views and his abdication. The author also examines Galerius' endeavour to take control of Diocletian's empire, his failures and successes, against the backdrop of Constantine's remorseless drive to power.

The work is built from the premise that the "Tetrarchy", which Diocletian is often thought to have crafted as a revolutionary alternative to unstable military monarchy, is a creation of modern scholarship and does not actually emerge from the ancient sources. Instead, Leadbetter argues that Diocletian was seeking to craft a dynasty along more traditional lines, using adoption (as had so many of his predecessors) as a tool of statecraft. Galerius, however, did not prove equal to his inheritance, which was ultimately usurped by the more astute and ruthless Constantine.

The first comprehensive study of the Emperor Galerius, this book offers an innovative analysis of his reign as both Caesar and Augustus, using his changing relationship with Diocletian as the principal key to unlock the complex imperial politics of the period.

Bill Leadbetter, School of Education, Edith Cowan University, Australia.

D1595793

ROMAN IMPERIAL BIOGRAPHIES

FOR MAIA
OPTIMA PUELLA

GALERIUS AND THE WILL OF DIOCLETIAN

Bill Leadbetter

Routledge
Taylor & Francis Group

LONDON AND NEW YORK

First published in hardback 2009
First published in paperback 2013
by Routledge
2 Park Square, Milton Park, Abingdon, Oxon OX14 4RN

Simultaneously published in the USA and Canada
by Routledge
711 Third Avenue, New York, NY 10017

Routledge is an imprint of the Taylor & Francis Group, an informa business

© 2009, 2013 Bill Leadbetter

Typeset in Garamond by Taylor & Francis

British Library Cataloguing in Publication Data
A catalogue record for this book is available from the British Library

Library of Congress Cataloging in Publication Data
Leadbetter, Bill.
Galerius and the will of Diocletian/Bill Leadbetter.
p. cm.
"Simultaneously published in the USA and Canada"–T.p. verso.
Includes bibliographical references.
1. Galerius, Emperor of Rome, ca. 260-313. 2. Emperors–
Rome–Biography. 3. Emperors–Succession–Rome. 4. Diocletian,
Emperor of Rome, 245-313–Influence. 5. Diocletian, Emperor of Rome,
245-313–Political and social views. 6. Constantine I, Emperor of Rome,
d. 337 7. Imperialism–History–To 1500. 8. Rome–Politics and
government–284-476. 9. Rome–History–Empire, 284-476.
10. Rome–History, Military–30 B.C.-476 A.D. I. Title.
DG314.L43 2009
937'.08092–dc22
[B] 2009031764

ISBN13: 978-0-415-40488-4 (HB)
ISBN13: 978-0-415-85971-4 (PB)
ISBN13: 978-0-203-86928-4 (EB)

Printed and bound in the United States of America by Publishers Graphics,
LLC on sustainably sourced paper.

CONTENTS

ACKNOWLEDGEMENTS

Humans gestate for thirty nine weeks. This book has taken somewhat longer. Its origins lie in an undergraduate seminar class that I took in 1978 at Macquarie University. Entitled "Rome under the Tetrarchs", it was led by Ted Nixon, at that stage beginning to make inroads into his long, and now seminal study of late Latin panegyric. It was then, and at Ted's suggestion, that I began to work on Galerius. That interest led to my 1994 Macquarie doctoral dissertation on Galerius, and thence to this work. At every stage, Ted's help, criticism, advice and counsel has been invaluable. He has been both mentor (in the best sense of the word) and staunch friend. I was also fortunate to be an undergraduate at a particular time in Macquarie's history. Edwin Judge taught me to look for what was actually in the evidence rather than impose a view upon it. The argument that this book adopts was formed in partial response to long reflection upon his lectures on the Augustan principate. Margaret Beattie taught me to be an acute critic of my own work; to read it carefully, and have it read, before seeking to rule the line of completion. I owe debts of different kinds to other friends and former Macquarie colleagues, in particular Lea Beness, David Clarke, Geoffrey Cowling, Alan Dearn, Tom Hillard, Sam Lieu and Alanna Nobbs.

Over the years, I have been fortunate in receiving support, advice, offprints and enjoyable conversation from scholars working in the field. I owe particular debts to Timothy Barnes, Alan Bowman, Peter Brennan, Simon Corcoran, Brian Croke, Hal Drake, Philip Esler, Walter Goffart, Jill Harries, Robert Hohlfelder, Mark Humphreys, John Matthews, Fergus Millar, Tom Parker, Roger Rees, Steven Sidebotham, Alan Walmsley, Bryan Ward-Perkins, Everett Wheeler and Greg Woolf.

In Perth, I have received some financial support from Edith Cowan University that allowed important visits to Thessaloniki in 1999 and 2007, as well as the leave that promoted the peaceful composition of some of the work in the congenial cylinder that is the Sackler Library. While in Greece, I enjoyed the facilities of the Australian Archaeological Institute in Athens, and access to the Library of the German Archaeological Institute through the good offices of its then director, Hermann Kienast. While in Oxford, I have been fortunate to have had the support of Wolfson College. I have also enjoyed the company, the friendship and the professionalism of Western Australian colleagues, most particularly Peter Bedford, Alex Jensen and David Kennedy.

I would also like to acknowledge the enthusiastic support of Mihailo Milinkovic, Mr Bora Dimitrijevic, Director of the National Museum of Zajecar, and Maja Zivic. Every scholar with whom I have spoken, corresponded and exchanged offprints about Galerius has contributed, no matter how indirectly, to this work. Its faults, infelicities and imperfections, however, remain my doing.

I first learned Ancient History at the feet of Mr Richard Rowling at Barker College in 1974 and 1975. His enthusiasm for his subject and his love for learning have provided me with a profound model for my professional life. My debt to him is incalculable. I continued to learn and teach Ancient History with the loving support of my late parents, Archelias Victor Leadbetter and Ruby Isobel Leadbetter. I wish they could have seen this book. I owe great thanks to Catherine Arends, who travelled with me when she could, bore my absences when she could not, provided me with decisive encouragement to finish and gave me my greatest treasure.

My partner, Margo, has been an enthusiastic source of support, and happily tolerated my lonely affair with the computer in my study. I owe her a great debt for her patience, her wisdom, her fortitude, her beauty and her love. My daughter Maia looked at me as I worked on this not long ago, and her eyes grew wide as she saw the number of words on the page. Even so, this work is for her.

ABBREVIATIONS

Abbreviations for the names of journals are those customarily used in similar works and can be found listed in any edition of *L'année philologique*. Other abbreviations used in the text and notes of this book but not otherwise customary are as follows:

ANRW	H. Temporini (ed.) (1972–) *Aufstieg und Niedergang der Romischen Welt*, Stuttgart
CAH XII	S.A. Cook, F.E. Adcock, M.P. Charlesworth and N.H. Baynes (eds) (1939) *The Cambridge Ancient History*, Vol. XII, 1st edn, Cambridge
CE	T.D. Barnes (1981) *Constantine and Eusebius*, Cambridge, MA
Chron Min	T. Mommsen (ed.) (1892) *Chronica Minora, Monumenta Germaniae Historicae: Auctores Antiquissimi,* Vols IX, XI, XIII, Berlin
CIL	*Corpus Inscriptionum Latinarum,* Berlin, 1863ff.
CLRE	R.S. Bagnall, Alan Cameron, Seth R. Schwartz and K.I. Worp (1987) *Consuls of the Later Roman Empire*, Atlanta
CJ	*"Codex Iustinianus"*, in S.P. Scott (1932) *Corpus Iuris Civilis,* Vols 12–17, Cincinnati
C.Th	C. Pharr (1951) *The Theodosian Code and Novels and the Sirmondian Constitutions: A Translation with Commentary, Glossary and Bibliography,* Princeton
FGH	C. Müller (1848–51) *Fragmenta Historicorum Graecorum*, Frankfurt-am-Main
ILS	H. Dessau (1892) *Inscriptiones Latinae Selectae,* 5 vols, Berlin
Jakoby *Fr Gr. Hist.*	F. Jacoby (1923–) *Die Fragmente der greichischen Historiker*, Berlin and London
NE	T.D. Barnes (1982) *The New Empire of Diocletian and Constantine,* Cambridge, MA

PLRE I	A.H.M. Jones, J.R. Martindale and J. Morris (1971) *The Prosopography of the Later Roman Empire*, Vol. I, Cambridge
RIC V1	P.H. Webb (1927) *Roman Imperial Coinage*, Vol. V, Part I, London
RIC V2	P.H. Webb (1933) *Roman Imperial Coinage*, Vol. V, Part II, London
RIC VI	C.H.V. Sutherland and R.A.G. Carson (1967) *Roman Imperial Coinage*, Vol. VI, London

Editions and translations of principal primary sources consulted

Ammianus Marcellinus (Amm. Marc.):

J.C. Rolfe (1950) *Ammianius Marcellinus with an English Translation*, 3 vols, rev. edn, Cambridge, MA

Aurelius Victor (Aur. Vict.):

H.W. Bird (1994) *Aurelius Victor: de Caesaribus. Translated with an Introduction and Commentary*, Translated Texts for Historians, vol. 17, Liverpool
Fr. Pichlmayr (1970) *Sextus Aurelius Victor: de Caesaribus*, Leipzig

Epitome de Caesaribus (Ep. de Caes.):

Fr. Pichlmayr (1970) *Sextus Aurelius Victor: de Caesaribus*, Leipzig, 133–76

Eunapius:

R.C. Blockley (1983) *The Fragmentary Classicising Historians of the Later Roman Empire*, Vol. II, Liverpool, 2–151
W.C. Wright (1921) *Philostratus and Eunapius: The Lives of the Sophists*, Cambridge, MA

Eusebius (Eus.):

F.C. Conybeare (1912) "Contra Hieroclem", in *Philostratus: The Life of Apollonius of Tyana*, Cambridge, MA, pp. 484–605
H. Delehaye (1897) *de Martyribus Palestinae: longionis libelli fragmenta*, Brussels
R. Helm (1956) *Die Chronik des Hieronymus*, Berlin
Kirsopp Lake (1926) *Eusebius: Ecclesiastical History*, Vol. I (Books 1–5), Cambridge

J.E.L. Oulton (1932) *Eusebius: Ecclesiastical History*, Vol. II (Books 6–10), Cambridge

E.C. Richardson (1890) "The Life of Constantine by Eusebius, together with the Oration of Constantine to the Assembly of the Saints and the Oration of Eusebius in Praise of Constantine", in P. Schaff and H. Wace (eds), *A Select Library of the Nicene and Post-Nicene Fathers of the Christian Church*, Vol. I, Grand Rapids, rep. 1979, 473–610.

Eutropius (Eutr.):

H.A. Bird (1993) *Eutropius: Breviarium: Translated with an Introduction and Commentary*, Translated Texts for Historians, vol. 14, Liverpool

H. Verheyk (1821) *Eutropii Breviarium Historiae Romanae*, London

P'awstos Buzanda:

N. Garsoian (1989) *The Epic Histories Attributed to P'awstos Buzand: Translation and Commentary*, Cambridge, MA

Festus:

J.W. Eadie (1967) *The Breviarium of Festus: A Critical Edition with Historical Commentary*, London

Jordanes (Jord.):

C.C. Mierow (1915) *The Gothic History of Jordanes in English Version, with an Introduction and Commentary*, Princeton, NJ

Lactantius (Lact.):

A. Cleveland Coxe (1979) *The Ante-Nicene Fathers*, Vol VII: *Lactantius, Venantius, Asterius, Victorinus, Dionysius, Apostolic Teaching and Constitutions, Homily and Liturgies*, rep. 1979, Grand Rapids, MI, 9–328

J.L. Creed (1984) *Lactantius: de mortibus persecutorum*, Oxford Early Christian Texts, Oxford

J. Moreau (1954) *Lactance: de la mort des persécuteurs*, Sources Chrétiennes, 39, Paris

Malalas:

E. Jeffreys, M. Jeffreys, R. Scott *et al.* (1986) *The Chronicle of John Malalas: A Translation*, Byzantina Australiensia 4, Melbourne

Origo Constantini Inperatoris (Origo):

J. Moreau (1968) *Excerpta Valesiana* (rev. V. Velkov), Berlin

Panegyrici Latini (Pan. Lat.):

E. Galletier (1952) *Panégyriques Latins*, 3 vols, Paris
R.A.B. Mynors (1964) *Panegyrici Latini*, Oxford
C.E.V. Nixon and Barbara Saylor Rodgers (1994) *In Praise of Later Roman Emperors: The Panegyrici Latini: Introduction, Translation and Historical Commentary*, Berkeley, Los Angeles and Oxford

Scriptores Historiae Augustae (SHA):

D. Magie (1921) *The Scriptores Historiae Augustae: With an English Translation*, 3 vols, Cambridge, MA

Zonaras:

M. Pinder (1841) *Ioannis Zonarae: Annales,* 2 vols, CSHB, Bonn

Zosimus (Zos.):

L. Mendelssohn (1887) *Zosimus: Historia Nova*, Leipzig
F. Paschoud (1971) *Zosime: Histoire Nouvelle*, Paris
R.T. Ridley (1982) *Zosimus*, Byzantina Australiensia 2, Melbourne

INTRODUCTION

This book is not a biography. The conditions for the construction of a coherent and meaningful biography do not, in this case, exist. We have none of the writings of Galerius, nor evidence of the kind of person he was, or of his reflections upon the events and personalities of his time. Rather, the principal focus of this book is what the life and career of Galerius can tell us about the events of his lifetime and, in particular, the nature and course of imperial politics. This is not a social history, nor does it (other than in passing) analyse the spiritual and economic crises of the period. The focus here is on imperial politics, not in some slavish adherence to a "great man" view, but because of a basic view that politics is important. Political history is a study of the ways in which individuals in positions of authority interact with contemporary social movements and, through that interaction, change their world. The Roman world was a very different place after Diocletian's abdication than before his accession. That is a reflection of the way in which he had affected his world.

Diocletian's "new empire" (as Gibbon called it) can be seen in retrospect as a critical period of transition for the Roman world. The year 284 is often taken (for good or ill) as the beginning of Late Antiquity. A.H.M. Jones, for example, defined it as such by taking that year as the chronological commencement of his history of the Later Roman Empire. It is also, famously, the year in which the Oxford Modern History syllabus commences, and therefore the year that Ancient History ends. Yet it did not seem so at the time. Just as Napoleon Buonaparte was not aware that he was commencing a period known in many textbooks as "Modern History", neither did Diocletian (nor any but the most prescient of his contemporaries) realize that an old epoch was fading away and a new one emerging. For a period which is so critical in the history of the Roman world it is not widely or accessibly treated. Most of the scholarly material is in languages other than English. There are some nineteenth-century studies of the period in German, although they are difficult to find and understandably dated. In the last century Ensslin published a superb study in the *Realenzyklopädie* and, in 1987, Frank Kolb published his book on the period 284–305, *Diocletian und die erste Tetrarchie: Improvisation oder Experiment in der Organisation der monarchischer Herrschaft?* In French, William Seston published his *Dioclétien et la Tétrarchie* in 1946. It was intended to be the first volume of a longer work, but no further volumes were ever published. His scholarly mantle was taken

1

up in the Francophone world by André Chastagnol. In Italian, G. Costa wrote a magisterial and highly influential entry on Diocletian in the *Dizionario Epigrafico* and, in 1979, Anna Pasqualini published her study of Maximian Herculius, *Massimiano Herculius: per un'interpretazione della figura e dell'opera*. In English, the scholarly work of T.D. Barnes has been fundamental, although that scholar preferred to concentrate his attention on the enigma of Constantine. Otherwise, there has been the derivative and unsatisfactory book by Stephen Williams, *Diocletian and the Roman Recovery*.

One of the purposes of this study is to provide a proper and scholarly analysis of the political and diplomatic history of the period for colleagues, students and others whose first and/or best language is English. There will be a necessary amount of rethinking and reinterpretation here. There is new evidence to be deployed, and old evidence to be carefully reread. Galerius has been a convenient device by which to explain two of Diocletian's less explicable acts: his instigation of the "Great" Persecution and his abdication. Much has been asserted about Galerius' negative role in forcing an unwilling college of colleagues to mount an attack upon the Christian community; likewise on Galerius' preying upon an enfeebled Diocletian in order to bring about the abdications of the Augusti in 305. The evidence for this is distorted by polemic and requires an approach which takes a wider perspective. Moreover, any progress to an understanding of the nature of Diocletian's empire must begin with the interrogation both of the basic working assumption which has marked scholarship for the best part of a century, the concept of "Tetrarchy", and also of the major sources which permit us to enter into analysis and discussion of the political world of the late third and early fourth centuries. Having proceeded with this initial analysis, the text will then be structured into diachronically defined chapters. The reader expecting detailed treatments of Diocletian's reforms will be disappointed. His military, economic and administrative reforms have been treated thoroughly in other contexts, and there is nothing that can be added here which cannot be read more elegantly elsewhere. But they are here in a sense. The will of Diocletian knew no convenient boundaries.

Narratives of Tetrarchy

Diocletian had by now matured his schemes for the division of imperial power and chosen the right men for his purpose, perhaps as early as 292, or 291, though the formal act of investiture seems to have fallen in 293. Constantius Chlorus, a Dardanian nobleman of high repute and tried merit, was appointed Caesar to Maximian in the West, while Galerius, a rough but able soldier took the same rank under Diocletian in the East. To bind both Caesars to himself and his colleague, Diocletian required them to put away their wives and marry the crown princesses. Constantius put away Helena,

mother of Constantine, and married Theodora, daughter of Maximian, while Galerius gave up his former wife to marry Diocletian's
daughter, Valeria. Thus was established the famous Tetrarchy of
Diocletian.[1]

So wrote Harold Mattingly in the first edition of the *Cambridge Ancient History*, published in 1939. These firm and confident sentences, with their florid
coda, have served ever since as a convenient summary of Diocletian's policies
and arrangements. Its clear and positivist certainty has provided generations
of readers with a kind of confidence in the political narratives of late antiquity that is entirely unmerited. The concept of the Tetrarchy has become
pervasive: there are studies of tetrarchic iconography, law, imperial policy.[2]
It has generated an adjective ("tetrarchic") that is regularly employed to
describe dates, objects and policies – a practice in which the present author
has also engaged. The reason is its simple utility. It can be an effective
shorthand for a vast and sustained period of reform between 284 and 337, a
half-century which has been more properly labelled a "new empire".[3] Its
repetition does not, however, reflect an undeniable historical truth, but a
more dubious verisimilitude.

The word "tetrarch" has a respectable history in antiquity. "Tetrarchs"
were independent rulers of portions of a kingdom, most famously post-
Herodian Judaea, divided between surviving sons.[4] Later in the century,
Pliny the Elder described tetrarchies as *regnorum instar singulae et in regna
contribuuntur* ("each is the equivalent of a kingdom, and also part of one").[5]
But at no point was the term ever employed to refer to collegial power: a
"tetrarch" was not one of four rulers but the ruler of a quarter of a discrete
region. It is hardly surprising to find that Diocletian, his colleagues and
successors were never referred to in antiquity as "tetrarchs". A late fourth-
century pastiche refers to them as *quattuor ... principes mundi*: "four rulers of
the world".[6] Ammianus represents Constantius II as reminding Julian that
the Caesars submitted to Diocletian and Maximian in the manner of servants.[7] Julian himself likened the four to a chorus clustered around a leader,
remarkable for their deference and unanimity.[8] Lactantius, a contemporary
and a deep ideological opponent, simply refers, rather testily, to a multiplicity
of rulers.[9]

It was Edward Gibbon who, in magnificent and laudatory prose, identified
the "new empire" as an entirely new system for the mediation of power.
Gibbon's Diocletian is a noble prince and wise politician, a man, above all,
of reason and moderation. His new system deployed pomp and ceremony
to defend an augmented imperial office, and he presided over an Empire
carefully and wisely redivided into regions and departments. The edifice was
built upon the sharing of power and its devolution. Colleagues were
appointed to share in rule since management of the whole was beyond one
man.[10] Gibbon's Diocletian is a man of reason and his arrangements are to

3

be comprehended as the constructions of a rational man. Gibbon's political analysis of Diocletian's entirely sensible, indeed clockwork, reform of the imperial office has been deeply influential and still provokes responses.[11] It was not, however, Gibbon who called it a "Tetrarchy".

Indeed, the term does not seem to have been devised for this purpose until the 1870s. A number of significant nineteenth-century studies of Diocletian passed without using it: Moriz Ritter, in 1862, wrote a dissertation on Diocletian's reforms omitting to employ it or even, since he wrote in Latin, the word *quattuorvirate*; Theodor Preuss, in 1867, employed a synonymous phrase, "der Regierung der vier Kaiser".[12] Twenty years later, however, Hermann Schiller, in his *Geschichte der Römischen Kaiserzeit*, wrote clearly of a system which he labels "die diokletianische Tetrarchie".[13] Schiller was a school principal and a professor of education and his two-volume work seems to have the quality of a handbook.[14] The term was not picked up swiftly or comprehensively. Indeed, scholars seem to have avoided it for a long time. Mommsen did not use it, although he also argued that Diocletian created a governmental system. K.-F. Kinch appears not to have heard of it since it would have provided a powerful shorthand for his discussion of the ideological imagery of relief-panels on the Arch of Galerius.[15]

In 1897, however, Otto Seeck employed it, and it is tempting to ascribe the wider circulation of the word to him.[16] Francophone scholars, in particular, seem to have picked up on it. In 1908, Jean Maurice published his hugely influential *Numismatique Constantinienne*, in which, citing Schiller, he both uses the term "tetrarchy" and gives a brief definition: "*Cet empereur était le chef incontesté de la tétrarchie, son system fut, comme l'ensemble de sa legislation, adopté dans tout l'Empire, et il y fut seul appliqué jusqu'a 309.*"[17] In the same year, J.-B. Mispoulet employed the term in a study of the chronology of the reign of Maximian, and, in 1912, the legal historian Goyau published a description of Diocletian's legal policy in which he employed the word in the title.[18] Costa, the great Italian scholar, in his mighty article on Diocletian in the *Dizionario Epigrafico*, citing Schiller, wrote of the tetrarchs of "*il nuovo regime*", and labelled this regime a tetrarchy.[19] Others were less eager. Kurt Stade, in his 1926 study *Der Politiker Diokletian und die letzte grosse Christenverfolgung*, preferred the clumsy term *Mitregentschaftssystem* to the more elegant "Tetrarchy".[20] In Anglophone scholarship, P.H. Webb wrote a long article on Carausius, published in 1907, which appears ignorant of the term; J.B. Bury referred to Diocletian's "throne system"; J.G.C. Anderson used the phrase "Diocletian's joint reign" in a 1932 article; Mattingly and Sydenham examined and catalogued the coins of Diocletian and his colleagues up until 297 without once referring to "tetrarchs" or "tetrarchy"; N.H. Baynes, always careful with terminology, confessed himself deeply sceptical about the whole proposition as late as 1948.[21]

The most significant study at this time to pick up on the term was that by Ernst Kornemann of collegiate emperors. His work, published in 1930, employed and expanded it, identifying no fewer than five different "tetrarchies".[22] Kornemann's ideas of a number of successive tetrarchies were subsequently brought into the world of Anglophone scholarship by H.M.D. Parker's highly influential narrative, published in 1935,[23] and its effect can be seen in the German-speaking academy in successive fascicles of the *Real-Encyclopädie*. The biographies of Diocletian, Maximian and Galerius were all written by Wilhelm Enßlin. Those of Maximian and Galerius appeared in a fascicle published in 1928, and that of Diocletian was published a full twenty years later.[24] As is customary for that vast undertaking, Ensslin trawled both the sources and the scholarship meticulously before constructing his entries. His entries on both Maximian and Galerius, both heavily citing both Seeck and Schiller, disclose only one use of the term "tetrarchy" apiece. His 1948 entry on Diocletian, however, places far greater weight on the concept, defining it in the following terms:

> *So war die Tetrarchie der beiden Augusti und ihrer Caesares zu einer teils fiktiven, teils wirklichen Herrscherfamilie geworden, und damit war zugleich die Nachfolgefrage geregelt.*[25]

> (Thus was the Tetrarchy of the two Augusti and their Caesars, being part virtual, part real ruling family, and, at the same time, the succession question was regulated therewith.)

By that time, the idea of the Tetrarchy was well entrenched. Enßlin not only cites the authorities of twenty years before, but adds Kornemann and Mattingly's ebullient *Cambridge Ancient History* article with which this introduction began. He might also have cited Straub's critical study of late antique imperial ideology,[26] his own 1942 monograph on Diocletian's eastern policy,[27] Seston's *Dioclétien et la Tétrarchie* (1946) or, – most interestingly – L'Orange's 1938 study of the Decennial monument in Rome which was, perhaps, the first reference to "tetrarchic art".[28] It is a curious thing that Mattingly might refer, in 1939, to the Tetrarchy as "famous", whereas a decade earlier he, like many other scholars, did not employ the term. Although invented by Schiller and deployed by Seeck and a number of French scholars, its fame is, perhaps, most due to Kornemann. His rearticulation of the idea, together with both a clear definition and succession of tetrarchies, provided a clear model for scholars either to react to or to employ.

One might ask, with some justice, if this matters. It does not insofar as the term is employed as a scholarly shorthand for the period of collegiate rule between 284 and (arguably) 324, and artefacts, architecture, texts or any other *testimonia* of the period. It does matter, however, if one mistakes the term for precision. A "dyarchy" very clearly signifies a joint sovereignty between two rulers, but for most of the "tetrarchic" period, such a symmetry of two (legitimate) Augusti and two Caesars was not in evidence. For 285–293,

Diocletian ruled collegially with Maximian only. From 310 until Galerius' death in 311 there were four Augusti (notwithstanding the failed attempt to content Constantine and Maximinus with the title *filius Augustorum*); from May 311 until July/August 313, there were three Augusti. From then until 324, there were two Augusti and three Caesars. While it is arguable that this simply reflects the breakdown of the tetrarchic system, it must be considered that there was never much of a system in the first place. There is very little evidence for one in fact, and what there is has been inferred from events. This is as true for Lactantius as it is for Gibbon.

It would, indeed, be surprising to find that Diocletian was the author of a radical and innovative restructuring of the imperial office. The contemporary evidence would seem to suggest a profoundly conservative man. The models of active (rather than nominal) collegial empire which existed were essentially dynastic: Marcus Aurelius with his adoptive brother, Lucius Verus; Valerian with his son Gallienus; Carus with his son Carinus; Carinus with his brother Numerian. Diocletian, however, had no son, nor is there any evidence for a brother. Adoption and association were ancient strategies to make good deficiencies of kinship. Augustus had employed it on numerous occasions and had himself been (posthumously) adopted by Caesar; Claudius had adopted Nero; Nerva had adopted Trajan; Hadrian's claim to legitimacy was a vague family propinquity with Trajan supported by a claim to adoption; Hadrian himself adopted, successively, Aelius Caesar and Antoninus Pius; Pius adopted Marcus Aurelius and Lucius Verus. As has long been settled, there was no "adoptive principle" nor an inherent meritocracy at work. These are the precedents, however, which conditioned Diocletian's policy. They lay firmly behind his thinking. Yet they were all essentially dynastic decisions. They kept power in the family by enlarging the family, with recruits from the imperial ruling class – principally the senatorial aristocracy. Were Diocletian's choices of colleague, then, of the same nature? Were they dictated by principle or did they make a virtue of necessity? It is this question that employment of the term "tetrarchy" can serve to obfuscate, implying that an essentially private dynastic arrangement was a constitutional form.

Narratives of Diocletian and Galerius

The primary sources give little clear guidance on this issue, although, as far as the quantity and quality of source material is concerned, we are better served for this period than for most of the third century. Most of the narrative material is, in some sense, polemical. Nor should it be assumed that, simply because an account purports to detail, it is well informed. There are three, essentially narrative, sets of sources which are directly contemporary: the works of Lactantius; the works of Eusebius; and the corpus of Gallic Panegyrics, eight of which were delivered at dates between 289 and 313. Each of these three *corpora* reflects a different perspective, or, rather, range of perspectives. Two of them are conditioned by the experience of persecution and partisanship for Constantine, while the third walks the perilous tightrope of simultaneously saying what an emperor wishes to hear and what the speaker wishes to say.

Lactantius

The most influential source has been Lactantius. His *de mortibus persecutorum* provides the only contemporary narrative account of imperial politics. Like many political narratives, it is a document which reflects contemporary political discourse. Just as the panegyrics provide a discourse on behalf of the powerful, Lactantius' narrative is redolent with the gloating bitterness of one who has long been in opposition. Little enough is known of Lactantius' life. Our fullest account is the brief notice in Jerome's *de viris illustribus*. This states that he was a student of Arnobius, presumably at Sicca in Africa, that he came to Nicomedia with the grammarian Flavius to teach rhetoric, suffered penury because of an ancient preference in that place for Greek letters and, in old age, was tutor to Constantine's son Crispus in Gaul.[29] Jerome also gives a list of his works, one of which was written in Africa and another about his journey to Nicomedia. Later works include the *de Ira Dei*, the *Institutiones Divinae*, an epitome of that work, one book *de Persecutione*, some letters, and the *de Opficio Dei*.

There are few fixed points in the chronology of his life. One is his education of Crispus. That prince's execution in 326 gives us a *terminus ante quem* of some kind.[30] Crispus was, by then, a young man who had already commanded a fleet and fathered a four-year-old child.[31] It is conventional to date the prince's birth to about 305, which is probably too late but neither impossible nor inherently implausible.[32] The suggestion that Lactantius was tutoring Crispus between about 316 and 319 may therefore stand. If this were his "extreme old age" then Lactantius must have been born in the decade between 240 and 250, which would place him in his late sixties or older during his tutorship of the young Caesar.[33]

Lactantius must have made a name for himself as a rhetorician in Africa. While the date of his journey to Nicomedia is unattested, it is probable that he went there on the summons of Diocletian.[34] There was evidently not much call for Latin rhetoric in Nicomedia, so Lactantius had few students and much time for writing. It is also most likely that he became a Christian here.[35] It can reasonably be inferred that whatever imperial patronage he received ceased with the commencement of the Great Persecution in 303.[36] He seems, nevertheless, to have remained in the city until at least 305.[37] After that there is only uncertainty until he is found in Gaul with Crispus over a decade later. This considerable lacuna in Lactantius' life is one which scholars have laboured hard to fill. There is simply no evidence, not even a hint from the man himself. He certainly thought it proper and prudent to flee persecution, so presumably he himself did.[38] His place of refuge presents another problem. Gaul and Italy suggest themselves as possibilities.[39] Certainly Lactantius' narrative in the *de mortibus persecutorum* of the years after 305 (*de mort. pers.* 27–33) focuses very much upon events in the west. This is notable given that this is a point in his narrative where he could say a great deal more about events in the east than he does, most particularly in relation to the policies of Maximinus Daza.

That the *de mortibus* is his authentic work, despite its peculiar provenance, has been beyond doubt for over a century.[40] The precise date and location of its composition remain obscure although some probability is possible. Lactantius' portrayal of Licinius gives a clear indication here. It differs markedly from that of his Christian contemporary Eusebius who advances a view that Licinius was a persecutor in disguise.[41] Lactantius has none of this, depicting Licinius as pro-Christian, despite his origins in the court of Galerius. Lactantius accords him a vision of an angel, a prayer of victory, and proper piety in victory. Likewise, according to Lactantius, he exhorted Christians to rebuild their churches, and Lactantius endeavours to put a positive slant to Licinius' executions of the children of his deceased colleagues.[42]

Lactantius' favourable view of Licinius must then mean a date of composition for the work prior to Constantine's first conflict with him in 314 and in a region in which Licinius' favour might be important.[43] Is it likely that Lactantius would return to the east? Lactantius' text of the Edict of Toleration is dated from Nicomedia and Nicomedia is the focus of reports about the death of Galerius. It was from Nicomedia that Lactantius had fled and, most probably, to Nicomedia that he had returned at the earliest opportunity, and penned the *de mortibus*, perhaps to seek to persuade Licinius against the course which he ultimately took.[44] Licinius' resumption of hostilities towards the church also provides the context for Lactantius' later movements. As a prominent Christian, he would scarcely have been welcome in the realm of Licinius after 314 and may have fled or been expelled.[45] The sensible place for him to have gone at this point would have been the court of Constantine, and his reputation ensured him appointment as Crispus' tutor.

The *de mortibus persecutorum*, however, remains a peculiar document. It has been called, with some justice, "the first attempt at a Christian philosophy of history",[46] since at its heart is a critical thesis, polemically expounded. God punishes those who persecute his people, most especially emperors:

> *de quorum exitu testificari placuit, ut omnes qui procul remoti fuerunt vel qui postea futuri sunt, scirent, quatenus virtutem ac maiestatem suam in extinguendis delendisque nominis sui hostibus deus summus ostenderit.*[47]

(I determined to testify to the deaths of these men so that those who are far away and those who are yet to come will know the extent to which the greatest god has revealed his grandeur and greatness in the annihilating and destroying the enemies of his name.)

Lactantius' explicit statement of purpose is critical in any reading of this work. It is both apologetic and triumphal, and hence, one suspects, the apparent ghoulish delight which the author takes in recounting the deaths of persecuting emperors. While such a text might have resonated well with believing readers, it also sounded a warning to any ruler who might be reconsidering a policy of tolerance and forbearance towards the church. Lactantius' formidable polemical skills were then deployed in order to establish characters who illustrated this theme. This was an urgent and important matter, in which theology, high politics and recent history all collided. His argument was based upon a particular understanding of God's involvement in history as the avenger of wrongs to his people. In this he drew upon Christian scripture and existing Christian and pagan concepts of divine retribution. Such retribution is consistently depicted in the book of *Acts*, which relates a number of occasions for divine vengeance: Judas Iscariot's death after a botched suicide attempt; Ananias and Sapphira, struck dead after defrauding the church; Herod Agrippa I who, having set himself up as an oriental monarch and persecuted the faithful, was struck down by the Angel of the Lord and eaten by worms.[48]

The Christian concept of divine vengeance has been well documented and studied.[49] But Lactantius was not simply a Christian; he was also a Roman Christian, deeply influenced also by classical models of retribution.[50] The idea of divine vengeance was one which he could deploy to both a Christian and a non-Christian audience, and one which made sense to him both as a Christian and as a Roman. Thus, his identification of "bad" emperors in the work is conventional, as are his criticisms of contemporary rulers. His reverence for senatorial tradition is clear in his criticism of Maximian for his extinction of its leading lights and the treatment of the nobility by both "good" and "bad" emperors (*de mortibus persecutorum* 8.4; 8.5–6; 37; 44.11). Likewise, he condemned Diocletian for his arrogance in seeking to construct a new Rome at Nicomedia (7.10). Lactantius' negatives also reveal his reverence for Rome. He did not merely portray Galerius as a bad emperor, but also as an enemy of the Roman name (27.8). This rhetoric emphasizing the barbarism of Galerius can be found at other points in the work. Lactantius, for example, noted that Galerius intended to change the name of the Empire from "Roman" to "Dacian", and was an enemy of tradition and culture (22.4). Moreover, his economic policy reflected his lack of respect both for the past and for the privileges of the city of Rome. Galerius was not Lactantius' only savage. He also described Maximin Daza as "half-barbarian" (18.13), and Maximian as the possessor of a "barbarous libido" (38.3). Similarly, Lactantius' praise for Constantine was genuinely Roman in its cast. He described Constantine as *sanctissimus adulescens*, handsome, a good soldier, decent in personal morality, affable and popular (18.10). Furthermore,

Lactantius depicted Constantine as properly respectful of the Senate. A significant feature for this relationship to Lactantius is the salutation of Constantine by the Senate and people of Rome as Emperor: "Constantine was received as *imperator* by the senate and people of Rome with great joy" (44.10). Not content with this mere acclamation, the Senate went further in recognition of Constantine's *virtus* and awarded him the right to have his name first in imperial titles, thus raising him in one stroke from the most junior of the Augusti to the most senior (44.11). For Lactantius, then, bad emperors were not merely enemies of God but, more particularly, enemies of Rome. By contrast, Constantine was honoured by the Senate for his quality.

These sentiments are not particularly Christian in themselves. Any writer operating within the canons of Roman historiography could have written them. There is little about piety or impiety here, but a great deal about respect for the *mos maiorum* by good emperors and disrespect by the bad. Astute readers of Lactantius have known this for a long time. As long ago as 1943 it was suggested that Lactantius was consciously trying to bring about a fusion of Christian and classical tradition.[51] While this probably goes too far in itself, the suggestion points to the basic fact that Lactantius was a trained rhetorician, more familiar with classical tradition than with Christian writing.[52] As such, it would be difficult for him to write in any other way. As a late convert, and a professional rhetorician, he was inevitably far more familiar with classical literature than he was with Christian writing. Moreover, he saw its value. He drew upon it when it suited his apologetic purpose. Just as Christian literature reflected theological imagery of a vengeful god, so too classical literature and historiography abounded with examples of divine vengeance.[53]

It must also be remembered in any discussion of Lactantius' work that he was, by both training and trade, a rhetorician. Words were his profession, in particular the language of praise and invective. He himself recognized this when he stated in the prologue to the *Divine Institutes* that, whereas before he had taught men to lie, thenceforth he would teach them the truth.[54] It is not surprising, then, to find a good deal of rhetorical technique used in the *de mortibus*.[55] Lactanius uses contrast (*sunkrisis*), accusations of sexual excess, and exaggeration. An excellent example of the latter is his account of Diocletian's provincial reorganization:

> *Et ut omnia terrore comperentur, provinciae quoque in frusta concisae: multi praesides et plura officia singulis regionibus ac paene iam civitatibus incubare, item rationales multi et magistri et vicarii praefectorum, quibus omnibus civiles actus admodum rari, sed condemnationes tantum et proscriptiones frequentes, exactiones rerum innumerabilium non dicam crebrae, set perpetuae, et in exactionibus iniurae nonferendaede.*[56]

(Moreover, to spread terror everywhere, the provinces too were cut up into bits; with a multitude of governors and even more officials burdening each region, and nearly every city; likewise many civil servants, judges, and deputy prefects, all of whom were rarely civil, but with such condemnations and frequent purges, they extracted innumerable taxes – I should say here, not merely often, but all the time – and in such collections the injustices were intolerable.)

A little earlier, he likewise states:

in quattuor partes orbe diviso et multiplicatis exercitibus cum singuli eorum longe maiorem numerum habere contenderunt quam priores principes habuerunt cum soli rem publicam gererent.[57]

([Diocletian] divided the world into four parts and increased the army with each of [the emperors] competing to have a larger number of soldiers even than earlier emperors who had ruled the state alone.)

Such claims are an evident exaggeration. Diocletian did not quadruple the size of the army, as is the rhetorical implication here. Nor did he chop the provinces into fragments. He did enlarge the army, and significantly increased the number of provinces. A contemporary administrative source known as the Verona List reveals, nevertheless, that they remained of notable size.[58] Libya Superior, Bithynia, Rhodope and Baetica were not quite the tiny tracts of land cursed with a multiplicity of officials that Lactantius endeavoured to portray. His hyperbole becomes almost absurd when he makes the simply impossible claim that more people were deriving their income from the state than were paying taxes.[59] In testing his assertions for rhetorical technique, it is clear that his judgements and characterizations are neither sober nor objective. But it is as unjust and misleading to label him a mere polemicist as it is to consider him a reliable historian. He was an apologist and philosopher who took historical events seriously since to him they had cosmological significance.

There is therefore a necessary amount of ratiocination in Lactantius' work. While he does not write deliberate falsehoods, he does construct narratives and invent conversations on the basis of what he thinks would have happened within the overall context of his thesis. The extended death narrative accorded to Galerius has long been established as a case in point, based as it is, not upon forensic or clinical reports, but upon the account of the death of Antiochus VI in 2 Maccabees. Galerius' death was, no doubt, lingering and unpleasant.[60] It was also far more gruesome that that of Diocletian, to which Lactantius devotes a few insipid lines. This suggests that Lactantius' "logic of retribution" led him to blame Galerius over Diocletian for the origin of the persecution and construct his narrative accordingly. Lactantius is not a simple writer to contextualize and interpret; the *de mortibus* is more complex than it first appears. It is an apologetic work, written by a rhetorician who dwelt firmly and ineradicably within the classical tradition. He was not consciously writing propaganda; he was writing an historiographical essay with a thesis, a method and a sophisticated cultural vocabulary. This needs to be borne in mind in any use of Lactantius' historical testimony. When his account and, in particular, his judgements stand at variance to those of alternative traditions, severe questions must be asked of Lactantius. Where he remains our sole authority he must be treated with care, not so much because he is prone to falsify, but because he uses history as the stage for his theology.

Eusebius

Like Lactantius, Eusebius has the primary value of being contemporary to the events which he describes. His work, however, is of a different quality and stamp. The documents which are most relevant in this context, the *Chronicle*, the *Church History*, the *Life of Constantine* and the *Martyrs of Palestine*, were each composed at different periods in Eusebius' life in quite different historical circumstances. Indeed the whole, and considerable, corpus of Eusebius' work was composed during a half-century of dramatic, even revolutionary, political and religious change in the Empire. In this, Eusebius himself played a minor part. It is unsurprising, therefore, to find that Eusebius' own thoughts, observations and perspectives change over this period.

Eusebius' most durable achievement was a whole new historical genre, that of ecclesiastical history. This soon found continuators and imitators, to the degree to which one might justly label Eusebius the "father of social history". He was one of a small group of Christian writers who were born into the faith. Most other Christian writers contemporary to Eusebius – notably Lactantius himself, Arnobius and Marius Victorinus – were converts.[61] Eusebius had been born a Christian, and educated by Pamphilus, who had in turn studied in Origenist Alexandria.[62] The tradition from which Eusebius emerged was both Christian and Platonic, an aspect for which Origen himself was savagely criticized both by pagan critics, such as Porphyry, and the Christian tradition which later (briefly) anathematized him.[63] Under the influence of such thinking, Eusebius came to see the world very much as an image of heaven and the stage upon which God's purposes were revealed and achieved.[64]

His earliest work was the *Chronography*, a world chronicle in which he set out his theory of history in tabular form, and the first seven books of the Church History. His earliest political ideas were set out in the prolegomenon to the Church History. Here he makes it clear that he thinks of the Roman Empire as a divinely ordained institution, the function of which is to reunite scattered humanity into one polity, and that the Christian revelation was truly ancient, as old as the pagan traditions which claimed the authority of antiquity.[65] It is significant that Eusebius' thought should tend in this way, twenty years before Constantine's promotion of Christianity. It is, perhaps, the fruit of the long truce between State and Church following the Edict of Gallienus in 261. Eusebius has no natural hostility to the Roman state unlike, say, Tertullian. Rather, he saw it as the work of God, and predicted in scripture.[66] While not hostile, he was not uncritical either. He formed his own judgements of emperors based on how they treated the Church, and any reading of the final three books of the *Church History* must be read with that in mind.

After the conclusion of the Great Persecution, Eusebius composed a pamphlet called *On the Martyrs of Palestine*, a shorter version of which became an appendix to Book Eight of the *Church History*.[67] This work, composed before the final version of the *Church History*, concentrates upon parochial events in Eusebius' own neighbourhood. This document was intended as hagiography, and not too much should be expected from it. Nevertheless, it remains a significant document of the Great Persecution: it attests the bitterness with which many Christians came to regard the state, and the regime of Maximinus Daza in particular.

The *Martyrs of Palestine* raised an important historical question for Eusebius. Why did persecution occur at all? His own view, like that of Tertullian in this matter, was that persecution was undertaken by "bad" emperors. Eusebius added to this view the same kind of logic of retribution that we find in the *de mortibus*, asserting that persecutors were punished by God.[68] Pilate, for example, was depicted as committing suicide; Herod Agrippa as smitten with worms; Decius as punished by God; Macrianus and his progeny as wiped from the face of the earth.[69] Linked with this, however, is the notion that persecution was also a divine punishment upon an errant church.[70] Eusebius came to view the Great Persecution as a judgement: as God punishing the Church for its indolence and sectarianism during the peace after 261.[71] That leads him to an ambiguity: while persecutors were exercising the just judgement of God, in so doing they were still creatures of the Devil. This is made clear in his view of Maximinus Daza who is consistently depicted as an agent of evil, acting on the prompting of the Devil but nevertheless in so doing, exercising God's will.[72] Eusebius' Maximinus suffers the just punishment meted out by God – perhaps less because of his divinely appointed role as chastiser of the Church, and more because of the cruelty with which he carried out his task. This can be particularly seen in the depictions of both Daza and Theotecnus in the *Martyrs of Palestine*. Both are characterized as wicked and justly punished, but also as having served "the mysterious decrees of God". In the same way, Eusebius sees the civil wars of the period from 312 to 324 as a punishment visited by God upon the state for the persecution.[73] Hostility to Galerius in Eusebius' work comes, then, as no surprise. Galerius had been a persecutor and therefore one of the wicked emperors used by the Devil to make war on God's people. Like Lactantius, Eusebius recorded a similar protracted narrative of Galerius' hideous death. Indeed these accounts are so similar that it is difficult to shake the suspicion that either one is dependent upon the other or that they are drawing upon a common source.[74]

More important, and indeed enduring, than Eusebius' portrayal of Galerius is his emerging view of Constantine. Eusebius developed an historical theology which placed Constantine and his court in the cosmological role as the earthly counterpart of the Heavenly Kingdom. For him, Constantine was far more than a patron, co-religionist and sympathetic ruler. Rather the victory at the Milvian Bridge was the epiphany of a divinely appointed ruler, honoured by God and a friend of God. Such a political theology leads to a necessary polarization. Constantine's enemies were also the enemies of God. Maxentius, who actually promoted a policy of toleration, was therefore depicted as a demonic persecutor of Christians, and Licinius as descending into the madness of evil.[75] This view finds its clearest expression in a late work, a speech in honour of Constantine delivered in the 330s. In it he depicts the emperor as an invincible warrior sent by God to rescue the pious and punish the wicked. As God in heaven himself punished the demons, so Constantine triumphs over their earthly allies, marking his victory by the toppling of statues and building of churches.[76] His final work, the *Life of Constantine*, composed after the death of Constantine in 337, and in the final months of Eusebius' own life (he died in 339), reflects a serious and sincere political theology. If the sentiments of the speech "In Praise of Constantine" might be dismissed as Episcopal flattery, the conclusions of a work composed after the death of Constantine, and in the shadow of the death of its author, compel the conclusion that Eusebius meant what he wrote. There was a certain urgency here. The transition from Constantine to his successors had been an unstable and a bloody one. Members of the dynasty had been purged, leaving the three sons of Constantine ruling the state. With the future uncertain Eusebius may well have seen this last work as an apologetic testament, urging the sons of Constantine to rule as their father had.[77] In the developed text of the *Life*, Eusebius' view of Constantine becomes elaborately theological. He sees Constantine as being prefigured by the biblical model of Moses. Both were raised in the houses of the enemies of God; both bore an irresistible talisman of divine presence – the Ark of the Covenant and the *labarum* respectively; both lured their foes to death by water, Maxentius in the Tiber and Pharaoh in the Red Sea. The parallels are clear: as Moses led the people of Israel from captivity into the edge of the Promised Land, so Constantine has led the new people of God from humiliation and persecution to freedom and favour. As such, Constantine's rivals become cosmological figures, wholly evil and relentless in their plotting against the godly emperor.[78]

Within the work of Eusebius, theology dominates history. He was convinced of the importance of the Church, not merely as a sub-community or sect, but as a polity in its own right.[79] Thus, he does not perceive persecution of the Church as an occasional policy imposed by wicked and hostile emperors, but as a war between rival kingdoms. But he also saw the Roman Empire as a divinely ordained unifying principle, reuniting the nations and peoples sundered at Babel in a single state. Within the parameters of this thought, Constantine became the key figure. The emperor united the two strands of this thought – the divine deliverer who both unites the Roman state and provides it with a godly and pious master. If all history is, for Eusebius, sacred history written on this scale, then his judgements are appropriately cosmological, and his characters always refracted through the prism of religion.

Eusebius' influence was also enduring. He inspired imitators and continuators. As the years went on, moreover, the years of the Great Persecution came to assume mythic significance for Christian historians. A tradition, deeply hostile to both Diocletian and his colleagues (with the exception of Constantius), emerged which remained deeply influential in forming views of this period. There are some documents to counter this, most particularly a corpus of speeches given by imperial panegyrists in Gaul, although they are even more tainted by partisan favour of their subjects: it was their job after all.

The Gallic panegyrics

These documents are of a completely different character and style to the documents already discussed. They appear in an anthology of speeches collected in the late fourth century. Eight of these were delivered to various emperors in Gaul – Maximian, Constantius and Constantine – between 289 and 313. These documents emerge from an ancient tradition of encomiastic oratory. As such, they had their own customs, strategies and critics.[80] A series of recent studies, notably those of Nixon and Rodgers and Roger Rees, have shed much light on the historical value of these texts. They are daring speeches: a subject is addressing the emperor on a ceremonial occasion and, within the customary language of praise, there might lurk an exhortation or an expression of purely parochial concern.[81] Principally, however, panegyrists were professional rhetoricians making set-piece speeches to and for an audience. It is not so much that they said what emperors wanted to hear (the speeches were delivered on public occasions); rather, they said what emperors wanted others to hear. They were finely calibrated diplomatic documents, and what orators chose to omit was every bit as significant as what they chose to include.[82]

These speeches, moreover, are not explanations of imperial policy, but celebrations of it. Mamertinus, for example, in delivering a panegyric to

Maximian in 289, praised the unity of the Empire and the brotherhood of the two Augusti without feeling the need to explain why there were two emperors in the first place. Likewise, his stress upon the Jovian nature of Diocletian and the Herculian nature of Maximian articulated rather than explained the divine imagery of imperial ranking. Mamertinus' task might, indeed, seem to be invidious here – that of praising the number two man. His solution is adroit and subtle, emphasizing fraternity and patrimony over charismatic authority while, whenever he can, portraying his subject as the real power in the land.[83] Such characterizations cannot be taken as genuine political statements. They are the product of the need to praise. One advantage of this need, and the speeches themselves, is their contemporaneity. Eusebius edited, re-edited and reworked his *Church History* a number of times. These speeches were given once. As Sabine McCormack has noted:

> Late antique panegyrics ... had a built-in obsolescence, for they addressed themselves to contemporaries, and then mainly to a particular group of contemporaries, that is to locals who were present to listen. It is thus important to realize the potential and limitations of the panegyrics. On the one hand a panegyric could crystallize in considerable detail and depth one specific moment in one specific place, but on the other hand, in its particularity lay its limitations.[84]

As such, they reveal the changing perspectives of the powerful, as circumstances and events occur. Mamertinus' panegyric on Maximian again provides a clear example. Having described the extent of Maximian's victory over Eruli and Chaibones, Mamertinus then says, "I pass over your countless battles and victories over all Gaul."[85] Why pass over these things? Surely because they are not worth praising – because they are the products of a civil skirmish with the Bagaudae.[86] Instead Mamertinus turns to the heroic: the assumption by Maximian of a consulship on the morning of 1 January 287 and his repulse of a German raid on the same afternoon. In the same way, the Gallic panegyrists omit events which were of recent memory or are not of local relevance, in particular the short-lived breakaway Gallic empire or, in 307, the tense political situation east of the Alps.[87]

The panegyrics which we possess were recognized in late antiquity as being of exemplary quality. They were not vapid and formulaic. They were skilful speeches, included in an anthology of the best of their kind.[88] No doubt many other speeches of a similar kind were given on similar occasions, but they have been deservedly forgotten. They are, in short, the best kind of primary source. Neither propaganda nor vehicles of policy, they are, rather, responses within conventional formulae of praise to the deeds and policies of their addressee. They are not intended to explain anything, but to praise what is, although there are exceptions. As will be argued in Chapter 6, the panegyric of 307 admits us to an historical event as it unfolds. But that is exceptional. By and large, they remain as snapshots of what passed for "political correctness" in one place at one time.

Other primary sources

While these three sets of documents form the principal corpus of contemporary narrative texts, a number of other texts and sources survive from antiquity which serve to give a much clearer picture of political events, policies and personalities between 284 and 311. One major collection of source material for this period lies in its published laws and decrees. We are also fortunate in possessing a number of random documents of different kinds preserved on fragile papyrus. In addition to these survivals, there are the more durable documents in stone and metal: the coins and inscriptions of the period furnish information about policy and propaganda, as do officially commissioned artworks, monuments and official buildings. Finally, this period was also of some interest to the generations which followed it. Historical works written in the late fourth century and beyond drew heavily upon works now lost to us, down to a very full narrative offered by the Byzantine writer John Zonaras in the twelfth century.

A significant number of official documents, of various kinds, survive from this period. The evidence for their preservation, textual quality and historical value has been exhaustively studied by Simon Corcoran, and his work will be drawn upon in the present study.[89] While some imperial enactments are recorded by the narrative sources, in general we depend for their preservation either upon insertion into various legal codes, or the random chances of epigraphic and papyrological survival. The *Edict on Marriage* and the *Edict against the Manichees*, for example, were conserved in a legal text comparing Roman and Mosaic law probably composed in the late fourth century.[90] The critically important *Edict on Maximum Prices* referred to by Lactantius has been preserved in a number of inscriptional copies of varying quality.[91] Many other documents found their way into the Theodosian or Justinianic Codes, probably via the codes of Hermogenianus and Gregorius.[92]

While a number of official acts were preserved on papyrus and in inscriptions, these media also preserved an enormous variety of other contemporary texts. In Egypt, papyrus documents record correspondence, taxation records, petitions and administrative memoranda.[93] Likewise, inscriptional texts from across the Empire, varying in quality from vernacular graffiti to elegant official dedications, all add to our picture of Diocletian's empire. Many of these are the dedications to public works commissioned and completed during this period. The dedication to the great Baths of Diocletian in Rome is a case in point.[94] T.D. Barnes, moreover, has used imperial victory formulae in official inscriptions to reconstruct much imperial campaigning under Diocletian and his successors. Even inscriptional texts of apparent local significance can add to our knowledge of imperial policy and its implementation.[95]

The buildings which some of these inscriptions celebrated are also important evidence for the period. Lactantius described Diocletian's massive public works policy as "an endless desire for building".[96] While Lactantius' more extravagant rhetorical flourishes can be discarded at this point, there was certainly an explosion in both military and civilian construction during this period. Rome itself was adorned with various triumphal monuments of which a fragment of the Decennial Monument survives, a vast baths complex and a new Senate House. New imperial palace structures were built in cities across the Empire: Mediolanum, Thessalonica, where a major triumphal monument popularly called "The Arch of Galerius" is preserved, Nicomedia, Antioch and Trier all provide significant archaeological *testimonia*, as do the retirement palaces constructed at Split and Gamzigrad. Likewise, recent archaeological projects at the edges of empire have revealed significant investment during this period in military and economic infrastructure.[97]

This period remained of great significance to the generations who followed. It marks the great and decisive conflict between ideologies. Christian monotheism replaced traditional polytheism, and the fight which that engendered led to both Christians and traditional Hellenists writing about the period with particular vim and venom. Christians, for example, mythologized the period, repeating and embellishing martyr stories as well as inventing new ones. Traditionalists looked back with nostalgia on a world which they had lost. Fourth-century writers like Eunapius and Nicomachus Flavianus, whose work is now lost to us, were sources for later writers like Zosimus, Peter the Patrician and John Zonaras.[98] Equally mysterious writers of the early fourth century, specifically Praxagoras of Athens and the anonymous *Kaisergeshichte*, also provided texts plundered by later writers such as the author of the *Anonymous Valesianus*, as well as the brutal late fourth-century abbreviators of history, Eutropius, Aurelius Victor and the author of the anonymous *Epitome de Caesaribus*.[99] This great multitude of sources provides us with a variety of voices and perspectives. It remains to make sense of them.

The date of Galerius' birth

The year of Galerius' birth is unknown. His encyclopaedists have estimated the year 250 as an approximation.[100] This is based upon a statement in Aurelius Victor:

> But the unity of these men proclaimed that integrity and sound military practice, such as had been instituted for them by Aurelian and Probus, was almost sufficient for virtue.[101]

This is slender evidence. Victor's comments are limited to the quality of the precepts of Aurelian and Probus, from which Diocletian and his colleagues learned. He does not actually say that they all served as soldiers under these emperors. Diocletian and Maximian may well have served under these emperors. Perhaps even Constantius. But Galerius was somewhat younger than his colleagues. Other evidence is at hand. In particular the eccentric evidence of John Malalas has been suggested.[102] Malalas gives the age of a number of emperors at death, including one whom he names "Maxentius Galerius".[103] Reading of the context does not inspire confidence: Malalas is especially confused at this point, giving "Maxentius Galerius" a short reign and a campaign in Armenia, which would therefore seem to describe Maximinus Daza (properly Galerius Maximinus). This does not fit Daza who is otherwise portrayed in the sources as a relatively young man.[104] It would seem more appropriate for Galerius who would then have been born in about 258.

While Malalas' testimony is better evidence than none at all, it does require some form of corroboration before it can be taken seriously. Lactantius may provide this. He makes much of Galerius' "barbarian" (specifically Dacian) origins. Of most relevance here is Lactantius' statement that Romula, Galerius' mother, had fled across the Danube to escape from the threat of the Carpi. Galerius himself was born in the province of Dardania, and it can be reasonably assumed that his father was a Roman citizen since Lactantius is silent on the subject, preferring instead to emphasize his Dacian descent through Romula.[105] The fact of Romula's migration should give us some clue as to the date of Galerius' birth since he came into the world south of the Danube. The Carpic incursions into Dacia must have occurred well before Aurelian's evacuation of the province in the early 270s since the date of Galerius' birth cannot be so late. Given that Galerius is most unlikely to have been born before 250, it is worth examining the known pattern of Carpic activity in the region between 250 and the death of Gallienus in 268.

The Carpi were a Dacian group, or confederation of groups, with a distinct and identifiable material culture.[106] It was the Carpi, rather than the Goths, who had infiltrated and settled trans-Danubian Dacia by the time of Aurelian's withdrawal south of the Danube, so that the raids which led to Romula's emigration could have occurred any time in the 250s or 260s.[107] Imperial victory titles, however, suggest more specific evidence of Carpic incursions during this period. The Emperor Philip took the titles *Carpicus* and *Dacicus* in the late 240s. Decius, Philip's successor, took the title *Dacicus* which might indicate a defeat of the Carpi in 250.[108] Moreover, Jordanes, the historian of the Goths, was quite specific that 3,000 Carpi joined the Gothic confederacy which defeated and slew Decius in 251.[109] Gallienus had also taken the title *Dacicus* by 257.[110] There is no subsequent appearance of the titles Dacicus and Carpicus in imperial victory titles until the time of Aurelian. These titles themselves are important pieces of evidence for imperial campaigning, since they provide a rough chronology and identification of the theatre of war. In this case, they indicate that there was consistent pressure on Dacia from the Carpi during the 240s and 250s followed by a period of relative quiet during the 260s and then a renewal of assaults in the early 270s. This observation is not greatly complicated by the usurpations of Ingenuus and Regalian, which occurred in the wake of the defeat of Valerian in Persia, and were swiftly suppressed by Gallienus.[111] Nor is there any evidence to suggest that Gallienus ignored problems in the Danubian regions, as his detractors might have suggested. Rather, there seems to have been a degree of peace, perhaps even the peace of exhaustion.[112]

While it is possible to identify these phases of conflict, the locus of each is not so straightforward. Philip's wars involving the Carpi seem to have been on the lower Danubian banks, opposite the Moesian provinces. These were, perhaps, free Dacians and many of these found their way into the force which later defeated Decius in Moesia Inferior. During his brief reign, nevertheless, Decius took the title *Dacicus Maximus*, and an inscription from Apuli in Dacia refers to him as *restitutor Daciarum*.[113] Lactantius adds that Decius' objective, in his final campaign, was to clear out the Carpi occupying Dacia and Moesia.[114] His ultimate failure and death led to an intensification of pressure upon the Danubian frontier, and the lonely provincial redoubt in Dacia was most vulnerable. Zosimus, in a dreary and highly rhetorical picture of the years that followed, mentions raids by the Carpi.[115] Zosimus' view is supported by the demonstrable instability of the imperial office, and the constant distraction of war with Persia, which prevented the development of a sustained response in Dacia and Moesia. Decius' immediate successor, Trebonianus Gallus, sought to buy time by paying off the invaders. Their withdrawal, however, was temporary. The Thirteenth Sibylline Oracle refers to raids by the Carpi at the same time that Shapur was victorious in Syria (253).[116] These raids were briefly halted by Aemilian, who then sought to exploit his success by acclamation as emperor. While Aemilian was able to defeat and kill Gallus, he was in turn defeated and slain by Valerian, who sought to bring some stability to the imperial office. The civil wars of 253 squandered whatever advantage had been won by Aemilian's victory. This left the frontiers vulnerable and the Carpi are specifically attested as exploiting this. There was certainly nothing to hinder them. Valerian's accession began the long, and punctuated, process of the Roman recovery. By 257, his son and colleague Gallienus had taken the title *Dacicus* which would indicate the return of a sustained imperial response to Carpic incursions into Dacia, probably in the years 254–6.[117]

If matters were in some degree settled towards the end of the 250s, then the most likely time for Romula to have fled from trans-Danubian Dacia will be in the years 251–5. While this remains a best guess rather than an evident certainty, there is some evidence as to Romula's destination. It is clear that she settled in Dacia Superior on a rural property which later took her name: Romuliana.[118] It was into this home that Galerius was born, and it was in the rolling country around what is now Gamzigrad that he herded sheep as a boy.[119] The first structure on the site, a small *villa rustica*, dates to the middle decades of the third century and may well have been built by Romula and her unknown spouse in a more settled environment than the circumstances of her immigration.[120] Such times existed after 256 from which time the middle Danubian provinces enjoyed a welcome respite from the threat of attack.[121]

There is no "smoking gun" here. The limits of the evidence have been tested, but no certainty can be offered, only a probability. What can be said is that a dubious literary source gives Galerius' age at death as 53, and therefore provides a birth year for Galerius of 257/8. Better evidence identifies his mother as a refugee from Carpic raids on trans-Danubian Dacia. These were a feature from the late 240s and reached a height of impunity after 253. Galerius' newly built childhood home in Dacia Superior implies a more settled and peaceful environment, as pertained after 256/7. These identifiable circumstances at least render Malalas' date plausible, even probable. It is reasonable, then, to accept his testimony and date Galerius' birth to 257/8, which would make him about 35 in 293 and the youngest of Diocletian's college, although by no means a youth.

Notes

1 Mattingly (1939), p. 328.
2 A standard bibliography of the period discloses the following examples: Seston (1946); Kolb (1987); Corcoran (2000); two numbers of the journal *Antiquité Tardive* are devoted to "la Tétrarchie" (II, 1994; III, 1995). Now see also Rees (2004) for a useful narrative and collection of relevant texts.
3 The term is from Gibbon (1896), Vol. I, p. 351; so also Barnes as "an implicit homage" (Barnes 1998: p. 178, n. 48).
4 Vollmer (1991).
5 Pliny *NH* V. xv. 73.
6 *SHA, Vit. Car.* 18.4.
7 Amm. Marc. XIV. 10.10; see Blockley (1972), pp. 451–6. When Julian was appointed to Gaul, Constantius famously said that he was not giving the Gauls a ruler, but a man who carried in himself the imperial image (Julian, *Ep. Ad Ath.* 278 A).
8 Julian, *Caesares*, 315, A–B.
9 Lact. *de mort. pers.* 7.1.
10 Gibbon (1896), Vol. 1, pp. 381–5.
11 For example, Kolb (1987) specifically addresses the issue in the subtitle of his work: *Improvisation oder Experiment in der Organisation monarchischer Herrschaft.*
12 Ritter (1862); Preuss (1869), pp. 47–52.
13 Schiller (1887), p. 119ff; Vollmer (1991) p. 443f.
14 Vollmer (1991), p. 443f.
15 Kinch (1890), esp. pp. 24–7.
16 Seeck (1897), p. 42. Strictly speaking, in his text, Seeck refers to the post-Diocletianic arrangement as *der neue Tetrarchie*, which would seem to imply the existence of an *alte Tetrarchie* also. This reading is confirmed through an examination of the volume of notes accompanying the text (Seeck 1898: p. 433).
17 Maurice (1908), Vol. I, p. xxxvii.

18 Mispoulet (1908), p. 436; Goyau (1912), and his earlier article Goyau (1893), p. 262.
19 Costa (1926), pp. 1807, 1813, 1816, 1835.
20 Stade (1926), p. 53, and ascribing the origin of the idea to Galerius. One of Stade's basic tenets was that Diocletian improvised constantly, rather than planned (p. 50ff.). E. Stein (1928: pp. 94–143) also avoided the term, although he surely knew it, preferring the terms "Thronordnung" and "Kaiserkollegium".
21 Webb (1907); Bury (1923); Anderson (1932); Mattingly and Sydenham (1933), pp. 204–19; Baynes (1948).
22 Kornemann (1930), p. 110ff.
23 Parker (1935), pp. 229–34, 240–6.
24 Ensslin (1928), (1928A) and (1948).
25 Ensslin (1948), p. 2437.
26 Straub (1939), pp. 36–55.
27 Ensslin (1942).
28 L'Orange (1938).
29 Jerome, de vir. ill. 80, n.b. 79 on Arnobius at Sicca.
30 PLRE I, p. 233, s.v. "Crispus".
31 Origo Constantini Imperatoris,1. 5. 23–7; C.Th.9.38.1.
32 PLRE I, p. 233; but see Palanque (1938) which argues plausibly for 303 as Crispus' birth-year. This creates its own difficulties, as Palanque freely admits that at that time Constantine was in Galerius' household. Also Barnes, NE, p. 83 on Crispus' activities. He evidently fought his first campaign in 319, at which time he should have been out of Lactantius' care.
33 Nicholson (1981), p. 14. Nicholson's suggestion that Lactantius came to imperial attention by delivering the panegyric upon Maximian's adventus into Carthage is entertaining and attractive but unlikely, given that Lactantius went to Nicomedia rather than to Milan. Nicholson's arguments for the date of Lactantius' journey to Nicomedia, however, remain strong.
34 Ibid.
35 For the view that Lactantius was converted before he came to Nicomedia, see Stevenson (1957). Both Moreau (1954, I, p. 14) and Palanque (1966, p. 711), consider Lactantius to have been a convert to Christianity but do not venture a view as to when this took place. Lactantius seems ignorant of the work of his old teacher Arnobius, and Ogilvie concludes that most of Lactantius' work was written after his move to Nicomedia (Ogilvie 1978: p. 90f.). It seems most probable that Lactantius and Amobius were both converted after they parted from one another. Amobius' own apologetic work was written late in his life after a sudden conversion to Christianity (Arn., Adv. Nat. 1.3.4). According to one tradition, he was converted through a dream, and the bishop of Sicca, mistrusting this change of mind after a lifetime of opposition to Christianity, required Amobius to write the Adversos Nationes (Jer., Chron. 326). This story of Amobius' late conversion tends to increase the likelihood that Lactantius and Amobius were converted apart. See also Corsaro (1978); also Monçeaux (1905), p. 109, states, "C'est presque son avènement à Nicomédie, avant le persécution de Dioclétien, que s'est converti Lactance." If he became a Christian in Nicomedia, he set about writing at once. His first Christian work is probably the de Opficio Dei and was written before 302. It predates the Institutiones Divinae (D.I .2.10.15) which were written during the persecution (D.I. 5.11; 5.2.2).
36 Moreau (1954), p. 14.
37 D.I. 5.11. Lactantius had evidently been in Nicomedia for at least two years following the outbreak of the Great Persecution. Digeser (2000), p. 135; Bowen and Garnsey (2003), p. 3.
38 D.I. 4.18.2; see Nicholson (1981), p. 44; (1989), p. 20. See Moreau (1954), p. 32f.

39 Bowen and Garnsey (2003), p. 3f., Digeser (2000), p. 133ff.
40 This old controversy has long been settled. The manuscript of the *de mortibus persecutorum* was first edited in 1679 by Etienne Baluze, who ascribed it to Lactantius. This identification was disputed for two centuries until René Pichon's (1901) study of Lactantius. Pichon's arguments demonstrated so conclusively that Lactantius had written the *de mortibus persecutorum* that Samuel Brandt (1897: pp. 1255–9), who had argued non-Lactantian authorship in his Vienna edition of the work, professed himself convinced by Pichon.
41 Eus., *H.E.* 10.8.4.
42 Lact. *de mort. pers.* 46.1. 28; 48.1. 30; 48.3; 50.7; Alföldi's (1948: p. 45) argument that this is a change of heart by Lactantius, demonstrating the brutality of Licinius and the author's sympathy for the women goes beyond the evidence. Whatever Lactantius may have meant, the text talks of a judgement of God, justly deserved because of the evil done by the persecutors. Here, Licinius is depicted as acting as an agent of divine vengeance, not as the impious murderer of those entrusted to his care.
43 There is no clear consensus as to the dating of the *de mortibus*. Barnes (1973), Christensen (1980) and Roller (1927) all argue for 313–14, although for differing reasons; Moreau (1954, p. 34f.) dates it to 317 and argues that it reflects Constantine's propaganda; Seston (1946) prefers a later date, *ca.* 321, during the "watchful peace" between Constantine and Licinius.
44 Contra Moreau (1954), p. 34ff., but see Barnes (1973), pp. 32–5.
45 Eus., *HE.* 10.8.10 on expulsion; 10.8.17 on those fleeing from Licinius' dominions. Of course, Lactantius need not have been expelled but may have fled of his own accord, or may even have been offered the Crispus job before the outbreak of hostilities.
46 Corsaro (1978), p. 27.
47 *de mort. pers.* 7.1.
48 Acts. 1. 16–20, 43; 5.1–10; 12.23.
49 Moreau (1954), pp. 63–4; see, more comprehensively, Trompf (2000).
50 Leadbetter (1998).
51 Alban (1943).
52 On Lactantius' classicism, see Loi (1965), p. 67; Corsaro (1978), pp. 25–49, 83; Ogilvie (1978), p. 98; Leadbetter (1998); Digeser (2000), pp. 7–14.
53 See Africa (1982).
54 *D.I.* 1.1.8. 85.
55 Corsaro (1978), pp. 34–6.
56 *de mort. pers.* 7.4.
57 *de mort. pers.* 7.2.2.
58 Barnes (1982), chapter XII, for a text of the list and discussion.
59 Lact. *de mort. pers.* 7.3
60 Gelzer (1937, repr. 1963); Africa (1982) p. 13f.
61 Leadbetter (1998), pp. 249–52.
62 Barnes (1981), p.84f.; Kannengiesser (1992).
63 Eus. *HE* 6.16.4–8. On Origen's view of history, *Contra Celsum* 2.30, 8.73; see also Milburn (1952), chapter III; Chesnut (1977), p. 153.
64 On this see Milburn (1952), pp. 70–3; Cranz (1952); Baynes (1955); Trompf (1983); Trompf (2000), pp. 126–32; Cameron and Hall (1999), pp. 34–9.
65 Barnes (1980); Mosshammer (1979), p. 31f.
66 Eus. *PE* 1.4; *DE* 7.1; *HE* 4.26.7 quoting Melito of Sardes.
67 There are two forms of the *Martyrs of Palestine*, the Long Recension (L) and the Short Recension (S). L was composed between May and November 311 as an independent work, but later edited into the S form and included in the subsequent edition of the *Church History* from which it was eliminated in the edition of 315. See Barnes (1980), p. 200f.

68 Trompf (1983).
69 Eus. *HE* 1.7 (Pilate); 1.10 (Herod Agrippa); 7.1 (Decius); 7.8. 8–10, 23.1 (the Macriani).
70 See, for example, his judgement at *HE* 7.30.21 that God had slain Aurelian in order to prevent a persecution, but it might yet happen if the Church strayed from the divine will.
71 Eus. *HE*. 8.1. 7–8.
72 *Ibid.*, 8.4.2.
73 *Ibid.*, 8.16.3–5; *de Mart. Pal. L. 3.6, 13.10; S. 1.2, 1.4, 3. 5–7.*
74 Eus. *HE* 8.16.3–5; *VC* 1.57.
75 Baynes (1955); Eus. *HE* 10.8.1; 10.8.5–9, 9.2; on Maxentius, see Drake (1975), p. 22f.; Cullhed (1994), p. 72f.; on Licinius, *HE* 10.8.3–10.
76 Drake (1975), pp. 30–40; Eus. *de laud. Const.* 7.12; 9.13.
77 Cameron and Hall (1999), pp. 9–13.
78 Eus. *VC* 1.5; 1.12; 1.20, 47; 1.37; 1.57–8, 2.7; Cameron and Hall (1999), pp. 34–9.
79 Cranz (1952), pp. 59–64.
80 Pichon (1906), p. 285f.; S. MacCormack (1975), p. 144; Nixon (1987), p. 2f.; on the nature of panegyric, see S. MacCormack (1975), pp. 146–8; Rees (2002), pp. 6–19; on its critics, Cicero, *Brutus*, 62.12; Augustine, *Confessions*, 6.6.9.
81 Nixon and Rodgers (1994), pp. 28–35.
82 On the origins of the panegyrists, Nixon (1987), p. 91f.; on the inclusions and omissions of the panegyrists, see here the important study by Roger Rees (2003).
83 Leadbetter (2004); Rees (2005). I am grateful to Dr Rees for a pre-publication copy of this paper.
84 S. MacCormack (1975), p. 159; see also B. Warmington (1974).
85 *Pan. Lat.* 2 (10).6.1. The translation is that of Nixon and Rodgers (1994), p. 63.
86 Here I agree with Seston (1946) and Galletier (1952) against Nixon and Rodgers (1994), p. 63 n.24.
87 Nixon (1990); Barnes (1981), p. 31; on the political agenda of the panegyric of 307, see Nixon (1993).
88 Pichon (1906), p. 244; S. MacCormack (1975), p. 144; Nixon (1987), p. 2f.; Rees (2002), pp. 22–3.
89 Corcoran (1996; 2000).
90 Corcoran (2000), p. 11.
91 Lact. *de mort. pers.* 7.6; Corcoran (2000), p. 178f.
92 Corcoran (2000), p. 28f.
93 For an interesting collection of papyrus texts from the period, including the very important archive of Aurelius Isidorus from Panopolis, see Rees (2004), pp. 148–60.
94 *ILS* 646; Rees (2004), p. 147; Platner and Ashby (1926), p. 527.
95 Mitchell (1988); Leadbetter (2003); on imperial titles and campaigns, see Barnes (1976).
96 Lact. *de mort. pers.*7.8 (*infinita ... cupiditas aedificandi*).
97 See, for example, Lewin (1990); (2002), pp. 91–101.
98 Paschoud (1994); on Eunapius, see Blockley (1981), pp. 1–26; Rohrbacher (2002), pp. 64–72.
99 On Praxagoras of Athens, Photius 62; Jakoby *Fr Gr. Hist.* no. 219. Ensslin dates the composition of Praxagoras' work to the end of Constantine's reign, or to the beginning of that of his sons (*RE* 22.2 1743); Seston (1946, p. 21 n.1) to somewhat later. The "Kaisergeschichte" was identified by A. Enmann in the nineteenth century. See Enmann (1884); Barnes (1970). On the fourth-century tradition, see H. Brandt (2006).
100 For example, Altendorf *RAC* V, *sv* "Galerius", 786; Ensslin *RE*, XIV 2517.

101 Aur. Vict. *de Caes.* 39.28: *sed horum concordia maxime edocuit virtuti ingenium usumque bonae militiae, quanta his Aureliani Probique instituto fuit paene sat esse.*

102 Barnes (1982), p. 46.

103 Malalas 12.47.

104 Lactantius (*de mort. pers.* 18.13) describes Daza as *adulsecens.* While this is no doubt tendentious, it does point to his youth.

105 Lact. *de mort. pers.* 9.1; 11.1; 27.4; on the flight across the Danube, 9.2.

106 See Bichir (1976).

107 *Ibid.*, Vol. I, p. 157.

108 Peachin (1990), p. 65; *CIL* II 4949.

109 Jordanes *Getica* 91.

110 *CIL* II 2200; VIII 1430; the date is secured in the inscriptions by reference to Gallienus as consul for the third time and in the fourth year of his tribunician power.

111 The date is controversial. The usurpation of Ingenuus is connected by Aurelius Victor (*de Caes.* 33.2) to the death of Valerian in Persia in 259/60 but the consensus of modern scholarship dates it earlier to the days following the death of the young Valerian II in 258. See here, for example, Fitz (1966), p. 27f.; Demougeot (1969), pp. 442–6; Potter (1990), p. 52. What is clear is that Gallienus defeated Ingenuus at Mursa (Aur. Vict. *de Caes.* 33.2; Eutr. 9.8; Zonaras 12.24) and then left for the Rhine frontier. A fresh threat from over the Danube then resulted in the proclamation of Regalianus in Upper Pannonia (Aur. Vict. *de Caes.* 33.2; *SHA* "Trig. Tyr." 10.1.4), but his failure to secure a swift victory led to his death at the hands of his own troops.

112 Blois (1976), p. 33f. He suggests that the provinces might have felt neglected. Gallienus had abandoned the policy of appointing a *dux* on the Danubian frontier, since so many challengers had used the office as a power base. The devastation after the raid of the Roxolani in 260, which Regalian had failed to stop, was considerable and has led to a suggestion that Gallienus carried out a major reorganization of the province in 262 (Fitz 1976: pp. 6–7). The mint of Siscia was opened at this time (*RIC* V 1, p. 22) and there was an undoubted period of stability, if not prosperity, between 260 and 267. On the raid of the Roxolani, see Fitz (1966), pp. 49–57.

113 *ILS* 517; *ILS* 514. Coins were also struck, at a number of mints, referring to victory in Dacia (*RIC* V3, pp. 120–50; nos 2, 12, 13, 14, 35, 36, 37, 101, 112, 113, 114).

114 Lact. *de mort. pers.* 4.3.

115 Zos. 1.27.

116 *Or. Syb.* XIII, 141–4; Potter (1990), pp. 46f., 310–13; (2004), p. 252.

117 *CIL* II 2200; VIII 1430; Peachin (1990) p. 325 no. 193; Kienast (1996), p. 218.

118 *Ep. de Caes.* 40. 16–17; the name of the site is given by the epitomator as "Romulianum", but Procopius *de aed.* 4.4 called the site Romuliana, a name now confirmed by an inscription. See Duval (1987); Srejovic and Vasic (1994).

119 According to the *Epitome de Caesaribus* (40.15–16) Galerius' nickname was "shepherd-boy" (*Armentarius*); see also Aur. Vict. *de Caes.* 39.18; Barnes, p. 38; Syme (1971), p. 226.

120 Srejovic (1983), pp. 21–3 (English abstract, p. 194); Srejovic and Vasic (1994A), p. 57f.

121 Blois (1976), p. 5.

1

DYNASTS AND OLIGARCHS

A democracy cannot rule an empire. Neither can one man, though
empire may appear to presuppose monarchy. There is always an
oligarchy somewhere, open or concealed.

Ronald Syme[1]

When the Emperor Augustus died in AD 14, the Roman world was a bright
and confident place. Romans themselves knew what their empire was for. It
was to bring peace and prosperity; security and good government; in Vergil's
words, "to crush the arrogant and show mercy to the vanquished".[2] This
Roman world endured and flourished for two centuries. It overcame the
incompetence of rulers, the predations of foreign foes; plagues and famines;
earthquakes, volcanic eruptions and terrible urban fires. Furthermore, the
ideology which underlay Augustus' new empire fed the minds of succeeding
generations. As the Empire persisted, and as it encouraged the creativity of
artists, and the comfort of municipal aristocracies, the idea of Rome became
a powerful and lasting one. By the end of the second century, the Latin word
romanitas had been coined, meaning "Roman-ness" – that very quality
exemplary of being Roman.[3]

The tumultuous events often referred to as "the third-century crisis" tried
and tested that ideology. Emperors came and went as the empire itself suffered from a series of major miltary defeats and secessions. The Persian king,
Shapur the Great, both in a great inscription at Persepolis and in a series of
rock reliefs, boasted of having humbled three successive Roman emperors:
one slain, one a supplicant; one a captive.[4] Another emperor, Decius, went
down in battle against the Goths, whilst still others fell on the swords of
their own rebellious soldiery.

When Galerius was born, in about 258, it was at a time when the idea of
Rome presented fewer certainties. His own parents were refugees who had
been forced to flee their home in trans-Danubian Dacia because it was no
longer secure from a barbarian tribe, the Carpi, which periodically raided the
region. They settled on a small farm near to the major centres of Serdica and
Naissus, and not all that far from the home which they had lost.[5] Their

26

status as refugees highlights the change which had taken place in the third century. Unrelenting pressure on the frontiers had taken a toll upon the resources of the empire. The province of Dacia, the conquest of which early in the second century was immortalized in the spiralling reliefs of Trajan's Column, was untenable by the middle of the third century. In the 270s, it was definitively abandoned by Aurelian, but Roman control beyond the Danube was, by then, a tenuous proposition.[6] Galerius' family, thus, was directly touched by the retreat of Rome.

By the time that Diocletian became emperor in late 284, the need for lasting solutions to the empire's problems had become even more acute. Military and political failure necessitated change. Much of the imperial ideology remained predicated upon peace born of victory. The empire had not seen much of either since the death of Septimius Severus in 211. Instead, it had seen presentiments of failure: not merely defeat, but secessionism; not merely invasion, but collaborationism; not merely the retreat of the imperial cult, but the growth of personal religion.[7] Documents of dissent were likewise produced, the most celebrated being the "Potter's Oracle" from Egypt, and the Syrian Thirteenth Sibylline Oracle.[8] These promised the overthrow of foreign rulers through plague, calamity and war. Such documents not merely reflect the desire for security in an insecure world, but also the failure of Rome itself to capture the imagination and loyalty of provincials. They sought their security apart from the empire, whether in the assertion of a narrow ethnicity or in the expectation of a saviour-king.

Many, although not all, of the empire's problems can be readily located within its political structure and especially in the relationship between three key institutions: the army, the Senate and the emperor. The army had always had the power to change the emperor. Augustus' position, and that of his successors, was based squarely upon the support of the army. Tacitus noted of the Year of the Four Emperors that it revealed the "secret of the empire": that emperors could be made in other places than Rome.[9] For many years, they were not. These were the slow and stable years of the Flavians and Antonines, during which time the army was the passive, mighty and unspeaking ally of the emperor. The emperor, in turn, was made by the Roman aristocracy with the quiet assent of the Praetorian Guard. Revolts were rare and resisted. Only in the principate of Marcus Aurelius was there a serious insurrection, and that was effectively suppressed.[10]

But the chaos which followed the death of Commodus saw a return to the uncertainty and instability of 69. The Severi sought to resolve this by allying themselves with the legionary soldiers, over and against potential senatorial rivals. They increased rates of pay and improved conditions of service. As he died, Septimius Severus is said to have told his sons: "agree amongst yourselves, enrich the soldiers, despise everyone else".[11] It was this renewed alliance between emperor and legionary which worked more than any other to destabilize the imperial office. This is precisely because the alliance became institutional rather than personal. Once the successors of Septimius Severus squandered the goodwill established by his dynasty with the legionaries, no individual person was able to establish the same relationship with the soldiers as a group. Rather, individual armies developed loyalty to their respective commanders, and those commanders in turn cultivated the favour of the soldiery. Thus, the allegiance of the soldiery was recaptured by the ambitious who used it to further their own political aspirations.

The commanders of the legions were still invariably senators. The Senate had never had very much power as a body under the principate and, ironically, seems never to have wanted it very seriously. What the Senate, taken collectively, had always wanted was respect and privilege. Emperors had varied in their approach to this, but had never varied in their need to use the senatorial class as a reservoir of talent.[12] This is where the problems generally arose. Even if the Senate as a body no longer sought to govern, it was composed of a class born to power whose individual members could and did exploit their positions and offices in order to defeat rivals and obtain supreme power.

The most straightforward way in which to do this was the capture of an army's loyalty, generally through victory in the field. Victorious generals were proclaimed emperor often enough for incumbents to need to take the field in person. It became a matter of course in the third century that emperors took the field themselves in major campaigns whether offensive or defensive. As a consequence, they became vulnerable both to the vagaries of war and the caprice of their armies. It is no accident that up until the time at least of Gordian III, no emperor had either fallen in battle or been taken by the enemy, yet after that both occurred within a decade of each other.[13]

Roman emperors were particularly vulnerable to overthrow. They were not monarchs in the traditional or tribal sense simply because the empire was never a monarchy of that kind. Rather, they were military dictators: generals or politicians who had achieved power, rather than having been born to it. Thus, the emperors did not in general possess the traditional safeguard of hereditary monarchy: dynastic legitimacy. From time to time, the principate could function dynastically and was at its most stable when it did so; but therein also lay the seed of instability. On more than one occasion the unworthy son of a great father was overthrown, and that overthrow occasioned civil war.

What, then, did the emperor do to justify his position? Fergus Millar once made the famous and thoroughly empirical statement that "the Emperor was what the Emperor did".[14] But it is not only what the emperor did; it is also what sustained him in doing it. It is crystal clear that the instability of the imperial office lies very much at the heart of the problems of the third century, either as symptom or effect, or even both. It is likewise undeniable that in some way the office of emperor failed to triumph over the challenges which it faced.

At the heart of this lies the role of the emperor as the defender and promoter of the empire itself. The empire was geographically vast and culturally diverse. The person of the emperor was a unifying factor more important even than the army. People were reminded of that daily as they counted out their change. On that coinage, the people of the empire were repeatedly told in word and symbol of the peace, piety, fruitfulness, social harmony and general happiness brought by the emperor. It is therefore no accident that the cults of Rome and of the emperor were inextricably linked from the earliest time. Augustus was not being coy when he insisted upon the twinning of the cults, but canny.[15] The cult gave the emperor the widest possible exposure across the empire without him having to lift a foot. It provided a focus of ideological loyalty and unity by ensuring the emperor a cosmological role as well as a merely political one.

This brought its own problems. Religious nonconformists were excluded from the imperial mainstream. Although Jews were tolerated because they were outside the perceived cultural continuum, other heterotheists such as Christians and, later, Manichaeans were not. More importantly, the cult brought added pressure to bear upon the emperor to succeed. If the emperor was no longer a mere mortal, neither were his failures. These implied the departure of the divine *genius*, that spark of deity that set the emperor apart from mortals, to another and worthier soul.

The imperial cult was one of two universal symbols of the emperor. The other was the coinage which not only bore the emperor's image and whatever message of peace and prosperity he wished to convey, but also functioned as a gauge by which to measure the economic success of the empire. Prosperity and secure trade routes meant a robust and stable coinage by which merchants and aristocrats could confidently exchange and store wealth. But the advent of the Severan military policy, together with the professionalization of the public sector, meant a considerable expansion of imperial expenditure at the same time as the economic base of the empire was declining.[16] This decline was the consequence of both pestilence and barbarian incursion. Rather than taking the unpalatable step of increasing the tax burden upon communities already economically troubled, emperors preferred to debase the coinage. The consequence was currency inflation, which fed a general lack of confidence in both the empire and an emperor whose likeness appeared on coins of ever-decreasing value.[17]

Despite these symbols or, perhaps, because they claimed so much, subjects remained sceptical. As Potter has remarked, the typical tendency was to believe the worst of emperors, not the best. The negative judgements upon various emperors encountered in the texts which he examines "do not reflect sentiment that can be regarded as anti-Roman; rather, they reflect sentiment that may be regarded as typically Roman".[18]

All of this meant that, more than at any other time, the imperial office was extremely vulnerable. Emperors were under pressure to solve abiding and structural problems in an instant. When they failed, they fell. Of necessity, this resulted in an increasing centralization of power in the hands of the emperor, as *principes* sought to extend their personal control in order to reduce the number of things that could go wrong. Emperors also became increasingly peripatetic. There was pressure upon the imperial office to respond personally to crises. Crises there were aplenty, as reflected by the number of claimants to the imperial office at any given time. All of the European and Asian frontiers of the empire were threatened more or less continually from 240 onwards. Westward pressure from the newly reconstituted Persian empire meant the collapse of the troubled entente which Rome had enjoyed with its Parthian predecessor. By the time of Galerius' birth, the emperor Valerian had been captured, and the empire humiliated, by the Persians. His ignominious end must have been a profound shock to Roman minds.[19]

It also represented something of a reversal of fortune. Valerian had come to the principate in 253 after a series of short-lived emperors had proven incapable of responding to the challenge of the times.[20] In 248, the emperor Philip had celebrated Rome's millennium with magnificent games.[21] This endeavour to reassert Rome's sense of imperial mission rang hollow. Philip had always held power uneasily. In 249, he was deposed and slain by an Illyrian senator and general, Decius. Decius saw the problems with which Philip had failed to deal, no doubt the primary reason for Philip's overthrow. His solution was to return to earlier certainties. He assumed the name of Trajan, the empire's most successful soldier-emperor, and commenced a self-conscious programme of restoration. An inscription from Dacia, still Roman, called him "the renewer of military discipline, the securer of the sacred city, the strengthener of Roman hope".[22] Furthermore, he sent out an edict that, in an act of old-time piety, all of the empire should sacrifice to the gods. The result was a needless persecution of nonconformist Christians.[23] Decius himself died in battle with Gothic invaders of Moesia within a matter of months.

Ephemeral successors failed to deal with the military crisis until Valerian seized power. The situation was grave enough. A Gothic breakout following the death of Decius had resulted in the ravaging of Thrace;[24] Shapur was undefeated in Persia; Germans were raiding across the Rhine.[25] Valerian reacted with energy and purpose. He appointed his adult son Gallienus to the purple, not merely to strengthen the nascent dynasty as his predecessors had done, but also to enable an imperial presence in two places at once. He articulated a firm and clear language of restoration, as Decius had done. Coins called him *restitutor orbis*, the restorer of the world, and more besides.[26] He recommended Decius' religious programme, and targeted the recalcitrant Christians quite specifically.[27]

Initially Valerian's wars went well. Gallienus went to the Rhine frontier where he met with great success.[28] Those victories were followed by his title of *Dacicus* in 257.[29] In the meantime, Valerian sought to confront the Persians. He was successful in his first campaign, in 254, but a Persian counter-attack in 257 obliged him to return to the east, where he was distracted by a large sea-borne Gothic raid which penetrated the provinces of Asia Minor.[30] His march against these raiding tribes seems to have exposed his army to an epidemic. From Cappadocia, Valerian marched his ailing army to Emesa, defeat and capture.[31] It was an ignominious end for a man with both energy and vision. As Potter has remarked, many of his policies seem to foreshadow those of Diocletian.[32] As it was, his death precipitated a grave crisis. Whatever precarious stability had been won in the years following Valerian's accession was now lost.

Gallienus has won the opprobrium of succeeding generations of historians seemingly because of his spectacular failures. Ironically, this is not just. It was rather because of his successes that he was hated in antiquity by the class which formed and recorded historical judgements.[33] Gallienus recognized the necessity of addressing the structural problems which had weakened the imperial office and its ability to deal coherently with the problems of the empire. For him the solution lay primarily in the promotion of the competent rather than the privileged.[34] Therefore, he completed a process long in train of professionalizing the senior ranks of the army. From Gallienus' time onwards, it was men of equestrian status who dominated senior posts, both military and civil. One ancient writer, Aurelius Victor, went so far as to speak of an "edict of Gallienus" which excluded senators from military posts.[35] While this has been rightly doubted by modern scholars, it cannot be denied that Valerian and his dynasty were the last emperors drawn from the Roman aristocracy for two centuries.[36] What was probably not an edict was undoubtedly a policy and it had the twin effects of creating a new professional governing cadre whose claim to office derived from competence, rather than birth, and protecting the imperial office from ambitious senators, the traditional main source of disloyalty. It did not, however, protect it from ambitious soldiers.

Like Severus before him, Gallienus was an aristocratic warrior. He wore both toga and *paludamentum*, and his power was based firmly upon the loyalty of his troops, most particularly the cadre of senior generals that emerged through his policies. He strengthened this corps of professionals by developing the corps of *protectores* as a new pool of talent for command posts. He was active in the field and an able general, apparently careless of his own person. Mostly successful in battle, he nevertheless suffered a decisive defeat when he sought to retain the secessionist Gallic empire under Postumus under Roman rule.[37] For the rest, he was able to juggle his limited manpower successfully by developing a strategic approach which Luttwak has called "defence in depth".[38] He displayed imagination in dealing with the various Danubian tribes, one of whom he pacified by the acceptance of the daughter of the chief as a concubine.[39] Moreover, seeing little advantage accruing in the persecution of the Christians commenced by his father, he put an end to it and ensured the restoration of property confiscated from churches and individuals.[40]

But however far-reaching and imaginative Gallienus' solutions were, he failed the ultimate test of unifying a fragmented empire. He lost Gaul, Britain and Spain.[41] In the east, the price of the repulse of the Persians from Roman territory was the cession of actual, although not titular, authority to Odenathus, client-king of Palmyra.[42] While Odenathus lived, he displayed loyalty to Gallienus. His murder in 267 in a palace coup brought to effective power his widow Zenobia, who swiftly displayed her ambition of converting the east into a Palmyrene empire.[43]

It may well be that this was the last straw for Gallienus' hitherto loyal officers. In 268, his cavalry commander and most trusted senior soldier, Aureolus, rebelled against him.[44] Gallienus was able to defeat him in the field and pen him up in Milan, but, during the course of the siege, he was murdered by a group of his own officers.[45] Some of the members of this group are known, including the future emperor Aurelian, the Praetorian Prefect Aurelius Herculianus, and the *dux Dalmatarum*, Cecropius, who struck the fatal blow.[46] They chose one of their own, Claudius, to succeed Gallienus. He piously persuaded the Senate to enrol amongst the gods the man whom he had supplanted and against whom he had conspired.[47]

This group of officers, largely anonymous, but nevertheless important, was the creation of Gallienus. He was the last emperor of this period to have been born into the senatorial class precisely because it was he who opened up the senior echelons of the army to men of talent but humble background. They then provided the senior generals who became emperors: Claudius, Tacitus, Aurelian, Probus, Carus. They were careful to ensure that no out-sider disturbed their dominance, and that it was they alone who controlled imperial succession.[48] What this meant was that professionalizing the army did not in itself serve to safeguard the emperor. The locus of potential dis-loyalty and, therefore, instability had passed from ambitious senatorial legates to the cadre of equally ambitious professional generals. Their presence can be glimpsed in Dexippus' account of an embassy of the Danubian tribe, the Iuthungi, to Aurelian in 270, shortly after the death of Claudius. He describes Aurelian amidst his army, arrayed as if for battle. The emperor himself is on a rostrum. Surrounding him are his senior generals, all on horseback and behind him were the symbols of the army. This is a spectacle clearly intended to intimidate the Iuthungian ambassadors, and does so. But it is also a remorselessly military set of images. There is no civilian present. The emperor's most senior men are not consuls or prefects. They are his warriors.[49]

These men were gifted commanders and administrators, and they sought to continue the work of restoration commenced by Decius, continued by Valerian, and apparently neglected by Gallienus. It is undeniable that the

empire was at the nadir of its territorial fortunes at the accession of Gallienus, with the loss of the east to the Persians and its subsequent effective
cession to Palmyra, and the Gallic provinces in the hands of Postumus. Eight
years of rule by Gallienus did nothing to ameliorate this. His successors saw
it as their priority.

The last year of Gallienus' life had seen a massive sea-borne invasion by a
Gothic confederacy which threatened Greece and the Balkans.[50] That the
barbarians were obliged to resort to a mode of transport foreign to them says
much for the security of the Danubian frontier under Gallienus. There is
some dispute as to whether Gallienus defeated one group of these raiders
before turning to deal with Aureolus. Whether this is the case or not, credit
for the defeat of the Gothic raid went to Claudius.[51] Indeed, Claudius began
a process of reassertion. He attacked the Gothic bands and defeated a major
group of them at Naissus.[52] It was this victory which really began the process of military recovery, a fact which probably led Constantine to claim him
as an imperial ancestor.[53] Nevertheless, it is to the credit of the departed
emperor that much of this success was due to Gallienus' reformed army with
its improved cavalry wing.[54]

Victory over the invaders meant that Claudius was the first emperor to
assume the title *Gothicus*.[55] Victories and titles did not guarantee immunity
from disease. He succumbed to illness early in 270. The clique of senior
officers asserted its claim to nominate the emperor over the dynastic expectations of Claudius' brother Quintillus. After a few days' reign, he was made
away with and Claudius' effective replacement was another senior officer of
Illyrian origin, Domitius Aurelianus.[56]

Aurelian's first task was no different from that of his predecessors: to
guarantee the frontier. He repelled raids by the Alemanni and Vandals.[57] A
fragment of the *Skythika* of Dexippus provides a tantalizing view of negotiations with the Vandals after the Roman victory.[58] They were obliged to
return home, leaving behind hostages and two thousand recruits for the
Roman army. Trade between the empire and the Vandal nation was to be
regulated by the local governor in a single market. This concluded, Aurelian
turned to swift and victorious war against the Iuthungi, after which it was
the turn of Zenobia's Palmyra.

Her generals had seized Egypt in 270, and the Roman governor there had
been killed.[59] Despite this evident hostility between Palmyra and Rome,
Zenobia may have sought negotiation. Aurelian still appears as Augustus in
documents from the east until 272.[60] But no territory was returned. Aurelian's march towards the east was a success. The march was disciplined and
he did not permit his troops to plunder.[61] Aurelian met Zenobia's army
outside Antioch and defeated it twice.[62] After a siege, Palmyra itself surrendered and Zenobia departed in captivity to adorn Aurelian's triumph and
marry a senator. A brief revolt by the city in the following year led to its
physical destruction.[63]

From the east, Aurelian returned to confront the now rickety *Imperium Galliarum*. Postumus, its founder and most skilled general, had been slain by his own men in 269.[64] A succession crisis supervened in which the Spanish provinces may well have returned to central authority, and in the following five years the Gauls had four emperors.[65] The last was an elderly Gallic senator named Tetricus who may have little relished his task. One tradition says that Tetricus betrayed his own army both in correspondence with Aurelian and premature personal surrender on the field of battle.[66] Like Zenobia, Tetricus survived his kingdom, was led in triumph by the emperor and given a local Italian governorship.[67]

Aurelian's military successes reunited the empire. With justice, he revived the theme of restoration which can be found in documents of Valerian's principate. Aurelian became the *restitutor orbis* – "restorer of the world".[68] Perhaps it was this very success which gave Aurelian the moral authority to retreat from Dacia and abandon it to the trans-Danubian tribes.[69] The settlement of the eastern frontier which he left behind after the destruction of Palmyra was, however, less than satisfactory. His restoration of the world was far from complete, but his victories, and those of Claudius, breathed into the Roman world a new confidence. No doubt it was a confidence that Aurelian shared. That which he failed to complete in the one year, he could always do in the next. First the frontiers, then the Palmyrenes, next the Gauls. The final project was the long-delayed Roman counter-attack on Persia.[70] This was the great war of national vengeance desired by many to expunge Valerian's disgrace and a half-century of retreat in the east.[71]

Aurelian's string of victories only gave the empire immediate physical security. His vision was broader than that. He also saw the need to tackle the problem of a steadily and continually debasing coinage. Silver was the main medium of exchange in the Roman world, but by early in his principate, the silver content of the coinage had dwindled to a very small percentage.[72] While the nature of Aurelian's currency reform has excited some,[73] there was certainly a revival of the bronze coinage which had all but disappeared under Valerian and Gallienus. He also improved the quality of the silver coinage and offered to exchange new revalued coin for the debased currency still in circulation.[74] He also uncovered large-scale embezzlement in the mint of the city of Rome, which led to a short and unpleasant siege of the Caelian Hill.[75] Another tradition records a similar revolt amongst the mint-workers at Antioch.[76] Indeed, there is clear evidence that he actively and mercilessly sought to combat corruption within all levels of government.[77] After all, Aurelian had his own need of money. He fortified the city of Rome, increased food rations to the citizen populace and gave cash donatives to the people.[78] Roads were repaired and there are isolated examples of building projects in Italy and Dalmatia.[79] He held a lavish triumph and, to consecrate his success, commenced the building of a temple to Sol.[80] All of this required a great deal of money, and Aurelian was implacable in collecting it.

The building programme in Rome has its own significance. It was a part of a wider and fundamental project to reassert *romanitas*. The city of Rome was the symbol of Rome's success. Aurelian's care for the city indicates a proclamation of the city's primacy. Likewise, Aurelian's new Rome had the approval of the gods. In restoring the empire, Aurelian proclaimed the restoration of that harmony between earth and heaven which had marked the Augustan age.

Aurelian's piety is representative of the changing nature of Roman religion. Augustus' patron deity had been Apollo; Aurelian's was *Sol Invictus* ("the unconquered sun"), whose cult originated in Syria.[81] Other options were nevertheless available. The growth of the cult of *Sol Invictus* occurred alongside the burgeoning cults of Mithras and Isis.[82] Mithraic temples dating from the second and third centuries can be found from Britain to Asia.[83] Mithraic and Isaic inscriptions abound.[84] Likewise, the worship of Jupiter Dolichenus and Jupiter Sabazius.[85] Even inscriptions from Africa call upon Saturn as a personal god.[86] Lactantius says that Galerius' mother worshipped "the gods of the mountains",[87] which has been taken to be a reference to Silvanus, Diana and Liber Pater.[88] Irrespective of her religiosity, there is a significant amount of inscriptional evidence for the celebration of *taurobolia*, rituals uniquely connected with the worship of Cybele.[89] Some people sought to draw nigh to the heavens through magic and oracles.[90] The fundamentally humanist philosophical schools of Stoicism, Epicureanism and Cynicism gave way to the neo-Platonic cosmological speculations of Plotinus and Porphyry.

Aurelian's promotion of the cult of *Sol Invictus* was both a reflection and a recognition of this. The army, from which Aurelian had come, was very much a vehicle for religious change and had long harboured adherents of the new cults.[91] As an individual, Aurelian was as much subject to this as any other soldier. What is significant is his attempt to impose political meaning and order upon the confused cosmos by the promotion of *Sol Invictus* as an imperial patron, as well as a personal one, since his most important need was public, not private, piety. A new, officially sponsored pontificate was established, and perhaps the first *pontifex Dei Solis* was the distinguished senator Virius Lupus.[92] Perpetual prayers were vowed to Sol for the welfare of the Emperor, whose *comes* he was.[93] By immediate implication, the empire was blessed by the association. But the new cult may have had a grander purpose, beyond the advertisement of personal piety. It may have been intended to provide a new religious, and therefore ideological, unity.[94] Cults of the sun could be found all over the empire in various guises. In a new and official umbrella-cult, piety and politics could serve one another. It comes as no surprise in this context to discover that Aurelian was contemplating launching a fresh attack on the Christians at the time of his death.[95]

Aurelian's murder in 275 was unexpected. He was on the march to Persia, hitherto blessed by every success. He was struck down, at the town of

Caenophrurium, as the result of the fears of an individual, rather than as the consequence of an orchestrated mutiny.[96] This was no meditated and carefully executed coup against a struggling leader: no one was ready to seize power. The officer cadre which had nominated Aurelian was caught by surprise, and found difficulty in reaching agreement on a candidate. According to the tradition, they referred the matter to the Senate, which chose the elderly Tacitus.[97]

The stories about Tacitus are mostly romantic legend. One almost entirely fictional biography of him describes him as a senior senator, and descended from the great second-century historian, Cornelius Tacitus.[98] Such traditions about Tacitus are fiction. He was, in all likelihood, a retired general and possibly of Illyrian birth. To the perplexed *viri militares* at Caenophrurium, he may well have seemed an ideal compromise candidate.[99] The death of Aurelian demonstrated to potential claimants that success was no guarantee of survival. Personal treachery, such as that of Aurelian's murderer, was still to be feared. Even if success unified the provinces and pacified the armies, the principate remained a precarious regime. A single dagger thrust could throw the world once again into chaos. The man and the office remained so completely linked that there was no institutionally provided instrument of vengeance upon Aurelian's murderers, and therefore no natural deterrent. Some of Aurelian's killers remained unpunished until a later emperor invited them to a banquet where they were surrounded, disarmed and slain.[100]

The reign of Aurelian's successor Tacitus was brief. He sought to follow the policies of Aurelian which had proven so successful.[101] Tacitus also sought to protect his rule through the promotion of kin: his half-brother Florianus was appointed Praetorian Prefect, and a relative named Maximus received the governance of Syria.[102] This last proved Tacitus' downfall. Maximus' rapacity made him hated. Tacitus himself was brought to the east to campaign against another sea-borne Gothic invasion. Victory in the field did not save him from the enemies of Maximus, who slew him at Tyana.[103] Once again, the imperial office had failed to save the incumbent from assassins with a private grudge. Florianus took charge by virtue of his command of that portion of Tacitus' army with which he had been entrusted for the war against the Goths in north-west Asia Minor[104] and was recognized by the western provinces.[105] The circumstances of the ensuing civil war are unclear. Zosimus gives the detail that the eastern provinces supported Probus, while those from Cilicia to Britain backed Florianus.[106] Tacitus was assassinated in Cappadocia, closer to Syria and the east than Florianus. It may well be that Probus had been one of the officers with Tacitus' army, and one of the senior generals who had dominated the nomination of emperors from the time of the murder of Gallienus. Resenting the self-proclamation of Florian, a clear challenge to their own pretensions, they nominated their own candidate. If so, then Probus' victory at Tarsus reinforced the power of the senior military cadre and their claim to determine the succession.

Probus' victory meant little in terms of change of substantive policy. The process of structural change initiated by Gallienus and Aurelian went on much as before.[107] These were, after all, the same men with the same ideas and approaches. Probus spent much of the early years of his reign shoring up the European frontiers, which had again become vulnerable owing to the protracted absence of the emperors in the east and the civil war of 276.[108] Despite his subsequent reputation as a mighty warrior, his rule was not as universally accepted as one might think. For the first time since Gallienus a number of pretenders arose. Although they were despatched with relative ease, their very existence indicates that there was no universal confidence in the emperor or his policies.[109]

There does seem to be one point at which the military policies of Probus differed from those of Aurelian. Although Probus was a vigorous defender of Roman territory, with victories in Gaul, Illyricum, Cilicia and Egypt, there is no evidence to suggest that he contemplated renewal of the war with Persia. Rather, it would seem that with the boundaries secure, he put the army into redeveloping the economic base of the European regions devastated by recent raids.[110] There is some evidence, dating from 279, in which Probus is given victory titles reflecting a victory of some kind over the Persians, but this is isolated, unsupported by other evidence.[111] This has led some, most plausibly, to suggest a peace treaty with Persia, negotiated and settled during the course of 279.[112] The existence of such a treaty would in any case support the contention that Probus had no apparent intention of going to war with Persia.[113] The emperor's better attested and celebrated statement, "soon it will not be needful for there to be any soldiers" (*brevi milites necessarios non futuros*), might not indicate an intention of universal disarmament, but it does bespeak a desire on Probus' part not to prosecute any aggressive wars.[114]

Probus' rule ultimately failed, perhaps because he was never entirely able to assert himself, which led to defensive policies. This would explain why, at the end of his life, Probus was deserted by his own men. Carus, his Praetorian Prefect, was powerless to prevent, and indeed may have encouraged, his own nomination to the purple by the troops under his command.[115] Carus certainly seems to have had some new ideas. The troops sent against Carus by Probus went over to the new claimant.[116] The soldiers still under Probus' command at Sirmium, whether weary of the task of rural reclamation assigned them, or anxious to avoid the prospect of fighting their friends in yet another civil war, or both, mutinied and the emperor was slain.[117]

One writer quite specifically blames the soldiery for the fall of Probus, and there is something to be said for this.[118] The fact that Aurelian intended war against Persia and Carus subsequently embarked upon it may be of significance, since Probus apparently had no such intention. The great war of revenge against the Persians had yet to be fought and Valerian's disgrace had yet to be expunged. Alternatively, Probus' pacific policy towards Persia might be explained by the many provincial revolts with which he had to deal. His absence in the east would have been an incentive to the disaffected in the west. If so, then the deficiencies of late third-century monarchy are nowhere better apparent than in Probus' shaky principate and history's favourable verdict upon him is more romantic than real.

It is to Carus' credit that he had a plan to deal with this very problem. He had two sons, one grown and one growing, whom he could use in the service of the empire. In so doing, he returned to the imperial strategies of Philip, Decius and Valerian to strengthen his hold on power and ensure a more universal imperial presence, by elevating his sons to the purple. His sons, Carinus and Numerian, became Caesars, both bearing the title "Most Noble Caesar" (*nobilissimus Caesar*), and Carinus at least also held the title *princeps iuventutis*.[119] Carus was another warrior, and his first campaigns were in the Danubian regions where the tribes may have taken advantage of the death of Probus to renew raids. A number of Latin sources report a campaign by Carus against Danubian tribes, the Quadi and Sarmatians.[120] It may well be from this campaign that Carus took and shared with Carinus the title *Germanicus Maximus*.[121]

Carinus was soon sent to the Rhine border and raised to the rank of Augustus, thus providing his father both with an imperial presence on the insecure European borders and a bulwark against revolt during his absence in Persia.[122] Carinus was no stripling who took an elder's advice, but a mature soldier in his own right. Numerian was intended to be protected by the wisdom of his father-in-law, the Praetorian Prefect Aper. If this Aper is to be identified with the epigraphically attested L. Flavius Aper, then Carus' choice fell upon a military colleague, perhaps one who had assisted his seizure of power. Flavius Aper had been one of the officers who had profited from Gallienus' new army, having served in the legions and as a military governor of Pannonia Inferior.[123] The political relationship with Aper, expressed through marriage, was intended to ensure the succession of Carus' sons. Should Carus meet a premature end, there would be an experienced man to guide the younger generation. It must also have been intended to ensure that the Prefecture went to a safe man. Carus cannot have forgotten that it was from that office that he himself was elevated to the purple.

After settling the Danube frontier and sending Carinus, who was probably raised for this purpose to the rank of Augustus, to the Rhine, Carus set off for Persia. At first, he was successful. He exploited his own ability as a commander, together with the uncertain political situation in Persia, to march beyond the Persian capital, Ctesiphon.[124] It was a mighty achievement. For the first time since the Severi, a Roman emperor had not only taken the conflict to the Persians but done so successfully. *Persicus Maximus* was added to the victory titles.[125] It seemed that Rome was at last to be avenged for the defeats of Gordian III, Philip and Valerian. At the height of this success, Carus suddenly died. Rumour spoke of fire from heaven, but there is no reason to suspect foul play.[126] Deep in Persian territory was the worst possible place to attempt a coup, and hard to justify in the face of Carus' successes. In any case, the events speak for themselves.[127] There was no seizure of power in the camp of Carus, but the orderly elevation of Numerian to his late father's rank.

Numerian wisely, and probably upon the advice of Aper, decided to call a halt to the invasion and return to Roman territory. Ample reason could have been adduced to explain this, not the least the young prince's inexperience of command. Carus' scheme to protect the stability of the imperial office seemed to have worked. Two young emperors ruled, guarding both east and west. The contemporary pastoral poet Nemesianus seems to have reflected an optimistic mood when he wrote in his *Cynegetica*:

> Hereafter I will gird myself with fitter lyre to gird your triumphs, you gallant sons of deified Carus, and will sing of your sea-board beneath the twin boundaries of our world, and of the subjugation by the brothers' divine power, of nations that drink from Rhine or Tigris or from the distant source of the Arar or look upon the wells of the Nile at their birth; nor let me fail to tell what campaigns you first ended, Carinus, beneath the northern bear with victorious hand, well-nigh outstripping even your divine father, and how your brother seized on Persia's very heart and the time-honoured citadels of Babylon in vengeance for outrages done to the high dignity of the realms of Romulus' race.[128]

While the commanders united to extricate the army from Persia, their support for Numerian may well have been equivocal. Imperial blood-relatives had not prospered in recent years. Quintillus and Florian had both sought power on family grounds and been rejected. Carus had sought to establish a dynasty but also to guarantee it through intermarriage with the family of a military colleague. Self-interest dictated that Aper's task, upon Carus' decease, was to ensure the safe return of his son-in-law and the army with him. In this he failed. The new emperor led the army back from Persia as far as the safety of the Bosporus but Numerian himself was seldom seen on the march.

Aper had much to manage. The world had changed again, and the dynastic claims which he sought to promote conflicted with those of experienced and ambitious officers. In Pannonia, the *dux*, Sabinus Iulianus, revolted and, taking the imperial *nomen* Aurelius, made a bid for empire.[129] Moreover, Aper was betrayed by men whom he needed to trust. The man most directly responsible for the young emperor's safety was C. Valerius Diocles, the commander of the *protectores*, the elite officer corps instituted by Gallienus to train commanders of the future. At some point in the westward progress of the army, Numerian, complaining of ophthalmia, had taken to a closed litter. Soon afterwards, he quietly died. In all likelihood, once informed of this, Aper decided to play for time. Emperors' deaths had been concealed before in order to advantage their successors.[130] From time to time, he issued encouraging bulletins about the emperor's health. Diocles foiled Aper's attempt to bring the army home safe and loyal by accusing him of encompassing the squalid death of Numerian (he had certainly concealed it).[131] When the army had marched as far west as Chalcedon, the decomposing body of Numerian was conveniently discovered by those who had been guarding his enclosed litter for weeks. At a public assembly of the troops, Diocles affirmed his own innocence of the death of Numerian and, accusing Aper, slew him at once.[132] Such a conspiracy of silence demanded the complicity of the guards themselves, and Diocles, their commander. It also gave Diocles the time he needed to organize his own coup. Given the circumstances of a public assembly with other senior officers present on the podium, what followed was less opportunism than a carefully planned manoeuvre. For all we know, some may have seized Aper (he must also have been armed) and held his arms while Diocles stabbed him. That much is pure, if reasonable, inference. What is not inference is that the silence which followed Aper's death was broken by someone hailing Diocles as emperor. The rest of the army followed suit. The status of the new claimant was advertised by his new name: Caius Valerius Diocles became Caius Aurelius Valerius Diocletianus.

Diocletian was a member of the new generation of commanders. No aristocrat, his background was, like so many of his contemporaries, humble. There is no certain knowledge of his *patria* or early life. He probably came from Salonae on the Dalmatian coast, in what is now Croatia. His father may have been either a freedman or a scribe — or perhaps a freedman who was a scribe. His mother may have been named Dioclea. It can be sensibly inferred that he had joined the army as a youth and made his way upwards through the ranks, and coming to command the elite corps of *protectores*, the cadre of gifted trainees and emperor's private bodyguard.[133] It was that office which he had exploited to craft his nomination as emperor.

It is tempting to think that the *protectores* and officers who assisted Diocletian in his ambition included some of his future colleagues. Maximian was quite probably with him in Syria; perhaps too Galerius who by now will have been a senior officer in the army.[134] These two were of similar origins to Diocletian. Maximian was the son of a Sirmium grocer, and even more can be discerned about Galerius' origins.[135] He was a peasant. Some Latin sources record an instructive nickname: *Armentarius*, the shepherd-boy.[136] Lactantius accuses him of being the son of trans-Danubuan refugees, Romanized Dacians, who then settled in north-east Pannonia.[137] Lactantius names the place as Romulianum; archaeology has identified it, but as Romuliana. Sheep are still run in the rolling and gentle hills near modern Zajecar, which were the pastures of Galerius' youth. If he enlisted at the normal age, it was during the non-stop wars of Aurelian, Tacitus and Probus.[138] It was a good school in which to learn soldiering.

At the same time as Galerius was succeeding in a military career, the imperial office was failing to sustain itself. Victory alone could not protect the emperor. It could not save Aurelian from the paranoia of his assassin, nor Probus from disaffection and mutiny, Tacitus from assassination or Florianus from civil war. That great second-century consensus which had made Rome seem eternal had dissipated with the failures of the mid-third century. It could no longer either protect the emperor or sustain the empire. It had been Aurelian who had seen this most clearly. He had sought to restate the primacy of Rome through public works and a programme of largesse. Furthermore, he sought to refocus the spiritual core of the empire by his new emphasis on the sun cult. It is no surprise that Christians thought him contemplating a persecution. His coinage proclaimed the emperor as "Lord and God" (*dominus et deus*),[139] emphasizing the Roman world's theology of temporal power. In this respect, also, currency reform was mandatory as he sought to tackle the totality of the imperial malaise.

Aurelian's vision had been bold but pragmatic. It was also more vulnerable even than the fragile daring of the anachronistic philhellenist, Gallienus. Gallienus had sought to protect himself with both dynastic and military guardians, and he had succeeded for longer than any other emperor since Severus. Aurelian, on the other hand, could secure the frontiers, attempt to stabilize the currency and thereby stimulate the economy, and provide an imperial ideology, but it was all personally dependent upon him. If he had a plan for the succession, he kept it to himself. Turmoil, uncertainty and more civil war ensued. His successors failed to impart his determination and energy, either because of age, or, as in the case of Probus, because they never really had a secure grip on power.

A daring programme was needed, time in which to implement it, and peace in order to reap its benefits. There remained a universal need for the presence of the emperor in trouble-spots. There remained a need for a revitalized and restructured economy, the recultivation of deserted fields, the safety of the seas for trade, a stable coinage. And a coherent imperial theology of power consonant with contemporary late antique religion. All of these matters weighed upon the minds of the officers at Chalcedon who conspired with Diocletian and sought to make him emperor.

Notes

1 Syme (1939), p. 346.
2 Vergil, *Aeneid* 6. 853.
3 The earliest use of the word seems to have been by the Christian writer, Tertullian (*de Pall.* 4).
4 On the reliefs, see MacDermot (1954); Shapur's claims can be found more explicitly on the grand inscription from Persepolis generally known to classical scholars as the *Res*

Gestae Divi Saporis, and to orientalists as SKZ. A complete edition, though with limited circulation, was published in Chicago in 1953: Sprengling (1953). An edition of the Greek text in translation into French by Mariq (1958) was published in *Syria*, Vol. 35, 1958, pp. 295–360. A complete English translation of the Persian text has also been published by Frye (1984: Appendix 4, pp. 371–3) and extracts of the text have been translated by S.N.C. Lieu (Dodgeon and Lieu 1991: 2.1.3, 2.1.5, 2.2.3, 3.1.4, 3.2.6). On the psychological effect of Valerian's capture and its subsequent place in Roman thinking about Persia, see Julian, *Caesares*, 313C; Pet. Pat., fr.13.

5 Lact. *de mort. pers.* 9.2; Eutr. 9.22.1; *Ep. de Caes.* 40.16.

6 Bichir (1976), Vol. I, p. 157f.

7 For a comprehensive treatment of the secessionist *Imperium Galliarum*, see Drinkwater (1987); on Palmyra, see Stoneman (1992). On collaborationism with both domestic bandits and foreign invaders, see MacMullen (1966), pp. 196–8; Ste Croix (1982), pp. 474–9. On religious changes, see below.

8 Two texts of the Potter's Oracle are datable to the third century: *P. Rainer* 19813; and *P. Oxy* 2332. Although the text was composed in an earlier period of Egyptian history, it is significant that it was recopied and circulated during the third century. On the Thirteenth Sibylline, see Potter (1990).

9 Tac. *Hist.* 1.4.

10 Epitome of Dio Cassius, 72. 17–27; for a discussion of the revolt of Avidius Cassius, see Astarita (1983); Birley (1987), pp. 185–9.

11 Dio Cassius, *Ep.* 38, 15.2; Birley (1988), pp. 196–8; Grant (1974), pp. 254–61.

12 Talbert (1984: p. 490f.) has argued that, up until the time of Marcus Aurelius, the Senate exercised an active partnership in power with the emperor. Even if this is so, there is no question but that the emperor was the senior partner, and that there was little incentive, as Hopkins (1983: pp. 176–93) argues, for families to remain in politics once they had obtained the status of senator. See also Ste Croix (1982), 2nd edn, pp. 378–81, for a considered and realistic appreciation of the role and general expectations of the Senate in the imperial period.

13 The emperors in question are, of course, Decius and Valerian (not counting those emperors killed by their own men or in civil war). Indeed, if the propaganda of Shapur the Great is to be believed, Gordian III is also to be included amongst those who fell in battle (Macdermot 1954: pp. 76–90).

14 Millar (1977), p. 6.

15 Tacitus, *Annals* 4.37.3–5; Dio, 51.20.7.

16 For a general survey of the economic state of the Roman Empire during the third century, see Rostovzeff (1957), Chapter XI.

17 *RIC* V, pp. 5–15; on the progress of coin debasement in the third century, see Walker (1978), pp. 129–36.

18 Potter (1990) p. 140. This approach has subsequently been doubted by Ando (2000), who argues for a more nuanced approach to provincial loyalty/disloyalty, and a greater level of consensus, cohesion and loyalty throughout the Roman polity.

19 On the psychological effect of Valerian's capture and its subsequent place in Roman thinking about Persia, see Julian, *Caesares* 313C; Pet. Pat. fr.13.

20 Zos. I. 27–9.

21 Eutr. 9.3.

22 *AE* 1891, 46; Peachin (1990), p. 245, no. 37: *reparator disciplinae militaris fundator sacrae urbis firmator spei Romanae.*

23 For the most recent discussion of the Decian Persecution, see Potter (1990), pp. 261–8; also Knipfing (1923); Clarke (1969); Keresztes (1975); Leadbetter (1982).

24 Zos. I 29.2; see also Wolfram (1988), p. 46; Demougeot (1969), p. 416f.

25 Zos. I. 30.2.

26 *RIC* 5.1, pp. 116, 117, 118, 119, 149, 220, 286.

27 See Potter (1990), p. 68f.

28 *Ibid.*; see also Blois (1976), p. 6.

29 *CIL* II, 2200; VII, 1430; Blois (1976) p. 5.

30 Valerian evidently went to the east in 254 in order to oppose the Persians who had captured Antioch (Zos., I. 27.2). The local priest-king of Emesa, Uranius Antoninus, who may be the Sampsigeramus reported by Malalas (XII, pp. 296–7), had apparently already successfully opposed the Persians (*ibid.*; *IGLS* I 799; *RIC* IV iii, p. 203f.). It has been generally concluded that the operations of Uranius Antoninus represented an attempted usurpation, largely on the strength of the coinage (*RIC* IV iii, p. 203f.; Isaac 1992: p. 227f.), although this has been recently doubted by Potter (1990: p. 48f.). It is evident from the acount of Zosimus that the Persian invasion of 253/4 ended with a Persian withdrawal, leaving Valerian to pick up the pieces (Zos. I. 32.3). On the second and fatal campaign, see Zos I. 36. 1–2; *SKZ*. ll. 19–37 (Greek text); Potter (1990), pp. 331–7. For a recent treatment, see Millar (1993), pp. 162–6.

31 Zos. I.36. 1–2.

32 Potter (1990), p. 49.

33 See Boer (1972), pp. 75–86; also Blois (1976), pp. 57–83, 206f.

34 Blois (1976), pp. 83–7.

35 Aur. Vict. *de Caes.* 37.5.

36 Blois (1976), p. 40.

37 *Ibid.*, p. 26.

38 Luttwak (1976), pp. 130–45, although this view has been questioned by Isaac (1992), pp. 374–418. Isaac's arguments have themselves been recently criticized by Wheeler (1993).

39 Aur. Vict. *de. Caes.* 33.6; Ep. *de Caes.* 33.1.

40 Eus. *H.E.* 7.13.

41 Blois (1976), p. 7; Potter (1990), p. 52f.

42 Potter (1990: Appendix IV, pp. 381–94), restating the view of Clermont-Ganneau, has argued that Odenathus was in fact granted the title of *corrector totius Orientis*, but that this title in essence was ambiguous, and that an especial consequence of this was Palmyra's war with Rome. The *SHA*, *Vita Gallieni* 3.3 and 10.1 calls Odenathus *totius Orientis imperator*, perhaps a confusion of the actual title and a further indication of its uncertain meaning. On Odenathus' role in the east after the defeat of Valerian's army, see Zos 1.39.2.

43 Zosimus (1.39.2) states that Odenathus was assassinated while visiting Edessa, a murder for which Eutropius claims Zenobia herself was responsible (*Brev.* 9.13), although Potter (1990: p. 55) prefers George Synkellos' account in which Odenathus was killed in battle against Gothic raiders. Stoneman (1992: p. 108f.) has preferred the tradition that he was murdered. Vaballathus took the title "King of Kings" and *corrector totius Orientis* (*CIS*. II 3971; see Dodgeon and Lieu 1991: p. 84f.), associating Zenobia with him in inscriptions as Queen-mother (| mlkt' 'mh dy mlk mlk'|); see Potter (1990), p. 391.

44 Zos. I.40.1; Aur. Vict. *de Caes.* 33.17.

45 Zos. I.40; Aur. Vict. *de Caes.* 33. 19–21; the Ep. *de Caes.* gives Gallienus' age at death as 54 (33.3).

46 On Heraclianus, see Zos. 1. 40; on Aurelian, Aur. Vict. *de Caes.* 33.21, identified for no good reason by the editors of *PLRE* I as Heraclian (p. 417); on Cecropius, SHA *Vit. Gall.* 14.4–9. On the conspirators in general, see Syme (1971), p. 210.

47 Zos. 1. 40 implicates Claudius in the conspiracy; the Ep. *de Caes.* 34.32 has Claudius absent at Ticinum. Syme (1971: p. 205) sees here a pious fiction, deriving in all probability from the *Kaisergeschichte*, which perhaps had cause to ensure that no ill was recorded of Constantine's putative ancestor. On the deification of Gallienus, see Boer (1972), pp. 79–83.

48 Much of the assertion here about an "officers' group" is inferential, but there is later evidence of such a council of commanders which, after the death of Julian, made Jovian emperor and, upon the death of Jovian, appointed Valentinian (Amm. Marc. 25.5. 1–4; 26.1.3–6).

49 Dexippus, fr. 6, 456–60; Jacoby (1923–), no. 100; Millar (1969), pp. 24–6; on the chronology of the campaigns, see Saunders (1992).

50 Zos. I. 42–3; Demougeot (1969), pp. 425–8; Wolfram (1988), pp. 52–6 n. 45; Potter (1990), p. 57f. n. 174 *contra* Alföldi (1939).

51 On a victory by Gallienus at "Nessus", Synkellos, s.a. 467, see Potter (1990) on the reputation of Claudius who certainly seems to have earned the title of *Gothicus*.

52 Zos. I. 43.2

53 Syme (1971A).

54 Wolfram (1988), p. 54; Blois (1976), p. 29; Demougeot (1969), p. 425f.

55 On the significance of this at the time, see Wolfram (1988), p. 55f. Certainly, Claudius was a hero to his contemporaries. Upon his death, the Senate itself ordered not merely his deification, but also the erection of a golden shield (perhaps a *clipeus virtutis*) in the curia, and a golden statue upon the Capitol (Eutr. 9.11.2). Quintillus was apparently in Italy (*SHA Vit. Aur.* 37.5) when Claudius died. The circumstances of his death are unclear. Eutropius 9.12, the *Ep. de Caes.* 34.5 and the *SHA Vit. Claud.* 12.5 and *Vit. Aur.* 16.1 all relate murder by soldiers in a mutiny. Other sources allege suicide (Zos., 1. 47), and natural causes (*SHA Vit Claud.* 12.7, citing Dexippus). Aurelius Victor decided, wisely enough, to pass over him altogether and move straight on to Aurelian. On the date of Quintillus' passing and the undisputed accession of Aurelian, see Watson (1999), 221–4.

56 *P. Oxy.* xl. 23–4.

57 Zos. 1. 48–9; for the most recent discussion of the scale and speed of Aurelian's border wars, see Saunders (1992).

58 Dexippus, fr. 24, Müller (1849 [1975]), pp. 682–6.

59 Zos. 1. 44; for Probus' rank, see *AE* (1934), 257; for the date, see Potter (1990), p. 59.

60 Potter (1990), p. 61; *RIC* V, p. 573.

61 *SHA,Vit. Aur.* 22.4–23.2; *Anonymus Continuator Cassii Dionis* 10.4, *FGH* IV, p. 197.

62 Zos. 1. 50. 2–52.4; Stoneman (1992), pp. 169–71.

63 Zos. 1. 60–1.

64 Aur. Vict. *de Caes.* 33.8; Eutr. 9.9; Drinkwater (1987); Demougeot (1969), p. 501.

65 Postumus was killed in an insurrection after defeating a usurper named Laelianus in Moguntiacum (Aur. Vict. *de Caes.* 33.8; Eutr. 9.9; *SHA Trig. Tyr.* 3.7); for the coins of Laelianus, *RIC* V2 p. 372f.; his successor was the short-lived Marius (Aur. Vict., *de Caes.* 33.11–12; Eutr. 9.9.2; *SHA Trig. Tyr.* 5.3, 8. 1–2. 31.2). Marius was in turn overthrown by Victorinus (Aur. Vict. *de Caes.* 33.12; *SHA Trig. Tyr.,* 6.1–3; *ILS* 563; *RIC* V2, p. 316f.). For a comprehensive discussion of the succession crisis in Gaul, see Drinkwater (1987), pp. 33–8. On the return of the Spanish provinces to central authority, *ibid.*, p. 120f., also Pond (1970), p. 158. It is also worth noting in this context that the city of Autun likewise attempted to return to central authority and withstood a six-month siege before its final capture by Victorinus (*Pan. Lat.* 5.4; Ausonius, *Parentalia* 4.8ff.; Drinkwater 1987: pp. 78–81).

66 Zos. 1.61.2; Aur. Vict. *de Caes.* 35.3–4; Eutr. 9.13. the story of Tetricus' *literae occultae* is common to Victor, Eutropius and the *SHA Trig. Tyr.,* 24.2.4, and, in particular, Eutropius and the *SHA* are close echoes of one another, including, for example, the same Vergilian quotation (*Aeneid* 6. 365). Mutual dependence on a common source, the so-called *Kaisergeschichte*, is thereby rendered probable, although not certain.

67 Aur. Vict. *de Caes.* 35.5; Eutr. 9.13; *SHA, Vit. Aur.* 39.1; *Ep. de Caes.* 35.7; it is worth noting that the *SHA, Trig. Tyr.* 24.5 calls Tetricus *corrector totius Italiae*, since, on the

appearance of the evidence, this would appear more likely than the otherwise attested rank of *corrector Lucaniae*, given that regional correctorships do not appear in Italy until the time of Diocletian (see Jones, 1964: p. 45).

68 For the many variations in this theme in Aurelian's titulature, see Pond (1970), p. 171; Peachin (1990), pp. 382–403.

69 Eutr. 9.15; see also Demougeot (1969), pp. 452–62.

70 Zos. 1. 62.1; *SHA*, 'Vit. Aur.' 35.4; Isaac (1992), p. 32.

71 Nemesianus, *Cynegetica*, 69–75.

72 *RIC*. V1, p. 8.

73 *Ibid.*, for a full discussion of Aurelian's coinage reforms, Callu (1969), pp. 230–36.

74 Zos. 1. 61.

75 Aur. Vict. *de Caes*. 35.5–6; Callu (1969), p. 231f.

76 Malalas, 12.30, = 301.1.

77 Aur. Vict. *de Caes*. 35. 8–10.

78 *Ibid.*, on the fortifications, see Todd (1978b), pp. 21–46.

79 Pond (1970), p. 174f.

80 Aur. Vict. *de Caes*. 35.6–7; Zos. 1.61. 2.

81 There was an ancient sun-cult of sorts during the republican period and into the early empire. This was an autochthonous Roman cult, largely twinned with the worship of Luna (Varro *de re rustica* 1.1.5). On this, see Halsberghe (1972), pp. 26–38; on the Syrian origin of the later cult, see *ibid.*, pp. 45–57.

82 On Mithraism, see Vermaseren (1963), pp. 35–6; MacMullen (1981), pp. 122–7; on Isis, see Vidman (1970), pp. 106–24; although Malaise (1972) considers that the cult of Isis, largely eclipsed by the sun-cult, was in decline during this period.

83 See Vermaseren (1963), pp. 43–67.

84 The inscriptions of Mithras have been collected by Vermaseren (1960); those of Isis and Sarapis, by Vidman (1969).

85 On Jupiter Dolichenus, see Speidel (1978), who notes the general appeal of the god, rather than its restriction to members of the military; on Jupiter Sabazios see Cumont (1911), p. 64f.; Ferguson (1970), p. 102.

86 Frend (1965B), p. 451f.; but see Lane Fox (1986), p. 581.

87 Lact. *de mort. pers*, 11.1.

88 Moreau (1954), Vol. II, pp. 267–8; Creed (1984), p. 92; curiously, there appears to be a *fossa sanguinis* at the Gamzigrad site, which would indicate devotion to Cybele (Srejovic *et al.*, 1978; Srejovic, 1983: p. 196).

89 Duthoy (1969), pp. 112–21; Vermaseren (1977), pp. 101–7.

90 On the use of magic and astrology in the classical period, see Liebeschuetz (1979), 119–39; MacMullen (1966), pp. 95–163; it is worth noting that, towards the end of the third century, Porphyry wrote a work entitled *Philosophy from Oracles*; and long ago Rostovzeff (1957: p. 479) pointed to an Egyptian papyrus containing questions to an oracle (*P. Oxy.* 1477). See also Brown (1978), p. 5. Certainly the great oracles at Delphi (see Fontenrose 1982: p. 5f.) and Didyma (Lact. *de mort. pers*. 11.7) were still in receipt of petitions from the perplexed.

91 Daniels (1975); on religion in the army in general, see von Domaszewski (1895); E. Birley (1978); also Helgeland (1978); Nock (1933), p. 67.

92 *CIL* VI. 31775 (*ILS* 1210). He served as consul twice, the second time with Probus as his colleague in 278, and later as urban prefect. He also had a number of provincial governorships to his credit. The *PLRE* (I. p. 522, no. 5) notes his ancestry and descent. On the college of priests see Halsberghe (1972), pp. 145ff; Pond (1970), pp. 210–12.

93 *CIL* VIII. 5143; Halsberghe (1972), p. 152.

94 Halsberghe (1972), pp. 103f., 136.

95 Eus. *HE.* 7.30. 30–1; Lact. *de mort. pers.* 6. 1–2. Lactantius actually says that he commenced persecution, but was killed before the process could get very far. The *Liber Pontificalis* 27 records a tradition that Pope Felix was martyred on the orders of Aurelian in 274, presumably in late May since the same source records his burial on 30 May. Augustine (*de civ. dei* 28.52) also lists Aurelian as one of the persecutors. See also Frend (1965), p. 444f.

96 On the death of Aurelian: Aur. Vict. *de Caes.* 35. 7–8; Zos. 1.62.1; *Ep. de Caes.* 35.8; Eutr. 9.15; *SHA, Vit. Aur.* 36.4–5; see also Syme (1971), p. 242 ff.

97 See Syme (1971), p. 242ff.

98 *SHA, Vit. Tac.* 3–4, 10.3.

99 Syme (1971), p. 247.

100 Zos. 1. 65.

101 Pond (1970), p. 216f.; see also Syme (1971), p. 247.

102 Zos. 1. 63.2 (Maximus); Aur. Vict. 36.2 (Florian), the *SHA, Vit. Tac.* 14.1. attests Florian as *frater germanus* to Tacitus. Syme (1971: p. 246) argues that this confusion of the Latin tradition as to the precise nature of the relationship between the two means that it ought to be rejected in favour of the Greek writers who attest no family relationship but rather identify Florian simply as Tacitus' praetorian prefect (Zonaras, 12.29).

103 On Tacitus' campaigns, see Zos. 1.63. 1–2; Zonaras, 12.28; *SHA, Vit. Tac.* 13.2–3; RIC V1, p. 337, no. 110, p. 346, no. 199. On his death, Zos. 1. 63.2, Aur. Vict. *de Caes.* 36.1, *SHA, Vit. Tac.,* 13.6, which reports in addition a variant tradition, which also occurs in the *Ep. de Caes.* 36.1, that he died of illness.

104 Aur. Vict. 36.2; Zos. 1.63.1.

105 Zos. 1.64.1; it would seem, in support of Zosimus' testimony, that only mints west of Cyzicus struck for Florian (*RIC* V1, pp. 350–60), which is especially significant given that he and his army were in the region of Cyzicus, and nearer Antioch, which did not strike for Florian, than Lugdunum, which did.

106 Zos. 1.64.1.97.

107 Pond (1970), pp. 235–8; M. Kennedy (1952), pp. 231–6.

108 Eutr. 9.17.1; Zos. 1.67.1.

109 Eutr. 9. 17; Aur. Vict. *de Caes.* 37.3; Zos. 1.66.2, *Ep. de Caes.* 37.1; *RIC* V2, p. 591 (Saturninus); Aur. Vict. *de Caes.* 37.3; *SHA, Firmus, Saturninus, Proculus and Bonosus,* 14–15; Eutr. 9. 17; *Ep. de Caes.* 37.1; *RIC* V2, p. 592 (Bonosus); the details of the account in the *Historia Augusta* can be largely dismissed as fiction (Syme 1971: pp. 268–73); Eutr. 9. 17; *Ep. de Caes.* 37.1 (Proculus). Zosimus also records provincial revolts in Isauria (1.69.1–70.4) and Egypt (1. 71.1).

110 Aur. Vict. *de Caes.* 37.3; Eutr. 9.17; *Ep. de Caes.* 37.2.

111 Peachin (1990), p. 440f. nos. 134–7 for the titles. Probus was certainly in Syria in 279 (M. Kennedy 1952: p. 225), and it may be that a treaty of some sort was concluded at this time and thus reflected in the papyri. The absence of any other evidence, as well as the indefinite nature of the victory titles themselves (variously *Persicus Maximus, Parthicus Maximus* and *Medicus Maximus*), tend to rule out the possibility of a major campaign against Persia. A treaty, on the other hand, as suggested by Kennedy, would certainly explain Probus' subsequent lack of interest in Persia in that he may well have thought the situation in hand.

112 *SHA, Vit. Prob.* 17.4; M. Kennedy, 1952: p. 225; Peachin (1990), p. 97.

113 The testimony of the *SHA, Vit. Prob.* 20.1 should be dismissed as fictitious, as is most of that document; see Syme (1971), pp. 217–19.

114 Eutr. 9. 17; also found in slightly different words in Aur. Vict. *de Caes.* 37.3; *SHA, Vit. Prob.* 20.5; the similarity of these sources on this matter does not compel the conclusion of a genuine *obiter dictum,* rather, mutual dependence on the *KG* (Syme, 1971: p. 224f.).

115 A Greek tradition, represented by Zonaras (12.29) and Ioannes Antiochensis (160), avers that Carus was proclaimed Augustus against his will and sought advice and aid from Probus before Probus' troops took matters into their own hands. This is far outweighed by the testimony of the Latin sources, which mention no such correspondence, and the Anonymous Continuator of Cassius Dio, who quite specifically ascribes responsibility for the revolt to Carus (fr. 11). For a full discussion of the tradition, see Meloni (1948), pp. 46–53.

116 Ioannes Antiochensis, 160.

117 Aur. Vict. de Caes. 37.4; Eutr. 9.17.

118 Aur. Vict. de Caes. 37.5–7.

119 On the titles of Carinus and Numerian, see Peachin (1990), pp. 451–71; Pond (1970), p. 241.

120 SHA, Vit. Car. 9.4; Eutr. 9.18; Pond (1970), p. 239.

121 Peachin (1990), p. 98f.; Pond (1970), p. 239.

122 Aur. Vict. de Caes. 38.2; Eutr. 9.19.1; Pond (1970), p. 239; Peachin (1990: p. 98) suggests that Carinus was made Augustus in the spring of 283; see also Meloni (1948), pp. 61–79; on Carinus' task in the west, see ibid., pp. 79–87.

123 The name "Aper" is certain, attested by the literary sources (e.g. Aur. Vict. de Caes. 38.6; Ep. de Caes. 38. 4–5; Zonaras 12. 30–1), possibly to be identified, as the editors of the PLRE suggest, with L. Flavius Aper, a senior vir militaris of about this period (PLRE I, p. 81, no. 3); see also Howe (1942), p. 83.

124 Aur. Vict. de Caes. 38.3; Festus, Brev. 24; Eutr. 9.18.1; Zonaras 12.30; Christensen (1939), p. 113; Frye (1984), p. 305; Dignas and Winter (2007), p. 27. For a full collection of the sources, see Dodgeon and Lieu (1991), pp. 112–21.

125 SHA, Vit. Car. 8.1; Peachin (1990), p. 99.

126 Aur. Vict. de Caes. 38.3; Eutr. 9.18.1; SHA "Vit. Car." 8.

127 Contra Bird (1976).

128 Nemesianus, Cynegetica, 64–73; Duff and Duff (1934), 491–3.

129 Leadbetter (1994).

130 There were traditions in antiquity about the concealments of the deaths of both Augustus and Trajan. For Augustus, see Dio Cassius 56.30.5; Suetonius states that Tiberius did not announce the demise of Augustus until Agrippa Postumus had been slain (Vit. Tib. 12). For Trajan, Dio 69.1; SHA Vit. Had. 4.10 suggest that Plotina kept Trajan's death quiet until the adoption and succession of Hadrian could be announced (see Syme 1958: Vol. I, p. 240).

131 The accounts of antiquity do not vary in recounting this tale: Aur. Vict. de Caes. 38.6; Ep. de Caes. 38.4; Eutr. 9.2.20; SHA, Vit. Car. 12–13; Jerome, Chron. p. 225 (Helm); Zonaras 12. 30–1. They also invariably ascribe responsibility for Numerian's death to his socer, the Praetorian Prefect Aper. The story was rightly doubted by Seeck (1897), Vol. I, pp. 3–4, and has recently been the subject of some interesting speculation by Bird (1976), rightly rejected by Kolb (1987), pp. 11–15.

132 Aur. Vict. de Caes. 38.6; Ep. de Caes. 38.4; Eutr. 9.2.20; SHA, Vit. Car. 12–13; Jerome, Chron. p. 225 (Helm); Zonaras 12.30–1.

133 Barnes (1982), NE, p. 31.

134 Ibid., p. 33.

135 On Maximian, see Ep. de Caes. 40.10.

136 Aur. Vict. de Caes. 39.24; Ep. de Caes. 39.2.

137 Lact. de mort. pers. 9.9.

138 If Galerius were born in ca. 258, he would have been of age for recruitment in about 275.

139 These coins only appear from the Serdica mint; RIC VI p. 299, nos. 305–6; see also Peachin (1990), p. 384, no. 11, p. 387, no. 29. Peachin also notes four inscriptions upon which Aurelian is hailed as deus (Ibid., p. 383, nos 2–3).

2

IOVIUS AND HERCULIUS

On 1 March 293, the emperor Diocletian raised Galerius to the status of Caesar. Galerius had become a member of a college of rulers – four men, two Augusti and two Caesars, who between them ruled the Roman world. This college, the Tetrarchy as it has become known, seems at first glance to be a peculiar response to a series of stimuli. It has, in the past, invited suspicion from scholars. Otto Seeck, for one, could not conceive of this arrangement as a conscious creation and preferred instead to argue that it was a series of ad hoc responses and characterized by disunity and mistrust. Others, puzzled by the contradictions of collegial power in a monarchic empire, have followed him.[1] Partnerships of mutually suspicious men seem more credible and do have precedents in Roman history. They tend, however, not to be good precedents. They are either ephemeral, like that of Pupienus and Balbinus, or fratricidal, like the "Second" Triumvirate, or the brief joint rule of Caracalla and Geta.

Imperial collegiality, then, seems to reflect an abrogation of authority, a dangerous dilution of the imperial office and an open invitation to civil war. Suspicion of the cordiality amongst Diocletian and his colleagues would seem well founded, but other and happier models also exist from the Roman past. Dynastic partnerships had been effective: Augustus with Agrippa and then Tiberius; Marcus Aurelius with Lucius Verus. Diocletian's arrangement, of course, was not at first glance dynastic, but such a perception does not stand scrutiny. The Caesars were adopted as the sons of the Augusti: they had already married their daughters and fathered their grandchildren. As such, the arrangement mimicked the imperial adoptions and collegialities which had kept the empire stable for most of the second century. There was no adoptive "principle" at work – Diocletian made a virtue of necessity (like Augustus, he had one daughter and no sons), and in so doing founded a new dynasty which ruled the empire until the death of Julian in 363. Moreover, this new imperial *domus* was successful. It won most of its wars and enabled Diocletian to superintend a comprehensive programme of administrative and economic reform. Here is the conundrum. The mischievous and sardonic author of the Augustan History described the arrangement in glowing terms:

48

quattor sane principes mundi fortes, sapientes, benigni et admodum liberales,
unum in rempublicam sentientes, perreverentes Romani senatus, moderati,
populi amici, persancti, graves, religiosi, et quales principes semper oravimus.

(Four such rulers of the world: strong; wise; kind and entirely generous, of one mind in the state, highly respectful of the Roman
Senate, moderate, friends of the people, very pious and devoted; such
rulers for whom we always pray.)[2]

None have contradicted this luminous assessment until modern times. Eyes
unclouded by the dust of Diocletian's propaganda machine have seen a
different empire. But then propaganda is not always to be entirely dis-
believed, merely scrutinized and criticized. Some further caution is merited:
20 November 284 is often seen as one of those moments in history which
constitutes a turning point. A glance at any library of Roman history will
find that most studies of "the Roman empire" end with Diocletian's
accession, and most treatments of "the Later Roman empire" or "Late Antiquity" begin with it. Like the Fall of the Bastille on 14 July 1789, it is
one of those dates which has been used as a chronological line in the sand.
While periodization is a useful heuristic device, it leaves the impression that,
when the Roman world woke on the morning of 21 November 284, it too
shared in the knowledge that from that point its world would be profoundly
different. But neither Diocletian himself, nor his entourage, knew anything
of the sort. In constructing an image of the way in which Diocletian's
empire worked, and the ways in which the dynasts related to one another, we
must proceed warily through the sources, mindful both of their ability to mask
reality with the slogans of ancient spin doctors, and of our own temptation
to impart greater significance to them than they would otherwise merit.

Diocletian's eyes were not on the future, but on the immediate past. His
accession to power had been neither uncontroversial nor uncontested. He had
been one of those who had prospered through Gallienus' changes to the
Roman officer corps. Before he was Diocletian, he was Valerius Diocles, a
Dalmatian of humble birth, perhaps even the son of a freedman.[3] By dint of
talent and hard work, he had made his way into the senior officer cadre
which had produced every emperor since Gallienus. It is a reasonable speculation that he, like Flavius Aper, had been amongst the officers loyal to
Carus in 282 when Probus had been overthrown. Even if the details of
Diocletian's early career are not known,[4] inscriptions attest Aper as a *praepo-*
situs of two legions under Gallienus and, later, *praeses* of Pannonia, the region
in which Probus was slain.[5] Aper was rewarded for his loyalty with the
Praetorian Prefecture, Diocletian, with the command of the *protectores*. Seen in
this way, both Aper and Diocletian, like Carus himself, are products of a
military caste, the oligarchy of senior officers which had seized the empire
from Gallienus in 268.

The deaths of Numerian and Aper did not mark a decisive seizure of power, merely the staking of a claim. Others too had a claim. The elder of Carus' sons, Carinus, Augustus since April 283, remained in the provinces of the west, in command of a significant army. He had campaigned on the Danube and in Britain. His military exploits, like those of his father, were celebrated by at least one contemporary poet.[6] In his portraiture, both on coins and in sculpture, he displays a marked likeness to Gallienus, with the same "phil-Hellenic" beard which replaced the soldier's stubble of his father. In his portrait bust, he gazes upward into the distance.[7] He was a fearsome competitor with a family of his own to protect. His wife, Magna Urbica, carried the title Augusta. She had also, perhaps, borne him a son, Nigrinianus, who seems to have died in the course of 283–84.[8]

Carinus was not the only claimant to power. The news of the death of Numerian and the usurpation of Diocletian at Nicomedia had provoked another, Sabinus Iulianus, a commander on the Upper Danube, to proclaim himself Augustus and seize the two Pannonian provinces.[9] The result of the affair was by no means clear-cut. Rather, it was an open grab for empire like those of 68/9 and 193/4. In any such competition, the institutions of the empire came into contention. The senatorial class in Rome, long marginalized from active participation in politics was still wealthy and important enough to court. In 275, they had been deferred to by a divided and uncertain officer class after the death of Aurelian. This was only a decade later. Diocletian's first consulship, in the interval between 20 November 284 and 1 January 285, was taken with a senior senator Ovinius Bassus as colleague.[10] By taking such a colleague, Diocletian implicitly offered the senators of Rome the hand of friendship and alliance. It was worth having; subsequent senatorial historiography castigated Carinus with all of the rhetoric of depravity at its disposal.[11] The author of the *Scriptores Historiae Augustae* is surely representative in this, claiming nine wives in all for Carinus.[12] For his part, Carinus sought to woo the order with the appointment of a senator, Aurelius Aristobulus, as Praetorian Prefect.[13]

What followed was, in every sense, a civil war. Just as previous civil wars had been contests for dominance amongst the empire's senatorial class this was a serious conflict within the emergent military aristocracy. Unlike the perfunctory suppressions of Quintillius and Florianus this was a hard and bloody struggle. Carinus was an able general. He defeated Iulianus' invasion of Italy near Verona.[14] Some months later, the armies of east and west met at the Margus near Viminacium on the Danube. Carinus evidently had the best of the battle, but, at the moment of triumph, he was assassinated by an officer, whose wife he had allegedly seduced.[15] The motive is transparent. A coin struck at Siscia, soon after Diocletian's victory, depicted the emperor receiving the globe from a figure in military dress. The legend reads "FIDES MILITVM".[16] The date of the issue and location of the mint are significant: these coins were designed for both the victorious and the defeated soldiery. It told them that the power to bestow the empire was theirs. In a sense it was. Again, they had been guided by the treason of a senior officer, unwilling to permit the victory of Carinus over the candidate of Carus' senior officer corps.

Diocletian's support amongst Carinus' administration may well have run deeper than one act of treason. Aurelius Aristobulus was retained as Praetorian Prefect, and his designation as *consul ordinarius* for 285 was honoured. He went on to a proconsulship of Africa and an urban prefecture. Such notable honours in the new regime represent a reward for talent, loyally employed.[17] A similar reward should be discerned in the ordinary consulship held by Pomponius Ianuarius in 288. Ianuarius had been Carus' *praefectus Aegypti*.[18] His support must have been crucial for Diocletian in 284. His colleague as consul was the emperor Maximian and, like Aristobulus, Ianuarius crowned his career by tenure of the urban prefecture.

Diocletian's early consular bounty to the senatorial establishment is notable. Emperors had dominated the *fasti* from the time of Aurelian.[19] Carus and his sons had held all of the ordinary consulships while they were in power. Diocletian nominated two senior senators as consuls for 286: Vettius Aquilinus and Iunius Maximus. For Maximus, it was his second consulship, and the honour was made sweeter by tenure of the urban prefecture.[20] It was perhaps too at this time that the *clarissimus*, Turranius Gratianus, was sent off to Achaea as *corrector*. He was later awarded an urban prefecture without the distinction of having been an ordinary consul.[21]

Diocletian's initial respects to the Senate were conveyed by Ovinius Bassus, his first consular colleague, who was sent on to Rome after the Battle of the Margus to take office as the urban prefect.[22] Soon he offered them more directly, making a swift visit to Rome in 285. A rare *quinarius* records his *adventus* into the city, as does an *adventus* issue from Ticinum, in northern Italy,[23] and a stray reference from Zonaras.[24] The visit was swift; other priorities demanded his attention.

By the middle of 285, Diocletian was master of the Roman world. There had been seven months of civil war and that had its price. Gaul and Britain had been stripped of troops by Carinus, who had probably also incorporated into his force the defeated Pannonian army of Iulianus. Diocletian had led a force perhaps inferior in numbers from the east. This all had its logical results. Whereas, scant years before, Probus could boast that a minimal number of soldiers were needed to maintain the borders, and set the greater part of them to public works, by 285, soldiers in arms were needed everywhere.[25]

From Rome, Diocletian headed to the east via the Danubian provinces. There, he fought a campaign against marauders from over the river.[26] By the beginning of 286, fourteen months after he had been proclaimed emperor there, Diocletian had returned to Nicomedia. Here, at what became his favourite residence, he wintered before returning to the task which had been abandoned in favour of civil war: that of making a permanent peace with

Persia.[27] He did so, secure in the knowledge that a crisis elsewhere in the empire was being managed by competent and loyal hands. This crisis is one about which our sources confess a degree of embarrassment and uncertainty. In Gaul, something of an insurgency was in progress. It was not a military revolt, but a mutiny it seems of an entirely different stamp. In 291, a panegyrist of the emperor Maximian dilated upon the ruler's early career in Gaul.[28] He referred to the problem of the "two-formed monsters" (*monstri biformia*), whose turbulence was quelled by the magnanimity of the emperor and described these rebels as farmers who had assumed the guise of soldiers. Our sources call these rebels "Bagaudae",[29] a word better known from a similar insurgency over a century later.[30] The coyness of the panegyrist disguises a deeper problem. Some scholars have seen the Bagaudae as the dispossessed, bandits on the pattern of earlier Roman Robin Hood figures, like Maternus and Bulla.[31] For others, the Bagaudae are a more specific consequence of the uncertainties of the late third century. Usurpation and invasion had disrupted agricultural patterns: large landholders had benefited; smallholders lost out. By the 280s the dispossessed were something more than highwaymen: they had become *bagaudae*.[32] These arguments have asserted that the lines of social fracturing were horizontal, determined by economics and by class. An alternative approach sees the lines of fracture as vertical: landowners arming hordes of client dependants and looking to their own defence.[33] The most recent approach to this question has been to abandon an understanding of the term "bagaudae" as anything other than a term of abuse applied to both rebels and bandits.[34]

If there is any resolution to the conundrum which the reticence of our sources has bequeathed to us, it must lie in two things: the perceived seriousness of the revolt, and the measures taken to suppress it. The revolt does not seem to have been perceived as a minor affair. Its ringleaders are known: Aelius and Amandus. Unlike the depredations of the robber Bulla Felix a century earlier, coins were struck on this occasion and an emperor proclaimed.[35] Moreover, these coins were struck in a particular context. The provinces of Gaul had only been reunited to the central empire for a decade. For some years prior to that, they had looked to their own defence. Emperors, as Miller and others have pointed out, were more afraid of their own subjects than they were of any foreigners.[36] The secessionist Gallic empire had been ruled by mutinous generals and Gallic magnates; it had fed upon fear of foreigners and the apparent neglect from Rome's rulers.[37] If the Bagaudae of the late third century are correctly seen as local militias led by disgruntled magnates, then the seriousness with which Diocletian reacted to their appearance is merited. They threatened to renew the secession of the Gauls.

It is worth noting that, even following Aurelian's defeat of Tetricus, the Gallic provinces were far from secure. Soon after the provinces were reintegrated into the empire, there was a brief revolt.[38] The uncertainty which came after Aurelian's death in 275 seems to have provided Gaul's predators with an opportunity for raids on an unprecedented scale.[39] Probus spent a significant proportion of his time there and restored a large number of cities.[40] Invasion was not his only problem. At least two of his generals were acclaimed emperor by their troops after Probus had left Gaul.[41] While the circumstances are far from clear, what is certain is that no emperor could afford to leave the Gauls to themselves. Carus had appointed Carinus to the task, who had performed diligently and effectively. No doubt the departure of Carinus from the region, together with a substantial army with which to combat Diocletian, had given both the timorous and the disloyal good cause to embrace local leaders.

The nature of Diocletian's response is of particular significance. He did not appoint a general to the task of securing the Gauls. In the past, that had been the path to secession and civil war. Instead, he appointed an old friend, Maximian, to the purple as Caesar. Comparatively little is known about Maximian's early career. Born in Sirmium, son of a stall-holder, he had risen through the ranks with Diocletian. He had been in Syria with the army of Carus and Numerian and, therefore, an officer in the rebellious army. He may well have taken a wife while in Syria, and he certainly had a son.[42] Diocletian had owed the officer-corps of the army of Carus his initial proclamation as emperor. Had they chosen to support Carinus, Diocletian's ambition would have been stifled, perhaps fatally. While we can only guess as to the identities of those in the cabal which surrounded Diocletian, one who can be most plausibly identified is Maximian. Maximian was not appointed to mollify an ambitious colleague. It is clear that a long-standing bond of trust and friendship had built up between the two imperial colleagues.

Maximian's appointment as Caesar was, in the end, brief enough. This is made clear by the paucity of the evidence for it. There are no coins, a few ambiguous inscriptions, and a sparse literary testimony.[43] Moreover, the date of his appointment is significant. When Diocletian raised Maximian to imperial office, he must have already determined and announced the consular nominations for the following year, perhaps during his visit to Rome. His nominees were two aristocrats, Iunius Maximus and Vettius Aquilinus. It would be most irregular for any new emperor (senior or junior) not to signify their accession by the assumption of an ordinary consulship. Maximian's complete omission from this scheme is best explained by the proposition that he was not nominated to the rank of Caesar until after the consular nominations had taken place. Diocletian was then in no position to vary arrangements long made for the consulships of the following year without running the risk of alienating a Senate so assiduously cultivated. Thus Maximian had to wait until the following year (287) to take his first consulship.

A plausible date for Maximian's nomination has been argued by Frank Kolb. On the basis of a reference in Lactantius, he has suggested 13 December,[44] a date which fits well with the evidence of regnal formulae attested on papyri and inscriptions.[45] Even if the date is not completely secure, the weight of the evidence suggests that Maximian was appointed later in 285 rather than earlier. This in turn brings its own implication: Diocletian had not planned for this nomination from the beginning of his rule. It was a product of circumstance and necessity.

The Gauls most certainly needed to be secured; their problems were deep and long-standing. But they did not represent the only urgent item on Diocletian's agenda. Pannonia had again become prey to trans-Danubian tribes; the coasts of Britain were being raided by Saxon pirates;[46] Numerian's diplomatic settlement in the east needed to be consolidated or it would have been fleeting. In addition, Diocletian had his own victory to consolidate. He had no desire to be yet another evanescent soldier-emperor, hostage to a fickle soldiery and the self-obsessed plutocrats of Rome, and he was in great measure beholden to both for his victory.

Diocletian's appointment of Maximian also reveals another detail about his political approach. In appointing Maximian as Caesar, Diocletian was careful to retain his own superior authority through the differential in rank. Certainly there was more to the difference than mere titles. At least since the time of Septimius Severus, Caesars had not counted tribunician authority (*tribunicia potestas*) in their titulature.[47] Gallienus is a notable example of this;[48] the sons of Decius are notable exceptions.[49] Maximian followed the customary model and did not hold tribunician power as Caesar.[50] This clearly articulated the superiority of the Augustus over the Caesar and ensured that, while Maximian could embody the image of the emperor to the Gauls, the empire still only had one ruler.

A panegyric delivered to Maximian, very probably in 289, enables us to reconstruct something of the next few years. Panegyrics are not critical histories, and must therefore be treated with caution, but they do supply both reference to events and a chronological structure.[51] Maximian's appointment to the rank of Caesar, and his commission against the Bagaudae, date from the end of 285. His successful campaign belongs to the following year,[52] as does his defeat of a German raid.[53] The Bagaudae were suppressed swiftly, and attention was directed towards remedying the most egregious of their grievances.[54] Moreover, Maximian made plain his commitment to the defence of the Gauls by taking up residence in the city of Trier.[55] It was in Trier that he took up his first consulship in January 287 and, on the same day, made a demonstration of his defence of the Gauls through the repulse of a midwinter raid.[56] Some suspicion has been attached to this display. Wightman has labelled it "a carefully planned action".[57] If so, then it was an action calculated to impress the Gauls with imperial prowess and commitment to their protection.

Maximian could also display the enhancement of his own status. During the course of 286, probably in April, he had been raised from the status of Caesar to that of Augustus.[58] His promotion reflects a response to a need.

Although it is conceivable that Maximian's victorious army hailed him as Augustus, and Diocletian acquiesced for the sake of stability,[59] such a proposition is inherently unlikely. Had Maximian's promotion been his own initiative, it would have left him in a position of power over Diocletian, able to dictate terms and policy, which he never exercised. Far from this being so, Maximian was a dutiful but subordinate colleague.[60] The origin of Maximian's promotion must therefore be seen as a reflection of Diocletian's own purposes. The rank of Augustus carries with it independent and absolute authority. With the needs of the empire acute, Diocletian may well have anticipated a long absence from the critical Rhine frontier. The death of Numerian and Diocletian's departure to the west had created a degree of instability in the eastern provinces. There is some evidence to suggest that the Persians reoccupied territory which had been taken from them by Carus.[61] This would certainly make sense of Diocletian's presence in Syria and Palestine in 286.[62] If Carus, anticipating a long absence in the east, had raised Carinus to the rank of Augustus,[63] then Diocletian could do no less.

In raising Maximian to the rank of Augustus, Diocletian had created a constitutional problem of sorts. While Maximian had been Caesar, Diocletian's superior rank had been apparent. As Augustus, Maximian was Diocletian's coeval. Yet clearly too Maximian's authority had come from Diocletian, who was the senior partner in the imperial college. In devising a way to express the seniority of his role, Diocletian initially drew upon earlier experience. Where two Augusti had ruled together in the past, with a clear junior and a clear senior, the titles of Augustus and nobilissimus Caesar had both been held by the junior partner.[64] A collection of inscriptions from Africa reveals that, early in his reign, Maximian held the two titles together.[65]

This formulation was abandoned within a matter of months. It may have proved too clumsy and ambiguous for regular employment. In its place, a far more durable charismatic titulature of power was adopted. In 286, coins began to appear featuring Hercules as the conserver of the state (HERCVLI CONSERVATORI) while other issues featured Jupiter in the same role.[66] Before too long the titulature was reflected in inscriptions.[67] In 289 much is made of the titles by Mamertinus, a Gallic rhetorician, in a panegyric to Maximian which might suggest their utility.[68] This way of differentiating imperial roles was entirely new. Emperors had claimed particular divine companions in the past, but had never employed them to define their earthly relationships with one another. Moreover, it provided an economic ideological formulation, linking earth and heaven and also the emperors with one another. Its adjectival form (Iovius/Herculius) makes it clear too that the emperors are not claiming actually to be these gods incarnate, but are establishing a mimetic relationship with Olympus. Diocletian acts like Jove: his law and the thunderbolts of his legions rule the empire; Maximian labours and assists. In 289, Mamertinus sets this relationship out with a commendable and uncharacteristic brevity:

Ut enim omnia commoda caelo terraque parta, licet diversorum numinum ope nobis provenire videantur, a summis tamen auctoribus manant, Iove rectore caeli et Herculi pacatore terrarum, sic omnibus pulcherrimis rebus, etiam quae aliorum ductu geruntur, Diocletianus facit, tu tribuis effectum.

(For just as all things in heaven and on earth seem to be provided for us through the work of a diversity of divinities, yet ultimately proceed from the supreme creators – Jupiter, the ruler of Heaven, and Hercules, pacifier of the Earth – so too all the most splendid deeds – even those accomplished under the command of others – Diocletian devises, and you put into effect.)[69]

By the time that Mamertinus delivered his speech, however, the successes of the partnership between Diocletian and Maximian had generated imitators. The Panegyrist makes only oblique mention of Carausius, *ille pirata* cowering in Britain.[70] Otherwise, and properly, Maximian's victories are stressed: his battlefield initiation to the consulship in a sortie from Trier;[71] this was followed by his defeat of tribes across the Rhine and a raid deep into barbarian territory. Delighted, Mamertinus declared:

quidquid ultra Rhenum prospicio, Romanum est.

(Whatever I behold across the Rhine is Roman.)[72]

The usurpation of Carausius is quietly glossed over in the speech. Maximian's most egregious failure neatly sidestepped as the unfinished punishment of a bandit. Yet it had more to do with Maximian than Mamertinus hints. Maximian had been concerned to protect the provinces of Britain from the raids of Saxon pirates. According to Aurelius Victor and Eutropius, Maximian appointed Carausius to the task of clearing the English Channel of Saxon raiders. He did so, but was accused of having allowed the raiders through on their way to England and then, in true buccaneering fashion, intercepting them on their loot-laden return and keeping a proportion of the recovered British booty for himself.[73]

This is too obviously simplistic and propagandist. The implication is that he had been robbing the people of Britain by permitting them to be raided by Saxons and then keeping the loot for himself. The accusation was no doubt a contemporary one and well-enough known, since its public circulation would have well suited Carausius' imperial enemies. But the British provincials themselves chose either not to believe it or to ignore it. Herein, of course, lies a very significant question of the Carausian usurpation. It was not merely successful because of the Channel; it was also successful because he received the support of British soldiers and civilians alike.

At the furthest western periphery of the empire, Britain was even more vulnerable to predation than the Gallic provinces. It had joined them in the secessionist enterprise of the 260s,[74] surely because Gallic emperors represented a more proximate and therefore more secure imperial presence. The evidence suggests that one of the first acts of Postumus, the first of the Gallic emperors, was to visit Britain in 261.[75] This reversed a trend of apparent imperial neglect and removal of resources from the province apparent in the 250s.[76] Britain remained an integral part of the *Imperium Galliarum* until its reincorporation into the empire. Coin hoards and inscriptions both indicate the loyalty of the British provinces to the rebel regime, which apparently looked after them well enough. The second stage of the Saxon Shore forts may have commenced at this time. At Burgh castle, for example, the earliest coins uncovered by the excavators were from the late 250s, which should indicate construction and use some time in the 260s or early 270s.[77]

This interest in the British provinces came to an end with the fall of the Gallic empire in 274. Neither Aurelian nor his successor Probus visited Britain, despite a major Frankish incursion into Gaul in 276.[78] It was left to Carinus to visit the provinces in 284.[79] By that time there was certainly the need. The evidence of the continued construction of the Saxon Shore forts indicates that the Saxon threat had intensified after the fall of the Gallic empire, and the need for a remedial imperial presence had become acute. That need cannot have receded when Carinus withdrew both his presence and significant troop numbers in order to combat the usurpations of Julianus and Diocletian.

The British provinces must certainly have felt neglected. They were wealthy and productive. A panegyrist, speaking in praise of Constantius I, proclaimed in 297 that Britain is "a land so abundant in crops, so rich in the number of its pastures, so overflowing with veins of ore, so lucrative in revenues, so girt with harbours, so vast in circumference".[80] Even allowing for the customary magniloquence of panegyrical language, the image of a wealthy and prosperous Britain is clear. Romans had always been aware of the natural wealth of the island: in the first century Strabo knew of a number of British exports: "it [Britain] produces grain and cattle, gold, silver and iron. These are exported along with hides and slaves and dogs bred specifically for hunting."[81] These exports were still a feature of the British economy in the fourth century. Ammianus makes it clear that Julian's army in Gaul was dependent upon British corn, and Zosimus states that, at one point, Julian constructed 800 grain transports in Lower Germany in order to ensure its arrival.[82]

Despite such economic value to the empire, Britain had nevertheless been subject to a progressive withdrawal of imperial resources.[83] The garrison of Wales had been steadily denuded of troops from the middle of the second century, as it became apparent that they were needed elsewhere.[84] A clear case of this is seen in an inscription from the Roman legionary fortress of Moguntiacum on the Rhine, attesting the presence there of a detachment from the XX Valeria Victrix, based at Chester.[85] The clearest evidence of redeployment within the province comes with the establishment of the first of the Saxon Shore forts. The first wave of these fortifications was in the 230s with the construction of the forts of Reculver and Brancaster, watching over the estuaries respectively of the Thames and the Wash.[86] Reculver's garrison at least was the I Cohort Bataesiorum, originally stationed at Alauna in the north.[87] This makes it clear that there was no new commitment of troops to the British provinces. When trouble came, they had to fend for themselves, transferring troops within the provinces as the need arose. In one case, an entire legion was transferred. The II Augusta, stationed for many long years at Isca, was transferred in the course of the third century to the newly commissioned Saxon Shore fort at Richborough (Rutupiae).[88] The transfers within and outside the British provinces were such that one observer has estimated that the total garrison of the provinces was depleted from a total of one-eighth of the entire Roman field army in the first century after the conquest, to about one-thirtieth in the fourth.[89]

This is despite both the wealth of the province and its own vulnerability to attack. A series of imperial campaigns during the second century had minimized the threat from the north. Furthermore, the construction of Hadrian's and the Antonine walls created a buffer zone in between. This was the land of the Votadini, whose friendship with Rome was guaranteed by regular trading contacts.[90] Other threats remained. The Scotti from Ireland continued to be a persistent thorn in Rome's side. The greatest danger, however, came not from the British Isles themselves, but from the Saxon pirates based in modern Denmark. The threat may have been made plain by raids in southern Britain as early as the late second century. Coin-hoard evidence, together with clear remnants of burning in the archaeological record, indicate the violent destruction of a number of sites in Essex in the late second and early third centuries.[91] The logical inference is sea-borne raiders, and this is confirmed by the construction of the first of the Saxon Shore forts in the first part of the third century.

The British provinces were peculiarly vulnerable to such attacks. British mines, for example, produced both silver and gold, but there was no mint on the island until Carausius opened one. Bullion therefore had to be shipped to the Gallic mints, coined there, and then re-exported to Britain. That made them a very tempting target to the pirates of the North Sea. The forts of the Saxon Shore were built in order to combat this particular menace, and the British fleet was certainly still active into the middle of the third century.[92] After this time, the record from Britain falls briefly silent. Carausius, to whom Maximian entrusted the security of the provinces, was Menapian from Gallia Belgica by birth. He had been a professional sailor before he embarked upon a military career. His naval expertise was perhaps decisive in

Maximian's choice of him.[93] But the choice seems to have been a poor one. The propaganda tale of Carausius' malfeasance was for domestic consumption. The provinces, rich and productive yet long neglected and starved of resources, had good cause to look to their own defence. Carausius became that defender.

The date of the usurpation is a problem and has long been fought over. Scholars disagree as to whether the revolt took place in 286 or 287.[94] Recently, the arguments for the earlier date have been restated with clarity and vigour by P.J. Casey.[95] The literary testimony is vague and imprecise. Great weight has been given to it in the past simply because it provides the only clear dates which we possess. The expectation that these sources – themselves either epitomators or chronographers, seeking to express information with more brevity than precision – will produce an exact chronology is a highly optimistic reading of their accuracy. Complementing the literary testimony has been the numismatic evidence, more empirical perhaps, and possibly even more precise. A coin minted before 290 proclaims Carausius as COS IIII.[96] Barnes dates the revolt on this evidence to 286.[97] The argument is a strong one. If Carausius had claimed the consulship (as Diocletian had) as soon as he had been proclaimed Augustus, and then held the consulship for each of the years following, then his fourth consulship would fall in 289. It is probable that if the revolt took place in 286, then it did so in the latter part of the year, after the campaigning season which had seen Maximian's promotion, the suppression of the Bagaudae, and Carausius' successful expedition against Saxon pirates.

Carausius' revolt had broad implications. Much of coastal north-west Gaul seems to have gone over to him without a struggle.[98] But Carausius had limited ambitions: he did not seek the entire empire, merely his corner of it. He sought to legitimize this through acceptance as a third imperial colleague. His coins proclaimed "PAX AVGGG" and, even more telling, one issue shows a triple portrait of the three Augusti with the legend "CARAVSIVS ET FRATRES SVI".[99] Carausius' attempt to graft himself into the imperial college makes it clear that there was no necessary public ideology of dyarchy. Such a discourse did emerge, but only after Carausius' usurpation.[100] It is therefore arguable that Diocletian did not institute a diarchy in 285; Carausius did.

Maximian's and Diocletian's refusal to accept Carausius as a colleague is unsurprising. The essence of the arrangement between the two was hierarchy and unanimity. Carausius' self-promotion threatened both. War followed. Campaigns in 287 and 288 may well have recovered territory lost to Carausius in north-west Gaul. Mamertinus' panegyric alludes to successes in securing mainland territory, but the usurper remained secure on his island fastness from the wrath of Maximian.[101] In a broader context, however, the usurpation represented the only major problem which the dyarchy failed to solve. In a series of campaigns, Diocletian and Maximian had stabilized the

Rhine and Danube frontiers. In a major diplomatic victory, Diocletian, perhaps aided by civil strife, had wrested the hegemony of Armenia from the Sassanids.[102] Carausius remained. In 289 the grand fleet which Maximian had prepared for the *reconquista* was shattered in a storm.[103] Maximian never again challenged Carausius himself.

Early in 288, Diocletian and Maximian met and conferred with one another, probably somewhere in Rhaetia.[104] Doubtless Carausius was a significant item on the agenda. Another event may also have occupied their counsels. Mamertinus, in his panegyric of the following year, alludes to Maximian's desire for harmony (*concordia*), a desire so great that for its sake he had bound the holders of highest office to himself by bonds of amity and kinship.[105] The allusion is clearly to a wedding, but Mamertinus is too coy to say whose. The "holder of the highest office" (*potissimum officium*) can only be Maximian's Praetorian Prefect. One possible identification is a marriage between Maximian himself and Eutropia, the first wife of the Praetorian Prefect, Afranius Hannibalianus.[106] This is entirely plausible. Maximian had a step-daughter which indicates a wife who had herself been married earlier.[107] It seems, however, a very bold statement to make, even by an accomplished Panegyrist, that an emperor marrying the ex-wife of a Praetorian Prefect constituted a bond of family and friendship. Indeed, Mamertinus even went further than this, claiming that the match inspired devotion:

> *id pulcherrimum arbitratus adhaerere lateri tuo non timoris obsequia sed vota pietatis.*

> (adjudging it is the most wonderful thing, to have them fast by your side, not from the obsequiousness of fear but from the solemn vows of proper duty.) [108]

Maximian was certainly married to Eutropia, but it is far more likely that, by 289, they had long been married.[109] Theodora was more probably the daughter of Maximian by an earlier marriage, rather than a step-daughter.[110] It is here that the family connection with the Hannibaliani is better found. There no doubt was one. The onomastic evidence is too strong to deny. If Maximian's first wife were a member of that illustrious family, another tantalizing detail emerges from the shadowy world of the powerful Illyrian marshals who, between them, ran the Roman world. Hannibalianus' tenure of the office of Praetorian Prefect is also significant. It is most likely that he was not Maximian's prefect in 289. Numismatic evidence makes it more likely that he had served Diocletian in that capacity soon after Maximian's departure for Gaul.[111]

The marriage alluded to in 289 is more properly understood as a reference to the wedding of Maximian's step-daughter Theodora and another senior

member of the Illyrian cadre, Flavius Constantius.[112] Other sources, themselves drawing upon a common source of information, date this match to
293.[113] The literary testimony is not, however, unanimous. The author of
the *Origo Constantini* does not link the marriages and promotions in the same
fashion. Here, the word *enim* is used in such a fashion as might suggest that
Constantius' promotion was the consequence of his marriage, rather than the
reverse.[114] Prosper Tiro gives the date for the marriages and elevations as
288, the only date in his chronicle for this period, which might otherwise
seem to be badly wrong.[115] These divergent traditions provide clear evidence
for an earlier match. The alternative evidence of the *Kaisergeschichte*, upon
which many of the narratives of this period have been based, is tainted by
the suspicion that that document largely reflects Constantine's version of
history.[116]

The bridegroom was sufficiently distinguished:

protector primum, exin tribunus, postea praeses Dalmatiarum.

(first protector, then tribune, and after that, governor of the
Dalmatians.)[117]

He was, moreover, an Illyrian from Naissus. The arrangement is a significant
illustration of the way in which the military establishment maintained and
shared the power which they held. Like the senatorial class of old, it was
through a matrix of office and marriage. Hannibalianus too was a part of this
charmed circle, both in terms of office holding (he was Praetorian Prefect,
consul and urban prefect[118]), as was Julius Asclepiodotus (long-time Praetorian Prefect and consul[119]). Identifying the marriage alluded to in the
Panegyric of 289 with that of Constantius and Theodora admits another of
this military cabal. The marriage of Constantius with Theodora is linked in
the sources with that between Galerius and Diocletian's daughter Valeria.
Might this marriage too belong to 289? It should also be the case, then, that
Galerius was Diocletian's Praetorian Prefect in 288.[120]

One family detail tends to confirm an earlier date for the marriage
between Galerius and Valeria. Their daughter, Valeria Maximilla, was married to Maxentius at some time prior to 304.[121] She was also a mother before
Maxentius' usurpation on 28 October 306.[122] It is therefore improbable that
Valeria Maximilla would have been born as late as the end of 293 – the very
earliest possible date for her birth if the marriage of her parents took place in
March 293. The year 289 is more plausible for her birth and clearly permits
the linkage of Galerius' marriage with that of Constantius.[123] Thus, when
Diocletian and Maximian met in 288, they conferred about Carausius and
devised a method to deal with him. They were also determined to join their
daughters in wedlock to their Praetorian Prefects, thereby extending and
consolidating the new dynasty which they were crafting together.

Diocletian and Maximian had survived for longer than most of their immediate predecessors, but they were still vulnerable to usurpation. They needed to surround themselves with a rampart of loyal men whose fate was bound to theirs. The Panegyrist's comment that such men would be bound to Diocletian and Maximian out of loyalty rather than fear (*non timoris obsequia sed vota pietatis*) should be taken at face value. There is much here to proclaim. Praetorian Prefects had proven costly traitors in the past: Aristobulus had deserted Carinus for Diocletian; Carus had overthrown Probus.[124] Carus himself had recognized the need to prevent the recurrence of his own coup when he ensured that his own prefect was closely tied to his family through the bond of matrimony,[125] although that did not prevent Diocletian from blaming Numerian's death upon a perfidious father-in-law.

This was not intended to be a grand constitutional scheme, but neither was it the nervous policy of uncertain men. The principal intention of the marriages was the protection of the regime through the bonding of the most powerful men in the empire with the strong cement of dynastic self-interest. Moreover, this evolving *domus* of rulers, while not preventing ambition, made it far more complicated. This element was emphasized when the sons-in-law were given commands: Constantius on the Rhine; Galerius on the Danube.[126] Their loyalty and skill enabled Maximian to concentrate upon the elimination of Carausius and Diocletian to commence the immense task of the renovation of the eastern frontier.[127]

The genesis of the so-called "Tetrarchy" therefore is to be found long before 293. It existed in fact, if not in formal arrangement, from 288. The years that followed vindicated the wisdom of this decision. Although the fleet being fitted out by Maximian was destroyed in a great storm,[128] there was also a period of peaceful consolidation and preparation. For four years (289–293) Diocletian took no victory titles: in the circumstances, more indicative of an absence of conflict than failure in the field. That peace was in itself a critical indicator of Diocletian's immediate success; it permitted the recovery of a measure of confidence, not to mention prosperity.

In late 290 or early 291 Maximian conferred with Diocletian in Milan.[129] It was a public occasion: men of rank and position were permitted to enter the palace and behold the sacred countenances of the emperors.[130] This was another critical aspect of the elaborate political network constructed by Diocletian to defend both himself and the office of emperor. Far more successfully than his predecessors he insisted upon a complex court ceremonial. One source, repeated by many others, noted that Diocletian was the first emperor successfully to insist upon the receipt of formal adoration, and to wear vestments and shoes adorned with jewels.[131] This was not megalomania but policy. It created a significant symbolic barrier by making the emperor more remote and inaccessible. Moreover, it expressed in more tangible terms the theology of power already implied by the adoption of the titles of *Iovius* and *Herculius*. The emperors were not remote and bejewelled figures because it suited their vanity: it was the consistent result of the assertion that the imperial office was the point at which divinity and humanity uniquely met. The emperor was surrounded by divine companions and advisers, his *comites*. Such a status could not be frivolously or wantonly claimed; it was granted by the gods, not grasped by ambitious men.

With such bulwarks in place, Diocletian could proceed to remake the empire. The peace of the following years enabled him to embark upon a programme of administrative reform which saw radical changes in provincial structure and a new complexity of government. Lactantius, recruited to be a teacher of rhetoric at Nicomedia during this period of reform and renovation, was also its bitter critic:

> *Et ut in omnia terrore complerentur, provinciae quoque in frusta concisae: multi praesides et plura officia singulis regionibus ac paene iam civitatibus incubare, item rationales multi et magistri et vicarii praefectorum, quibus omnibus civites actus admodum rari, sed condemnationes tantum et proscriptiones frequentes exactiones rerum innumerabilium non dicam crebrae, sed perpetuae, et in exactionibus iniuriae non ferendae.*

> (So that every place might be filled with terror, the provinces too were cut up into pieces; a multitude of governors and bureaux watching over each region and virtually every town, and with them numerous financial officials and managers and deputies of prefects – all of whose acts were rarely civil, engaging instead in condemnations and frequent purges, and numberless confiscations, not just repeatedly, but perpetually such that in their commission, there were unbearable injustices.)[132]

It seems surprising, then, that, in the midst of what seems to be vigorous peacetime policy, Diocletian and Maximian raised their sons-in-law to the rank of Caesar in March 293. The promotion was well planned: the day was chosen with care, and there is evidence of an elaborate ceremonial which required a degree of stage management. The date upon which Galerius and Constantius were elevated was 1 March.[133] This day was the traditional feast of Mars.[134] The birthday of Mars, for such it was, had been the day of great festivities for centuries, including the dance and banquet of the Salian priests. It was still celebrated in the time of Diocletian, appearing in the *Feriale Duranum* – a select list of some of the more important festivals of the mid-third century.[135]

The auspicious nature of the day cannot have been lost on the principal participants in the ceremonial. These were all soldiers. The ceremonies, which took place in Milan and Nicomedia, are alluded to by Lactantius. Ammianus describes a similar ceremony twice: once for Constantius' nomination of Julian, and again for Valentinian's nomination of Gratian. Upon a platform, in the midst of the assembled soldiery, the Augustus outlines his proposal for the creation of a new Caesar, and then proceeds to nominate him. The troops roar their approval and applaud by banging their knees with their shields and the Caesar is then clothed in purple by the Augustus who exhorts him to wear it worthily.[136] This elaborate piece of political theatre needed to be planned and staged in advance, particularly since there was not one such ceremony but two, both happening on the same day in widely separate parts of the empire.

There has been some suggestion that events moved slightly differently: that only Constantius was nominated on 1 March, and Galerius was not made Caesar until slightly later, on 21 May.[137] This suggestion, while supported by slender evidence, has found powerful scholarly support.[138] There are two items which can be adduced to support this suggestion. The first is the explicit nomination of 21 May as the date for the creation of the Caesars by the Paschal Chronicle.[139] On its own, this is a weak reed upon which to build a historical interpretation: chronicles are less precise than this might imply. Moreover, T.D. Barnes has pointed out that the date may simply be the one upon which the news of the double accession became current in Egypt.[140] The other problem is weightier. Within the imperial college, Constantius was senior to Galerius, despite the fact that Galerius was Caesar to Diocletian, and, as such, Iovius Caesar. Constantius' superiority is reflected in the imperial titulature in which he is always listed before Galerius. Yet, if one comprehends the arrangement not as a formal "Tetrarchy", but as a dynastic household, an explanation is to hand: Constantius was senior by the simple reason of his age. He may have been as much as fifteen years older than Galerius and his attested career includes provincial governorships.[141] Nothing of the sort is known for Galerius. An older man with a more distinguished record naturally outranked the promising newcomer in an army where seniority had always counted. A final and decisive argument for the date may lie in the words of the Panegyrist of 297, who praised 1 March as adorned with the beginnings of the reigns of eternal emperors. In the circumstances, he can only be referring to Constantius and Galerius.[142]

A natural question arises at this point: Why did Diocletian take this momentous step? The question was a live one at the time with one theory finding its way into an influential historiographical tradition. In this version, Diocletian simply found himself beset by too many problems for merely two Augusti to cope with. Eutropius, one of this view's more influential adherents, sums it up thus:

> *Ita cum per omnem orbem terrarus res turbatae essent, Carausius in Britaniis rebellaret, Achilleus in Aegypto, Africam Quinquegentiani infestarent, Narseus Orientem inferret, Diocletianus Maximianum Herculium ex Caesare fecit Augustum, Constantium et Maximianum Caesares.*

(And so, when the whole world was in turmoil, with Carausius rebelling in Britain and Achilleus in Egypt, with the Quinquegentiani troubling Africa and Narses bring war to the East, Diocletian raised Maximian from the rank of Caesar to that of Augustus and made Constantius and Maximianus Caesars.)[143]

This version is repeated by Aurelius Victor, the *Epitome de Caesaribus* and other sources either dependent upon them or their common source, the so-called *Kaisergeschichte*.[144] This particular version of events has led to what might be called the "crisis theory" which explains the emergence of a quadripartite imperial college as a response to a series of military emergencies. When, however, one examines the context in which these nominations were made, what is striking is the lack of urgency. Three of the four crises, moreover, mentioned by the ancient crisis theorists had, in March 293, not yet occurred, and the fourth (that of Carausius) was being responded to so successfully that, in the course of 293, Carausius was assassinated by one of his bureaucrats, Allectus, who then ruled in his stead.[145] In the north-west, it was the rebels who were experiencing a crisis of confidence, not the loyalists.

The price of rejecting the verdict of a source tradition so readily adopted by later writers (and by many modern scholars[146]) is that one is left, apparently, with no version at all. But this is to ignore the nature of the regime. The kind of dynastic junta which Diocletian was inventing was one of both status and also of rank. As sons-in-law, Galerius and Constantius had status but no guaranteed rank. They were no longer Praetorian Prefects: Hannibalianus and Asclepiodotus had taken their places. So the imperial household was augmented through the device of adoption: Maximian adopted Constantius; Diocletian, Galerius. A process had been completed: the cabal had become a dynasty, bound to one another with informal ties of family fealty (*concordia*) and, at the same time, the beginnings of a succession arranged.

One of the cardinal features of the imperial ideology as it was now proclaimed was the unanimity of the imperial college. The famous group of porphyry statues from the porch of St Mark's in Venice remains iconic of the regime (see Figure 1, overleaf). It depicts the four emperors together. Each Augustus embraces his Caesar in a statement of unity through devotion to duty and family piety. Their readiness to defend the empire is expressed by the simple fact that each emperor's left hand firmly grasps his sword hilt.[147] The world was safe under the watchful care of this united college, these *quattuor principes mundi*. A fragment of a head from Naissus is almost identical to the Venice group.[148] It may well be that this and the Venice group are the remains of a number of copies of this statue which found their way into the major centres of the empire. Thus the unity and readiness of the imperial college was proclaimed far and wide. In another symbolic act, silver busts of the new emperors were added to the praetorian insignia.[149]

Figure 1 "Venice Group": this porphyry statue of the four emperors, with their arms draped around one another, emphasizes the unity and harmony of the new dynasty (photo: the author).

The dynastic links of these military oligarchs were entangled even more comprehensively by the betrothals of the children of the Caesars. Constantine, the bastard son of Constantius, now a young man beginning a military career of his own, was betrothed to Maximian's daughter, Fausta. Maximian's young son, Maxentius, was promised to the infant daughter of Galerius and Valeria, Valeria Maximilla.[150] This was a useful piece of dynastic economy. The relationships between the hard men of the imperial *domus* were further cemented through marriage and betrothal, continuing the process of transforming a junta into a dynasty. It also generated expectations about the succession: if the Caesars were the designated successors to the Augusti, their own replacements were now being publicly bred, educated and trained. Large dynasties have their own problems; this one was united by familial and filial loyalty, the *concordia* of the imperial domus. That necessitated the senior Augustus to be a consensual focus of loyalty. While that worked for Diocletian, it did not for his immediate successors.

What was the nature of the power being endowed upon the Caesars? There was no clear precedent here. Many Caesars of the past had been children. The few who had exercised discretionary power, principally the sons of Decius, had not survived long enough to set a clear example. Certainly the Caesars held a formal rank of the highest kind: their names on laws and in dating formulae; their heads and titles on coins; inscriptions were dedicated in their honour; they wore purple cloaks; they held multiple consulships. These, however, are symbols. Any child emperor could be so honoured.

Yet for at least one knowledgeable observer, there was little distribution of power. The Emperor Julian, in his satire *The Caesars*, depicts the four emperors entering the Saturnalia feast of Jupiter together. Maximian and the two Caesars hold one another by the hand, forming a chorus around Diocletian who approaches in splendour. When they attempt to do him honour and form a bodyguard for him, Diocletian prevents them, allowing himself no greater honour than they. And thus:

ephgaosthesan hoi theoi ton andron ten homonoian.

(the gods marvelled at the harmony of these men.)[151]

A more contemporary view comes from Eumenius, a Gallic orator. In a panegyric, he praises a fine race of military princes:

Nunc enim, nunc demum iuvat orbem spectare depictum, cum in illo nihil videmus alienum.

(For now, now it is a joy to behold a map of the world, for nothing which we may see is foreign.)[152]

In both of these documents, we find the same themes as in the Venice group: unity and purpose. These kinds of source build a picture of an imperial college both united amongst themselves and also united in their common personal loyalty to Diocletian. Here the observation of Julian is of particular acuity: to him, they did not share power, it merely seemed as if they did. For Julian, discretionary power remained effectively with Diocletian, and the empire continued as a *patrimonium indivisum*. His contemporary, Aurelius Victor, however, noted a more formal fourfold division of the empire:

> *Et quoniam bellorum moles, de qua supra memoravimus, acrius urgebat, quadripartito imperio cuncta, quae trans Alpes Galliae sunt, Constantio commissa, Africa Italiaeque Herculio, Illyrici ora ad usque Ponti fretum Galerio; cetera Valerius retentavit.*

(and so because the sheer number of conflicts strongly pressed, as we have recounted above, all of Gaul beyond the Alps was committed to Constantius; Herculius received Italy and Africa; the Illyrian region up to the Pontic Straits went to Galerius; Diocletian kept the rest.)[153]

The ultimate source for this may be the *Kaisergeschichte*.[154] Curiously, the author of the Epitome *de Caesaribus*, a writer with access to the Greek tradition, makes no such statement. Nor does the author of the *Origo Constantini Imperatoris*, although it might be argued that he had cause to.

One Greek writer who does comment upon the division is Praxagoras of Athens, although here he displays a curious confusion. His work is only preserved in Photius. He records that:

> the father of Constantine, Constantius, ruled in Britain, Maximianus in Rome and all Italy and Sicily, the other Maximianus [Galerius] in Macedonia, Greece. Hither Asia and Thrace and Diocletian, the eldest of them, was master in Bithynia, Libya, Arabia and Egypt.[155]

It is a peculiar statement. Gaul, Pannonia, Syria and Africa have no part in the scheme. It might be argued that Pannonia could be implicitly included in what a Greek like Praxagoras might think of as Macedonia. A similar confusion can be detected in the allotment of "Hither Asia" ("kato Asia", a curious term possibly meaning Asia Minor), to Galerius, and Bithynia (demonstrably within Asia Minor) to Diocletian.

Praxagoras was a young Athenian. He wrote this work, a life of Constantine, in about 326, at the age of twenty-one. Constantine had only just become sole emperor, having deposed Licinius in the previous year. Praxagoras, born about 305, the year of the abdications of Diocletian and Maximian, had only ever known a collegiate empire in which divisions of territory were sharply delineated and tension between imperial colleagues made such boundaries explicit. Tension over territorial rights had been the *casus belli* for the second war between Licinius and Constantine.[156] The death of Galerius had seen a furious land-grab by both Licinius and Daza.[157]

Praxagoras' natural inclination, based upon his own experience of collegiate empire, would have been to find divisions of territory in situations which seemed to him analogous. Thus, he divides the Diocletian's empire into areas which seem to him to be logical. Constantius received Britain, which he indeed recovered from Allectus, and where he died in 306. Maximian received Italy and Sicily. Given that he spent much of his time there and retired to an estate in Lucania, that is also a reasonable conclusion.[158] Galerius is not surprisingly associated with Thessalonica in Macedonia, where he lived for some years, and a triumphal arch and palace were built that now bear his name. Again, this was a natural association for Praxagoras to make. If "Hither Asia" can be stretched beyond the Taurus, reference may also be found here to Galerius' Persian campaigns. Bithynia was the place of Diocletian's capital, Nicomedia. He had also campaigned in Egypt in 298, defining its southern border.[159] The inclusion of Arabia and Libya is curious. Diocletian did confront the Saracens in about 290,[160] but that did not even merit a victory title, and was more likely a diplomatic arrangement.[161] If "Libya" means the rest of Africa, then there is an inconsistency here, since Victor explicitly awards it to Maximian, and Maximian actually campaigned there at the end of the 290s. Diocletian certainly never went there.

Thus, the earliest account of the territorial division is confused. Victor's is the more logical and coherent. It defines strict spheres of operation. Further, Victor's analysis has been accepted almost unanimously by modern commentators, following the lead of Otto Seeck.[162] The difficulty is that neither the definition given by Victor nor that of Praxagoras actually describe the way that the regime worked in practice. This is most clearly seen in the case of Galerius. Soon after he was made Caesar, he was sent to Egypt to quell a revolt in the Thebaid. His most notable military victory was not upon the banks of the Danube at all, but in Persia, far from the Carpi and Sarmatians.[163] Indeed, it was only after that victory that Galerius went to the Danubian regions at all for any length of time. In 302/3, Galerius spent the winter at Nicomedia, in the court of Diocletian. In 305, he was with Diocletian again for some months.[164]

Diocletian also crossed the boundaries without difficulty. He campaigned in Egypt while Galerius was in Persia, and even before that had jointly conducted the campaign with Galerius for a time. After the campaign, he and Galerius met to confer at Nisibis. Somewhat later, he toured the Danubian provinces, perhaps even campaigning against the Carpi.[165] It would thus appear that in the east the territorial divisions were fairly fluid. Unarguably, Diocletian could go anywhere that he willed. But Galerius did not live a settled existence either. In the light of this alone, it is necessary to revise traditional definitions of territorial responsibility. This has already been essayed by T.D. Barnes, who has argued that Victor's divisions are only valid for the period after the Persian War. He maintains that it was only from this time that Galerius ruled the Danubian regions. Prior to that, he had responsibility for the east and it was only after the Persian victory that the territorial arrangement between Diocletian and Galerius was reversed.[166] The solution is ingenious, but perhaps a little too contrived. It does not account for Diocletian's activities in the Balkans in 303 and 304, tasks which, under this scheme, were surely within Galerius' portfolio.[167] Nor does it account for Galerius' frequent visits to Diocletian's capital on the Asian side of the Bosporus. It is more convincing, and makes more sense, if the notion of territorial responsibility is abandoned altogether. The difficulties of explicit attestation must still of course be overcome. Praxagoras, it has already been argued, wrote with the hindsight of a divided collegiate empire in which each ruler was master of his own patch but had no authority elsewhere. His own territorial allotments were predicated upon his expectation of what they would have been on the basis of the geographical associations known to him.

Aurelius Victor, as has been argued, may have derived this information from the *Kaisergeschichte*, a document not reputed for the accuracy of its testimony, where it can be detected. Just as Praxagoras wrote in conditions coloured by the experience of a divided empire, so did the anonymous author of the *Kaisergeschichte*. Writing either late in the reign of Constantine, or early in that of his sons, the author was aware of a multiplicity of emperors. Certainly, if he wrote after 337, the empire in which he lived had been split yet again between Constantine's sons. Further, this occurred after a particularly vicious purge of the imperial family in Constantinople which spared only two children, one of them because he was not expected to live long.[168] Such territorial divisions were thus particularly acute to the writer of the *Kaisergeschichte*.

Like Praxagoras then, the experience of the divided empire was natural for the author of the *Kaisergeschichte*. This does not ignore the fact that for thirteen years, between 324 and 337, the empire had been united under Constantine, who never formally ruled alone. But his colleagues, except for in his final year, were all his children.[169] There was certainly no *de facto* collegiality. This situation may not have been analogous to the author of the *Kaisergeschichte*. Constantine and his sons seemed a different kind of college from one formed by a group of Illyrian warriors bound by marriage and mutual trust, rather than by blood, although in effect, they represent the completion of dynastic creation commenced by Diocletian in 285. The reason for the territorial divisions to be found in the *Kaisergeschichte* thus derive from the same chain of reasoning evident in Praxagoras. They reflect centres of major activity by the emperors but not, in reality, a formal territorial division of the empire.

A further complication in any theory of territorial division of the empire between Diocletian and his colleagues is the uncertainty of what this actually entailed. In later times, when the emperors dwelt in mutual suspicion, each ruled their lands as virtual independent states, but that suspicion does not appear to characterize Diocletian's arrangement. An emperor controlled finance, foreign policy, religious policy, military organization, provincial government and the judiciary. Were all such divided into four parts? Clearly not. Diocletian's military, provincial and financial reforms embraced the whole empire. Diocletian's control of foreign policy was also absolute. He took over negotiations following Galerius' victory over the Persians. The Caesar may have won the war, but the Augustus imposed the terms of the peace.[170] Diocletian also sent a rescript to a governor of Africa on a point of religious policy.[171] There is also evidence that the emperors did not control inviolable armies. Reinforcements were sent to different trouble spots in the empire on two identifiable occasions.[172] The evidence of considerable reforms embracing the whole empire suggests that, in practical terms, the emperors themselves were not conscious of any division. In 286, when Maximian had become Augustus, there had been no formal division of the empire. Diocletian had campaigned in the west in 288. Then, the Herculian servant of the Jovian emperor had done what he was told. Diocletian was not unsubtle. He held conferences with his colleague, but he also held the reins of power. In 291, a panegyrist boasted that the empire, despite having two rulers, was an 'undivided estate' (*patrimonium indivisum*).[173] Certainly, Julian considered it to be so.

The Caesars, as Caesars, could hardly operate in a situation where they had the same honours and functions as an Augustus. In rank, they were inferior to Maximian. As such, the Caesars had no Praetorian Prefect. This has been a question of some dispute. T.D. Barnes considers that there were four Praetorian Prefects during the period 293–305. He assigns Flaccinus, the Prefect who demolished a church in Nicomedia in 303, to Galerius.[174] Since the action occurred in Nicomedia, however, it is more likely that Flaccinus was the Prefect of Diocletian. Asclepiodotus, the Praetorian Prefect generally identified as that of Constantius, is a more difficult problem. Asclepiodotus was undeniably Praetorian Prefect. His role in the recovery of Britain from Allectus was so prominent that both Eutropius and Jerome omit to mention the role of Constantius.[175] Victor says that Constantius and Asclepiodotus *qui praetorianis praefectus praeerat* divided the fleet between them for the final assault.[176] There is in fact no direct link between Constantius and Asclepiodotus except that they commanded together in this campaign. An unnecessary attempt has been made to distinguish this Asclepiodotus from the consul of 292, who was by then already Praetorian Prefect.[177] Asclepiodotus may either have served until 296 or, as a *vir militaris*, been recalled for a second term at a time of dire need. That would, of course, make it more probable that he was Maximian's Praetorian Prefect. On this basis,

Asclepiodotus' participation in the campaign against Allectus is actually an argument against there having been four Praetorian Prefects. Maximian would hardly 'lend' his Praetorian Prefect to Constantius if Constantius already had one of his own. Indeed, the participation of Asclepiodotus is also an argument against territorial divisions. Maximian clearly perceived sufficient unity so as to order both his Caesar and his Praetorian Prefect to work together to dislodge Allectus.

Two inscriptions confirm the matter. An inscription of the *vices* of a Praetorian Prefect, Septimius Valentio, dated to the period 293–96, employs the abbreviation *praett praeff*.[178] The conventions of Roman epigraphy dictate that at the time there were two Praetorian Prefects. Had there been four, the abbreviation *praetttt praeffff* would naturally have been employed.[179] A text of the Praetorian Prefect Aurelius Hermogenianus, perhaps the author of the law code, is securely dated to the period 293–305 and confirms that there were only two Praetorian Prefects at this time.[180]

If the Caesars had no Praetorian Prefects, then clearly their competence was limited. The Prefect was a vital figure in the imperial administration; by this time much less a military official than a civil one.[181] Without one, it is difficult to see how the Caesars could have exercised much major independent authority at all. Yet they were honoured with the title of *proconsul* and awarded tribunician power, as Maximian had not been. Clearly they were intended actively to be doing something. Their principal tasks, inferred from what we know of what they did, seem to have been the exercise of military commands. The evidence of the panegyrics would indicate some civil authority of a local and derivative kind,[182] but in general Constantius and Galerius went from one trouble spot to the next. From them come few, if any, rescripts.[183] They had courts, before which orators spoke in praise, but no *corps* of *protectores* apiece.[184]

The experience of a later Caesar is instructive here. Constantius II, in dealing with Julian's brother Gallus, then a recreant Caesar, reminded him in correspondence:

> *quod Diocletiano et eius collegae, ut apparitores Caesares non resides sed ultro citroque discurrentes.*

> (for Diocletian and his colleague, the Caesars acted in the fashion of servants, not residing in one place, but travelling hither and thither.)[185]

If these are not the actual words of Constantius, they are certainly those of Ammianus, who records the incident and has a view similar to that of Julian. The Caesars were servants to the Augusti, not tied down by territorial barriers, but, conversely, free to go wherever sent. Like servants (*apparitores*) they did the bidding of their imperial superiors in the college.[186] Thus, although the Caesars were in name the colleagues of their Augusti, featuring on coins, on inscriptions, on the preambles of laws, in reality they exercised no independent executive power. From the movements of the Caesars and the evidence of both Ammianus and Julian, it would seem that the best way in which to analyse the power dynamics of the Diocletian's empire is to see the Caesars as servants rather than colleagues. Their position was simply that they were instructed to perform certain tasks, going wherever they were most needed to do so. They went where the Augustus was unable to go, the living face of the emperors. That they had discretionary power is indicated by the title of *proconsul* and the possession of tribunician power, but such discretionary power was limited by the terms of reference set them by their Augusti.

The new dynasty was held together by loyalty and concord. The coinage of Alexandria in particular stresses *"homonia"*,[187] and a figure clearly labelled "OMONIA" stands behind Galerius as he is depicted offering sacrifice on a panel of the Arch of Galerius.[188] Even Julian, sixty years later, says that the *homonia* of the tetrarchs was a matter of wonder even to the Gods.[189] This *homonia* sprang not from a unity of mind and spirit, but from loyalty to Diocletian, the *auctor imperii* and *paterfamilias* of this new imperial *domus*. He was brother and father, the Jovian lord, the guiding spirit; the other ruling members of the family were the agents of his benevolent mastery.

Notes

1 Much of the historiographical discussion on this point is well summarized by Kolb (1987), pp. 3–8.
2 *SHA Vit. Car.* 18.4.
3 Lact. *de mort. pers.* 9.11; Eutr. 9.19.2; Zonaras 12.31; Barnes (2008), *NE*, p. 30f.
4 Zonaras (12.31) offers the detail that he was *doux Musias*. This, however, is a late and uncertain detail.
5 Howe (1942), p. 83, no.57; *PLRE* I, p. 81.
6 Nemesianus, *Cynegetica*, pp. 63–75.
7 Museo del Palazzo dei Conservatori, Rome, inv. no. 850; see *Spätantike und frühes Christentum*, Liebeghaus Museum alter Plastik, Frankfurt-am-Main, p. 399; p. 56 Abb 30. Cf. the short soldier's beards of Probus (*Ibid.*, Abb 29), Claudius Gothicus (Abb 28), Decius (Abb 23) and Philip (Abb 22); also the "philhellenic" beard and style of the portraiture of Gallienus (Abb 25–27). This style of beard can also be found in the portraiture of Nero.
8 Both are known from coins and inscriptions. Magna Urbica was Augusta (*RIC* V2, pp. 181–5). Nigrinianus (*PLRE* I, p. 361, no. 1) is styled NEPOS DIVI CARI, so he was not necessarily the son of either Carinus or Numerian, but possibly of their sister Paulina (*SB* 7028, *PIR2* A 1665, *PLRE* I, p. 675, no. 1).
9 *PLRE* I sv. "Iulianus" nos. 24 and 38; Barnes (1981), *CE*, pp. 4–5; Leadbetter (1994), pp. 54–9.
10 *AE* 1964, 223; see Barnes, *NE*, p. 97. Bassus had already held a consulship, the major urban priesthoods, and a number of important offices, including a proconsulship of Africa. He had accompanied Carus to the east as a *comes* (*PLRE* I, p. 156, no. 18).

11 Aurelius Victor was particularly savage (*de Caes.* 39.11). Zosimus referred to his cruelties and sexual misdemeanours (1.73), echoing a Eunapian tradition found also in the *Ep. de Caes.* 38.7. Only Eutropius (9.19) was in any way equivocal. See Kolb (1987), p. 17f.

12 *SHA, Vit. Car.* 16.7.

13 Aristobulus was an ordinary consul in 285, and therefore designate to that office in 284, during which time he must have had senatorial rank; see Bagnall *et al.* (1987), p. 104f.

14 *Ep. de Caes.* 38.6; Zos. 1.73.3; Leadbetter (1994), p. 56.

15 Eutr. 9.20.2; Zos. 1.73.3; *Ep. de Caes.* 38.8; Aur. Vict. *de Caes.* 39.11.

16 *RIC* V2, p. 247, no. 266.

17 For his career, see *PLRE* I, p. 106; Chastagnol (1962), pp. 21–5. This consulship shared by an emperor and a *privatus* was significant enough to be remarked upon by Ammianus (23.1.1).

18 *PLRE* I, p. 452f., no. 2.

19 *Ibid.*, p. 1041f.

20 *Ibid.*; see also Barnes, *NE*, pp. 98, 110.

21 See *PLRE* I, p. 402, no. 3; Chastagnol (1962), pp. 14–17.

22 Barnes, *NE*, p. 97.

23 *Ibid.*, p. 50, *contra* Seston (1946), p. 53f. On the coin issue, see Mazzini (1956), p. 247. This *adventus* must be dated to before 286, since the reverse legend reads "ADVENTVS AVG". The plural is invariably used when there is more than one Augustus, irrespective of how many enter the relevant city at a time. Clear examples are Maximian's entry into Lugdunum (*RIC* V2, p. 222, no. 11; p. 261, no. 347); Numerian's (expected?) arrival at Cyzicus (*RIC* V2, p. 177, no. 317, p. 201, no. 462); cf. Carinus' *adventus* into Ticinum after the death of his brother (*RIC* V2, p. 175, no. 294).

24 Zonaras 12. 31.

25 *SHA, Vit. Prob.* 20.5; Eutr. 9.17.3; Aur. Vict. *de Caes.* 37.3.

26 Barnes, *NE*, p. 50 and (1976) p. 178.

27 Barnes, *NE*, p. 50f.

28 On the date and occasion of the panegyric, see Nixon and Rodgers (1994), p. 42f.

29 Aur. Vict. *de Caes.* 39.17; Eutr. 9.20.

30 Thompson (1982), pp. 311ff.; Drinkwater (1989), pp. 192ff.

31 Thompson (1974).

32 This view has been principally argued by Drinkwater (1984) and (1989).

33 MacMullen (1966), pp. 192–221; Wightman (1978) and (1985), p. 199f., Van Dam (1985, pp. 24–33; see also the thoughtful analysis of Miller (1996).

34 Rubin (1995).

35 On Bulla and his *bon mot* to Papinian (Dio Cassius 77.10.7), see Ste Croix (1982), p. 477; Thompson (1982), p. 309f.

36 Miller (1996), p. 165f.

37 Drinkwater (1987), pp. 24–41.

38 Zonaras 12.27.11; Drinkwater (1987), p. 91.

39 Wightman (1985), p. 198f.

40 Julian *Caesares* (403) says that Probus restored seventy cities. There is some archaeological evidence to suggest that the fortification of many of the cities of Gaul postdated the end of the Gallic empire. See here Wightman (1985), p. 222; Drinkwater (1987), pp. 229–31.

41 Aur. Vict. *de Caes.* 37.2 mentions one (Bonosus) by name. Other sources link the defeat of the Köln-based Bonosus with Proculus (Eutr. 9.17; *Epitome de Caesaribus* 37.2). For coins for Bonosus, see *RIC* V2, p. 591. Syme has decisively demonstrated that the biographies of these usurpers in the *Historia Augusta* are almost entirely fiction. See also Barnes (1972).

42 Maximian had trained in the armies of Aurelian and Probus (Aur. Vict. *de Caes*. 39.28) and had served on the Danube frontier before he went to Syria (*Pan. Lat*. 2.2.4–6). On his origin, *Ep. de Caes*. 40.11, *Pan. Lat*. 3. 5–6; see also Barnes, *NE*, p. 32f.

43 For discussion of the evidence, see Leadbetter (1998B), pp. 216–21.

44 There is a vast bibliography on this issue, but see most recently Kolb (1987), pp. 28–31; see also Nixon and Rodgers (1994), p. 47; Leadbetter (1998B), pp. 219–21.

45 Rousselle (1976), pp. 448–50. One inscription cited by Rousselle is to be rejected. *CIL* VIII 22187 is unclear. Rousselle reads COS II[I] PROCOS II[I] in the titulature of Diocletian, but the inscription is unbroken, merely mistaken. It also calls Diocletian PP II[I], and hence is not to be trusted. See also Chastagnol (1967); J.D. Thomas (1971); R.E. Smith (1972); Leadbetter (1998B), p. 220.

46 In his last year, Carinus took the title *Britannicus Maximus*, which is clear evidence of a campaign in Britain (*CIL* XIV 126 = *ILS* 608). This evidence has been rejected by Meloni (1948: p. 151 n.5) for no good reason, but accepted without elaboration by Barnes, *CE*, p. 287 n. 15.

47 Neumann, *RE* 3.1(1887), 1287, sv. Caesar.

48 See *ILS* 538, where Gallienus is *trib. pot. IV* and Valerian *trib. pot. V*. A subsequent augmentation is suggested by *ILS* 539.

49 *ILS* 518, 520 show the exceptions to be the sons of Decius.

50 Pasqualini (1979), p. 27f.

51 Rees (2002), pp. 19–26.

52 Against the dating of these events by Barnes (*NE*, pp. 10, 57) to before the end of 285. Clearly this cannot be so if Maximian was not Caesar until December, and must therefore belong to Spring 286. This has its own logic. If the campaigns belong to 285, then there is no evident military activity for Maximian in 286; rather peculiar, given the apparent urgency of the situation. But this hiatus is an artificial one.

53 *Pan. Lat*. 2.5. *Pan. Lat*. 2.4; Pasqualini (1979), p. 31f.; Nixon and Rodgers (1994), p. 61f.

54 Rubin (1995), p. 142f.

55 Barnes (1982), *NE*, p. 56; Wightman (1971), p. 58f.

56 *Pan. Lat*. 2.6. The city may not be Trier (see Barnes, *NE*, p. 57), but it seems the obvious choice.

57 Wightman (1971), p. 58.

58 Barnes, *NE*, p. 4 n. 6; Kienast (1996), p. 268.

59 Seeck (1897), p. 26.

60 Leadbetter (1998), pp. 224–6.

61 See Frye (1984), p. 305.

62 Barnes, *NE*, p. 50f.

63 *RIC* V2 pp. 152–79; *ILS* 607.

64 Pflaum (1966/7); Leadbetter (1998B), pp. 222–8.

65 Jones (1964), Vol. III, p. 3 n. 3; Seston (1946), p. 63; see also Pasqualini (1979), p. 17. Most of the relevant African inscriptions can be taken to refer to Galerius (*Ibid*., p.19). Only *CIL* VIII 10285 refers unambiguously to Maximian. The imperial title *proconsul*, which it bears, first appeared under Trajan (Hammond 1957: p. 20), although it was not used regularly until the Severan period (*ILS* 458 illustrates the changes particularly clearly). It appears to have been unique to the Augustus, only being assumed by a Caesar upon elevation to the higher rank (Seeck 1897: Vol. I, p. 14ff.).

66 Bastien (1972); Leadbetter (1998B), p. 223f. Kolb (1987; 2001) has used this evidence to argue that the Iovian/Herculian ideology was in place from the start. The evidence of the African inscriptions, however, makes clear an intermediate stage when the terminology was not employed.

67 The earliest datable inscription referring to Diocletian as *Iovius* and Maximian as *Herculius*, *ILS* 617, is from 288.

68 *Pan. Lat.* 10 (2).1;11;13 and *passim.* Rees (2002), pp. 39–49.
69 *Pan. Lat.* 10(2) 10.6; on a textual crux, see Nixon and Rodgers (1994), p. 71f.
70 *Pan. Lat.* 10 (2). 12.1.
71 *Ibid.*, 6.3; Barnes, *NE*, p. 57, suggesting other locations as well, but see Wightman (1971), p. 58. Some modern scholars have been unkind enough to suggest that this event was carefully choreographed to enhance Maximian's prestige (*Ibid.*; Drinkwater 1996: p. 22f.).
72 *Pan. Lat.* 10 (2). 7.7.
73 Aur. Vict. *de Caes.* 39. 20–1; Eutr. *Breviarium* 9.21.
74 On the *Imperium Galliarum*, see especially Drinkwater (1987).
75 *Ibid.*, p. 168f.
76 *CIL.* 3. 3228 = *ILS.* 546.
77 S. Johnson (1976), p. 40.
78 Zos. 1.67.
79 *CIL* 14. 126 = *ILS* 608. The coupling of Carinus' name on the inscription with that of his brother fixes its date to between July 283 (when their father Carus died) and November 284 (when Numerian died), which makes the summer of 284 the most likely occasion for the British campaign. Meloni (1948: pp. 151–2) argues against Carinus' presence in Britain, however. He interprets a reference in Nemesianus to refer to Carinus' campaigns in Germany. His greatest difficulty, however, lies in the interpretation of the Ostian inscription, which attests Carinus as *Britannicus Maximus.* He prefers to see this as a victory over Gallic *Bagaudae* and not over Saxon pirates. But this explanation is unsatisfactory.
80 Nixon and Rodgers (1994), 8.11.1 (C.E.V. Nixon, trans.).
81 Strabo, *Geography*, 4.5.2.
82 Amm. Marc. 18.2.3; Zos. 3.5.2.
83 On the wealth of Britain, see Todd (1978); Salway (1981), p. 280; Millett (1990), pp. 157–80.
84 Salway (1981), pp. 255–6.
85 *CIL.* XIII. 6780.
86 S. Johnson (1976), pp. 17–18.
87 Frere (1987), p. 329.
88 S. Johnson (1976), p. 68.
89 Higham (1992), p. 50.
90 Salway (1981), p. 386; S. Johnson (1980), pp. 72–7.
91 S. Johnson (1976), p. 15f.
92 *CIL* XII, 686.
93 See *PLRE* I, p. 180f.
94 Webb (1907) argues for 287, and has been followed by E. Stein (1957: p. 67) and Jones (1964: Vol. I, p. 38). Others have preferred 286, notably Seeck (*RE* III 1570f.), Seston (1946: p. 74f.), Chastagnol (1982: p. 95f.) and Barnes (1982: *NE*, p. 11). Shiel (1978: p. 202) is non-committal.
95 Casey (1994), pp. 39–45.
96 *RIC* V2, p. 497, no. 393. For the date, see p. 451.
97 Barnes, *NE*, p. 11.
98 For the breadth of Carausius' revolt, see Shiel (1978), p. 3ff. Shiel argues that Carausius' Gallic holdings were not particularly extensive, although they certainly included Gesoriacum (Bononia). For a different view, see Casey (1977).
99 *RIC* V2, pp. 442, 550, no. 1. Carausius also issued coins in the names of Diocletian and Maximian (*ibid.*, pp. 551–6).
100 Most clearly articulated in the panegyric of 289. See here *Pan. Lat.* 2(10), 9.3–5; Rees (2002), pp. 52–4.

101 *Pan. Lat.* 10 (2) 11.7 appears to make reference to a campaign by Maximian in which Carausius' forces have been driven from Europe. See Nixon and Rodgers (1994), p. 72; Casey (1994), p. 91.
102 See Frye (1984), p. 305.
103 *Pan. Lat.* 4.12.2; see Shiel (1978), pp. 9–10; Seston (1946), p. 104f.
104 *Pan. Lat.* 2.9.1; Barnes, *NE*, p. 57.
105 *Pan. Lat.* 2.(10). 11.4.
106 Seeck, *RE* IV 1041. The argument with respect to the name "Hannibalianus" is a strong one. Constantius I and Theodora had a son to whom they gave the name, as did another of their sons, Dalmatius (*PLRE* I, p. 407, nos 1 and 2). A second item is of circumstantial value. Gallus Caesar, grandson of Constantius I and Theodora, spent a part of his youth relegated to Tralles, before being sent to join Julian in internal exile in Cappadocia (Julian *Ep. ad Ath.* 271B). The family of Hannibalianus had a hereditary connection with Tralles (see Groag 1907: pp. 282–99, esp. 288f.; Barnes, *NE*, p 34). If Gallus' time in Tralles had been spent at a family estate, as would seem likely, then might not such a property have come into the family's possession via Hannibalianus?
107 Eutr. 9.22.1; Aur. Vict. *de Caes.* 39.25. Similarity of wording confirms an origin in the *Kaisergeschichte*. In each case, Theodora is described as Maximian's *privigna*.
108 *Pan. Lat.* 2.11.4.
109 Leadbetter (1998A), p. 76; Barnes, *NE*, p. 34.
110 *Origo* 1.2; Barnes, *NE*, p. 33.
111 *ILS* 8929 is the evidence for Hannibalianus' prefecture. It exhibits problems. It dates from between 285, when Diocletian first took the victory title *Germanicus Maximus* which appears on the inscription (Barnes, 1976: p. 178) and 292, when Hannibalianus was consul with Asclepiodotus. On the basis of the victory title, Chastagnol (1962: p. 28 n. 13) prefers a date *terminus ante quem* of 290. In this, he is followed by the *PLRE* (I, p. 407, no. 3). Given that the only victory title in the inscription is *Germanicus Maximus*, it ought properly to belong quite early in Diocletian's reign, and Howe (1942: p. 51, n. 67) argues that it belongs to the first twelve months. Howe's argument is weakened by his assumption that Diocletian's *tribunicia potestas* was not renewed until November 285, whereas it was augmented on 10 December, nineteen days after he seized power. This inscription cannot date from so early in Diocletian's reign, when his titulature was uncertain (*AE* 1973, 540; *P.Oxy* 3055), and in any event, its provenance (Oescus, on the distant Danube, where news might not reach so swiftly) should settle the matter. On the matter of whose prefect Hannibalianus was, his primacy in the inscription would indicate Diocletian, rather than Maximian (Barnes, *NE*, p. 124).
112 Barnes (1982), *NE*, p. 33; Nixon and Rodgers (1994), p. 70; Leadbetter (1998A), pp. 76–8.
113 Eutr. 9.22.1; Oros. 7.25.5; Aur. Vict *de Caes.* 39.25; *Ep. de Caes.* 39.2; Prosper Tiro, *Chron.* sa. 288 (= *MGH* IX.1, 1892, p. 445). This coincidence of sources make dependence upon the common tradition of the *Kaisergeschichte* a compelling inference (see Enmann, 1884: pp. 444–5).
114 *Origo* 1.2.
115 It is worth noting that Prosper's account of Diocletian's reign differs from that of Jerome in significant particulars. Most noteworthy is his omission of the catalogue of woes in connection with the creation of the Caesars.
116 Leadbetter (1998A), pp. 77–9.
117 *Origo* 2; also *CIL* III 9860, which attests him as *praeses* of Dalmatia. The *SHA* (*Vit. Car.* 17.6) also states that Constantius was a governor under Carus. If the date is correct, a doubtful proposition when the evidence is from the *SHA*, most likely he was governor during the civil war between Diocletian and Carinus. If so, his loyalty to Diocletian had already been of crucial importance.

118 Barnes, *NE*, p. 124; Chastagnol (1962), pp. 27–9.

119 Barnes, *NE*, p. 124 (incorrectly discounting the identification of the Asclepiodotus of 296 with the Praetorian Prefect of the 280s; Ockam's razor, discretely applied, discloses one man and two instances); *PLRE* I, p. 115f.

120 As conjectured by Barnes, *NE*, p. 136.

121 Lact. *de mort. pers.* 18.9 for the date.

122 For the date of the usurpation, Lact., *de mort. pers.* 44.4. Maxentius had held power for six years exactly when he was defeated at the Milvian Bridge (*CIL* I2, p. 274).

123 Thus Valeria was a bride at fifteen and a mother before she was seventeen; both reasonable propositions. Two objections to this solution must be overcome. First, it is possible that Valeria Maximilla was the child of a first wife, as Theodora apparently was. Lactantius' statement that Valeria, Galerius' wife, was incapable of bearing children (*de mort. pers.* 50.2) lends support to such a view. The evidence of the nomenclature, however, suggests otherwise. The name of Valeria Maximilla contains elements of both Galerius' name ("Maximilla" – Galerius may have been called Maximinus before his elevation to the purple: Lact., *de mort. pers.* 44.1) and that of his wife Valeria. As to the issue of the elder Valeria's sterility, Lactantius, strictly speaking, is referring to the mid-290s when Candidianus was born. Such a reference does not preclude an earlier child, with Galerius' resort to concubinage a subsequent development as a result of his desire for the son which his wife could no longer give him. Lactantius shows no sympathy for Valeria. He finds peculiar satisfaction in her later execution at the hands of Licinius (*de mort. pers.* 51). His gibe at Valeria's sterility might then be another piece of rhetorical nastiness, as was his reference to Diocletian's cowardice (see Barnes, *NE*, p. 38). *ILS* 674 gives the immediate imperial ancestors of Valeria Maximilla's son, Romulus. Unfortunately, the text breaks off after an *ac* which might well have added the fact that the deceased boy was also the great-grandson of Diocletian, thereby clinching the matter.

124 *Pan. Lat.* 2.11.4. Carus had been Praetorian Prefect under Probus (Aur. Vict. *de Caes.* 38.1) and was commanding in Rhaetia and Noricum at the time of his revolt (Zos. 1.71.4). This revolt provoked the mutiny in which Probus lost his life (Zos. 1.71.5).

125 Arrius (?) Aper, whose daughter was married to Numerian (*PLRE* I p. 81, no. 2). The date of the marriage is unknown, but the coincidence of kinship and office underscores Carus' determination to keep the prefecture in the family (see Howe, Probus 1942: p. 81f.).

126 For Constantius, see n. 117 above; for Galerius, Lact. *de mort. pers.* 18.6. Here (in 304) Galerius complains that he has been fighting on the banks of the Danube for fifteen years, i.e. from 289. Seeck (1897: Vol. I, p. 438) has sought to emend the *quindecim* of the text to *duodecim* purely on historical, rather than textual, grounds. Moreau (1954: p. 310) has retained the reading of the manuscript, arguing that Galerius spent the remaining three years on the Danube *before* he became Caesar. There is no reason to reject the figure of fifteen as unhistorical. Creed (1984: p. 97f.), however, maintains that the figure is intended to be more rhetorical than exact.

127 *Pan. Lat.* 2.10.3.

128 *Ibid.*, 4.12.2; see also Shiel (1978), pp. 9–10.

129 *Pan. Lat.* 3.11.1.

130 *Ibid.*, 3.11.2.

131 Eutr. 9. 26; Amm. Marc. 15.5.18; Aur. Vict. 39.2; Jerome, *Chron.* s.a. 296; Zonaras 12. x; see the comments of Bird (1994), p. 161f.

132 Lact. *de mort. pers.* 7.4.

133 *Ibid.*, 35.4; Hydat., *Conss. Const.* s.a. 291.

134 Scullard (1981), p. 85ff.

135 Fink *et al.* (1940), p. 43 (*Fer. Dur.* Col. I. 19).

136 Amm. Marc. 15.8. 4–15 on the acclamation of Julian; cf. 27.6.4–15 on Gratian's nomination as Augustus by Valentinian.
137 Seston, 1946, p. 92ff.
138 *Ibid.*, p. 88ff.; König (1974), p. 567ff.
139 *Chron. Pasch.* s.a. 293.
140 Barnes, *NE*, p. 62 n. 73.
141 Galerius was born in about 258 (Barnes, *NE*, p. 37f.); on seniority as a factor in the ranking of the emperors, see Eus. *VC* 1.26, Lact. *de mort. pers.* 25.5.
142 *Pan. Lat.* 4.3.1.
143 Eutr. 9. 22.1.
144 See here Bird (1993), p. 148.
145 For the date, see Casey (1994), p. 42.
146 Seston (1946), p.88f.
147 On the identification of the emperors, see Chastagnol (1982), p. 100. On the *similutudo* of the group, see Rees (1993), pp. 182–5.
148 See *Spätantike und frühes Christentum*, Liebeghaus Museum alter Plastik, Frankfurt-am-Main, 1983, p. 409ff.
149 Künzl (1983), p. 385ff.
150 *Pan. Lat.* 5.6.2. The marriages certainly later occurred, although Constantine's was not celebrated until after Maxentius' usurpation. In the meantime, he had consorted with Minervina, who bore him Crispus (*PLRE* I, p. 602f.). On Constantine's legitimacy, see Leadbetter (1998A).
151 Julian *Caesares* 315, A, B.
152 *Pan. Lat.* 5.21.1–4.
153 Aur. Vict. *de Caes.* 39.30; the text here is from Pichlmayr's Teubner edition, following Freudenberg's suggestion of *quadripartito* for an obscure abbreviation in the manuscript (Pichlmayr 1970: p. 119).
154 Eutr. 9.22–3.
155 Phot. *Bib.* 62.
156 *Origo* 5.21.
157 Lact. *de mort. pers.* 36. 1–4.
158 Barnes, *NE*, p. 59f. He retired to a villa in Lucania (Eutr., 9.27.2).
159 Procopius, *Hist.*1.19.34; see Bowman (1978), p. 30; van Berchem (1952), p. 62.
160 Barnes, *NE*, p. 51; *Pan. Lat.* 3.5.4.
161 See here Leadbetter (2004A).
162 Seeck (1897), Vol. I, p. 32; Ensslin, *RE* XIV 2519; Altendorf, *RAC* 8.786; E. Stein (1957), p. 68; Seston (1946), p. 184; Jones (1964), Vol. I, p. 39f.; cf. Barnes (1976); Chastagnol (1982), p. 100.
163 Lact. *de mort. pers.* 8.6; 18.1.
164 Barnes, *NE*, p. 56.
165 *Ibid.*, p. 186.
166 Barnes, *NE*, p. 56.
167 For example, see Syme (1971), p. 321f.; Barnes (1982), *NE*, p. 33, Barnes (1978), p. 92f.
168 Julian, *Ep. ad Ath.*, pp. 270–1; Gallus was not expected to live long (Socrates 3.1; Sozomen 5.2.9).
169 His nephew Dalmatius became Caesar in 335 (*PLRE*, I, p. 241, no. 7), while Constantine contented his half-brothers with the meaningless rank of *nobilissimus* (Zos., 2.39.2).
170 *Pet. Pat.* fr. 14.
171 *Mos. et Rom. legum collatio* 15.3 (the "Edict against the Manichees"); see here Corcoran (2000), p. 135f.
172 Danubian legions were sent to Egypt by 295 (*P.Oxy.* 43 *recto*; see Bowman 1978: p. 11); and to the Persian war (Aur. Vict. *de Caes.* 39.34; Eutr. 9.24; Jordanes, *Getica* 21).

173 *Pan. Lat.* 2.6.3.
174 Barnes *NE*, p. 126.
175 Eutr. 9.22.2; Jer., *Chron.*, p. 227a (Helm).
176 Aur. Vict. *de Caes.* 39.42.
177 Barnes *NE*, p. 126.
178 *CIL* VI 1125 = *ILS* 619, found in the Roman forum.
179 Howe (1942: p. 61) does not regard this as decisive, suggesting that the abbreviation referred to two Prefects of Maximian. This is unconvincing. For further arguments as to a dual rather than quadripartite prefecture, see Mommsen, *Ges. Schr.* VI, p. 287ff.; Ensslin, *CAH* XII, p. 389.
180 Chastagnol (1989); Corcoran (2000), p. 85f.
181 Palanque (1933), p. 1; Howe (1942), p. 62.
182 For example, Constantius' resettlement of the barbarians of Batavia (*Pan. Lat.* 4.8.4; 21.1–2); his appointment of Eumenius as *praeceptor* of the schools of Autun (*Pan. Lat.* 5.14.1) and his possession of something of a court of his own (*Pan. Lat.* 5.14.1). The settlement of a salary of 600,000 sesterces upon Eumenius also bespeaks some independent financial control (*Pan. Lat.* 5.14.5).
183 See Corcoran (2000), pp. 268–74.
184 *P. Oxy.* 43 *recto* attests the presence a *protector* of an Augustus, but it had been Galerius who had visited Egypt (see Bowman 1978: p. 27).
185 Amm. Marc. 14.11.10.
186 See Blockley (1972), pp. 455–7.
187 See Poole (1892), nos 2511, 2559–68, 2608, 2615.
188 See Kinch (1890), p. 36; Pond Rothman (1977), p. 440f.
189 Julian *Caes.* 315. A,B.

3

AUGUSTUS AND CAESAR

The men whom Diocletian chose to promote were men accustomed to authority. Maximian, Constantius and Galerius were soldiers who had risen through the ranks in a hard school. The loyalty which they owed towards Diocletian was repaid by his trust, in particular in the exercise of command. While all of Diocletian's colleagues were in one sense his reflections, exercising power on his behalf, they were entrusted with tasks of great magnitude and given considerable freedom to act. In this they differed from their successors as Caesars, Gallus and Julian, who were fenced with the officials of the profoundly suspicious Constantius II. The scale of the commissions entrusted to Diocletian's colleagues has, in the past, led to the illusion that power was formally divided. It was argued in the last chapter that this was never the case during the First Tetrarchy. This proposition will be more fully explored in this chapter as Galerius' military activities in the years of his Caesarship (293–305) are examined.

Convention has placed Galerius on the Danube between 293 and his Persian campaign, whence he returned to his European duties.[1] Based upon the political description of the regime provided by Aurelius Victor, there was little reason to doubt the accuracy of this proposition until, in 1976, T.D. Barnes demonstrated that Galerius had spent the years 293–299 in the eastern provinces. Barnes' arguments were based upon the victory titulature of the emperors.[2] They shared their victory titles. If one won a victory, it was added to the nomenclature of all, thus subtly proclaiming the charismatic unity of the college. These titles could be either geographic (e.g. *Persicus Maximus*, *Britannicus Maximus*) or ethnic (e.g. *Carpicus Maximus*, *Sarmaticus Maximus*). In some cases titles were claimed, but abandoned. Diocletian, for example, abandoned his initial salutation as *Gothicus Maximus* in the interests of diplomatic necessity.[3] Two titles that Galerius bore after Diocletian's abdication which he had been forbidden before were *Thebaicus Maximus* and *Aegyptiacus Maximus*.[4] The evidence of these titles led Barnes to place Galerius in Egypt in 293 in response to a revolt in Upper Egypt. This argument was confirmed by the publication of a papyrus which attested the presence of Alogius, an *adiutor memoriae* in Galerius' *comitatus* in Egypt in late 293.[5]

Galerius' first war as Caesar was a local affair. Two Egyptian towns defied the empire. The principal source, Jerome's Chronicle, reports tersely:

> *Busiris et Coptos contra Romanos rebellantes ad solum usque subversae sunt.*

(Busiris and Coptos, rebelling against the Romans, were utterly destroyed.)[6]

The very brevity of this reference and apparent lack of other evidence caused many scholars to identify these events with another, and later, revolt, although in Lower Egypt.[7] Other papyrological evidence adds detail. One document from Oxyrhynchus, most likely dated 23 December 293, mentions *equites promoti* of the emperors.[8] Three legionary *vexillationes* and an imperial *protector* are attested at Oxyrhynchus in January 295. These were drawn from the IV Flavia, the VII Claudia and the XI Claudia.[9] Another papyrus document records the presence of a detachment of the V Macedonica.[10]

Other literary sources add little to Jerome's account save for the detail that both towns were in the Thebaid. Moreover, Galerius' temporarily abandoned victory title, *Thebaicus Maximus*, clearly refers to a specific victory in Upper Egypt. This has led to the postulation of an otherwise unknown Egyptian Busiris in the region of Coptus.[11] Alan Bowman, however, has identified the town recorded by Jerome as "Busiris" as a community in the Thebaid recorded as "Boresis" in an inscription of Cornelius Gallus, rather than as one of the five towns named "Busiris" otherwise known.[12] While the actual site of Boresis has eluded identification, the evidence is clear that it still existed into the fourth century.[13]

The Thebaid was a region both distant and important. Coptus itself stood at the head of the Wadi Hamammat and commanded secure routes to the Red Sea ports of Berenike and Myos Hormos, the former in particular. The Coptus–Berenike road passed porphyry quarries, emerald mines and gold mines. An inscription discovered at Coptus lists the costs of travel permits to the Red Sea ports.[14] Desert wayfarers included sailors, artisans and wagons with various loads, including masts, yardarms, corpses and women. Prostitutes were charged a considerable sum, indicating the profitability of a trade plied in remote communities.[15] A series of ostraka lists some of the articles flowing eastwards through Coptus as a consequence of the trade: wheat, barley, oil, hemp, skins, bullion and coins.[16] The natural consequence of this had been that Coptus held a place as an important centre of Roman trade. Its wealth was reflected in great buildings and embellishments.[17] It was also the home to a garrison. Troops from the III Cyrenaica were permanently stationed there until they took their expertise in desert patrols to Arabia Petraea.[18] They were replaced by a unit of Palmyrene horse archers.[19] Other detachments came through from time to time to build or repair the fortifications along the desert road.[20]

These troops not only ensured the safe conduct of commerce. They were also a naked reminder of the reality of Roman power. This was of some significance in Upper Egypt which had long been a region where nativist Egyptian aspirations had flourished.[21] Coptus itself had been one of a confederation of cities which had revolted against Roman control in the very earliest days of the Roman occupation.[22] In the late 270s the town of Ptolemais, aided by the desert-dwelling Blemmyes, revolted against Roman control.[23] The towns of Upper Egypt had reason for disloyalty. The glory days of prosperity were long past. Piracy on the Red Sea was already a problem in the second century. The trade itself seems to have dried up by the early third century.[24] The latest evidence of imperial *euergetism* in the town dates from the time of Caracalla. Shabby and down-at-heel after decades of recession, it still remained of great strategic and economic significance. The southern sea route through Berenike or Myos Hormos bypassed the Persian Empire entirely, avoiding both a number of tariff barriers and the closure of borders in times of war.[25] Unlike other caravan cities, however, Coptus lay within a highly regularized and bureaucratic structure designed primarily to benefit the central treasury.

It would, furthermore, be easy to underestimate the economic significance of the destruction of Palmyra by Aurelian. The influence of Palmyrene merchants went far and wide, even to Coptus itself where there had been a troop of Palmyrene cavalry and a number of Palmyrene traders. Such merchants ensured the safety of the caravans which tried to cross the Syrian desert from Mesopotamia and Antioch.[26] Once the protective penumbra of Palmyra was withdrawn, traders had to shift for themselves or find alternative routes. At the end of the 280s the nomadic tribes of the Arabian desert gave them further encouragement to do so. These tribes, known collectively as *Saraceni*, posed a particular threat to ordered commerce and, on at least one occasion, Diocletian himself was obliged to mount an expedition against them.[27] It may be in this context that the legion X Fretensis was moved from Jerusalem to Aila (modern Eilat) at the head of the Red Sea. In noting its presence there, Eusebius stated of Aila:

Ailam, en eschatois esti (Palaistinis) paracheimeni ti pros mesembrian eremo kai tis pros auti erythra thalassi ploti ousi tois te ap' Aigyptou perosi kai tois apo tis Indikis.

(Ailam at the far bounds of Palestine, by the southern desert and the Red Sea, which is sailed by those coming from Egypt and India.)[28]

Eusebius' observation illustrates the economic significance of the southern route and the need to protect it. It is in this context that the expedition to Coptus must be perceived. Moreover, Coptus' economic significance went far beyond its historic place in the eastern trade. The eastern desert of Egypt was a major quarry for the empire. Monumental buildings were embellished with the grey granodiorite from the Mons Claudianus; imperial statues were carved from the rich red porphyry of the Mons Porphyrites; luxuriant emeralds and other precious stones were hewn from the region known as Mons Smaragdus.[29] It was not simply an operation designed to quell the disloyalty of distant peoples. It was much more determined by the economic role which had been played by Coptus in the past and might be again in the future. Imperial panegyrists were well aware of the economic significance of Galerius' campaign. In 297, a panegyrist proclaimed:

> dent veniam trophaea Niliaca sub quibus Aethiops et Indus intremuit.

(May the Nile trophies under which the Ethiopian and Indian quaked pardon me.)[30]

The invocation of the Indian and the Ethiopian refer specifically to the role of the Thebaid as gateway to the Red Sea, the principal arm of communication with east and south. Galerius himself recognized the importance of the consolidation of Roman control over this region through his employment of *Thebaicus Maximus* and *Aegyptiacus Maximus* in his victory titles.[31] Diocletian, for his part, preferred not to highlight this counter-insurgency operation in a remote but strategic frontier. He did not permit Galerius to employ the titles which he had claimed, perhaps because they implied the conquest of Roman citizens, not foreign foes.[32] Despite this reluctance, Diocletian took the whole matter very seriously. Galerius marched up the Nile at the head of a considerable force. To the units already identified must be added the *Ala II Hispanorum* since it later became the garrison.[33]

Galerius' remit was to find a workable solution to the problem of regional disloyalty in a strategically critical region. Less obviously, he may well have been required to commence the renovation of infrastructure which had fallen into desuetude. He certainly sought to impose a drastic settlement. Jerome records the complete destruction of Coptus. Subsequent references to the city by name, however, indicate that this is perhaps an exaggeration. As early as 297 the private correspondence of Paniskos, who was in the force of the rebel *corrector* Achilleus, was sent from a place still called Coptus.[34] Papyrological evidence casts some light on to this difficulty. A papyrus of 300 mentions a fort named "Potecoptos".[35] The name simply means "once-Coptus" or "formerly Coptus". It is used elsewhere.[36] Evidently in 299 there was a garrison of mounted archers at this fort under the command of a *praepositus*. The remains of this fort may well have been observed by Sir Flinders Petrie during his excavation campaign there. A brick wall of Roman date, and its collapse, was recorded by Petrie who only narrowly avoided being buried by it. It was originally a curtain wall constructed of baked brick and flanked by round bastion towers.[37] Round bastions became a regular feature in Roman fortifications only towards the end of the third century.[38] It is likely that the wall belongs to the period after the revolt of 293/4, although it is impossible to be more precise.

Construction of the fortress combined with the refoundation of the town. Not too far distant from Coptos, probably at Cainopolis (modern Qena), arose the newly named town of Maximianopolis.[39] Nomenclature renders its origin evident: "Maximian" is Galerius' regnal name. Resettlement of a population amounted to the refoundation of a town, hence the new name. Galerius' foundation flourished, although obscurely, well into the sixth century.[40] If the identification is correct, a further detail can be added to Galerius' reorganization of the region. A Roman road runs northeast from Caenopolis/Maximianopolis. It leads through the quarry region known as the Mons Porphyrites to a fortified port facility on the Red Sea now called Abu Sha'ar.[41] This fortress was long thought to be of Ptolemaic date, but it has recently been shown to have been constructed in the last decade of the third century.[42] Numismatic evidence from the site provides Alexandrian coinage of Galerius struck before the monetary reform of 296.[43] The desert road is fortified on the model of a desert *limes*, and carried traffic between the Red Sea and the Nile and also connected the Nile with the porphyry quarries.[44]

Galerius may well have also supervised a more drastic change in the structure of Egyptian administration. The province of Thebais was in existence by September 298.[45] Its earlier existence is probable. *P. Oxy.* 43 *recto*, although fragmentary, can be restored to refer to a *praeses* of the Thebaid in February 295.[46] Similarly, *P. Lond.* 958 can be interpreted as referring to a *praeses* of the province of the Thebaid on 28 September 296.[47] If these restorations are correct, then there is an attested governor of the province of the Thebaid as early as February 295. Since no separate province of Thebais existed prior to the revolt of Coptus in 293, the connection between the suppression of the revolt and the creation of the new province is highly likely. Apart from Diocletian's established policy of increasing the number of provinces, such a step at this point will have recognized the unique regional character of the Thebaid. Only a few years later Diocletian had to face a general revolt in Egypt which seems to have had regional origins.[48] For his part, Diocletian was less subtle in his response to parochial particularism. A military camp was constructed in the heart of the old and abandoned Temple of Amen-Re at Luxor. The shrine holding the imperial standards was located in an audience hall of the Temple of Amen constructed by Amenhotep III.[49]

The investment in the region was nevertheless fruitful. Although some Red Sea ports did not recover from the third-century recession, there is good evidence that at least one did.[50] Economic life resumed at Berenike, the southernmost of the ports, in the course of the fourth century.[51] Evidence from Arikamedu in India also indicates a renewal of the maritime trade from the fourth century onwards.[52] Coptus too was reborn. It was simply in too convenient a position for it to be abandoned. By the middle of the fourth century it was once more a town of some size with its own bishop. By the end of the century, a legionary garrison was stationed there.[53] Warmington's old description of the late Roman attitude to the maritime trade as uninterested is no longer sustainable.[54] Diocletian was in fact very interested in securing the eastern trade. After the Persian War one key point of the peace settlement was the establishment of Nisibis as the sole point of entry for the eastern caravan trade. The Persians for their part were content to relinquish territory, but baulked at that condition.[55]

Galerius' expedition to Upper Egypt cannot be seen as an isolated incident. While there are particularities unique to the situation, when placed in a wider context it encompasses far more than a merely punitive expedition against a distant and rebellious region. It was, instead, a part of a process which was already under way to renovate and revitalize the mercantile economy and its infrastructure throughout the Roman east. This was a process commenced by Diocletian in his negotiations with the Saracens, in which context, perhaps, the X Fretensis was redeployed to Aila.[56] It was continued by Galerius in Egypt and, in the following eighteen months or so, in Roman Palestine and Syria.

There are few firm dates for imperial activity in the east between the end of this Egyptian campaign and the outbreak of the Persian War. On 1 May 295, an Edict on Marriage was issued from Damascus.[57] In the course of the following year, war with Persia broke out.[58] The gaps can only be filled by supposition and inference. Unless new and decisive evidence is brought to light, any account of these years is necessarily tentative. A number of clues do assist here, however. The first is a heavily scrutinized inscription from Qasr al-Azraq which attests detachments from the IV Flavia, the VII Claudia and the XI Claudia engaged in roadworks on the desert frontier.[59] Vexillations from the same legions are attested at Oxyrhynchus in January 295, and the appearance of these vexillations in two adjacent locations within a few years of each other cannot be simple coincidence.[60] The likelihood is that these were the same units, and that they belonged to Galerius' mobile field army.

The inscription from Qasr al-Azraq attests works on a network of roads between centres on the edge of Roman Palestine. From there, roads ran north and west into Roman territory. From there also ran a long and important road through the Wadi Sirhan to Dumata (modern Jawf). From there, this road continued to the Persian Gulf, and was used in antiquity as both a military road and a trade route.[61] In many ways, the situation in this region was as vulnerable and important as that on the Red Sea coast. Both regions carried considerable long-range caravan traffic; both regions lacked a strong military presence to ensure the safe conduct of trade. This region of the *limes Palestinae* was hardly going to be an invasion highway for a Sassanid army. Soldiers stationed in the fortified centres were not the first line of defence against the ancient enemy, but peacekeepers in a different and irresolvable conflict.[62]

Further evidence of Galerius' involvement in the renovation of the eastern frontier comes from nomenclature. Less than one hundred kilometres north of Qasr al-Azraq lies ancient Saccaeum. During Diocletian's rule it was elevated to the status of a city and renamed Maximianopolis.[63] As in Egypt with Kainopolis, Galerius took an opportunity to stamp his own name upon the geography of the empire, thereby creating a memorial of sorts of his own contribution to Diocletian's greater work. Indeed, a third place also bears Galerius' name: Capharcotna in the Jezreel Valley, the settlement which had accumulated around the sometime camp of the VI Ferrata, also took the name of Maximianopolis.[64]

These activities of Galerius which can be inferred from this slight evidence were not isolated, but part of a grander plan which Diocletian was implementing for the eastern frontiers. The eastern provinces were of critical concern to Diocletian. He had become emperor in the east in the aftermath of an unfinished war; once free to, he had spent considerable time in Palestine and Syria. In 286, he was in Palestine.[65] In 287, he was back in the east, possibly residing at Antioch.[66] In May 290, he was in Palestine again, overseeing his campaign against the Saracens.[67] After this, he appears to have remained on the Danube detained by problems there.[68] The work which he had begun was deputed to Galerius to continue.

Work in the region commenced early in Diocletian's reign. Little had been done for years and there was much to accomplish.[69] Milestones have been recorded which identify roadworks in the area before 293.[70] The bulk of epigraphic material, however, is from the time of Galerius. Dedicatory inscriptions from completed fortifications belong to the period 293–305, except that at Dar el-Khaf which belongs to 305/6.[71] A new legion, the IV Martia, was raised and stationed at Betthoro – modern Lejjun.[72] Fortification occurred also at Ummel-Jimal and Umm el-Quttein at one end of the Limes Arabicus, and the stockades of the Wadi Aravah at the other.[73] Milestones dating between 293 and 305 are to be found on the roads running between Phaeno and Damascus;[74] Philippopolis and Petra;[75] Damascus and Galilean Maximianopolis;[76] Palmyra and Bostra;[77] and between Emesa and Damascus.[78] In addition, the fortress at Palmyra was probably completed during the 290s.[79] Diplomatically, links with the Lakhmid Arabs and their king 'Amr ibn 'Ali were perhaps strengthened.[80] Fortifications were also built and refurbished on the road from Damascus to Palmyra and, at some stage, on the roads from Palmyra and Sura. From the evidence of the milestones and the Palmyrene inscription of Hierocles, it most likely occurred at this time.[81] Such activities are what one might expect of a loyal and hard-working deputy accustomed to responsibility. Benefits too came to the Caesar. His name had now been bestowed on three cities and he will have become acquainted with Sossianus Hierocles, later a key adviser to Diocletian in religious matters.[82] He also fathered a son, although not by his wife.[83]

The result of this work was a web of roads and fortresses from the Red Sea to the Euphrates. Damascus was the key. It linked the *limes* of the south, which protected traders and farmers from predatory nomads of the Arabian desert, with those that ran to the Euphrates which apprehended the grander threat from Rome's imperial rival. According to Malalas, Diocletian established an arms factory there.[84] On 1 May 295 Diocletian issued an edict at Damascus on marriage which fixes his presence there at that time.[85] The likely context for such a visit was a consultation between Augustus and Caesar. The two had not met since Galerius left for Egypt in the latter part of 293. It is reasonable to suppose that Galerius would be asked to report in person to his Augustus. Such consultations featured in Diocletian's relationship with Maximian during the period of the dyarchy. The panegyrics attest at least two such "summit conferences".[86]

It is most likely that the principal discussions of the two emperors focused upon the plans and logistics for the building programme. Diocletian had good reason to believe that he had settled the problem of the Persian frontier for the foreseeable future. The import of Carus' great victory over Persia has been largely obscured by subsequent events. It was Rome's first genuine victory in the east since the time of Severus, reversing a history of defeat and humiliation for Roman arms.[87] Shapur I had depicted three Roman emperors in varying attitudes of subjection (dead, captive and suppliant) on his victory monuments.[88] His great inscription near Persepolis, the so-called *Res Gestae* of Shapur, provides a clear text: Gordian III defeated and slain; Philip I, obliged to make a humiliating peace; Valerian captured, and his army annihilated.[89] The captured and plundered towns of Syria and Cappadocia are listed too.[90] Despite the frustration offered by the Palmyrenes, Persia seemed strong and gaining in strength. The Arsacid King of Armenia, Chosroes, had been slain and replaced by a Sassanid prince. Chosroes' son, Tiridates III, fled to the protection of Gallienus.[91] The Severan province of Osroene too may have reverted to Persian suzerainty.[92]

The great war of revenge had been a project for a succession of rulers. Aurelian was murdered while leading his army to Persia and the war was abandoned.[93] It was left to Carus, seven years later, to take up where Valerian had left off. But, by then, the glory days of Shapur were over. A series of disputes over the succession caused Seistan to break away from central Sassanid control for much of the 280s. The more central Adiabene may also have been independent for a brief period at this time.[94] As a result, the young Sassanid Great King, Vahraran II, was largely preoccupied by internal warfare. Carus' campaign struck at this moment of weakness and distraction. His death, and the withdrawal of the Roman army from Mesopotamia, left Vahraran free to suppress these revolts.

It was into this situation that Diocletian first came when he arrived in the east in 286. No peace had been made with Persia following Carus' victory. The Euphrates was still the frontier between the two empires.[95] Negotiations may have commenced in that year. If so, they must have continued into 287 when Diocletian was in Antioch. Vahraran was in no position to drive a hard bargain. In 290, a panegyrist proclaimed to Maximian:

> *rex ille Persarum numquam se ante dignatus hominem confiteri, fratri tuo supplicat totumque, si ingredi ille dignetur, regnum suum pandit.*

(the King of the Persians, who has never before confessed himself a mere man, humbles himself to your brother and throws open all of his kingdom to him, should he condescend to enter.)[96]

A settlement was evidently reached, substantially on Roman terms. Armenia, wholly Persian since the time of Shapur, was partitioned. The Persians retained control of the larger, eastern portion, ruled by Narseh, the surviving son of Shapur. The western portion was granted to the Arsacid claimant, Tiridates.[97] In addition, Rome again pushed her boundary with Persia beyond the Euphrates. The new frontier is uncertain. It was either the Tigris–Singara–Circesium line, or one further north which substantially followed the line of the Balih river. The latter is more probable, since Nisibis remained in Persian hands until the end of the 290s.[98] Edessa was certainly in Roman hands again. Diocletian established an arms factory there for the needs of the newly recovered province.[99]

By this peace, something of the old Roman hegemony in the region was re-established. The vulnerability of Persian arms had been proven by Carus and exploited by Diocletian. It was nevertheless still something of a compromise. Rome had not recovered all of its lost territory or all of its ancient dominance. It was also precarious, depending as it did upon the weakness of a Persia as distracted by civil war as Arsacid Parthia had been. Diocletian celebrated the conclusion of the treaty by taking the title *Persicus Maximus*.[100] It was abandoned when the peace failed. In 293, Vahraran II died. He was succeeded by his son, Vahraran III, but this was not without dispute. Vahraran was a minor, but his claims were supported by a powerful noble, Vahunam, as well as the King of Mesene. Vahunam's power over the young king may have disturbed others at court who feared the consequences of his influence. Certainly a large number of them, including the Zoroastrian High Priest Kartir, and members of the old Parthian Suren and Karen families invited Narseh to lead the opposition to Vahraran and his powerful minister.[101] Their success was swift. Vahunam was captured and executed. Without his direction, Vahraran followed soon after and Narseh was invited to assume the kingdom of his father. Diocletian made no attempt to interfere but sent his congratulations to the new Great King.[102]

Diocletian presumed too much on the goodwill, or the distraction, of the new king. In the middle of 296, Narseh broke the fragile peace with Rome by invading Roman Osroene and Arsacid Armenia.[103] There had been a critical failure of intelligence: the Roman forces were unprepared; Diocletian himself was far afield in Pannonia.[104] He hastened to the east, bringing reinforcements.[105] Galerius was in the region and thus was able to take charge of the situation quickly. He had few troops at his disposal; Eutropius speaks of only a slight force (*parva manu*).[106] It was left to him initially, with such slender resources, to confront the Persians and blunt the force of their attack until Diocletian could arrive with reinforcements.

Some commentators assert that Galerius, attacking rashly, was routed by the Persians and lucky to escape with his life.[107] The sources permit a more nuanced and less clumsy reading of what must have been a genuine military crisis in the Roman east. Eutropius' full narrative is useful:

> *Galerius Maximianus primum adversus Narseum proelium insecundum habuit inter Callinicum Carrasque congressus, cum inconsulte magis quam ignave dimicasset; admodum enim parva manu cum copiosissimo hoste commisit.*

> (At first, Galerius Maximianus, coming against Narseus between Carrhae and Callinicum, suffered a defeat, although he fought foolishly rather than ignobly, since he came against a great and most numerous army with a small force.)[108]

Other sources provide similar narratives. Lack of immediate resources meant that the Romans could only respond with cunning and guile. Aurelius Victor relates the events of the campaign thus:

> *Interim Iovio Alexandriam profecto provincia credita Maximiano Casesari, uti relictis finibus in Mesopotamiam progrederetur ad arcendos Persarum impetus.*

> (Meanwhile, Iovius having departed to Alexandria, the task was assigned to Maximianus Caesar that he should proceed across the border into Mesopotamia in order to hinder the assault of the Persians.)[109]

A frontal battle was out of the question. Galerius' advance into Mesopotamia was only intended as a holding action. The sources refer to a number of battles in the vast area "between Carrhae and Callinicum".[110] Callinicum, which had been recently refortified by Diocletian may have been Galerius' base of operations.[111] Orosius states that three battles were fought, of which the last was the decisive defeat of Galerius' force.[112] These are, no doubt, records of skirmishes rather than pitched set-piece battles. Roman tactics, in the circumstances, must have been similar to those of other generals in the same region with the same objectives. The Parthian general Suren, for example, had also harassed rather than confronted, eroding the morale of Crassus' army until it collapsed. Suren, unlike Galerius, had a considerable cavalry advantage over Crassus' legionaries. That enabled him to avoid battle. In Galerius' case it was more likely that Narseh enjoyed the advantage in mounted troops, and so could locate, pursue and destroy Galerius' skirmishing force. Despite the loss in the field, the campaign was not a failure. Narseh's force did not cross into Roman territory. Persian success was elsewhere, perhaps indicating their immediate aims. In 297 Narseh occupied Armenia, expelled Tiridates and reclaimed the territory ceded by Vahraran in 287.[113] The Romans were unable to protect their client since their focus was, for the moment, on other matters. Reinforcements were urgently needed in the east. Galerius was sent to the Danube to gather them; Diocletian himself remained in Syria to prepare for the following year's campaign. Galerius' mission could not be completed swiftly.[114] He was not merely calling up old soldiers but also raw recruits who required some training. In addition, Jordanes attests that he enrolled some Gothic mercenaries and this surely required some negotiation.[115] Roman problems were augmented by another revolt in Egypt. Persian victories no doubt tempted the provinces' many disaffected into rebellion.[116] An emperor of their own, Domitius Domitianus, was proclaimed.[117] Diocletian was obliged to take his Syrian army and march on Alexandria in order to quell the revolt. Galerius was left to continue the war alone.

By winter 297, Galerius was in position at Satala in the Cappadocian uplands with an army of 25,000 men (see Figure 2, overleaf).[118] The relative paucity of this force reflects the haste with which Galerius was compelled to break off the process of raising and training it and bring it into action. It must nevertheless have been reinforced by the Armenian royal army.[119] The Roman force was composed of perhaps four legions plus cavalry and auxiliary cohorts.[120] It may be that no other legions were used as whole units, but twin *vexillationes* were drafted from the Danube as had occurred for Galerius' Egyptian expedition.[121] Satala, a legionary base, was a logical base for an invasion of Armenia.

The Persians themselves were consolidating their rule in Armenia. The Great King and his household were firmly established.[122] Two relatives of Narseh are also attested as present: Shapur and Ohrmazd.[123] An inscription of Narseh's which records his accession identifies Shapur as holding the rank of *hargbad*, a high official of the royal family whose brief seems to have been primarily financial.[124] Ohrmazd ought to be identified with Narseh's son of that name who, as his father's heir, may well have been given the kingship of Persian Armenia in 293, and was now therefore the vassal lord of the newly conquered territories.[125] Perhaps the Persians considered themselves sufficiently secure, complacent at an easy victory. They were certainly taken by surprise by Galerius' counter-offensive. Galerius himself had much to do with that surprise, as Festus reports:

Figure 2 Detail from the Arch of Galerius. Galerius sets out from Cappadociato to do battle with the Persians (photo: the author).

in Armenia maiore ipse imperator cum duobus equitibus exploravit hostes.

(in Armenia Maior, the emperor reconnoitred the enemy himself, along with two horsemen.)[126]

This might be considered folklore if it did not originate from a sober, if laconic source. Moreover there is independent attestation from the Armenian writer P'awstos, who fills out gaps in a surprising and intriguing fashion.[127] In his narrative, Galerius chose two Armenian nobles (Andovk and Arshavir) who were known to him and, disguising themselves as peasants – market-gardeners selling vegetables – they gained entry to the Persian camp and spied out its weaknesses. In particular, they noted that the royal enclosure was not strongly guarded and therefore particularly vulnerable. One might be tempted to reject this tale as folkloric invention but it occurs in two entirely separate historical traditions with little possibility of interdependence.[128]

P'awstos continues that, on the emperor's return to his own camp, he roused his army and fell upon the Persians, aiming for the royal enclosure. Ammianus adds the detail of a favourable portent.[129] P'awstos' account is entirely plausible. The Persians were completely surprised. In a letter to Constantius II half a century later, Shapur II complained:

Ideoque Armeniam recuperare cum Mesopotamia debeo, avo meo composita fraude praereptam.

(And so I am under obligation to recover Armenia, along with Mesopotamia, both of which were torn from my grandfather by a trick.)[130]

The defeat rankled years later, not least because it was achieved by subterfuge rather than a set-piece battle. It was a most effective ploy. According to P'awstos, the Romans raided the Persian camp soon after dawn, taking it totally unawares. A number of Persian grandees were captured but, most significantly, the household of the Great King, including his wives and concubines, fell into Roman hands.[131] The camp was looted and Narseh's queen, Arsane, captured, as were others of the Great King's women. The Great King himself escaped and fled to Persia proper.[132]

The major non-narrative sources for Galerius' Persian campaign are the panel reliefs on the Arch of Galerius in Thessalonika (see Figure 3). This artefact and its copious reliefs have been the subject of a number of studies since the late nineteenth century.[133] While the extant reliefs clearly focus upon the course of Galerius' Persian War, only three piers remain of what was originally an octopyle construction – more rotunda than arch in fact. Of those three piers, only two still carry reliefs. Potentially, therefore, only one quarter of the original decoration remains. One can only speculate as to what appears on the remaining panels, but what that means in terms of contemporary analysis

Figure 3 The Arch of Galerius in Thessalonica (photo: the author).

93

is that any narrative which scholars seek to construct from the surviving images is tentative at best, and that no real interpretative conclusions about imperial politics can be inferred from the fact of the Arch – although extant images do provide clear ideological messages.

This does not mean that the Arch cannot be employed as a source, merely that it has the same limitations as any fragmentary document. Diocletian and Galerius certainly took pride in the defeat of the Persians. It would not be surprising if the scenes which they chose to depict were well enough known to need little interpretation. The "adlocutio" scene, for example, where Galerius addresses his troops shows a city gate in the background which might reasonably be taken to be Satala (see Figure 4). The mountains in the background confirm the impression. As he speaks, the cavalry are being led out. In another scene, he and the same cavalry are depicted as heroically victorious in a scene which might represent the sack of the Persian camp; in another the victorious Romans accept the surrender of the Persian nobles and the harem of the Great King.[134] Figure 5 shows a battle.

Galerius' victory left the Persians helpless. He was able to drive the last of them out of Armenia, forcing them across the Tigris.[135] The rest of the war is summarized by Galerius' victory titulature. The first title taken, *Armeniacus Maximus*, refers to his victory over Narseh.[136] A first salutation as *Persicus Maximus* may also be attributed to this victory.[137] The title of *Armeniacus Maximus* was followed in quick succession by *Medicus Maximus* and *Adiabenicus Maximus*. These were neither fruitless bombast nor vacuous hyperbole: they reflect campaigns.[138] Galerius crossed the Tigris and marched down its left bank, taking cities in Atropatene and Adiabene.[139] His success took him down the river as far as Ctesiphon and possibly further. What is more likely is that he crossed the Mesopotamian plain at its narrowest point and

Figure 4 Detail from the Arch of Galerius: Galerius addresses the troops before battle (photo: the author).

94

Figure 5 Detail from the Arch of Galerius: the emperor in battle (photo: the author).

marched up the Euphrates.[140] In returning he did not march straight back to Roman Osrhoene but seems to have turned aside at the Khabur River in order to go up to Nisibis and thus complete the work of reconquering the old Severan province. Nisibis was recovered from the Persians before September 298.[141] He probably decided to rest and winter there. It was here that he received a visit from Appharban, a friend of the Great King's sent to negotiate a peace.[142] Peter the Patrician provides a most discursive tale of the encounter, a story which he probably picked up from the work of Eunapius.[143] It is one of the few anecdotes about Galerius that can be related with any confidence. Peter relates that Appharban, approaching the Caesar, endeavours to remind him of the fickleness of fortune — an empire victorious one day may be in the dust of defeat on the next. Moreover, he pleads, Rome and Persia are the eyes of the world. Extinguishing one would lessen the other. He praises Galerius' victory over a great foe, a victory that demonstrates Galerius' own inherent merit. Accordingly, he pleads, Rome should not push her luck but be merciful to the defeated, and especially those in captivity. This line of approach only serves to anger Galerius. According to Peter, Galerius trembles with fury as he rejects Appharban's diplomatic arguments and reminds him of the humiliation of Valerian by the Persians. In any event, Galerius had no powers to make peace with Persia. Such a matter, its terms and conditions, was for Diocletian to determine. Galerius' dismissal of Appharban's embassy is therefore not altogether surprising. Nevertheless, they may have concluded a truce which permitted the subsequent negotiations to proceed.[144]

Diocletian had completed his victory in Egypt in the middle of 298. His long siege of Alexandria was followed by a tour up the Nile and a settlement of the borders of the Egyptian provinces. Having done this, he returned to Syria and was in Antioch on 5 February 299.[145] From there, he went to Nisibis where he conferred with his victorious Caesar.[146] He instructed the *magister memoriae*, Sicorius Probus, to lay down the terms of a peace which permitted no negotiation.[147] The peace reflected Diocletian's own preference for a carefully regulated and controllable border region between the empires. His demands were moderate but firm, and gave the Persians no room for negotiation. They gained some territory, and asserted Roman control of trading relations by specifying Nisibis as the sole location of trade contacts between the empires.[148] This treaty reversed over half a century of Roman humiliation, and was built upon the hard work of the Caesar. His surprise attack had reaped rewards. Nor was it surprising, in retrospect, that Galerius should have chosen to attack the Persians in this way given his numerical inferiority. He entirely avoided fighting a set-piece battle against the larger army and, even with a small army, kept the momentum of his victory going by marching down the Tigris. In turn, this placed the Romans in a superb diplomatic position as well as a commanding military one. In addition, the Romans had possession of hostages of the highest rank, ultimately housed in all honour at Daphne near Antioch.[149] But Galerius did not seek to exploit this victory in any political struggle with Diocletian. Perhaps, even before negotiations were complete, his task was done and he had proceeded to the Danube, perhaps with much of the army that he had raised there. Fresh trouble had broken out with the Sarmatian Marcomanni raiding into Illyricum.[150]

The conclusion of the peace between Persia and Rome, together with the restoration of some stability on the Danube, permitted Galerius' brief return to the east in 300 in order to take part in the celebrations.[151] Rank dictated that the honours belonged to Diocletian. The Augustus rode through Antioch in a *quadriga* parading the results of Galerius' victory. Alongside in the place of honour walked the Caesar – a gesture which has long been misinterpreted.[152] The parade of victory included the captives and concluded with a grand ceremony of sacrifice in thanksgiving. This sacrifice is shown in one of the best preserved panel reliefs on the Arch of Galerius (see Figure 6). Diocletian is in civilian dress. Galerius is attired as a soldier. They stand in front of a colonnade, flanking an altar on which appear the reliefs of Jupiter and Hercules. Diocletian watches as Galerius sprinkles incense upon the altar. Between the emperors are the figures of *Eirene* and *Oikoumene*. *Homonoia* may also be present, a arm linked with that of Galerius. Behind Diocletian stands *Aion*, the figure of the ages.[153] The ideological statement is clear. Despite his complete victory over the empire's traditional

Figure 6 Detail from the Arch of Galerius: Diocletian and Galerius sacrifice together in thanksgiving for the victory (photo: the author).

enemies, Galerius was the servant of his master, linked by a filial bond of *concordia*.

The chronology of the next few years can be fixed by an examination of the emperor's victory titulature.[154] If one won a victory, it was added to the nomenclature of all, thus subtly proclaiming the charismatic unity of the college. As before, the titles could be somehow either geographic (e.g. *Persicus Maximus, Britannicus Maximus*) or ethnic (e.g. *Carpicus Maximus, Sarmaticus Maximus*). In some cases titles were claimed but abandoned. Galerius was neither *Thebaicus Maximus* nor *Aegyptiacus Maximus* until after Diocletian's abdication, since it was not customary to celebrate victory in a civil war,[155] and Diocletian abandoned his initial salutation as *Gothicus Maximus* in the interests of diplomatic necessity.[156] Victory titles were also numbered. As such, they no longer signified the successful conclusion of a war lasting several seasons, but the conclusion of the campaign of one season or a major victory in the field. Although this devalued the traditional significance of such titles, they have become an invaluable guide to warfare during this period. On this basis, a chronology of those conflicts has been firmly established and will largely be followed here.[157]

The security of the Danubian provinces was clearly to be Galerius' next task. It had long been a troubled frontier and the circumstances of Diocletian's accession only exacerbated that trouble.[158] Soon after his accession, Diocletian took the titles of *Germanicus Maximus* and *Sarmaticus Maximus*.[159] The first should indicate a campaign against a Germanic people and, since there is no evidence of Diocletian campaigning on the Rhine (rather, he sent Maximian to Gaul), a campaign upon the Upper Danube frontier, perhaps against the Marcomanni or Quadi, ought to be inferred.[160] Trouble along the *ripa Sarmatica* is attested by the second salutation.[161] These campaigns did little to resolve border tensions. Sometime between 285 and 293, the title of *Sarmaticus Maximus* was taken once again.[162] Maximian was no less busy in the north.[163] In 291, a panegyrist spoke of *trophaea Germanica*, a victory in Rhaetia, *Sarmatiae vastatio*, and a decisive destruction of Saracen tribes in the east.[164] In 289, Gennoboudes, King of the Franks, had already sought and received a peace settlement from Maximian.[165] One of the *Germanicus Maximus* salutations may also belong to a campaign by Diocletian against the Marcomanni in which a bridgehead was constructed on the barbarian side of the Danube.[166] In 294, Diocletian had toured the Lower Danube. This was Carpic territory. The pattern of settlement of the Carpi during this period displays a concentration in the trans-Danubian region opposite Moesia.[167] Just as they had earlier threatened Dacia, now they bore down on the Lower Danube, particularly along the border of Moesia Inferior.[168] It was precisely this area that was the focus of Diocletian's attention in 294. Thanks to the pioneering work of Mommsen, the course of Diocletian's journeys of that year can be followed. He spent much of the summer of 294 in Sirmium, perhaps supervising the construction of fortresses across the Danube.[169] When the autumn of that year arrived, he abruptly quitted this residence for a rapid tour of the lower Danube frontier.[170]

A series of inscriptions from Transmarisca, Durostorum and Kladovo attest a renovation of frontier fortifications at about this time. Diocletian certainly visited these places in the course of 294.[171] To this journey ought to belong the renovation of Danubian fortresses. These rebuilding activities were completed at varying times, but the first seems to have been either Durostorum or Kladovo, which were completed before the Persian victory, followed by Transmarisca soon after.[172] The victory title *Carpicus Maximus* does not appear on any dedicatory inscriptions, which might indicate an uneasy peace and a diplomatic settlement in the area.[173] Along with these specifically attested frontier sites, there is evidence of similar work at eight other sites along the Danube at this time.[174]

The years in which Diocletian concentrated his attention in Illyricum saw an extensive renovation and reconstuction of the Danubian defences.[175] Some claims for this period may be doubted. Jerome dates a transfer of Carpi and Bastarnae to Roman territory to 295.[176] This may be doubted, since Diocletian was in Damascus in May 295.[177] Diocletian evidently returned to the Danube from whence the Persian crisis recalled him to the Orient.[178] Perhaps as a preventative measure he raided across the Danube before his departure, assuming his first acclamation of *Carpicus Maximus*.[179]

A panegyric of 297, which passes tactfully over the Persian defeat, speaks of the felicity of *proxima illa ruina Carporum*.[180] The orator spoke too soon. The work of the early part of the decade had been partial and incomplete.[181] More wars were to follow and no fewer than four acclamations as *Carpicus Maximus* were assumed between 301 and 304.[182] The general in charge was Galerius. Lactantius, unwittingly, gives some evidence of his labours. In describing the household of Maximinus Daza, he states that it was largely composed of barbarians:

> *Nam fere nullus stipator in latere ei nisi ex gente eorum qui a Gothis tempore vicennalium terris suis pulsi Maximiano se tradiderant.*

(For there was barely anyone in the bodyguard other than men of those people, who, having been thrust from their lands by the Goths at the time of the *vicennalia*, had yielded themselves to Galerius.)[183]

Given the number of Carpic salutations won at this time, it is legitimate to identify the tribe in question as the Carpi. On this basis, Brennan has redated the transfer of the Carpi to 305, and this solution, while not resolving the difficulty posed by the specific attestation of the Chronicle, would seem to be the best.[184]

It was not the Carpi who summoned Galerius from his victory celebrations, but the Sarmatians. In 297 a panegyrist had proclaimed the virtual annihilation of the Sarmatians.[185] Such triumphalism was premature. In the middle of the following year, Eumenius was curiously silent about the Danubian frontier.[186] Trouble was brewing. A coin struck at both the Heraclea and Thessalonica mints points to the course of action undertaken by Galerius. It proclaims *"VICTORIAE SARMATICAE"*.[187] The fact that it was struck by both of these mints means that the victory in question can be dated with some precision. The Thessalonica mint was not opened until Galerius took residence in that city.[188] This mint superseded the operations of the Heraclea mint which was now closed down.[189] That the coin was struck by both mints indicates that it was amongst the very last of the Heraclea issues and the very first of those at Thessalonica. Of necessity, this would date the Sarmatian victory to a time immediately before Galerius' move to Thessalonica, where he was well and truly ensconced by 300.[190] Thus this Sarmatian victory ought properly to belong to late 298 or 299.

Thrice Diocletian had struggled with the Sarmatians, penetrating their lands and establishing bridgeheads deep into their territory.[191] Since then, however, Roman activity on the *ripa Sarmatica* had been negligible. The Carpi had demanded attention but the energy of both Diocletian and Galerius had been concentrated in the east. To this end, the Danube frontier had been weakened, of both recruits and veterans.[192] While the Gothic tribes had been conciliated Diocletian must have judged that his earlier defeats of the Sarmatians were sufficient for the moment.[193] That situation could not endure long. Pressure from the north-east and a weakened frontier are strong inducements for any trans-Danubian tribe to break the frontier peace. The surprise is that Diocletian's ad hoc settlement lasted as long as it did.

Nevertheless, it was felt to be safe enough to denude the Danube of troops for more pressing needs. In the winter of 296/7, Galerius arrived in the region to collect reinforcements for the Persian War.[194] The Goths were conciliated and they provided troops.[195] Roman soldiers were also gathered, both recruits and veterans.[196] It was a temporary measure, reflecting the gravity of the situation, since Diocletian had been diverted to Egypt by revolt.[197] The new drafts in all likelihood returned with Galerius, bearing the spoils of the east.

It was back to the Carpic problem that Galerius turned after the resolution of the Persian War. Lactantius alleges that, in 305, Galerius complained to Diocletian that he had been fighting barbarians on the banks of the Danube for fifteen years, while his colleagues took their ease in less troublesome quarters.[198] Galerius had been running Diocletian's errands for as long as that, although not always in Illyria. Nevertheless, the five years or so prior to this alleged conversation were years of unremitting conflict in that region.[199] During this time the title *Sarmaticus Maximus* was taken twice more and there were no fewer than four further salutations as *Carpicus Maximus*.[200] Fighting was so intense and victories proclaimed so often, that an embittered and sardonic Christian, upon reading the first edict of the Great Persecution in 302, exclaimed:

victorias Gothorum et Sarmatorum propositas!

(impending Gothic and Sarmatian victories!)[201]

Galerius' return to the frontier in 298/9 marks a return to the vigorous defence of the region commenced by Diocletian early in his reign. His new task was to hold the Danubian line and, if possible, to eliminate threats from across the river. It was to be the military task which would occupy much of the rest of Galerius' life.

This new task is reflected in Galerius' change of abode. Before 299, his main centres of activity had been Damascus and Antioch. His move to the Danube was heralded by the opening of the mint at Thessalonica and the commencement of the construction of the palace there. It was never intended to be his permanent residence. That was elsewhere and seldom visited.[202] It was nevertheless a useful and strategic place for an emperor to lay his head in the winter months. A chronicle reports a victory over the Marcomanni, a Sarmatian people, in 299.[203] In the following year, Diocletian took the title *Germanicus Maximus* for the sixth time.[204] This seems to have settled the problem on the Upper Danube. The three other *Germanicus Maximus* titles which were taken between 301 and 306 are to be credited to Constantius.[205] The main focus of Galerius' activities in the following years lay further down the Danube.

There had been peace of a sort in this area after Galerius' defeat of the Sarmatians in 299. No further Sarmatian or Carpic titles were taken before December 301.[206] It was in 302 that the storm broke. In this year the Thessalonica mint ceased operations altogether. Its place was taken by a new mint at Serdica.[207] This mint struck only base metal coinage and lacks the S(acra) M(oneta) mint-mark, thereby indicating that Galerius did not shift his residence there.[208] Rather, it is to be understood that the purpose of this mint was purely functional, as the nearest to Galerius' centre of activities. He spent the summers fighting and wintered in Nicomedia where proximity to his father brought political advantage.[209]

The immediate pressure came from the Carpi. Carpic lands across the Danube were being encroached upon by the Goths.[210] The tribe must have been desperate to seize Roman land in order to restore their livelihoods. They did not assault the border as raiders, but as invaders. The savagery of the conflict is reflected in the victory titulature. Between the beginning of 302 and the end of 303 the title *Carpicus Maximus* was augmented four times.[211] This bitter dedication to war bore fruit. In 303/4, the Carpi surrendered and submitted to Rome. The date is provided by Lactantius, who adds the detail that many of the hitherto hostile tribesmen were accepted into the household of Galerius.[212] It is to this time that the transfer of the Carpi to Roman territory is to be dated. Whether this was a policy which originated from Galerius or from Diocletian is immaterial. Diocletian certainly approved it and to him the historical credit accrued.[213] A final struggle in 303 preceded this surrender. In March 303, Galerius was with Diocletian in Nicomedia, but was hurriedly called away. Lactantius states that Galerius put his sudden departure down to fear of being burned alive in the palace after two fires had broken out within it.[214] More likely, he was summoned by the more urgent flames of war. In June of that year, Diocletian paid a visit to Durostorum before proceeding to Rome.[215]

A grand celebration awaited him. By 20 November he was in Rome for his *vicennalia*.[216] Galerius may have accompanied him. There is no evidence that he was anywhere else. It is certainly likely that Maximian was present for the great event, and it is not implausible that he was accompanied by Constantius.[217] In a sense, it would be strange if all the *quattuor principes mundi* were not present for the consecration of their achievements. Attention was focused upon Diocletian, but their fealty was indispensable to the new world order.

It was during this year that Diocletian arranged the settlement of the Carpi. He spent the summer of 304 in a tour of the provinces of the Danube.[218] In the main, the Carpi were not settled on the border that they had plagued but rather in Pannonia Valeria, where their descendants dwelt around Sopianae.[219] Some fewer may also have been settled in Moesia Secunda. Ammianus speaks of a *vicus Carporum* in the vicinity of Marcianopolis, although this village may be a vestige of a similar trans-Danubian settlement of the Carpi by Aurelian.[220] It is to this diplomatic triumph that, in all likelihood, Diocletian's fifth and final salutation as *Carpicus Maximus* belongs.[221]

Diocletian's personal involvement in the settlement of the Carpi is not surprising. Upon Galerius' destruction of the Persians, Diocletian arrived at Nisibis to take charge of negotiations with Appharban. His policy in this case reflects the same concern with dictating the terms of victory himself. Nothing illustrates the impotence of a Caesar more profoundly. Galerius had won both wars by dint of hard fighting and skilful generalship, but his rank compelled him to surrender the fruits of this work to his superior. In any case, Galerius was required in another quarter. The Sarmatians yet again demanded attention. Concentration upon Carpic affairs had led to the neglect of this vexatious nation. Galerius had defeated them in 302 in the course of his Carpic wars, but not decisively. In 304 he was again compelled to take the field against them.[222] These were his last few months as Caesar. Diocletian's abdication impended, with the political advantage which would accrue to him. It fell to him at the end of 304 and the beginning of the following year to protect that prospect from an unexpected danger.

That peril came from Diocletian himself. He had fallen gravely ill during the latter stages of his Danubian journey.[223] On 20 November 304, the twentieth anniversary of his accession, he had to be carried to the dedication of the circus at Nicomedia.[224] On 13 December he lapsed into a coma, and it was feared that his death was imminent.[225] Galerius did not hasten to the old man's bedside. Other tasks took his attention. Diocletian was the physical bond which bound the quadripartite power structure into charismatic unity. His premature death might well have the effect of splitting the empire. Diocletian had already extracted an oath from Maximian that he would abdicate with Diocletian in the following year.[226] His demise would negate an oath which Maximian had been loath to swear. Galerius journeyed to Maximian and confronted him. He possessed the prestige of the Persian and Carpic victories and the authority of one with Diocletian's ear. He made it clear to Maximian that, if an abdication was not forthcoming in due time, he invited civil war.[227]

With frontiers and colleague secured, Galerius could at last travel to Diocletian's sickbed.[228] Lactantius has taken Galerius' presence in Nicomedia as a cynical and successful attempt to exploit the weakened Diocletian.[229] There was more to it than that. When Galerius set out, there was no expectation of Diocletian's recovery. Anything could happen in the imperial household upon his death. Lactantius, well informed on contemporary gossip, refers to fears in Nicomedia of military insurrection in the case of that event.[230] Diocletian had himself exploited a similar situation in order to seize the purple. Thus Galerius wished to forestall another claimant, take whatever advantages accrued to him from being Diocletian's son, son-in-law and his faithful servant, and be at the centre of power when the crisis came. The anxiety for Diocletian's health was premature. He recovered to outlive all of his colleagues.[231] Doubtless Galerius' demonstrated *pietas* reaped him further political advantage, but he had to wait yet a few months longer to achieve the station to which he aspired.

Notes

1 For example: Mócsy (1974), p. 268f.; Seston (1946), Chapter VI; Mattingly, *CAH* XII, p. 334f.; Ensslin, *RE* XIV 2518–21; Altenorf, *RAC* 8, 786–7; Jones (1964), Vol. I, p. 39.

2 Barnes (1976), pp. 174–93, revised in (1982); *NE*, p. 27; Arnaldi (1972).

3 As argued by Brennan (1984).

4 See Barnes (1976), p. 182.

5 *P. Bod. inv. no. Ms gr class C.* 126 (P); see Rea *et al.* (1985).

6 Jerome, *Chron.* p. 226 (Helm), s.a. 293; see also Zonaras, 12.31; Cedrenus, p. 226D (*SHB*); Theophanes, *Chron.* s.a. 282.

7 Notably Seston (1946), pp. 141–2; also Chastagnol (1982), p. 102.

8 *P. Grenfell* II, 110. The document is dated VII Ides of January 293.

9 *P. Oxy,* 43, *recto*; see Bowman (1978), p. 27; van Berchem (1952), p. 105f.

10 *P. Oxy.* 2953.

11 Kees, *RE* III, 1074, no. 3; Ensslin (1942), p. 27.

12 Bowman (1984), pp. 33–8. The difficulty for this hypothesis, and Bowman acknowledges this, is that Galerius took two victory titles from this campaign: *Aegyptiacus Maximus* and *Thebaicus Maximus* in that order (Eusebius, *HE*. 8.17). This would suggest that there were two campaigns rather than one; the first in Lower Egypt, the second in the region of the Thebaid. Bowman suggests that the two titles might reflect the fact that the initial victory was won before Egypt was divided, but admits the possibility offered here. Rules for tetrarchic victory titulature are difficult to identify (see Barnes, 1976: p. 182). It is not really possible to lay down hard and fast rules for its usage in all cases. No explanation is immediately obvious, for example, for the dropping of victory titles after they are taken. In Diocletian's case, three victory titles were taken and subsequently abandoned: *Britannicus Maximus* (*ILS* 615) in 285; *Persicus Maximus* (*ILS* 618) in 289/90; and *Gothicus Maximus* (see Brennan 1984: 142–6). Similarly, there is no ready-made reason for Galerius' iteration of the title of *Persicus Maximus*. See Barnes (1976), p. 182.

13 *P. Erlangen* 52.

14 First published by Petrie (1896), p. 27f.

15 Bernard (1984), p. 199f., no. 67; see also Johnson (1963), times the average cost for a man.

16 Johnson (1963), p. 391f., no. 230. For the instability of bullion prices in Coptus, see *P. Geiss.* 47.

17 See Weill (1911), p. 110f.; Petrie (1896), Chapter IV. The latest piece of sculptural embellishment is a head of Caracalla.

18 *CIL* III, Supp 2. 13580.

19 See Petrie (1896), p. 33; also Reinach (1911: pp. 46–50) lists a number of Palmyrene grave stelae found at Coptus.

20 *CIL* III, 6627; Bernard (1984), p. 178 no. 56.

21 Frankfurter (1993), p. 264f.

22 *Inscr. Phil.* II. 128; see Strabo, 17: 782, 815.

23 Zos. I. 71; on Coptus' history as a focus of revolt, see Leadbetter (2000B).

24 See Sidebotham (1989).

25 B.H. Warmington (1974), Chapter I; NB also the map in the endpapers.

26 Raschke (1978), pp. 643–5; Matthews (1984), pp. 166–9; Isaac (1992), pp. 144–6.

27 *Pan. Lat.* 3 (11) 4.4; S.T. Parker (1986), p. 136; for the date, see Barnes, p. 51.

28 Eusebius, *Onomastikon* (E. Klostermann, ed.), p. 6; on the date of the *Onomastikon*, see Barnes, pp. 106–11, a dating most recently accepted by Millar (1993), p. 175f. Roll (1989) prefers a Constantinian date for the transfer of the legion, based on the absence of inscriptional evidence from the Tetrarchic period. He does not, however, challenge Barnes' earlier dating for the *Onomastikon*, now well accepted.

29 Meredith (1952); Peacock (1992); Shaw *et al.* (1999); R.B. Jackson (2002), pp. 35–73; Sidebotham *et al.* (2008), pp. 70–93, 124–34.

30 *Pan. Lat.* 4.5.2. The translation is that of Nixon (1994). Nixon's identification of "*Aethiops et Indus*" with the peoples of southern Egypt (*ibid.*, p. 116) is plausible but ignores the role of the Thebaid as an economic link with both India and the Horn of Africa.

31 The titles only appear in full in Eusebius' text of the Edict of Toleration. Barnes (1976B: pp. 277–9) argues that they can also be reconstructed from a very fragmentary inscription from Tlos which he dates to 310. Otherwise the titles seem not to appear elsewhere, which may indicate that they were not taken until Galerius became ranking Augustus in 306.

32 Barnes (1976), p. 181f.

33 See van Berchem (1952), p. 105f.; the inclusion of the I Illyricorum and the III Gallica are probably premature. Certainly there was a legionary garrison of troops from the III Gallica in Coptus early in the fourth century, but a date for its deployment prior to the revolt of Domitius Domitianus would imply the defeat of a major legionary force in the course of that revolt. Coptus was in the hands of the rebels for about seven months during the course of that rebellion and was its major centre in the south, as the Paniskos archive makes plain (see J.D. Thomas 1976: p. 266f.). Rather, it is more likely that the legionary garrison came to the area as a consequence of the second revolt, the auxiliary garrison having proven inadequate.

34 P. Mich. 214ff. It is worth noting that the letter is from Paniskos, at that time a rebel in the army of the corrector Achilleus. As such, the use of the name "Coptus" may be a deliberate archaism. Athanasius lists the city as a bishopric in the middle of the fourth century (see Lallemand 1964: p. 104f.) and Phoibammon, the Bishop of Coptus city, was a signatory to the acta of the Council of Ephedus in 431 (Amélineau 1893: p. 214).

35 *P. Beatty Pan.* II, 162; Skeat (1964: p. 145) also notes the existence of a *kastra Koptou* (*Stud. Pal.* xx. 84 *verso* 1.5). Skeat's conjecture as to the origin of the name does not take into account the adjacent and newly founded Maximianopolis.

36 See Bowman (1978), p. 27; *P. Oxy.* 2673.9.

37 As described by Maspero (1885), p. 68. One particularly old and crumbling section of the wall collapsed while Petrie's party was encamped nearby (Petrie 1896: p. 1).

38 A. Johnson (1983), p. 92f.; Lander (1984), pp. 255–7.

39 See Meredith (1953), p. 132.

40 Two cavalry units are recorded as stationed there in the *Notitia Dignitatum* (Or. 31.29, 48), see Kees, *RE* XIV, 2484f.

41 Sidebotham *et al.* (1991).

42 *Ibid.*

43 *Ibid.*, p. 144. The authors note that, so far, this coin is unique, the only evidence that the Alexandrian mint struck for Galerius.

44 Sidebotham (1991); Sidebotham *et al.* (1991), p. 158.
45 *P. Beatty Pan.* 1. 30ff.
46 See Skeat (1964) p. xviiif.; *PLRE* I, p. 427, no. 1.
47 See J.D. Thomas (1976), p. 269.
48 As argued by J.D. Thomas (*ibid.*); *contra* Schwartz (1975).
49 Kalavrezou-Maxeiner (1975); Golvin and Reddé (1986), pp. 171–7; Bagnall (1993), p. 263; for the date, see Lacau (1934), p. 32f.
50 Leukos Limen (modern Quseir al-Qadim) was abandoned by the early third century and was not reinhabited until the Islamic period. See Meyer (1991), pp. 6–7. This earlier date has, however, been questioned by Zitterkopf and Sidebotham (1989: pp. 187–8), who consider a later date for the abandonment of Leucos Limen more probable.
51 Sidebotham and Wendrich (1996), pp. 153, 443.
52 Begley (1993).
53 *ND* Or. 31.38.
54 E.H. Warmington (1974), p. 139 n. 30.
55 *Pet Patr.*, fr. 14; see also the discussion *infra*.
56 Isaac (1998: pp. 71–4) has suggested that a newly discovered road through the Wadi Aravah was constructed in connection with this transfer; on the agreement with the Saracens, see Leadbetter (2002).
57 *Mos. et Rom. legum collatio* 6.4 = *CJ* 5.4.17.
58 For the date, see Barnes (1976), p. 182.
59 Kennedy and MacAdam (1985), pp. 100–104; Speidel (1987); MacAdam (1989); Lewin (1990), p. 152f. A subsequent reinterpretation of this text which seeks to redate time of Aurelian is plausible, but unconvincing (Christol and Lenoir 2001); see Lewin (2002) for a thorough contextualization of this text.
60 *P. Oxy.* 43. *recto*; see Ensslin (1952); Bowman (1978), p. 27f.; Rea *et al.* (1985) p. 108.
61 Speidel (1987), p. 213.
62 For an overview of this situation and survey of the scholarship, see S.T. Parker (2002).
63 *SEG* VII (1927) 1055; Millar (1993), pp. 184, 543f.
64 *It. Burd.* 586.3; Avi-Yonah (1976), p. 170; Isaac (1992), p. 432f.; Tepper (2002).
65 See Barnes, *NE*, p. 50f., n. 25.
66 *Ibid.*, p. 51; Malalas records that Diocletian built a palace at Antioch (*Chron.* 305).
67 Barnes, *NE*, p. 51; *Pan. Lat.* 1.9.1.
68 Barnes (1976: pp. 186–7; 1982: *NE*, p. 63) suggests on the evidence of the victory titulature that, in 295, Galerius was already campaigning in Persia. The *Persicus* title in question, however, was assumed by Diocletian after his diplomatic victory of 287. The title appears in 290 (*ILS* 618), thus predating (and obviating) an extra and otherwise unattested campaign in 295.
69 The previous great fortification of this frontier was under Septimius Severus and, although attempts were made in the intervening years to strengthen the frontier, it was left to Diocletian to actually achieve this (see Bowersock 1983: Chapter VIII, p. 131ff.). On the Roman garrison in the region, see D. Kennedy (2004), pp. 47–9.
70 *CIL* III, 6267 (between Palmyra and Edessa); 14152. 48a (between Amman and Petra); 14382 (near Gerasa); *AE* 34.262 (between Palmyra and Emesa); 77.833 (near Bostra). For other milestones of 287–293 in the region of Bostra, see Littmann *et al.* pp. xx–xii, xxiv, xxvi–vii (1921–2); for milestones of 293–305 near Umm al-Quttein in Northern Jordan, see Kennedy and Abdul Gader (1996).
71 For example: *CIL* III, 6661; *AE* 30.105; 31.86; 57.272, Kennedy and Falahat (2008).
72 See Speidel (1978B). The suggestion that the legion's name reflects some relationship between Galerius and Mars and thus belongs to this period is enticing, but must be rejected. The question of Galerius' divine *comes* is a difficult one, complicated, rather than clarified by work in the field (e.g. see Nicholson (1984). On Lejjun, see S.T. Parker (1986), p. 136f.).

73 S.T. Parker (1986A); on the Aravah, see Isaac (1998), pp. 74–7, and for an overview Lewin (2002).
74 *CIL* III. 197.
75 *CIL* III. 14149, 34, 36, 54b(?).
76 *AE* 7.145; 33.144, 145; 36. 145.
77 *AE* 31.101–10.
78 *AE* 34.262.
79 *CIL* III. 6661.
80 See Bowersock (1983), Chapter X. It is possible that at this time 'Amr died. He was apparently long-lived and appears on the Paikuli inscription of Narseh in 293. He must have died not long after and was succeeded by Imru'l-qais.
81 This is an inference from the fact that in 303, Hierocles was *ex vicario* and *praeses* of Bithynia (Lact. *de mort. pers.* 16.4). The dedication in all probability predates 300. Further, it is reasonable to assume that work ceased on the *limes* during the Persian War when troops were more urgently required to meet the threat of Persia and, later, the revolt in Egypt. Therefore, the dedication at the fortress of Palmyra should be dated to the period 293–96.
82 See *PLRE* I, p. 432, no.4; Barnes (1976A).
83 Lactantius gives Candidianus' age in 305 as nine (*de mort. pers.* 20.4). He must therefore have been conceived in 295 or early in 296.
84 Malalas, *Chron.* 306.
85 *Mos. et Rom. legum collatio.* 64; *CJ.*5.4.17. Barnes' (*NE*, p. 62, n. 76) argument that the edict was issued by Galerius on the instructions of Diocletian, simply because of a visit by the senior emperor to Damascus, seems difficult to fit in at this time and is not compelling. Diocletian was in Nicomedia on 18 March of that year. Damascus is less than six weeks from Nicomedia by road, and Diocletian's whereabouts in the intervening period are unknown. It is therefore quite possible for Diocletian to have been in Damascus by early May. For further discussion which does not rule out Barnes' argument, see Corcoran (1996), p. 270. It is worth noting that, if the edict were issued by Galerius, it is the only case of a Caesar issuing an edict on his own, Barnes' response that he was doing so at Diocletian's direction is simply unconvincing.
86 *Pan. Lat.* 2: 9.1 speaks of a conference with Maximian at an unknown location, pehaps in Rhaetia. *Pan. Lat* 3: 8.1 speaks in grander terms of the better-known conference between the two in Mediolanum.
87 For useful summaries of Sassanid relations with Rome from 228 until 282, see Dignas and Winter (2007), pp. 18–32; Frye (1983), pp. 124–8; for an earlier and fuller account, Christensen (1944), pp. 206–27.
88 See MacDermot (1954), pp. 76–80.
89 His success was proclaimed in an inscription upon the so-called Ka'aba of Zoroaster at Persepolis (*KKZ*), the Greek text of which is published with a French translation by Mariq (1958). An English translation of the Parthian and Middle Persian text can be found in Sprengling (1953), and Frye (1983), Appendix 4. The Greek text is that which is referred to here.
90 *KKZ* 5–9.
91 For an excellent discussion of a confusing tradition, see Chaumont (1969), Chapter II. Much of the tradition is made difficult by the hagiography surrounding the escaped prince Tiridates, who became the first Christian king of Armenia. One clear example of this is Agathangelus' statement that Tiridates was sheltered in the empire by a nobleman named Licinius, the later emperor. Presumably he has confused this Licinius with Gallienus, whose full name was P. Licinius Egnatius Gallienus.
92 Lightfoot (1981), p. 4; also Frye (1983), p. 305.
93 Lightfoot (1981), p. 4.

94 *Pan. Lat.* 3.17.2; cf. Ensslin (1942), p. 9. The secession of Adiabene is attested by the dubious Chronicle of Arbela (see Frye 1983: p. 305 n. 56).

95 *Pan. Lat.* 2.7.5.

96 *Ibid.*, 10.6.

97 Ensslin (1942: p. 12ff.) denies the conclusion of any such treaty. The evidence in favour is simply too strong to ignore (for discussion, see Nixon and Rodgers 1994: p. 69). Moses of Chorene, for example, states that Tiridates was restored to his throne in the third year of Diocletian (II, 82), and other sources give a similar date (see Chaumont 1969: p. 95). Tiridates must have been restored by 293 when he appears on the Paikuli inscription of Narseh (cited as Paikuli §92).

98 Nisibis was not recaptured until 297/8 (*Chronicle of Joshua the Stylite*, trans. W. Wright, p. 6).

99 Malalas, *Chron.* 8. 306.

100 See Barnes, *NE*, p. 51.

101 The account is to be found on the inscription of Narseh at Paikuli. The inscription is fragmentary, but enough can be made of it to determine the course of events. See Humbach and Skjaervø (1983).

102 Paikuli § 91.

103 For the date, see most recently Lightfoot (1981), p. 4; also Barnes (1976) p. 186ff., *NE* p. 63 n. 77.

104 Festus, *Brev.* 2.5; NB the comments of Eadie (1967), p. 147. See also Orosius, 7. 25.9; cf. Aur. Vict. *de Caes.*, 39.34.

105 *P. Argent.* 480; see Barnes (1976), p. 182; *NE*, p. 54. Barnes has argued most plausibly, against a previous consensus, that both emperors were responsible for the conduct of the first campaign.

106 Eutr. 9. 24.

107 For example: Ensslin, *RE* XIV 2521; Mattingly, *CAH* XII p. 336 reads far too much into the sources; Jones (1964), Vol. I, p. 39 (a peculiar statement).

108 Eutr. 9. 24.

109 Aur. Vict. *de Caes.* 39.

110 Orosius (7.25.9) and Eutropius (9.24.1) give the region as between Carrhae and Callinicum.

111 Amm. Marc. 23.5.2.

112 Orosius 7.25.9.

113 When Galerius attacked the Persian army, it was on the frontiers of Armenia from which Narseh had expelled the Arsacid dynasty (P'awstos Buzand 3.21; *FHG* V2, p. 232). Although P'awstos has here confused the chronology greatly (cf. Moses of Chorene III. 17) he is clearly referring to Galerius' Persian War (see Chaumont 1969).

114 Barnes (*NE*, p. 63) allows a year, but this is over-generous.

115 Aur. Vict. *de Caes.* 39.34; Jordanes *Getica* 21.

116 Diocletian seems to have suspected it when he issued the order to persecute the Manichaean sect which originated in Persia. See Seston (1946), pp. 146–59; a view justly criticized by Brown (1969), p. 92f.

117 The complexities of this revolt need not detain us here. They have been thoroughly and controversially discussed by Schwartz (1975). For the date of the revolt, see J.D. Thomas (1976).

118 The figure is given by Festus (*Brev.* 25). See Chaumont (1969), p. 117. The location is given by the Armenian historian P'awstos (3.21). See here Garsoian (1989), p. 265f.

119 P'awstos 3.21.

120 The IV Parthica was probably raised for this campaign. The XV Apollinaris at Satala would also have been brought into action, and possibly also the I and II Parthica from Osroene. The I and II Parthica became the garrison units in Mesopotamia (*Not. Dig.* Or.

36.29f.) as they had been in the time of Severus. The IV Parthica became the garrison unit of Osroene and was raised at this time (see *RE* XII. 1556; *Not. Dig.* or. 35.24).

121 See H.M.D. Parker (1933), p. 181.

122 As most sources note, e.g.: Aur. Vict. *de Caes.* 39.35; Eutropius 9.25.1; Malalas 12. 308; P'awstos 3.21.

123 Eutropius 9.25.1; Paikuli §14; 32.

124 See Frye (1984), p. 306; also Christensen, *CAH* XII, p. 114f.; the title goes back to Parthian times and indeed the word *hargbad* is Parthian in origin and not Middle Persian. The position was of such a senior rank that Humbach and Skjaervø (1983: 3.2, pp. 39–44), the latest editors of the Paikuli text, consider it possible that this Shapur may have been Narseh's elder brother.

125 An Ohrmazd also appears on the same inscription (Paikuli §14.32), but not as a member of Narseh's family. He is Ohrmazd Waraz, i.e. not a Sassanid. No Sassanid Ohrmazd appears on the KKZ inscription of Shapur I. Therefore, this Ohrmazd must have been born after 260. Narseh was certainly succeeded by an Ohrmazd, and it was customary for a senior member of the dynasty to hold the fief of Armenia (Humbach and Skjaervø 1983: 3.2, p. 10f.). The son and successor of Shapur, Hormizd-Ardashir, appears as Great King of Armenia in the KKZ inscription. The Paikuli inscription makes it plain that Narseh was Great King of Armenia prior to taking the diadem of the King of Kings. According to Agathangelus, the Armenian Great King held the second place in the Sassanid realm (see Frye 1950). According to Ammianus (23.5.11) Galerius was invading "enemy" territory, although it had recently not been so. The implication is that the Persians, considering all Armenia theirs, were in the process of civil consolidation.

126 Festus, *Breviarium*; Eutr. 9.28.1.

127 P'awstos 3.21.

128 Synesius tells the more plausible story of an unnamed emperor exploring the Persian camp, while disguised as an ambassador (*de regno* 17). Dodgeon and Lieu (1991) identify this emperor with Galerius. See also the discussion by Austin and Rankov (1995: p. 62f.).

129 Although not without taking omens. See Ammianus 23.5.11.

130 Ammianus 17. 5.6.; Lactantius describes it as an ambush (*de mort. pers.* 9.7).

131 Eutropius 9. 25.1; also Zonaras 12. 31.; Amm. Marc. 22.4.8; P'awstos 3.21; see Malalas XII, 307 for the name. According to the Arab historian Tha'alibi, Narseh was remarkably restrained, having only two wives and two concubines. Malalas may be mistaken as to the queen's name. The KKZ inscription gives the name of Narseh's wife in the 260s as Shapurdukhtak (*KKZ* 20f.). Of course, things may have changed in the intervening period.

132 P'awstos 3.21.

133 The conclusions of Kinch's (1890) pioneering study have largely been controverted by those of von Schönebeck (1937) and Laubscher (1975), which in turn have been questioned by Pond Rothman (1977).

134 Using the relief numbers given by Pond Rothman (1977: pp. 427–54), relief (1) depicts the Roman army setting forth from Satala to commence the campaign; relief (5) shows a complete battle scene in which the emperor, his *paludamentum* flying behind him, scatters the enemy with the impetus of his charge; relief (9) shows Galerius, seated, receiving the Persian surrender; relief (2) the receipt into captivity of the Great King's household.

135 Relief (3) on the Arch of Galerius shows the Emperor pursuing the Persians across a river clearly labelled "*POTAMOS TIGRIS*".

136 For example, *ILS* 642.

137 Galerius and Constantius were both *Persici maximi II*. This indicates that both salutations were won after 293. Disregarding the possibility of a campaign in 295, it is clear

that the two acclamations of *Persicus Maximus* resulted from this war, perhaps the first for the specific victory over the Persian army itself and the second for the diplomatic settlement. The only remaining question is why Diocletian and Maximian were not *Persici Maximi III*. Diocletian may have dropped the title in 296 because of the breakdown of the diplomatic settlement which it celebrated.

138 See Arnaldi (1972).

139 Panel (II) on the Arch shows the submission of various Persian cities. Their identities must remain conjectural since the inscriptions are lost (see Pond Rothman 1977: p. 437).

140 The *SHA, Vita Cari*, 9.3 states that Galerius advanced as far as Ctesiphon. This makes sense since Galerius passed through Anatha on his return (Ammianus 24.1.10). In addition, Constantine had seen the ruins of Babylon (*Oratio ad sanctos* 16). He had been attached to the court of Diocletian for some years and had served with some distinction in Asia (*Origo* 2.2). It is reasonable to conclude on this basis that Constantine saw the ruins of Babylon in the course of Galerius' expedition (see Barnes, 1976: p. 184f.). Lightfoot (1981: p. 4) argues that Galerius turned south from Armenia and took Nisibis, rather than campaigning down the Tigris. This anecdote from Ammianus and the victory titulature provide clear evidence to the contrary.

141 Joshua the Stylite, *Chron.*, p. 6 (W. Wright, trans.).

142 Joshua the Stylite (*Ibid.*) gives the date of the capture of Nisibis as before September 298. Given Galerius' campaigns along the Tigris, it would most likely be later rather than earlier in that year. In the following year, Diocletian conferred with him at Nisibis (Pet. Patr. fr. 14). Von Schönebeck (1937: p. 362) considers the *adventus* scene on the Arch (Relief 7) to be that of Diocletian at Nisibis, but Pond Rothman (1977: p. 437) suggests more reasonably that it is Galerius.

143 Pet. Patr. fr. 14 (= *FHG* IV, p. 188f.). The scene is depicted on the Arch of Galerius (Relief 16).

144 Winter (1989) has argued that the peace treaty of 298 represents a political victory for Diocletian over his more ebullient and expansionist Caesar. There is no serious evidence to indicate that the peace treaty was an affront to Galerius.

145 On the movements of Diocletian, see Barnes, *NE*, p. 55.

146 Pet. Patr. fr. 14. Galerius' winter activities included the foundation of yet another Maximianopolis, this time in Mesopotamia. It later (and rather ungratefully) changed its name to Constantia (Malalas 12.47; 13.12). The existence of two towns in Mesopotamia named Constantia is attested by the *Notitia Dignitatum* (Or. 36: 22, 24, 29). The other was a Severan foundation renovated by Constantius II (Amm. Marc. 27.7.9; 9.1).

147 Pet. Patr. fr. 14. Peter reports that when Narseh sought to question the terms regarding Nisibis, Sicorius Probus, the Roman envoy, replied that he had no authority to negotiate. The "take it or leave it" implication is unmistakable, and Narseh took the hint.

148 See here Winter's (1989) discussion.

149 Malalas, 12. 308.

150 *Cons. Const.* s.a. 299 (*Chron. Min.* I, p. 230).

151 The year of these celebrations seems fixed at 300. This makes sense of the chronology herein established and is made more attractive by the likelihood that Diocletian presided at the Antiochene "Olympic Games" held in 300, perhaps with Galerius as his coadjutor (Malalas, 12. 307). What better way to conclude the celebrations than having the victorious Augustus and Caesar preside at the Games? (Libanius *Or.* II. 269; see Downey (1961) for the identification of the Emperor as Diocletian; cf. Nicholson, 1984B: p. 136 n. 12.).

152 The humiliation tradition appears to derive from the *KG* (Eutr. 9. 24; Festus *Brev.* 25; Jer. *Chron.* p. 227: Helm). Ammianus accepted it (14. 11.10); see Eadie (1967), p. 147f. Seston (1940) has argued that this kind of distinction was a feature of the tetrarchy. His

arguments have been examined by G.S.R. Thomas (1969). The latter's conclusions have in turn been called into question by Schwartz (1974) who has strongly restated Seston's original position. A significant argument against the humiliation tradition is the silence of the polemical Lactantius on the question.

153 The identification of these figures is aided by inscriptions now totally abraded but noted by Kinch (1890: p. 36f.). Kinch incorrectly identified the figure behind Diocletian as Jupiter. The zodiac vault within which it is depicted clearly marks it as Aion (Laubscher, 1975: p. 55).

154 Arnaldi (1972); Barnes (1976), pp. 174–93, revised in *NE*, p. 27.

155 See Barnes (1976), p. 182.

156 As argued by Brennan (1984).

157 Barnes (1976), as revised in the tables in *NE*, pp. 254–8.

158 Although Probus had boasted but a short time before of the security of the empire (Aur. Vict. *de Caes*. 37.3), it had been necessary for a vigorous defence of all of the frontiers in the time of Carus. Aurelius Victor (*de Caes*. 38.2; also *ILS* 608) gives the victory titles of Carinus and Numerian as *Germanici Maximi, Brittannici Maximi, Persici Maximi*. For Carus' titles, see *PIR2* A 1475. On the circumstances of Diocletian's accession, see Leadbetter (1994).

159 Diocletian has one more of each salutation than Maximian in his titulature on the Edict on Maximum Prices. On this basis, Barnes (*NE*, pp. 50, 255) dates these campaigns to 285. Unless otherwise stated, Barnes' chronology is followed in this chapter.

160 This is largely inferred from the following considerations: the title cannot be as a result of Maximian's activities in Gaul since otherwise it would appear in his titulature also, since he went there as Caesar to campaign against the Bacaudae; it must therefore pre-date Maximian's campaigns on the Rhine for which further titles were subsequently taken; there is no evidence of Diocletian himself having gone to Gaul at this time, and the evidence which we do possess places him in the Danubian region or Rome (Barnes *NE*, p. 50; see Chapter 2, p. 51 on Diocletian's visit to Rome in 285). The Marcomanni and Quadi are both Germanic people, for campaigns against which Marcus Aurelius had taken the title *Germanicus* (see Birley 1987: p. 174) and there is evidence of Marco-mannic warfare in the following decade (Jerome, *Chron*. p. 226: Helm); *Pan. Lat*. 2.9.1; 3.7.1, delivered in 289 and 291 respectively refer to recent victories in Rhaetia in tandem with the Sarmatian wars.

161 Barnes (*NE*, p. 50): on 2 November 285 Diocletian was in Iovia, in Pannonia Superior, perhaps overseeing the end of the campaign.

162 The titulature is based upon the Aphrodisias copy of the Edict on Maximum Prices (see Erim and Reynolds, 1971: p. 100).

163 Barnes (*NE*, p. 255 n. 1) attributes the first three *Germanicus Maximus* salutations to victories won by Maximian on the Rhine. This view does not take into account the difference of one in *Germanicus Maximus* titles held by the two. The solution offered here is that the panegyrist's Rhaetian victories were won by Diocletian in 285, soon after the Battle of the Margus.

164 *Pan. Lat*. 3.5.3–4.

165 *Ibid*., 2.10.3.

166 See Brennan (1980), p. 564 n. 39.

167 Bichir (1976), Chapter XII; Map III.

168 On the earlier threat of the Carpi to Dacia, Lact. *de mort. pers*. 9.2; Moreau (1954), p. 256 n. 6.

169 The *Consularia Constantinopolitana* records for 294 *his consulibus castra facta in Sarmatia contra Acinco et Bononia*. This has generally been taken to mean that a trans-Danubian fort was built opposite Aquincum (see e.g. Langyel and Radan (1980: p. 37), where the claim is made that the Diocletianic fort has been discovered under modern Budapest).

Mócsy (1974: p. 269; 1974A) doubts any claims that these fortifications have been found. The Bononia in question ought to be identified quite clearly with the port of Sirmium, rather than the Bononia further down the Danube (Mirkovic, 1971), but not on the *Ripa Sarmatica*, which means that the "Acincum" in question might be identified as Acumincum, close by the Sirmium, rather than Aquincum (but see Brennan 1980: p. 558f.).

170 See Barnes *NE*, p. 53f. According to the evidence collected by Mommsen and re-examined by Barnes, Diocletian was in Sirmium for nearly a year, until the latter part of August 294, whence he journeyed to Nicomedia along the Danube. He is found in Nicomedia in the middle of November, some three months after he set out.

171 Barnes *NE*, p. 53f. Diocletian was at Transmarisca on 18 October, and at Durostorum on 21–22 October. Diocletian would have been in the vicinity of Kladovo between 5 and 8 October, perhaps resting there on the evening of the 6th.

172 The Durostorum and Transmarisca inscriptions are so similar as to be virtually identical, the only difference in their wording being that the Durostorum inscription has *Gothici Max* where the Transmarisca text records *Persici Max II* (on the Durostorum inscription, see Brennan, 1981: p. 144). Both of these inscriptions record *Sarmatici Maximi IIII* and *Germanici Maximi V*, which dates them to the end of 299 or the beginning of 300, after Galerius' campaign against the Sarmatians of 299, and before his campaign against the Marcomanni later in that year (see below). The Kladovo inscription cannot be securely dated, because it records only victory titles taken against the Germans and Sarmatians, and those without numeration.

173 Brennan (1984) suggests that the apparent abandonment of *Gothicus Maximus* as a victory title was the consequence of a diplomatic agreement with the Goths. The same policy may have applied here in Carpic territory.

174 See Gudea (1974).

175 Mócsy (1974), p. 268f.; *CIL* III, 6151 (= *ILS* 641); *AE* 1936.10; *AE* 1979.519; see also Gudea (1974).

176 Jer., *Chron.* p. 226 (Helm).

177 *Mos. et Rom. legum collatio* 6.4 = *C.J.* 5.4.17. On Barnes' (*NE*, p. 62) view that the emperor who issued the edict in question might have been Galerius, acting in Diocletian's name, see my arguments earlier in this chapter.

178 *P. Argent* 480; see Barnes (1976), p. 182.

179 Barnes (1976), p. 187; *NE*, p. 54.

180 *Pan. Lat.* 3.5.3.

181 Kolendo (1969).

182 *AE* 1973.526a (Edict on Maximum Prices), cf. *AE* 1961.240 (Military diploma, dated to early 306); Barnes, *NE*, pp. 18ff., 257.

183 Lact. *de mort. pers.* 38.6.

184 Brennan (1984), p. 565.

185 *Pan. Lat.* 4.5.1.

186 Eumenius, the author of the Panegyric of 298, summarizes the victories of the emperors in his peroration (*Pan. Lat.* 5.21) and mentions Maximian's victories in Africa, those of Constantius in Batavia and Britain, Diocletian's business in Egypt, and Galerius' victories against Persia. *Nunc enim* says Eumenius, *nunc demum iuvat orbem spectare depictum, cum in illo nihil videmus alienum*, except, it seems from an equally eloquent silence, on the Danube.

187 *RIC* VI Index II, p. 705.

188 Brennan (1984), p. 510f.

189 *RIC* VI, p. 55.

190 *Ibid.*, p. 501f. See also Barnes (1976), p. 187, and *NE*, p. 257, although curiously this campaign was omitted from Barnes' account of Galerius' movements at this time (*ibid.*, p. 63).

191 The "thrice" is inferred from Diocletian's three Sarmatian titles. On activities across the Danube, see Brennan (1980).
192 Aur. Vict. *de Caes*. 39.34.
193 Jordanes, *Getica* 110; see also Brennan (1984).
194 Eutr. 9. 25; Aur. Vict. *de Caes*. 39.34; Festus *Brev*. 25.
195 Jordanes, *Getica* 110; see also Brennan (1984).
196 Aur. Vict. *de Caes*. 39.34 speaks of an army composed *e veteranis ac tironibus*.
197 Barnes, *NE*, p. 54.
198 Lact. *de mort. pers*. 18.6.
199 *Ibid*. The text of *de mort. pers*. has been called into question at this point by Seeck (1897: Vol. I, p. 438), who has sought to emend the manuscript reading XVm to XII. Both Moreau and Creed reject the emendation (Moreau 1954: p. 98; Creed 1984: p. 28). There is no reason for it other than convenience, and therefore Moreau and Creed ought to be followed. One could as easily (and more plausibly) emend to V, since that would follow the historical scenario, but the reading is not in real doubt.
200 For the dates, Barnes, *NE*, p. 257.
201 Lact. *de mort. pers*. 13.2.
202 At Romuliana, which Galerius was rebuilding in style at this time (see "Galerius Augustus", (pp. 236–241)).
203 *Fast. Hydat*. s.a. 299 (*Chron. Min*. III. p. 230).
204 Barnes, *NE*, p. 255.
205 Barnes, *NE*, p. 60f.; 1976: p. 179) gives Constantius all three German victories. These are well attested from the panegyric of 310 (*Pan. Lat*. 6. 6, 2–4). Barnes (*NE*, p. 255 n. 3) adds here that a fourth victory referred to by the panegyrist resulted in a *Germanicus Maximus* victory title taken between 297 and 301. However, he seems since to have withdrawn (and probably rightly so) from that position.
206 As is clear from the titles recorded in the Edict on Maximum Prices. See Barnes (1976), p. 175f. for the date.
207 See Sutherland, *RIC* VI, p. 501.
208 *Ibid*., p. 491f.
209 Galerius wintered in 302/3 in Nicomedia rather than in Thessalonica (Lact. *de mort. pers*. 10.6; Barnes: *NE*, p. 64). It was there that he took part in discussions with Diocletian on the policy of persecution of the Christians. Although this was a serious enough affair, the two will also have had discussions about the Danube frontier, as subsequent events bear out, since the policy of resettlement of the Carpi seems to have been put into effect in the following year.
210 Lact. *de mort. pers*. 38.6.
211 Barnes, *NE*, p. 257.
212 Lact. *de mort. pers*. 38.6.
213 Amm. Marc. 28.1.5.
214 Lact. *de mort. pers*. 14.7.
215 Barnes, *NE*, p. 56; *CJ* 5.73.4.
216 Barnes, *NE*, p. 56 ; Lact. *de mort. pers*. 17.1–3.
217 This is certainly implied in *Pan. Lat*. 7.15.4–6 and Eutropius 9, 27.2, and made certain by the attestation of a joint triumph by Jerome (Helm, p. 227f.). Barnes (*NE*, p. 59) concurs; see also Nixon (1981). On Constantius, Barnes (*NE*, p. 61) dates his victory over Germanic tribes near Vindonissa (*Pan. Lat*. 7.6.3) to this year. His movements are sufficiently unclear after this to permit a visit to Rome. Jerome's attestation of a double triumph celebrated by Diocletian and Maximian, rather than a quadruple one of all of the tetrarchs, need not mean that the Caesars were not in Rome. Their subordinate status may well have prevented their enjoyment of this supreme accolade of victory.
218 Lact. *de mort. pers*. 17.3–4; Barnes, *NE*, p. 56.

219 Amm. Marc. 28.1.5.
220 *Ibid.*, 27.5.5. On the possibility of Aurelianic settlement, Bichir (1976: p. 17) argues that there was no settlement of Carpi on Roman soil by Diocletian or any of his colleagues. This view is surely untenable, given the weight of testimony in our sources, including that of Lactantius, a contemporary observer.
221 Suggested by Barnes, *NE*, p. 56 n. 43.
222 *Ibid.*, p. 257, although this date is conjectural since it lacks explicit testimony in the written evidence. At least it has the merit of fitting the chronological pattern.
223 Lact. *de mort. pers.* 17.3–5.
224 *Ibid.*, 17.4.
225 *Ibid..*, 17.9.
226 *Pan. Lat.* 7.15.6.
227 Lact. *de mort. pers.* 18.1. It is interesting to note that Maximian then sent to Diocletian an account of his own version of the conversation, presumably to blacken Galerius' character and thus persuade the old man to withdraw from his determination that both Augusti should retire (Lact. *de mort. pers.* 18.7).
228 Galerius arrived at Nicomedia early in March 305 (Lact. *de mort. pers.* 18.1), in fact after the crisis of Diocletian's illness was largely over and the Augustus was on the mend. Only unavoidable military matters can have kept Galerius from Diocletian's extremely politically sensitive bedside.
229 Lact. *de mort. pers.* 18.1–2.
230 *Ibid.*, 17.7.
231 On the date of Diocletian's death, see Moreau (1954), p. 420ff.; Barnes (1973), p. 37ff. Both traditions identified by Moreau place Diocletian's death well after the death of all of his erstwhile colleagues.

4

GALERIUS AND DIOCLETIAN

In the course of the last two chapters, it has been argued that the Diocletian created, or at least sought to invent, a dynasty that was intended both as a bulwark of stability and a means of governance. To the senior emperor, his colleagues were his kin. When they exercised power, they did not do so on their own account but through their dynastic propinquity to Diocletian: purple was always granted by Diocletian; he was senior, Jovian. The other three were junior, Herculian. This was seen most particularly in the case of Galerius, whose movements were traced from campaign to campaign. He waged wars for Diocletian in Egypt, Palestine, Syria, Armenia, Persia, Moesia and Pannonia. But it would be naïve to expect that, in the midst of the constant travel and seemingly endless campaigning (over twenty victory titles were taken between 293 and 305), he and his colleagues were not also politicians.[1] But to these hard military statesmen, who had seen the emperors of their youth come and go, victory and mutual loyalty were the guarantors of their survival. Moreover, their loyalty was not merely to a man, but also to his cause. Diocletian was an enormously hard-working emperor. Amid his own journeying and campaigning between 293 and 299, he also found time to respond to petitioners, reform and regulate the tax base for the entire empire, and restructure the administration of the provinces.[2] All of these achievements were immense, and involved the collection, processing and interpretation of detailed demographic, economic and geographic information from across the empire. To oversee all of this, the imperial civil service had to be restructured and augmented.[3] This was accomplished on the back of an overhaul of the legal system in which Diocletian endeavoured to rationalize the conduct of legal business. In order to achieve this, a team of jurists began, in the course of the 290s, to collect imperial rescripts in two significant legal codices, the Codex Gregorianus, which seems to belong to 292, and the Codex Hermogenianus, the first edition of which appears to have been in 295, but thereafter undergoing a number of augmentations.[4] It is easy to overlook the magnitude of the reforms and the volume of work which they imply. Like the reconstruction and reinforcement of the frontiers, they were not swiftly accomplished and required a network of collaboration

114

which stretched from Hadrian's Wall to the Red Sea. It is in this that the cause of the new imperial family is most clearly seen, and where they were most obviously at one.

Not everyone, however, was so enamoured of Diocletian's cause and the new empire which he was constructing. The Christian writer Lactantius penned a savage critique:

> Diocletian was an author of crimes and deviser of evils; he ruined everything and could not even keep his hands from God. In his greed (*avaritia*) and anxiety (*timiditas*), he turned the world upside down. He appointed three men to share his rule, dividing the world into four parts and multiplying the armies, since each of the four strove to have a far larger number of troops than previous emperors had when they were governing the state alone. The number of recipients began to exceed the number of contributors by so much that, with farmers' resources exhausted by the enormous size of the requisitions, fields became deserted and cultivated land was turned into forest. To ensure that terror was universal, provinces too were cut into fragments; many governors and even more officials were imposed on individual regions, almost on individual cities, and to these were added numerous accountants (*rationales*), controllers (*magistri*) and prefects' deputies (*vicarii*). The activities of all these people were very rarely civil; they engaged only in repeated condemnations and confiscations, and in exacting endless resources
>
> (de mortibus persecutorum, 7. 1–4; J.L. Creed, trans.)

Lactantius continues in a similar vein, criticizing Diocletian's economic policies, his building policy (or *cupiditas aedificandi* as he puts it) and his colleagues – Maximian for his insatiable *avaritia*, both for property and for the slaking of his baser lusts; Galerius for a foreign and savage barbarism, which made him the worst of the four. Of Constantius, he says nothing other than that he was worthy of sole rule.[5] Lactantius' critique is profoundly personal; it is a venting of rhetorical spleen which gets more strident as it proceeds. This umbrage is not sectarian; it is political. Lactantius, it has long been recognized, was the promoter of a Christianized idea of Rome.[6] His Rome is as traditional and aristocratic as his Latin is Ciceronian.[7] Lactantius trained as a rhetorician, ironically with another late convert and Christian controversialist, Arnobius of Sicca.[8] Lactantius' sense of Rome has been explored recently by a number of commentators, and initially by Francesco Corsaro.[9] Corsaro's study of the *de Mortibus Persecutorum* argues that Lactantius attempted what was impossible in the late third century, of being both a lover of Rome and of the implacable Christian God.

Lactantius' pamphlet, "On The Deaths of the Persecutors" (*de mortibus persecutorum*), however, remains our only extended narrative source for much of this period, in particular the commencement of the Great Persecution and of the abdication of the Augusti.[10] Contemporary judgements of Lactantius' reliability have varied. Most recently, T.D. Barnes has been a champion of his veracity.[11] Frank Kolb, in contrast, has been less generous.[12] In any examination of Lactantius' work, it is worth asking what exactly the author expected of his readers. There is a considerable corpus of Lactantius' work, and more is listed by Jerome. He wrote poetry, theological treatises, apologetic works and epistles.[13] Jerome's catalogue does not include a work of narrative history precisely because Lactantius never wrote one. Like his African predecessors Tertullian and Cyprian, Lactantius was a warrior for his faith. Like them, his works were apologetic, pastoral or polemical.[14]

This brings us back to Lactantius' account in the *de mortibus persecutorum*. This is a tract, one man's theology of history. It is not an affidavit; it is an apologetic document. Lactantius declares this in his prologue when he writes:

> *de quorum exitu nobis testificari placuit, ut omnes qui procul remoti fuerunt vel qui postea futuri sunt, scirent quatenus virtutem ac maiestatem suam extinguendis delendisque nominis sui hostibus deum summus ostenderit.*

(I resolved to bear witness to the deaths of these men, so that all who were far distant or those who are to come after us should know how much the Greatest God has displayed his excellence and his grandeur in snuffing out and annihilating the enemies of his name.)[15]

Lactantius' declaration makes his polemical and apologetic purpose perfectly clear. His theologically determinist and retributive views determine his conclusions.[16] He may reproduce circumstantial details with candour and authenticity,[17] but it has long been recognized that his interpretations are of dubious accuracy.[18] What can be said with certainty about Lactantius' narrative is that it reflects the views of a survivor of the Great Persecution, who consciously sought to marry Christian belief with classical culture. He despises barbarians and accepts Tertullian's precept that only bad emperors persecute;[19] his image of a retributive god was one which drew upon both Christian and pagan models. None of this explains why Lactantius chose to cast Galerius as his villain, but it does enable a more sharply focused response to the question.

In chapter 33 of the *de mortibus persecutorum* Lactantius constructs a sordid and prurient narrative of the death of Galerius. The malady he describes is lingering, excruciating and malodorous. This is not a falsification. Galerius did die unpleasantly. Zosimus (probably following Eunapius) called it an infected wound as did Aurelius Victor (*vulnere pestilenti consumptus est*).[20] Disease or wound is not the issue here. What is important is that it was serious, prolonged and necessarily involved infection and putrefaction of living flesh. For Lactantius this fitted a salutary model. He had set out to prove that the enemies of God met a miserable end, and Galerius' death certainly fitted his case. He was not a witness. Galerius died at, or near, Romuliana; Lactantius was elsewhere.[21]

Despite this, Lactantius has presented an account of Galerius' final illness which has been taken so literally that some have ventured a diagnosis across seventeen centuries.[22] This is a risky business. The account of Galerius' death bears marked similarities to death-narratives of other foes of God with which Lactantius would have been familiar.[23] II Maccabees, for example, records a protracted account of the death of Antiochus Epiphanes which has important similarities to Lactantius' version of the death of Galerius.[24] Acts records the passing of Herod Agrippa I from "being eaten by worms", and a variety of Christian traditions attest the pathetic but condign suicide of Judas Iscariot.[25] Tertullian tells of Claudius Lucius Herminianus and Vigellius Saturninus who received divine punishments for mistreating Christians; Herminianus' fate bore a close similarity to that of Antiochus, Herod and Galerius.[26] Josephus also lists enemies of God struck down by unpleasant disease, notably Apion and the anti-Semitic governor of Libyan Pentapolis, one Catullus.[27] In some cases, these are clearly tales which grow in the telling. Antiochus Epiphanes is given a far wormier death in II Maccabees than in I Maccabees.[28] The author of *Acts* embroidered the account of the death of Herod Agrippa I; the narrative of the death of Judas Iscariot became more and more complex. Disease has such a place in religious polemic that one cannot take such accounts literally. They reflect more about the beliefs and purpose of the writer than the actuality of events.

The similarities between these accounts of retributive death and Lactantius' own account of the death of Galerius are striking. Motifs recur: the worms; the stench; the rotting flesh. There is a relationship here between purpose and description. Lactantius, in endeavouring to prove that God metes out vengeance upon the foes of his people, was in no actual position to know anything of the detail of Galerius' final illness. The sources do agree that it was unpleasant and Lactantius surely knew that. It was still left to him to reconstruct the details of the illness, and thus he drew upon the polemical tradition of retributive death. Lactantius sincerely believed that this was the judgement of God. Fundamental to his theology was a providentialism which saw God directly intervening in history to the benefit of his people. Implicit in this is what has been called "the logic of retribution".[29] Lactantius could draw no moral or providentialist lesson from the death of Diocletian, the only other possible culprit for the persecution. Compared with the spectacular passing of Galerius, Lactantius' narrative of his death comes as somewhat of an anti-climax.[30] Lactantius' account of the origins of the Great Persecution emerges from this analysis as theological, rather than historical, ratiocination. Faced with the difficulty of not knowing who began the Great Persecution, Lactantius could discern the hand of God in the unpleasant demise of Galerius. With a little Maccabean embroidery, common enough in the ancient historiography of retribution, and some rhetorical commonplaces, he convinced both himself and his audience that the impetus to persecute came not from Diocletian but from Galerius.[31]

This left him the problem of finding an explanation for Galerius' hostility towards the Christians. He found one shaped by the rhetorical tradition of which he was a part – the picture of a savage, egged on by his barbarian mother.[32] To him, Galerius is not merely a barbarian, but an enemy of all that is Roman (27.8). This rhetoric of the barbarism of Galerius can be found at other points in the work. Lactantius, for example, noted that Galerius intended to change the name of the empire from "Roman" to "Dacian" (27.8), and was an enemy of tradition and culture (22.4). Likewise, his economic policy reflected his lack of respect for the past, and the privileges of the city of Rome (23). Moreover, his brutishness is reflected in his pleasures. He possessed pet bears (he had names for them) to which condemned criminals were fed piecemeal while Galerius dined (21.5–6). And in appearance, Galerius was as ursine as his pets, a big bear of a man, capable of intimidating Diocletian by his size, looks and voice (9.3–4).[33] His primitivity, furthermore, is further stressed by dependence upon his mother, whose savage superstition Lactantius sees as the source of Galerius' own *animus* against the Christians (11.1–2). Galerius' mother, Romula, may well have been a devoted follower of her nature deities.[34] Galerius was certainly a dutiful son, building a fortified villa on the site of the family farm and naming it Romuliana in her honour.[35] This was the demand of *pietas*, although Lactantius prefers to see it as a primitive dependence upon the maternal.

While this trope of barbarism is not confined in Lactantius' narrative to Galerius, Galerius is certainly his principal savage.[36] In order for Lactantius to demonstrate his thesis, his narrative of the past ignores, manipulates and recontextualizes. Lactantius believed in an ordered historical process. There would only be a certain number of persecutions. "Good" emperors did not persecute. Therefore, the events in Lugdunum in the time of Marcus Aurelius are ignored; and Trajan's ambiguous attack upon Christianity, which Tertullian had shown up as a rhetorician's playground, was entirely passed over.[37] Aurelian, who did not actually persecute Christians, is included because he is said to have intended it (6.1: *illi ne perficere quidem quae cogitaverat licuit*). It is a matter of simple logic that if Lactantius' presentation of his past is determined by his thesis, so is his narrative of events in his own time. That does not mean that Lactantius' narrative has no historical utility. It does mean that its utility is limited by Lactantius' polemical purpose and must be used with proper caution, where possible being measured against other accounts, or at least historiographical traditions.[38]

Certainly that also means that Lactantius' treatment of Galerius must be regarded with care. The centrality of the Lactantian polemic to any historical narrative of the period has led to either the replication of his highly charged views or an emphatic rejection of them. The critical benefit which Lactantius has provided is his reminder that the emperors were not simply soldiers: they were also politicians. Lactantius portrays Galerius as deploying his humiliation of Persia, together with his hard and successful war with the Carpi, and his physical proximity to Diocletian, to good effect. It would be simply naïve to expect that Galerius – long a member of the inner circle of power and the father of Diocletian's grandchild – was merely the bluff and hearty soldier. He was compared in antiquity with Tiberius;[39] perhaps Agrippa would have been an equally plausible conceit. Galerius the politician is at two key historical points in Lactantius' narrative. The first is in the events concerning the origin of the Great Persecution (10.6–15.6). The second is the apparent dynamic between Diocletian and his Caesar in the matter of the abdications of the senior members of the dynasty in favour of the junior, an apparent *coup de main* for Galerius (18.1–19.6). In his accounts, Lactantius' *animus* against Galerius is as evident as his polemic is consistent: the claim that Galerius' Persian victory gave him a moral ascendancy over Diocletian that his elder could not exorcise depicts both a naturally bellicose and savage Galerius dominating a timid and timorous Diocletian.

It is an attractive notion, and might explain a great deal. Certainly, Lactantius has convinced a considerable number of subsequent commentators that his version of events is more plausible than any other.[40] But alternatives are possible: Lactantius was a partisan and a polemicist. His view was formed by his intellectual opposition to Diocletian's project, shaped by his experience of persecution, and coloured by his adherence to the cause of Constantine, at whose court he ultimately prospered. Moreover, events show that the truth was more nuanced. Diocletian had moral capital of his own to draw upon; while Galerius won wars, Diocletian invariably made peaces and took the credit. He did so both in the east and on the Danube. Nevertheless, a great deal needs to be explained. Two events in the latter years of Galerius' Caesarship are in many respects the key occurrences by which he has been judged: the Great Persecution, and the imperial abdications of 305. In both cases, the critical narrative is that of Lactantius and, in both cases, Galerius is the villain.

The Great Persecution

Matthias Gelzer wrote most perceptively of the sources of the Great Persecution:

> Denn es bedeutet für die geschichtliche Würdigung sehr viel, ob der alte Diocletian sozusagen sein politisches Lebenswerk abschliessen wollte mit der Beseitigung der christliche Kirche, oder ob der rohe Landsknecht Galerius dem Oberkaiser wider dessen besseres Wissen den Kampf aufzwang.

119

(For it means a great deal in terms of historical understanding, whether the elderly Diocletian, desired, as it were, to complete his life's work by the elimination of the Christian Church, or whether the rough warrior Galerius imposed the conflict upon his overlord against [Diocletian's] better judgement.)[41]

In identifying this dichotomy, Gelzer offered a choice – was it Diocletian, seeking to seal his transformation of the Roman world by the destruction of the Church; or was it the bullying of the rough and savage Galerius? This whole issue has generated such a deal of discussion in the past. The first summary of the controversy was provided in 1926 by Kurt Stade in his study of the matter. His own conclusions are prefigured in his choice of title: *Der Politiker Diocletian und die letzte grosse Christenverfolgung*, although, as Gelzer noted, Stade found himself in the unenviable position of controverting Lactantius, the oldest and apparently best-informed source.[42]

The debate in fact advanced little from 1937, when Gelzer published his own article, until 1989, when P.S. Davies further developed his arguments. Gelzer drew up the battle lines by showing precisely how Lactantius could be controverted and Davies has explored a wider range of evidence. Other studies on the persecution of the Christians in the Roman world by Frend, Molthagen and others say nothing new.[43] A 1977 colloquium on Lactantius, held at Chantilly (the proceedings of which are published as *Lactance et son Temps*), did little more than clarify arguments long adumbrated. Is there, then, anything new to say? Perhaps not, but it is certainly necessary to re-examine the evidence in this context, given the strong tradition of Galerius' role in its origin. Most recently, Elizabeth DiPalma Digeser has sought to refocus upon the group of philosophers around Diocletian, in particular Porphyry and Sossianus Hierocles, as agents of religious conservatism.[44] In so doing, she has sought to emancipate herself from the strong Galerius, weak Diocletian/weak Galerius, strong Diocletian polarity which has emerged in the scholarship over the years. Yet this will not entirely do. The intellectual coterie which she correctly discerns as gathering in Nicomedia in the winter of 302/3 did not make the ultimate decisions. They can be seen either as lobbying the emperor to persecute, as Digeser seems to suggest, or as presenting an intellectual *apologia* for a programme of persecution already decided upon.

Religion was not an imperial afterthought; Diocletian's imperial ideology had been suffused with religious concepts and images from the beginning. Religious terminology was first and foremost used to denote rank – the *Iovius* and *Herculius* titulature. In matters of ceremony and ritual, Diocletian displayed a public devotion proper to the *pontifex maximus*.[45] Lactantius, rather cheaply, labels this *timor* in his depiction of the senior emperor as an anxious *scrutator rerum futurarum*, but it is nothing more than the customary public religiosity of a Roman emperor. Lactantius describes not *timor* but *religio*; not an obsessive reader of entrails, but a proper taker of omens.

Other evidence suggests the seamless support, from Diocletian and his colleagues, for the structures, traditions and rituals of traditional religion. The surviving plinth of the *decennial* monument in Rome depicts a *suovetaurilia*.[46] A Temple of Sol was constructed at Comum *iussu Augustorum*.[47] The Temple of Hadrian at Ephesus was extensively restored and redecorated with contemptary motifs.[48] Malalas states that at Dafne, near Antioch, Diocletian restored the Temple of Apollo and built an underground shrine to Hecate.[49] These are not isolated instances in a long reign. In 291, a panegyrist indicated the reverse, that they represent a wider phenomenon:

> *nam primum omnium, quanta vestra est erga deos pietas! quos aris simulacris, templis donariis, vestris denique nominibus adscriptis, adiunctis imaginibus ornastis, sanctioresque fecistis exemplo vestrae venerationis. nunc enim vere homines intellegunt {quae sit} potestas deorum, cum tam impense colantur a vobis.*

(For, first of all, how great is your devotion to the gods! These, with altars, statues, temples and gifts, ascribed under your names and also adorned with your likenesses, you have made more sacred through the example of your piety. For now men truly comprehend the power of the gods when they are honoured by you at such cost.)[50]

Notwithstanding the customary grandiloquence of a panegyrist, this is a clear statement of the public religious face of the regime. The last sentence quoted above even has a curious evangelical ring. This religious element in the ideology of rule cannot be ignored: even Libanius, writing sixty years later, observed that Diocletian had given the imperial gods pre-eminence.[51] It is possible to go even further than this. This political theology was new, explicit and far-reaching. When the dyarchs took the titles *Iovius* and *Herculius*, they claimed a particular relationship with the divine. Digeser and Kolb have both argued that these titles imply a claim to participate in the divinity of these gods.[52] While this takes the evidence too far, there is no doubt that a special relationship with these gods was claimed, although not an earthly manifestation of divinity.[53] The emperors are not the agents of the gods; they are their friends. Their concern over the peoples of the empire is paternal. After all, they must remain approachable to the free population of the empire who are entitled to ask for their intervention and opinion in matters of legal dispute.[54] Thus, in the Edict of Maximum Prices, the emperors claim for themselves the epithet *parentes generis humani*.[55]

Parenthood implies watchful care, a duty to protect the weak, both from the strong and from themselves. In this respect, the maintenance of public piety is most important. This sentiment can be seen very clearly in the pre-ambles to two imperial edicts, that on the prohibition of incest, and that proscribing the Manichaeans. The Marriage Law begins:

quoniam piis religiosisque mentibus nostris ea, quae Romanis legibus caste sancteque sunt constituta, venerabilia maxime videntur atque aeterna religione servanda.

(Because it seems to our religious and faithful minds, those things which were decently and sacredly enacted by Roman laws [are] greatly venerable, and worthy of preservation in perpetual devotion.)[56]

Thus, a commitment is made to hold to perceived traditions of the Roman past as acts of religious duty. There is a reason for this. The Edict continues:

Ita enim et ipsos inmortales deos Romano nomini, ut semper fuerunt, fauentes et placates futuros esse non dubium est, si cunctos sub imperio nostro agentes piam religiosamque et quietam et castam in omnibus mere colere perspexerimus uitam.

(For indeed, those same immortal gods who have ever favoured the name of Rome, will without doubt continue to be pleased, if we could observe all free peoples under our rule cultivating devoted, religious, quiet and chaste lives, in all ways pure.)[57]

Here the link between divine favour and general religious devotion is made explicit, and the emperor here asserts his oversight and guardianship of such general piety. This theme is pursued even more aggressively in the Edict against the Manichaeans, through which Diocletian sought to assert this mandate through the proscription of the misguided:

Sed dii inmortales providentia sua ordinare et disponere dignati sunt, quae bona et vera sunt ut multorum et bonorum et egregiorum uirorum et sapientissimorum consilio et tractatu inlibata probarentur et statuarentur, quibus nec obuiam ire nec resistere fas est, neque reprehendi a noua vetus religio deberet. Maximi enim criminalis est retractere quae semel ab antiques statuta et definite suum statum et cursum tenent ac possident.

(But the immortal gods through their providence have so ordained and disposed matters so that those things which are good and true should be agreed upon and fixed by the counsel and through the writings of many good, outstanding, indeed the wisest of men. It is not right either to oppose or resist these things, neither should ancient religion be despised by a new one. For it is the height of

122

criminality to reject those things which for all time were described and fixed by the ancients, things which hold and have their clear state and course.)[58]

Here Diocletian depicts traditional religion, and its theological formulations as divinely given and guided. Departures from it are therefore criminal – not in any trifling way, but as a felony of the highest order. These legal formulations are critical in understanding the way in which the new dynasty projected itself. This is not a theocracy; the emperors do not claim any sort of divinity for themselves. They do, however, claim to be the guardians, defenders and asserters of an absolute truth.

If Diocletian's public policy was assertive, through the ideology which underpinned judicial determinations, the direction of building policy and the motifs of imperial propaganda, his private faith was also clearly sincere. This indubitable private piety can be seen in the construction which most reflects his personality – his retirement palace at Split. Clustered around the central peristyle of his fortified villa, there are no fewer than four temples. The largest and greatest was the intended mausoleum of Diocletian himself and his wife Prisca.[59] The other three are smaller, and only one is in any state of preservation, having served as the Baptistery of the Cathedral. This temple was magnificently decorated and its lavish coffered ceiling is still largely intact.[60] The other two temples are smaller, and only fragments and foundations are preserved. Despite this state, they are reasonably certainly identified as temples of Venus and Cybele.[61] Diocletian was under no obligation to clutter his retirement palace with temples. If Diocletian's piety were token, surely one would have sufficed.

This religious ideology, however, only provides a framework within which to explain the outbreak of the Great Persecution. The question still remains as to why Diocletian waited until such a comparatively late date in his reign to commence a religious offensive. It is in fact this comparatively long delay in the beginning of persecution which has led some scholars to reject imperial ideology as the base of the Great Persecution and embrace the Lactantian view.[62] To do so is to adopt a rather simplistic approach. One must examine the nature of Roman religion and also the relative success of Christianity in order to make any kind of determination as to what made Diocletian into a persecutor. It is also necessary, and this is the point which has been missed by many commentators who have simply taken it as read, to examine, insofar as is possible, the nature of late third-century Christianity.

Diocletian and Roman religion

Diocletian's religiosity was in keeping with the spirit of the age. During the third century the ruler cult became of increasing importance in religious life. This even found a niche in the spectacular cosmologies of the oriental cults.[63] *Taurobolia* were celebrated *pro salute imperatoris*.[64] Aurelian's solar theology led to a revival of the cult of *Sol Invictus* and perhaps the first systematic attempt to impose a state religion.[65] None of this was lost on Diocletian who, in all likelihood, took the idea of *princeps a diis electus* and his own divine *numen* or *genius* most seriously.

There is much more to Roman religion, however, than the ruler cult. Its fundamental political importance often overshadows the swell of popular religious feeling which reflects the real spirituality of the age. Here we discover a polyglot of religions, to some extent intellectually syncretized, at least for the literate and intellectual social elite, by Pythagorean and neo-Platonist thinkers. Intellectual concern with a personal knowledge of the deity and the wonders which could be performed by such a God's most faithful servants seems an age away from the dry and distant deities who had ruled the heavens for so long. The traditional religion of the Roman Empire is not a phenomenon which can be easily defined. It was a vast agglomeration of cults, superstitions, speculations and devotion.[66]

It did possess outstanding intellectuals, and perhaps the ablest and subtlest of these in the third-century spiritual explosion was Porphyry. For Eunapius, the pagan biographer of the sophists, he was the only intellectual worth noting between Plotinus and Iamblichus. Eunapius justly devoted a significant amount of his work to this man, the intellectual heir to, and biographer of, Plotinus.[67] Porphyry was an acute critic of Christianity and in the 270s published an attack upon it.[68] The fact that there was an intellectual battle line drawn at this time is important in itself. Moreover, the angle of Porphyry's attack, such as can be determined from the extant fragments of his work, is revealing. His argument seems to have been aimed at the Christians themselves, rather than at those to whom Christianity was still a tempting possibility. Porphyry was certainly an acute critic. His conclusions about the Book of Daniel are still held as orthodoxy by sober biblical scholars.[69] It was perhaps a cherished hope of Porphyry's to recall Christians to the true gods by pointing out the inconsistencies and absurdities in Christian tradition while acknowledging the personal qualities of Jesus himself. At the same time, Porphyry had something positive to say about traditional religion. It was not merely right because it was old; it was also right (and venerable too) because it worked. In *de Civitate Dei*, Augustine criticizes Porphyry for his guarded support of theurgic practice.[70] While Christianity and neo-Platonism might have found a middle ground upon which to exist (at least one member of Plotinus' school became a Christian), Christianity and the discipline of theurgy were natural enemies.[71]

Theurgy is not in itself a religion. Rather, it is a mode of piety. Its emphasis was upon mystical communion with the divine through spectacular means. It went far beyond the simple taking of omens and questioning of oracles into the esoteric and occult. Signs and wonders were the hallmark of the movement, which had Pythagoras and Apollonius of Tyana as its mystical heroes. Theurgy was very much folk religion, as evidenced by its notorious charlatan, Alexander of Abonoteichos.[72] It held oracles as sacred and was no stranger to magic.[73] A book of collected oracles may have been circulating as early as the middle of the third century and a well-known and often-cited papyrus from Oxyrhynchus demonstrates the kinds of question which an oracle might receive:

Shall I be sold up? Shall I become a beggar? Shall I take to flight? Shall I be reconciled with my wife? Have I been bewitched?[74]

A mass of evidence of the nature and manifestation of theurgic practice has been collected and discussed by Ramsay MacMullen, and analysed by Peter Brown.[75] What is clear is that the pagan faith which is revealed by these kinds of data is intensely personal. This is not dry public cult, of perfunctory and unsatisfying interest to its practitioners; it is visceral and profound. But such communications with the divine also reflect a creeping universalism in pagan faith, as Garth Fowden has observed.[76] Such a religious universalism was as exclusive of the Christian communities (or any other totalizing belief system) as it was to the Christians of, and beyond, the empire. While Christians rigidly adhered to the notion of a single ruling God, whose communication with humanity was limited to prophets of antiquity and the person of Jesus Christ, theurgic paganism claimed direct links with the divine through *daimones*, the lesser spirits of the ether. For Christians, such demons were devils – agents of Satan who acted further to divide people from God rather than the reverse. There was no common ground here. For Christians, the prized oracles of the theurgists were voices of Hell, designed to sow mischief and discord, not to make the voice of God clear to the waiting world.

Theurgic theology and practice was a religion both of the fields and of the intellectual salon. Porphyry was not the only religious polemicist of his time. Sossianus Hierocles, an official high in the counsels of Diocletian, published a pamphlet on the eve of the Great Persecution, which compared Jesus unfavourably with Apollonius of Tyana.[77] The growing importance of the theurgic movement in the late third century can be perceived in the changing direction of Porphyry's thought. His biographer, Eunapius, noted that he did a great deal of rethinking towards the end of his life. This led him to espouse intellectual positions at variance with those which he had earlier espoused so eloquently.[78] At some stage, Porphyry produced a three-volume work entitled *Philosophy from Oracles*. This study stands out within the corpus of his work as a peculiar departure from the reasoning spirit of "Against the Christians" and has led some scholars to consider it as an early and immature product of his thought.[79] In reality, its title and the strident anti-Christianity evident in the fragments indicate a developed position in which, perhaps, Porphyry was seeking to reconcile his own philosophical conclusions with theurgic Hellenism and its own insistence upon oracles. In particular, he cites an oracle of Apollo to a man whose wife is a Christian. This oracle reflects the abandonment of any attempt to recall Christians to proper piety by the process of reason:

> You might find it easier to write printed letters on water, or bird-like, to fly through the air spreading gentle wings to the breeze, than to recall to her senses an irreligious and polluted wife. Let her go as she pleases, singing in lamentation for a god who died in delusions, was condemned by right-thinking judges and died the worst of deaths – a death bound with iron.[80]

Here, Porphyry reflects the despair of failure. The Christians now appear to him to be irrevocably trapped in the web of their own irrationality. Porphyry's abandonment of Christians to the consequences of their own folly does not make him a persecutor, but it does mean that he had been challenged in his thinking by those who were. The Great Persecution itself brought such people to the fore. Sossianus Hierocles has already been noted, but there was also Culcianus, Peucetius and Theotecnus.[81] These men were not mere functionaries. They were theologians, intellectuals and also theurgists.

The irony is that there was very little about the *religio* which Diocletian sought to protect and enhance that was *vetus*. Classical paganism had moved, whether of itself, or in response to the challenge to newer alternative traditions (or both) so that the cults which Diocletian asserted had moved far from those of Varro and Vergil. Nevertheless, Diocletian considered himself to be a vigorous defender of the faith. So much so that the Great Persecution has two critical preludes. The first is the persecution of the Manichaeans, already referred to. Seston sought to argue that the stimulus for this assault was secular rather than sacred.[82] This is to misunderstand the vigour and sincerity of Diocletian's religious ideology. The Edict sets out a clear claim to exclusive truth, and is deeply rooted in the neophobia of ancient religion, a fear based upon an assumption that what is old is hallowed and that novelty therefore offends the gods to the extent that they withhold their bounty from the people.

Christianity at the end of the third century

What of the Christians themselves? It would be superfluous to explore the long history of hostility between Rome and the new faith. It was never-theless a conflict which had been muted by Gallienus' Edict of Toleration and frustrated by the premature death of Aurelian. The long peace following Gallienus' Edict led to a much more comfortable Christianity than had prevailed before. An impressive basilica overlooked the imperial palace in

Nicomedia.[83] Squabbling bishops had appealed to Aurelian. Christian leaders no longer held services in private houses but in church buildings supplied with orthodox-approved copies of the scriptures.[84]

There is no empirical way of assessing how many Christians there were in the empire. The number was considerable, most notably in Asia Minor, Egypt, Palestine and North Africa. All of the major cities of the empire possessed bishops and certainly many of the minor ones. Ossius, Constantine's companion, came from Cordova; Eusebius from Caesarea Palestina; Phileas was Bishop of Thmuis. A letter of Dionysius of Alexandria in the 250s lists bishops of the major centres, but declines to enumerate the others in order to render his letter somewhat briefer and avoid the risk of boring his reader.[85] He nevertheless alludes to bishoprics in Galatia, Cilicia, Cappadocia, Syria, Palestine, Arabia, Mesopotamia, Pontus and Bithynia. One can at least say that the Christian community was large and widespread, stronger in some regions than in others. Size, peace and affluence did not necessarily mean torpor. Intellectual life amongst the Christians was a furiously active one. While the late third century produced nothing like the mercurial brilliance of Origen or Clement of Alexandria, there was nevertheless the learned and imaginative Eusebius whose output was prodigious. Lactantius and Arnobius, both late converts to Christianity (which indicates that Christianity had lost none of its intellectual attraction), were forerunners inasmuch as they were both rhetoricians rather than philosophers and concentrated upon rhetorical *apologiae* rather than speculative theology. All three, and many nameless others, were certainly involved in the long intellectual struggle with Hellenism.

This confident and assertive Christianity could even afford more public internecine squabbles. Perhaps the conflict over Paul of Samosata resolved by Aurelian was not peculiar. Eusebius, in searching for a theodicy of the Great Persecution, accuses his church of pride, complacency and disunity, with bishops attacking bishops and factions formed among the laypeople.[86] This is a Christianity which is not hunted and fugitive, but large and potentially powerful. Its adherents could be found at every level of the empire. Its centres of worship could loom over imperial palaces. Bishops guided congregants in the muddy villages of the Nile delta, in the dry Anatolian uplands, and in the *municipia* of Spain. Peace had given Christianity momentum as well as a breathing space. All things considered, it is not surprising that Diocletian decided to persecute. It was either that or seek to annex the Church, and Diocletian was too conservative for that option.

The purge of the army

Diocletian had no qualms about the initiation of a persecution in order to combat a pernicious novelty. Nor had he any about purging the army of

Christians, an event which Eusebius dates to 297.[87] Lactantius ascribes this persecution to the failure of an augury.[88] He deserves some credence since the occasion was a public one. His tale is that the persistent failure of the augural procedure prompted the Tages (the chief *haruspex*) to lay the blame upon *profani homines*, that is, Christians. Here, the imperative for persecution came from a religious official rather than from the emperor. Diocletian's solution was characteristic:

> *Tunc ira furens sacrificare non eos tantum qui sacris ministrabant, sed universos qui erant in palatium iussit et in eos, si detrectassent, verberibus animadverti, datisque ad praepositos litteris, etiam milites cogi ad nefanda sacrificia praecepit, ut qui non paruissent, militia solverentur.*

(Then, burning with rage, he ordered everyone to sacrifice – not merely those few who were serving in the temples, but all those who were in the palace – if any declined, they received a flogging. Then he sent letters to the commanders, ordering that the soldiery also should participate in the wicked sacrifices, and that any not partaking be cashiered from service.)[89]

Lactantius judges the mood of the emperor in terms of his polemic. It is *ira* born of *timor*. But this is not a tantrum; it is policy. Eusebius knows better. His summary makes it clear that this purge was conducted in a fashion which was far from impulsive. It reveals a systematic and carefully devised action, a deliberate inquisition and staff of inquisitors.[90]

In purging the army of Christians, Diocletian was undertaking no small task. It is impossible to ascertain what proportion of the army was Christian, but there is evidence to suggest that there were a substantial number of Christians in service. A military martyrdom from North Africa, the *Acta Maximiliani* makes it clear that Christians regularly entered the forces. The martyred saint, Maximilian, became the exception which revealed the norm. It is clear from the text of the *Acta* that Christians were present among the *protectores*, the elite corps of junior officers.[91] Moreover, a long inscription from a site near ancient Cotaeum in Phrygia bears out the claim of Maximilian's judges. This is the long and proud Christian military epitaph of Aurelius Gaius, a soldier who had risen through the ranks to be an *optio* in the *comites*. His epitaph describes a long and varied military career, in which time he had certainly served under Galerius, although, during his career, he had also visited Gaul, Spain and Mauretania.[92] At one point, he served as an *optio* in the imperial *comitatus*.[93] It is entirely possible that his was one military career cut short by Veturius' purge.[94] In his account of the purge, Eusebius asserts that there was a significant number of Christian soldiers who preferred dismissal to apostasy.[95] At the end of the second century, Tertullian had boasted:

128

> We have filled every place among you – cities, islands, fortresses, towns, market-places, the camp even, tribes, companies, palace, Senate, Forum – we have left nothing to you but your temples.[96]

By the end of the third century, such bragging might not have seemed quite so vainglorious.[97]

It has already been noted that there were Christians of relatively important rank by the end of the third century. Doubtless, the period of toleration after 260 permitted them to rise to such levels both unmolested and without fear of denunciation. Thus, they can be found, for example, within the key imperial corps of *protectores*, the officers entrusted with care of the imperial person and destined for high command.[98] It was from command of this corps that Diocletian had risen to the purple. It is quite possible that at the time that Maximilian was speaking at least one future emperor was a member of the corps.[99]

There is also evidence of Christians rising high in civilian administration. Eusebius specifically mentions three: Dorotheus, a eunuch and Christian intellectual who administered the imperial dye-works at Tyre; Gorgonius and Peter who both held unstated positions at the imperial court.[100] Eusebius also adds that large numbers of (unnamed) people at the highest levels in the court were also Christians.[101]

The forcible discharge of Christians from the army occurred at a time of considerable stress. Eusebius dates it to 297, a date which holds up well, despite suggestions to the contrary. Lactantius states that the orders were given whilst Diocletian was in the east.[102] A better and slightly earlier context can be established. At the end of 296, both Diocletian and Galerius were facing serious problems in the east. Narseh had routed a Roman army. The emperors conferred, probably in Antioch. Galerius was sent to the Danube to collect reinforcements while Diocletian remained in Syria. In the course of 297, however, it became necessary for him to take his army to Egypt in order to quell a revolt there. The two emperors did not meet again until Galerius returned in victory late in 298 whereupon he was sent almost immediately to the Danube. This leaves two possible contexts for the persecution. The first is the winter of 296/7, just after the Roman defeat, or the brief consultation between Diocletian and Galerius during the winter of 298/9. Happily, the *Chronicle* of Eusebius places it precisely in the first of these contexts – between the Persian campaigns.[103]

Such a context was one of considerable anxiety for the immediate future. In a time of peace and security, Christian eccentrics might be tolerated. But a Roman army, led by an emperor (admittedly an emergency force led by a Caesar), had been defeated by an old and feared enemy. It was a time of imminent crisis. The empire needed every scrap of divine favour which it could garner, and religious pluralism was tantamount to treason. Certainly this is how Diocletian perceived the disruption of hepatoscopatic ritual. As it transpired, the purge only affected the military.[104] It was well organized and systematic: a special commissioner, Veturius, was appointed.[105] He went through the army, camp by camp, garrison by garrison, station by station. Christians were weeded out. Some were discharged. Others were tortured in the hope of forcing a recantation. Some died.[106] But this is not merely a grim harbinger of things to come. It is in itself a strong argument that the Great Persecution was anything but an aberration.

Prelude to persecution

What has been identified here is a series of factors: an active traditional culture on the intellectual offensive, challenged by Christianity's forthright rejection of it and substantially unable to counter its appeal, despite the dedicated efforts of Porphyry and others. Likewise, the Christian communities had been strengthened by thirty years of toleration. They continued to make converts, some – like Lactantius – in high places. They had organization and a hierarchy running the breadth of the empire and beyond. The Christian communities stood not merely as a cohesive faith but as the largest alternative belief-system in the empire to the imperial office itself. Christians largely, and with notable exceptions like Lactantius, rejected the ideology of the empire. They were instead citizens of a state within a state with its own laws, customs, heroes and soldiers.[107]

Diocletian's principal, and driving, concern was to revive a moribund empire. He had succeeded on the frontiers; he had curtailed centrifugalism and disloyalty; he had reorganized provincial administration and the army on a massive scale. He could not tolerate any challenge to his new order for long, no matter how passive it was. He neither liked nor trusted the adherents of a foreign religion, especially one that would not bow the knee to traditional syncretism. Christianity's rejection of the traditional pantheon implied a rejection of imperial theology, of the Augusti as *Iovius* and *Herculius*, of the implied nexus between private piety and public religion.

The conference in Nicomedia

If this discussion has only mentioned Galerius *en passant*, the reason should be plain. It was neither his superstition nor that of his mother which generated the Great Persecution. It was the conflict of ideologies, of Church and State which compelled it. The emperor, surrounded by powerful pagan supporters, simply decided to put an end to a state of affairs which had prevailed for too long. He was prepared to use force. He had already done so in ordering the suppression of the Manichaeans. With Christianity eliminated, the empire would be truly restored, not merely to true worship, but to the unity of faith and purpose. It was a grand vision, but it excluded the Christians. What part did Galerius play in this war of ideas? Although the interpretations of Lactantius cannot be trusted, his circumstantial information remains good. Barnes has clearly demonstrated his reliablity on this question.[108]

In the winter of 302/3, Diocletian and Galerius conferred in Nicomedia. Here, Lactantius states, they held secret counsels to which no others were admitted.[109] They had much to talk about in any event, religious policy notwithstanding. Galerius was faced by a troublesome situation on the Danube, and they had to consider the consequences of the Edict on Maximum Prices, promulgated in the previous year. Moreover, Diocletian's *vicennalia* was approaching and some thought had to be given to its arrangement. It might even have been at this point that Diocletian raised his intention to retire with Galerius. He certainly had that in mind when he went to Rome later in the year.[110] Such a conference was not a peculiar event. Conferences were as important in the relationship between Diocletian and Galerius as they had been when Diocletian ruled only with Maximian, with whom he had conferred in Rhaetia in 288 and at Milan in 290.[111] He had likewise met with Galerius in the east in 295, either in Damascus or Antioch. It is likely that there was another conference after the qualified failure of the defensive campaign in Osroene the following year. They certainly conferred in Nisibis in 299, and they travelled to Antioch together which they entered in splendour to offer thanksgiving for the Persian victory in the previous year.

The priority given to the forthcoming attack upon the Christians is unclear. Diocletian had probably considered it for some years, certainly since the earlier purge of the army. It was not a measure to be undertaken lightly, but the appointment of Culcianus to Egypt, a major centre of Christianity, in the previous year indicates that Diocletian was making careful preparations. Culcianus was one of those with intellectual pretensions who proved in the following years to be an awkward foe of Egyptian Christians.[112] Sossianus Hierocles, active on the intellectual front, and an experienced official, was appointed *praeses* of Bithynia, technically a demotion since he had already held the vicariate.[113] Not only had Hierocles composed his treatise *Philalethes*, comparing Jesus unfavourably with Apollonius of Tyana, but he was also giving public readings of it in Nicomedia.[114] A Bithynian appointment kept him close to the emperor in Nicomedia, and also entrusted him with the oversight of a region with a large Christian community.[115]

While Lactantius' elaboration of the role of Galerius can be largely dismissed as fiction, at this point it would be premature to remove Galerius from any analysis at all.[116] When Diocletian convened his *consilium* to discuss the matter in 302/3, Galerius was present. Others also attended. Sossianus Hierocles was a likely participant.[117] It has now been more or less conceded that Porphyry was also present in Nicomedia, and involved in the same programme of anti-Christian polemic.[118] He was no doubt also consulted upon the formulation of imperial policy towards the Christians as it mutated into full-scale confrontation.[119] Porphyry's reading was from his new work *Philosophy from Oracles*, and it may have been his influence that persuaded Diocletian to seek oracular confirmation before proceeding with the initiation of persecution.[120] The Oracle of Apollo at Didyma, a few days, sail down the Aegean coast from Nicomedia, was consulted.[121] Once both gods and men had given their advice, Diocletian proceeded to issue the first edict. Galerius' role seems curiously bland. He was asked, but in all likelihood neither urged Diocletian to savagery, nor sought to moderate his policy.

The date and terms of the First Edict of Persecution are also of importance here. It was issued at Nicomedia on 23 February, the date of the ancient feast of *Terminalia*. Diocletian did not choose days by accident. The Caesars had been proclaimed on the Festival of Mars.[122] The *Terminalia* was the celebration of boundaries. Sacrifices and feasts honoured the *numina* of border-stones. It was an ancient festival – so ancient in fact that the sanctuary of Terminus was in the *cella* of the Temple of Jupiter Optimus Maximus on the Capitol, having been built over in the time of the Kings.[123] This close and antique association between Jupiter and Terminus led ultimately to a popular association between the two.[124] An inscription at Ravenna records a dedication to Jupiter Terminus.[125]

At the commencement of the persecution, Diocletian sought simply to assert the exclusion of Christians from the civil society of the empire. No text of this edict survives, although its punitive measures are well attested. Christian public buildings were demolished, Christian documents and literature declared contraband, and the legal status of Christians revoked.[126] Such an approach was entirely consistent with the view that the Christians had rejected the legal and political structures of the empire, and all of the responsibilities of civil citizenship, in order to constitute their own society. The sense of the preamble to the Edict can be reasonably suggested. The attested measures are consistent with the kinds of objective outlined by Galerius in the Edict of Toleration of 311: to make it plain to the Christians that constituting laws and customs for themselves necessitated public and judicial intolerance; the way to escape this being *ut ad veterum se instituta referent* (that they should return to the practices of the ancients).[127] The first martyrdom of the persecution was not long in coming. As soon as the Edict had been posted, it was torn down by a Christian, offended by its terms and as convicted as Lactantius himself of the barbarity of imperial policy.[128]

Lactantius, however, continues his narrative, blaming Galerius for the intensification of the Persecution. His narrative states that there were a series of fires, set by Galerius' secret agents, in the palace at Nicomedia. Diocletian apparently blamed the Christians and, alarmed, mercilessly purged his household.[129] To keep this pressure up, Galerius then had a second fire set after fifteen days. This was more swiftly extinguished, but on the same day Galerius departed from Nicomedia, declaring that he was leaving in order to avoid incineration.[130] The first fire has some independent corroboration.

Eusebius mentions it, although without ascribing it to Galerius.[131] More significantly, an eyewitness, the emperor Constantine refers to it but gives the cause as a lightning strike.[132] Lactantius is here carried away by the force of his own polemic. The story has a familiar ring. The first imperially sponsored persecution occurred as a consequence of the Great Fire of Rome. As Tacitus describes it, there were two stages. The first was the major conflagration. The second was less devastating, but had its origin on the property of Nero's favourite and Praetorian Prefect, Ofonius Tigellinus.[133] The parallel is striking and hardly coincidental.[134]

If Galerius sought to use these fires to persuade Diocletian to intensify persecution, he was hardly successful. While Christians seem to have been considered the arsonists, Diocletian's anger was directed at his own household and not the broader Christian community.[135] It was in this context that Dorotheus, Gorgonius and Peter suffered martyrdom.[136] This was wholly within the provisions of the first edict. The persecution was subsequently intensified, but not in the way which Lactantius describes. In the middle of the year, there were two minor revolts in the east. In Seleucia, a party of soldiers engaged in public works mutinied as a result of ill-treatment, proclaimed their commander emperor, and marched on Antioch after a bout of looting and drinking. The Antiochenes themselves surrounded and killed the mob of drunken soldiers, including the would-be emperor, Eugenius.[137] This in turn exacted a swift and bloody retribution from Diocletian who ordered the execution of a number of Antiochene *curiales*.[138] Perhaps he misunderstood their initiative or perhaps there is more to the story that the Antiochene rhetorician Libanius tells.[139]

In any case, Diocletian displayed no mercy in Antioch, and certainly none in another place. Eusebius states that a revolt also took place in Melitene, a remote city of Cappadocia.[140] A Syrian martyrology records two deaths at Melitene on 3 May 303, which would not be very long after the first Edict reached the district.[141] These may be connected with the rising. Christianity was certainly strong in neighbouring Armenia.[142] Religion does not obey secular boundaries, so it is quite likely that the Melitene district likewise had a significant number of Christians among the population. One might speculate at this point that the Edict was resisted in this remote district of the empire more resolutely than elsewhere. If so, the attempt was in vain and the revolt was crushed. According to Eusebius, it was this revolt which induced Diocletian to intensify the persecution. The second Edict was promulgated in the middle of 303, long after the fire, with Galerius absent and embroiled in war on the Danubian border.[143]

It is clear that Diocletian, at this point, was exercising sole responsibility for the formulation of imperial policy towards the Christians. Nor did this subsequently change. Galerius has also been cited as responsible for a fourth Edict of the persecution, although not by Lactantius, but by N.H. Baynes.[144] Diocletian had, in fact, sought to mitigate the effects of the persecution with an amnesty (in return for apostasy) at the time of the *vicennalia*.[145] When the possibilities of this process had been explored, the persecution was again intensified, with a fourth Edict, issued nearly in 304, which was the most far-reaching up to that point, imposing a sacrifice test upon all of the inhabitants of the empire.[146] Baynes, suggesting that at that time Diocletian was crippled by severe illness and hence incapable of ruling, has argued that responsibility for this Edict lay with Galerius.[147] Diocletian did indeed suffer from a serious illness in the course of 304 which was, at one point, life-threatening. However, the fourth Edict was issued while Diocletian was touring the Danubian frontier, long before his malady became acute.

It would nevertheless be a manifest absurdity to attempt to cast Galerius on the side of the angels in the matter of the Great Persecution. He collaborated in its planning and administration. When, as senior Augustus, he had the opportunity to stop it, he did not. He did not share the tolerant independence of his colleague, Constantius.[148] He was neither tolerant, nor independent of Diocletian. It should not be considered, however, that Galerius was simply going along with the policy for the sake of form. It has been suggested that Galerius was not "especially fanatical", a contrast to the more common picture of Galerius as "a fanatical pagan". Both images fundamentally mistake both the nature of classical paganism itself and the reasoning behind the Great Persecution. In the world of Diocletian, politics and religion were inseparable. Refusal to honour the gods of the empire was not a tolerable eccentricity; it was sedition. This was an ideology which Galerius himself represented and asserted. He was a part of its processes, its most loyal and effective apparatchik.

The abdication of the Augusti

If Galerius' role in the outbreak of the Great Persecution was as negligible as is argued here, then another conclusion follows inescapably. Many have argued, following Lactantius, that after the Persian War Galerius gained a personal ascendancy over Diocletian, of which the Great Persecution was but the first fruits. An even sweeter and greater victory was achieved through the compulsion of the Augusti to abdicate.[149] At the very least this reflects the perplexity and uncertainty which has been felt in approaching an act so difficult to comprehend as the voluntary renunciation of supreme power. The import of this deed cannot be sufficiently highlighted. Unprecedented in nature, apparently out of character, both contemporaries and later commentators have been nonplussed by it, seeking to find circumstances which compelled Diocletian's resignation, rather than assume that any emperor would freely and willingly divest himself of supreme power. Lactantius echoes the incredulity of his own time by spinning a tale based around his villain Galerius.[150] For his part, Constantine refused to believe that Diocletian was in his right mind, preferring to claim that he went mad due to the guilt he felt for initiating the Great Persecution.[151] For Constantine, power was too sweet to discard. Other ancient writers find an explanation in the deterioration of Diocletian's health.[152] He had, after all, been seriously ill in 304.[153] The contemporary Eusebius simply gives up and confesses his incomprehension.[154]

For the great foundation scholars of late antiquity, Diocletian's act was voluntary. To Gibbon, it was a glorious act, dictated by reason, long contemplated and wisely enjoyed. Gibbon ignores the testimony of Lactantius, arguing that it is "sufficiently refuted by an impartial view of the character and conduct of Diocletian".[155] For his part, Burckhart was no less rhetorical: "May we not conclude that he had always inwardly risen above the Oriental court ceremonies he introduced and that at Nicomedia he had often longed for his Dalmatian throne?"[156] Their successors tend to divide into two camps — those who see the abdication as a considered and deliberate act, and those who consider it one dictated by circumstances. These vary from scholar to scholar. For some, Galerius is the villain of the piece: Lactantius' account suffices.[157] Others follow the second explanation of antiquity: that of Diocletian's health. Mild variations on the theme can be detected in the pages of each.[158] Some seek to steer a middle course — that Diocletian always intended to retire, but the actual occasion was forced upon him.[159]

Interpretations of the event cover the full spectrum from romanticism to cynicism. No starker a contrast might be drawn than that between Burckhardt's view of the noble Diocletian and Henri Grégoire's dithering dotard. For Grégoire, the situation is analogous to Hitler's rise to power in 1933: Diocletian is the vacillating and intimidated Hindenburg figure; Galerius plays Hitler, and the palace burns like the *Reichstag*.[160] But if the argument which has been advanced throughout this book is correct, then neither of these extremes are satisfactory. While there was no "ascendancy" of Caesar over Augustus, nor was there a master plan with a timetable. Yet the question remains, to which the malign influence of Galerius has often been seen as a convenient answer: Why did Diocletian not merely give up power on his own account, but also compel Maximian to do likewise, and then, despite all of the temptations and blandishments to return to the purple, obstinately tend his garden in his fortified retirement villa?[161]

There is no question but that the principal beneficiary of Diocletian's retirement was Galerius. His nephew Maximinus Daza became a Caesar, as did his friend Severus. Galerius himself became Iovius Augustus, Diocletian's successor. By a peculiar twist, Constantius I, the Herculius Augustus, was the senior of the two. But he was far away from the apparatus of government. The departments, the secretaries, the administrators and bureaucrats were all centred in the east, which had been the hub of the empire for twenty years. The abdication of Diocletian was, for Galerius, a move from the shadow of power to its reality. He had run Diocletian's errands for longer than he had worn the purple and now he was reaping the benefit of faithful service.[162]

But wrapped into the question of why Diocletian abdicated at all, and why he also compelled the abdication of Maximian, is the issue of the nomination of the Caesars. How did they come to be chosen? Lactantius has a version, naturally tendentious.[163] Eusebius has a briefer, but equally coloured narrative.[164] Other accounts are even barer and sparser, and all are distorted by the immense weight of Constantinian propaganda and hagiography.[165]

The chronology of the events is reasonably clear. In 303, Diocletian celebrated his *vicennalia* in Rome. It was a grand triumph over the many defeated foes of the empire.[166] He probably inspected the progress of the grand baths which bear his name,[167]and, late in the year, in a consultation with Maximian, extracted an oath from him on the altar of Capitoline Jove that he too would abdicate.[168] Then Diocletian left Rome and toured the Balkan provinces. At some point he fell seriously ill and returned to Nicomedia more dead than alive.[169] His life was despaired of, but by 1 March 305, he was well enough to make a public appearance, probably to celebrate the *dies imperii* of the Caesars.[170] On 1 May, in a grand ceremony outside Nicomedia, Diocletian divested himself of his purple cloak and bestowed it upon Maximinus Daza. He immediately left for his palace at Split, not quite the Valerius Diocles he had once been, but certainly no longer a ruling emperor.[171] In a parallel ceremony in Milan, Maximian Herculius gave his purple to Severus Caesar and likewise retired, to an estate in Lucania.[172]

Age and ill-health are tempting reasons to account for Diocletian's sudden withdrawal from formal power. He had been seriously ill, and had ruled for longer than any emperor since Antoninus Pius. He had been the political colossus of his age, and it would only have been natural if he had felt weary of office. Not only, however, have these not been factors for others in relatively recent history, neither had they been factors which had influenced any of Diocletian's predecessors to retire from absolute power. Diocletian was, perhaps, about 65 when he retired.[173] While 65 is far from youthful, neither is it sunk into the depths of old age. On occasion, Roman emperors had taken the purple when older. Nerva had been perhaps a year older when called upon to rule in 96. Pertinax had been 67; Tacitus, a septuagenarian.[174] Neither had age prevented Augustus, Tiberius, Vespasian, Antoninus Pius or Septimius Severus from exercising rule.[175] For these men, imperial power was to be exercised until the last breathing moment. One can prove little by comparison, only that Diocletian's decision was atypical.

It is certainly true that Diocletian had been ill. His debilitating and almost fatal ailment in late 304/early 305 has been seen as a factor which determined, or at least influenced, the abdication, but it is clear that Diocletian had determined to abdicate before he was afflicted by disease. He fell ill during the course of 304 while he was touring the Danubian provinces, but it was in November of the previous year that he had secured from Maximian a promise bound by oath to join him in retirement.[176] Moreover, Diocletian was in fact convalescing from his illness when he abdicated. If the prolonged and serious nature of his ailment had prompted his decision, then the question must persist as to why he would wait until he was on the mend before he actually carried it out.[177] It was hardly the most propitious time, given that he was now in a position to resume, rather than resign, the direction of public affairs. If further argument be needed, it must be noted that Diocletian required Maximian to abdicate with him. Age and illness are individual phenomena. There is certainly no evidence that Maximian suffered ill-health. If Diocletian's decision had been made on purely personal grounds, then why oblige his colleague to follow him into retirement? Diocletian cannot have lacked any confidence in his colleague. Maximian had acquitted himself well enough, dealing with border problems and separatists in Africa.[178] The borders in the west were secure, the Bagaudae and Carausius were memories, the administration efficient. Maximian had even wrung valuable revenue from the tight-fisted and arrogant senatorial class in Rome.[179] Surely he had done his job and done it well.

These objections remain serious problems for the view that Diocletian abdicated purely for individual reasons. The very unprecedented nature of the act perplexed the historians of antiquity who recorded it. To them, it was inconceivable that one man should voluntarily renounce so great a power. The only reasons they could find were the superficially plausible ones of age and health, or the rhetorical one of derangement. Lactantius alone sought an explanation in the person of his villain, Galerius.[180] For Lactantius, this was a reasonable interpretation and as a contemporary, his views merit consideration and discussion. In some degree they must reflect the kind of uninformed gossip and speculation which normally accompanied unexpected political acts, particularly resignations.

Lactantius' explanation is that Galerius bullied an enfeebled Diocletian into resignation, having already threatened Maximian with war if he also did not meekly submit. Galerius' plan was to put his own creatures in place as Caesars (anticipating the early death of Constantius) and retire in his turn, secure that the empire was ruled by his friends and family.[181] This version is fraught with inconsistencies and illogicalities and is difficult to take seriously. Three simple points can be made in response. First, the whole edifice of the narrative is built upon the assumption that Galerius could and did exercise a personal ascendancy over Diocletian. While it is likely that Galerius was instrumental in forcing Maximian's retirement, he could not have brought any instrument of state into play against Diocletian even had he been willing to.[182] He simply lacked the prestige to carry it off. A military coup was out of the question. Galerius' Danubian army had itself been commanded by Diocletian in recent memory and thus Galerius could never take its loyalty for granted. Furthermore, the act itself would have been impious, a violation of the charismatic and family relationships which Diocletian had been careful to establish. Even had Galerius been able to trust his army, his colleagues were in a good position to oppose his drive for power.

He would inevitably have lost, and in so doing, have shattered the very *concordia* of collegiate rule which he had striven for so long to maintain. Yet even had he, by some major miracle, been successful in forcing the abdications of the two Augusti, the supremacy would not even then belong to him, but to Constantius.

Herein lies the second point in response to Lactantius' narrative. Constantius is often forgotten in discussions of this issue. Galerius might conceivably have been able to prevail upon Diocletian, and perhaps even Maximian also, to resign, but the expectation that he could bully a third colleague is surely fanciful. Lactantius endeavours to extricate himself from this predicament by a neat hindsight: Constantius was ill and not expected to live.[183] This is a complete ratiocination. Constantius was hale enough to win a victory over a marauding band of Germans at the end of 304, and to go to Britain in the following year to campaign against the Picts.[184] It was from Britain that Constantius imposed his will upon Galerius in the following year when he sent for Constantine.[185] Constantius was no invalid when these plans were devised, but an active and vigorous general who could be reasonably expected to exercise imperial authority with determination and skill. His later, admittedly premature, death cannot have been a factor in the counsels of 304/5, during which time he was chasing Germans and Picts from the northern marches of the empire.

Third, Lactantius makes the extraordinary claim that Galerius himself intended to abdicate upon the completion of his *vicennalia*. Not only does this image run counter to the beastly, uncultured and grasping picture which he had hitherto painted of the Caesar, but it also exposes the threadbare fabric of the polemic. There is good evidence of Galerius' intention to abdicate – the sprawling, elaborate and extravagant fortified villa at Romuliana.[186] The question which logically arises here is why Galerius forced Diocletian to abdicate for the sake of a post which he himself intended to hold for only a limited number of years. Lactantius suggests it was so that Galerius could enjoy a secure old age, surrounded by the walls of his villa and the bulwarks of Severus, Licinius, Maximinus Daza and Candidianus.[187] This is too much like special pleading. He could have spent a far more secure old age surrounded by *protectores* in any one of the many imperial palaces scattered about the empire.

If Galerius did not oblige his (adoptive) father to abdicate, then we are left only with the alternative explanation: that Diocletian abdicated of his own free will (Maximian somewhat less so), and left the control of the empire to new Augusti – Constantius and Galerius. This is not a counsel of despair. It fits the evidence and, taking into account the bias of Lactantius, is entirely reasonable. No greater indication of Diocletian's own intention to retire exists than his extravagant and fortified palace at modern Split. This was his retirement home, and within his crenellated walls could be found temples, barrack-rooms and a sea-front imperial residence with its own baths, jetty and vast cellars.[188] A long portico faced the sea along which the retired emperor might stroll in order to catch the sea-breeze. The villa was built into the side of a hill. It was made level by the simple expedient of building up the seaward side. This resulted in the creation of cavernous cellars, still not entirely excavated. Nevertheless, they give the basic floor plan of the palace living quarters, and, most importantly for our purposes, indicate both the grandeur of the edifice and the fact that it could not have been built quickly. The palace was meticulously planned by a great architect and constructed with care. It might be suggested that Diocletian's palace is not necessarily evidence of his intention to retire there, that it is to be placed in the overall context of a prodigious building policy which saw new imperial palaces in Antioch, Nicomedia, Thessalonica, Serdica, Sirmium, Mediolanum, Trier, even a small model built against a single visit in Upper Egypt.[189] The only inference that one can make from the structures themselves is that they were built for an emperor to live in, no matter how briefly, and were part of a network of imperial dwellings which enabled the emperors to be as peripatetic as they were. Such a view is fair to the physical evidence, but a basic point must be made in response. Our principal evidence for imperial palaces at places like Nicomedia, Milan and Serdica is literary and we can only conclude their existence through texts attesting imperial usage of these structures. There is, however, no evidence for any imperial usage of the villa at Split until after Diocletian's retirement. Up until 305, he did not go near the place, but had dwelt in Sirmium, Antioch, Nicomedia and Alexandria. When he did retire, he went straight there.[190] If the purpose of a place can legitimately be inferred from its use, then plainly we have a fortified villa built at (or near) Diocletian's birthplace, employed only after 305. If further evidence be needed, a domed octagonal structure surrounded by a temenos wall and adjacent to a handsome peristyle court and arranged axially with a Temple to Jupiter was clearly built (and employed) as Diocletian's mausoleum. He intended to stay.[191]

Diocletian's retirement home was planned well in advance of his actual abdication in 305. If his retirement home was planned so much in advance, and with a completion date of early 305 in mind, it follows logically that so was Diocletian's retirement itself. The very existence of the Split palace itself is firm evidence that Diocletian's retirement was a contemplated and deliberate act of policy but it does not necessarily follow that he intended to retire from the very beginning. Diocletian, it has been argued, was consistently seeking to build a firm imperial bulwark which could both provide dynastic security and stability and also ensure a smooth succession. Experimentation with titles and epithets is evident from the beginning, and one such experiment left a famous anomaly: when the Caesars were adopted, they took the names of their new fathers, including the epithets *Iovius* and *Herculius*. This in turn meant that the most junior of the new dynasty, Galerius, became *Iovius Caesar*, while Constantius, who ranked before him in all of the elements of imperial titulature, became *Herculius Caesar*. This reflected the dynastic relationship, and became a part of normal titulature, but did not reflect the rigid ranking of the college.[192] This charismatic relationship was important early in the collegiate empire for establishing the relationship between Diocletian and Maximian: the Jovian master and Herculean servant.[193] But at the point when Constantius and Galerius succeeded their fathers, an anomaly was created. Galerius, the youngest of the emperors, and therefore the lowest-ranking, became *Iovius*; Constantius, although senior, became *Herculius*. This mattered little while Diocletian headed the college. But upon the abdications, the contradications of an improvised dynasty were laid bare.

If Diocletian had not always intended to retire, then he can only have determined to do so at a later time. The earliest firm evidence of his intention to retire is his negotiation with Maximian in 303. This might have been at Rome during the celebrations of the *vicennalia*, although Barnes has suggested a slightly earlier conference of all four rulers in northern Italy.[194] It has been suggested earlier in this chapter that Diocletian might have raised his intention with Galerius during the winter conference of 302/3. The two were long closeted holding private discussions, a private conference which Lactantius took to be Galerius browbeating Diocletian into persecution.[195] This is as much as, and perhaps more than, the evidence will yield. The remainder can only be guessed or inferred from scraps of evidence and the ultimate outcome.[196]

Certainly Diocletian's reasoning remains a mystery. Diocletian had changed the imperial office more than any emperor since Augustus; he had created an elaborate ceremonial in which the emperors became both images and monopolists of power. This was yet another fence around the imperial office, to protect it from usurpation and civil war. Seen in this context, the principal reason which must have motivated Diocletian was that self-abnegation by the Augusti was a final way of securing the stability of the office of emperor. Regimes are at their most vulnerable at points of transition. When a strong leader departs, there is inevitably a struggle amongst subordinates to succeed. The strength of Diocletian's new dynasty was its many faces; but this could also be (as it proved) its fatal weakness. Abdication not only guaranteed that power would not be locked up in the bodies of ageing monarchs, but also enabled Diocletian to manage his own succession. This was intended to be Diocletian's final and grandest gesture to imperial stability. That the boldness of the move was ultimately frustrated by the ambitions of Maximian and Constantine was no fault of Diocletian's. He could not foresee that he would outlive the Augusti who replaced him. In particular, he could not foresee that the sudden death of Constantius would precipitate a long struggle amongst and between ruling members of the dynasty and those who sought to shoulder their way to power.

It is Galerius, again, who is generally blamed for this vast family quarrel. In antiquity, Lactantius accused Galerius of displacing the next natural college of Caesars (Constantine and Maxentius) with his own nominees, Severus and Daza.[197] This view is given some support by Julian's image of Galerius in the *Caesares*. In this heavy-handed satire, he imagines an imperial banquet in heaven, with emperors received according to their virtues. When it is the turn of Diocletian and his colleagues, the four enter together, with the three lesser emperors dancing attendance upon Diocletian like a kind of chorus. Hence, the gods honour the college for their unanimity, but soon Maximian (Galerius) proves intemperate and ambitious, and is banished for introducing discord.[198] It would be unwise, however, to attach too much weight to this image. Julian was the grandson of both Constantius (whom he deliberately refers to as his grandfather) and Maximian Herculius. He might therefore be expected to be a little more generous to his side of the family. Lactantius and Julian between them present one version of the story. Their version, moreover, is one which Constantine had every reason to promote since it is based upon the assertion that Constantine had a legitimate right to succeed as the son of a ruling Augustus. This is disingenuous. It omits the truth both of Constantine's viler origins (the son of Constantius' youth by a Drepanum barmaid) and the legitimacy of Constantius' vast family by Theodora.[199] The marriage had been fecund, producing three sons and three daughters. Moreover, Lactantius manages neatly to obfuscate the family relationship between Galerius and Maximinus Daza, whom he simply labels an *adfinis*, rather than nephew.[200]

It would, nevertheless, be naive to suggest that Galerius was not an ambitious man. Men who lack ambition do not become Roman emperors, even junior ones, and it would be unusual in the extreme if he did not seek to promote his own interests in the negotiations which preceded the dynastic transition. But he also had the scruples, common sense and *pietas* not to exercise that ambition at the expense of his adoptive father. Galerius had all the advantages of propinquity in this bloodless and mediated contest. He had, however, fewer inhibitions relative to Constantius whom he had rarely met and to whom he was only tenuously related.[201] The interests of Constantius in this matter are usually (and falsely) assumed to be identical with those of Constantine. Constantine was his eldest, but not his only son. He had three others, legitimately conceived and, moreover, grandsons of Maximian. These sons and their sisters, all young, needed to be protected and their future claims assured. When agreement was struck as to the succession, it took sufficient note of Constantius' interests that he could be content with the outcome. This was guaranteed by further adoption. When Severus was made Caesar, he also joined the *domus*, being adopted by Constantius, and taking the name Flavius Valerius Severus.[202] As such, he might reasonably have been expected to safeguard the succession of Constantius' sons, his new brothers. The flaw here was that Constantius had no particular reason to trust Severus to do so and, when the time came for him to make a choice, he preferred the son of his loins to one thrust upon him through negotiation.

Nevertheless, Constantius' sons needed protection, for they already had a grown rival in the person of Maximian's son Maxentius, for many years married deeply into the dynasty. Maxentius had long before been married to Valeria, the daughter of Galerius and grand-daughter of Diocletian.[203] By her, he was the father of Galerius' grandson Romulus, born before 306.[204] He had, however, already been rejected as a possible successor. Such a policy had evidently pertained earlier: the dynastic marriage united all of the imperial colleagues, and the blood of three of them ran in the veins of the portentously named Valerius Romulus. But, according to Lactantius, Maxentius was also a proud man, refusing his father-in-law the honours due to him.[205] This palace gossip has a ring of authenticity. Maxentius did not live close to Galerius, nor did he hold a senior military post, both of which might be expected of a designated successor. Rather, he was living the leisured life of a Roman senator, possibly the link between his father and that ancient body.[206] He also had private affairs to manage, as any nobleman did. The family had Italian estates, perhaps achieved through confiscation. It was a post of some honour, but no power, and might easily be understood as relegation.[207]

What of Constantine, the other putative successor? It is difficult to make a genuine assessment of his prospects since the sources largely reflect his ultimate victory. Some things, however, can be said with some clarity. Unlike Maxentius, Constantine had followed a military career and still held military office. He had served with Galerius in Asia, in the Persian campaign and on the Danube.[208] His rank was given in 305 as *tribunus primi ordinis*.[209] In the 290s he had been linked in dynastic propaganda with Fausta, the daughter of Maximian, although he actually lived with Minervina, the mother of Crispus.[210] As a *vir militaris* of some experience, and the son of a Caesar, he might logically have considered himself to be a candidate for the purple. Others did not, Diocletian amongst them. Constantine did not fit the dynastic paradigm which Diocletian had been so artfully constructing. He was its cuckoo, a bastard, married (if at all) to an outsider. There was no sign that he could be trusted. Although Constantine was a successful *vir militaris*, he was otherwise outside the *domus*, and his nature and ambition were, perhaps, well enough known to Diocletian and Galerius. The *Origo Constantini Imperatoris*, generally an excellent and reliable source, notes that Constantine was "a hostage with Diocletian and Galerius" (*obses apud Diocletianum et Galerium*).[211] The implication here is that Constantine was kept close to Diocletian, not because he was trusted (as Lactantius implies) but because he was not. That Constantine was a hostage at all, however, is highly implausible. Constantius had many more children who might be "brought up" at the courts of Diocletian and Galerius in order to ensure their father's continued loyalty or, at least, acquiescence. There is no suggestion in the sources that this was the case. Moreover, no equivalent arrangement existed for Maxentius, the son of Maximian.[212] Constantine's position has its own clear explanation. He was a mature man, holding a senior rank. He had served with Diocletian and Galerius in Egypt, Mesopotamia and on the Danube, but was no mere officer cadet, climbing the ranks of the service. He was an imperial bastard, who might reasonably expect responsibility and command.[213] Significantly, his active service was always in the immediate entourage of either Diocletian or Galerius. He never had an independent command: Constantine had entered Palestine in 295 with Diocletian;[214] had served then with Galerius in Armenia and Mesopotamia;[215] thence went to the Danube, again with Galerius;[216] and finally served with Diocletian as a tribune amongst the soldiery of the Nicomedian court.[217] It is, then, plausible to conclude that, if he were *obses* at all, it was against his own ambition, on the political principle of keeping one's friends close and one's potential enemies even closer.

The foundation of Diocletian's regime had been *concordia*, the harmonious and consensual obedience of princes to a single master. Diocletian was as aware, perhaps more so, of the importance of *concordia* as the basis of imperial unanimity as any of his contemporaries. Retirement without ensuring the continued *concordia* between the imperial colleagues would therefore have been pointless. Thus Diocletian sought to replicate the *concordia* of his own experience for his successors. The compromise between Galerius and Constantius was his arrangement, negotiated (no doubt) rather than demanded. It omitted the ineligible and the untrustworthy, and augmented the dynasty through a further adoption and betrothal.

The power struggle between Constantius and Galerius was polite, and resulted in an arrangement with which Constantius could live, but in which clearly Galerius was the winner. His nephew and his nominee were the Caesars, just as Diocletian's colleagues had all been his nominees. The identity of the new Caesars, then, does not reflect a political victory of Galerius over Diocletian, but of Galerius over Constantius. Galerius had been uniquely placed to take advantage of Diocletian's decision to retire. His consistent loyalty had borne its own fruit during the time of Diocletian's illness when for quite some time the senior emperor was incapacitated and certainly unable to rule.[218]

The direction of Diocletian's administration at this time can only have come from Galerius. Not only did Galerius thereby have the experience of running the administration for Diocletian, but the administration itself was centred in Nicomedia. To be sure, emperors were peripatetic, and their courts went with them, but the court of Diocletian, wherever it was, was the court of the senior emperor.[219] This was not a regional or subordinate court; it was vast and lavish, and the decisions made in its corridors affected the entire empire. Here was the *praefectus praetorio* of the senior emperor; the cream of the officer corps; the *a libellis* who drafted the laws which were posted over the entire empire; and, most importantly, but most subtly, the bureaucracy which had administered the empire for twenty years.

In transferring the focus of *concordia* from himself to Galerius, Diocletian's policy was moving in an unexpected direction. But it was one which Galerius could have argued with some strength. For his part, Constantius never gave anything other than reason to believe that he was an effective and loyal colleague. He was very much of the old school. He had been a *praeses* under Carus and, presumably, had supported Diocletian's coup.[220] He and Maximian were almost direct contemporaries, so much so that their sons were of an equivalent age.[221] He had been singled out for promotion by Maximian as *praefectus praetorio* and son-in-law. In this, Diocletian had acquiesced but essentially Constantius was under the imperial patronage of Maximian – a relationship which Maximian later sought to exploit and replicate with Constantine. Furthermore, as his policy towards the Christians indicates, he had firm ideas of his own which were not necessarily in harmony with those of Diocletian. Galerius' political victory in the matter of the appointment of the Caesars appears to be a consequence not merely of his own skills and self-advocacy, but also because he was one of the two possible successors upon whom Diocletian felt more that he could rely. Constantius could (and did) retain the notional rank of senior Augustus, while dynastic soldiers, whose loyalty was to Galerius, became Caesars. What Lactantius and Julian do allude to, however, is something inevitable at points of succession and that is the tussle for power amongst those closest to Diocletian. It is more than probable that, once Diocletian made his intention to retire clear, his junior colleagues both sought to inherit his mantle. The power struggle between Constantius and Galerius, and the solution ultimately arrived at, was moderated by Diocletian and confined to the imperial *domus*. It resulted in a kind of compromise between the two new Augusti, although one which favoured Galerius, who emerged after the abdications in an exceedingly strong position. Maxentius, the son of Maximian, and Constantine, Constantius' bastard, had not only been passed over, but had never been realistic contenders. Those raised to the purple were Galerius' men: Severus was described by the *Origo Constantini Imperatoris* as "base of morals and birth; a drunkard too and thus a friend of Galerius" (*ignobilis et moribus et natalibus, ebriosus et hoc Galerio amicus*).[222] Lactantius, significantly, echoes this tradition of Severus as an old drinking friend of Galerius, while adding the detail that he had faithfully fulfilled his duties as commander.[223] Daza was even closer to Galerius. By blood, he was Galerius' sister's son.[224] He took the name "Maximinus" at Galerius' request and was swiftly promoted through the ranks of the army: *statim scutarius, continuo protector, mox tribunus, postridie Caesar*.[225] The decision was made well in advance of the actual abdications: Severus had long been despatched to receive the purple from the hands of Maximian in Mediolanum.[226]

Galerius' political victory in 305 was both the result of his own efforts at self-promotion and the failure of Constantius to win Diocletian's trust. That does not mean that his efforts in self-promotion were marginal. While Lactantius' account of Galerius' bombastic cry "*quo usque Caesar*" is not necessarily credible,[227] there is a great deal implicit in Galerius' career of the good and faithful servant giving grounds for reward. He had performed his military tasks to satisfaction and accepted a subordinate role which sent him from the Nile to the Tigris to the Danube. In accepting the overall authority of Diocletian, he had been overruled on the matter of the Persian peace by his Augustus and had donated to him the laurels of his own victories.[228] Furthermore, he gave every indication that he was as dedicated to Diocletian's vision of the empire as Diocletian himself. He in fact risked war to ensure it, when he visited Maximian late in 304.[229] We know little of this meeting, and then only from Lactantius, but its point is said to have been simply to reiterate to a reluctant Maximian that retirement awaited him. If Maximian did not retire voluntarily, said Galerius, perhaps reminding the unwilling Augustus of the oath sworn in Rome, then he would be forced to. The origin of this conference may well have been the illness of Diocletian. Lactantius makes it clear that Diocletian fell into a coma on 13 December and was not seen in public until March the following year.[230] Galerius' visit to Maximian belongs to the period between Diocletian's arrival at Nicomedia and the following March. Quite possibly it belongs to the period when Diocletian was in a coma and not expected to recover. This might just have given Maximian hope that abdication might not in the end be necessary, and indeed that the job of Augustus *senior* might yet be his. Diocletian's death might nullify his oath, by removing the moral authority which constrained him, and allow him to succeed as the most senior emperor to the tasks of supreme rule.

Such a situation raised dangers for Galerius and, as far as the abdications were concerned, his interests and Diocletian's hopes coincided. Diocletian's death might mean that Galerius would (of necessity) have become an Augustus earlier than expected. In turn, this would have led to the unwelcome choice of loyalty to Maximian and the inevitable acceptance of Maxentius as his Caesar; or a refusal to accept the sovereignty of Maximian and the undertaking of a civil war to unseat him. It was with this second alternative that he threatened Maximian in 304. Maximian perhaps evaluated his position and consented to retire. He could have fought, but Galerius' position was strong. Not only was Galerius victor over Persia, but in all likelihood he also held the loyalty of the Danubian troops which he had been commanding since 299. Maximian had some support in Africa, where he had commanded with great success, and perhaps also in Spain.[231] For Gaul, Germany and Britain he needed the support of Constantius, who might either relish the prospect of himself becoming senior Augustus or drive a hard bargain with Maximian for support. Maximian was clever enough to realize when he was in a corner, and gave in.

Thus Galerius assured the passage of Diocletian's plans for the succession even while Diocletian was still Augustus. His mission to Maximian sealed the inevitability not merely of the abdications, but also of the successions.

Diocletian's subsequent recovery was fortuitous. Galerius' handling of the administration and the problem with Maximian vindicated Diocletian's choice of him as successor, at least to Diocletian's own satisfaction. Galerius had thereby won a major political victory over Constantius and Maximian by simply doing as he was told, and enforcing the will of Diocletian. It is significant that all of Galerius' acts as Caesar reflect exactly that same loyalty and obedience.

Diocletian's precarious health perhaps served slightly to delay the abdications. His presence was required at the ceremony, otherwise its validity and his intentions remained open to question. On 1 March he returned to public view, wasted and frail.[232] As he grew stronger, an auspicious day was found and preparations were made. The ceremony was held on the Kalends of May 305. Its martial flair was unmistakable. The army (in this case, Diocletian's guard and *comitatus*) gathered in assembly at Nicomedia and approved the changing of the emperors. Diocletian divested himself of his purple cloak, bestowed it upon Daza and, quietly and without fuss, mounted his carriage and began his journey to Split. It was Galerius' moment. Hailed by the army, endorsed by Diocletian and surrounded by loyalists, he tasted the fruits of a political victory over Constantius and years of loyal toil for Diocletian. Galerius was junior Augustus in name only. In reality, he had reached for and grasped the prize of supreme power in the Roman world.

Notes

1 Barnes, *NE*, pp. 255, 257.
2 While much of the legal work here was done for the emperor by the experts (see Corcoran, 2000: pp. 48–54), there is little doubt that an emperor like Diocletian would simply not affix his name to a rescript without knowing the basis for the decision he was about to make.
3 Diocletian's reforms are summarized and discussed by Jones (1964), pp. 42–68; for the date of the tax reform, *P. Cair. Isidor.* 1, see Barnes, *NE*, pp. 230–31, who suggests that the first application of the new tax structure might have been as early as 291; Corcoran (1996: p. 174f.), who prefers the date of 296/7, on the basis of dateable inscriptions of the Syrian *censitores*. It is worth quoting Corcoran (p. 176) here: "This surveying process provides good evidence for a tetrarchic measure being carried out effectively at a local level and shows that administrative system working at its detailed best." Barnes (*NE*, p. 225) dates the provincial reform to 293. This is a date of convenience, although with some support from numismatic evidence (see here Hendy, 1972: p. 75f.). The earliest attested *vicarii* in the new system dates to 298 (*Passio Marcelli*; *P. Oxy* 1469), and this led Seston (1946: pp. 334ff.), followed by Chastagnol (1960: p. 26), to date the reform to 297/8.
4 See Corcoran (2000), pp. 25–37; on the legal reasoning underpinning the codifications, see Digeser (2000), pp. 3–4.
5 Lact. *de mort. pers.* 7.8–8.7.
6 See Heck (1987); on Lactantius as polemicist, see Moreau (1954), pp. 208–28; Wlosok (1989), pp. 394–9; Leadbetter (1998); Digeser (2000), pp. 32–40.
7 Jerome (*Ep.* 58.10) said of Lactantius that his style was "a river of Ciceronian eloquence" (*fluvius eloquentiae Tullianae*).

8   Jerome, *de vir ill.* 80.1.
9   Corsaro (1978) and, most recently, Digeser (2000).
10 Lact. *de mort. pers.* 10.1–14.7
11 Barnes (1973), p. 30.
12 Kolb (1987: p. 138) argues that Lactantius would have been quite content deliberately to distort the facts to fit his purpose. Piganiol (1932: p. 48) depicts Lactantius as an uncritical propagandist for Constantine.
13 Jerome, *de vir. ill.* 80.
14 On the African tradition, see Heck (1987), p. 47.
15 Lact. *de mort. pers.* 1.7.
16 See Heck (1987); Leadbetter (1996), pp. 246–50.
17 Moreau (1954), pp. 44–51 and *passim* in his commentary from p. 187 onwards; Barnes (1981), *CE*, p. 13; Barnes (1972), pp. 29–46.
18 Stade (1926) was the first to put Lactantius aside, followed by a lengthy critical analysis by Gelzer (1937 [1963]). More recently, Kolb (1987) and Heck (1987), p. 221ff. have reached conclusions critical of Lactantius' accuracy.
19 Davies (1989), pp. 84–9.
20 Zos. 2.11.1; Aur. Vict. *de Caes.* 40.9.
21 *Contra* Lawlor, *Eusebiana* p. 242; on the whereabouts of Lactantius see Barnes (1973), p. 40.
22 For example, Trompf (1983), pp. 139–40, who suggests diagnoses for both Herod the Great and Maximin Daza. More to the point here, J.H. Smith (1976), p. 41, and Frend (1965), p. 121, venture diagnoses, Smith vaguely as "a multiple cancer", and Frend more specifically as "cancer of the bowels".
23 Africa (1982).
24 II Macc. 9.5a-7, 9–10.
25 *Ibid.*, 11; Acts 12.33; cf. Josephus, *Ant. Iud.* 19.8.2 on Herod Agrippa; on Judas, Matt. 27. 3–5; cf. Acts 1.8, Papias fr. 3.
26 Tert., *ad Scapulam* 3. Saturninus was struck blind, Herminianus was eaten by worms.
27 On Apion, Jos., *contra Ap.* 2.14. Apion died of an infection after a circumcision operation; for Catullus, see Jos., *Bell. Iud.* 7.11.4.
28 Africa (1982), p. 8; Jos., *Ant. Iud.* 12.9.1; cf. II Macc. 9. 5–10.
29 See Trompf (1983), pp. 139–40.
30 On the death of Diocletian, the *Ep. de Caes.* 37.9 records a melancholy suicide. Other sources record a natural death (see Moreau 1954: p. 420).
31 For the earliest expression of this argument, see Gelzer (1937 [1963]).
32 On Lactantius' cultural allegiance, see Corsaro (1978); Kolb (1987).
33 Galerius was certainly a large man and his size was emphasized in his own iconography and that of his later colleague, Licinius. See here R.R.R. Smith (1997). By way of contrast to Lactantius' depiction of Galerius' physical presence, the *Epitome de Caesaribus* (40.15) says of Galerius' appearance that he possessed "a fine form" (*pulcher corpore*).
34 As argued by Nicholson (1984), p. 261.
35 *Ep. de Caes.* 40.16.3.
36 Maximin Daza is described as '*semibarbarus*' (18.13), and Maximian (Herculius) as the possessor of a '*barbarem libidinem*' (38.3).
37 See Moreau (1954), pp. 55–7. For Tertullian's critique of Pliny *Ep.* 10. 96–7, see Tert., *Apol.*2.
38 For an excellent critique of an aspect of Lactantius' testimony, see Mackay (1999).
39 Aur. Vict. *de Caes.* 42.19.
40 E.g.: Altendorf, s.v. "Galerius" *RAC* 8. 787; Ensslin, s.v. "Maximianus (Galerius)" *RE* XIV, 2523; Barnes, *CE*, p. 18f.; Frend (1965), p. 489; *CAH* XII, p. 338 (N.H. Baynes), p. 668 (H. Mattingly). Grégoire (1964) is the most passionate, at points likening

Galerius to Hitler, Diocletian to Hindenburg and the fire at Nicomedia is called a *Reichstagsbrand* (p. 78f.); Barnes (1973), pp. 29–46; Barnes, pp 18–21. But see also Kolb (1987), p. 138, who has been less generous, arguing that Lactantius would have been quite content deliberately to distort the facts to fit his purpose. For his part, Piganiol (1932: p. 48) merely says that Lactantius uncritically repeated what he heard at the court of Constantine.

41 Gelzer (1937), p. 378.
42 Stade (1926); Gelzer (1937 [1963]).
43 Davies (1989) *contra* Frend (1965b); Molthagen (1975). Davies (1989: p. 66 n. 2) provides a useful summary of the scholarship on this point. He omits Sordi (1986), pp. 122–31; Lane Fox (1986), pp. 592–5; see also Portmann (1990).
44 Digeser (2000), pp. 2–9.
45 Lact. *de mort. pers.* 10.1.
46 See L'Orange (1938), pp. 67–8.
47 *AE* 1914, 249 (dated between 286 and 293).
48 See Brenk (1968).
49 Malalas, 12.307.
50 *Pan. Lat.* 3.6.1–2.
51 Libanius, *Oratio* 4. Libanius was no admirer of Diocletian (see *Oratio* 19.45). For another discussion of the religiosity of imperial ideology, see Digeser (2000), p. 27ff.
52 Digeser (2000), p. 27ff.; Kolb (1988), pp. 23–7.
53 Jupiter and Hercules, as principles rather than specific manifestations (see Liebeschuetz, 1981: pp. 392–5), are consistently described as *comites* of the Augusti. (For the significance of this, see Nock (1947), or the more exuberant view of Nicholson (1984) and (1984B)).
54 On this duty see Millar (1977), pp. 465–77; Corcoran (2000), pp. 43–62.
55 *EMP praef.* 7.
56 *Mos. et Rom. collatio* (Th. Mommsen, ed.), VI.4.1.
57 *Ibid.*
58 *Ibid.*, XV.III.2.
59 Marasovic (1982), 106–16.
60 Wilkes (1986), pp. 45–8.
61 Marasovic (1982), pp. 120–4; Wilkes (1986), p. 48; however, Mannell (1995) identifies the temple with the barrel-vaulted coffered ceiling as dedicated to Jupiter and the two round buildings (*monopteroi*) as ancillary to it, housing images of Diocletian and Maximian.
62 See especially Frend (1965), pp. 477–91; Barnes, *CE*, Chapter II; but see Davies (1989), pp. 92–4.
63 Notably in the development of the theology of a divine *comes* for the emperor. Such *comites* variously included Hercules (Commodus and Maximian), Sol Invictus (Gallienus, Probus and possibly Aurelian) and Sarapis (Gallienus). See Nock (1947).
64 See Duthoy (1969), pp. 115–18.
65 See Halsberghe (1972), pp. 131–55.
66 See MacMullen (1981), pp. 1–5; Fowden (1988), p. 176f.
67 Eunapius, *Vit. Soph.* 456–8.
68 Alan Cameron (1967), p. 384; cf. Barnes (1973B), Barnes (1976A) and Croke (1984); Digeser (1998: pp. 134) argues that Porphyry could have composed *Against the Christians* at any time between 270 and 295. See also Digeser (2000), p. 96.
69 For a discussion and bibliography, see Kaiser (1975), pp. 305–17.
70 Augustine, *de Civ. dei*, 10.9–11.
71 Aquilinus; see Eunapius *Vit. Soph.* 457; Porphyry, *Life of Plotinus* 16.
72 Satirized by Lucian as "Alexander the False Prophet". By various chicaneries, Alexander deceived the entire town of Abonoteichos into thinking him an incarnation of

Asclepius. Influential Romans were also impressed, and the cult of Glycon which he founded flourished for a time (see A. Stein, 1925 and also Lane Fox, 1986: pp. 243–50).

73 Augustine, *de Civ. dei,* 10.9–11.
74 *P. Oxy.* 1477; see the translation and discussion by Lee (2000), pp. 28–30.
75 MacMullen (1981), pp. 49–62; Brown (1978).
76 Fowden (1993), pp. 38–43.
77 On Hierocles, see *PLRE* I, p. 432, no.4; Barnes (1976A); Judge (1983); on the date, see Croke (1984), pp. 4–5; Digeser (2000), p. 5.
78 Eunapius, *Vit. Soph.* 457.
79 See Labriolle (1962), pp. 233–9; Wilcken (1984), pp. 136–7.
80 Fragment in Augustine, *de Civ. dei* 19.23.
81 Allies of Maximin Daza, executed in 313 at the orders of Licinius (Eus., *HE* 9.11). We know something of Theotecnus' activities through the testimony of Eusebius (*HE* 9.1–4) and of Culcianus who was the Prefect of Egypt who tried Phileas (*Actae Phileae et Philoromi*). He was appointed before the commencement of the Great Persecution (*P. Oxy.* 71.2). We only know of Peucetius from a bare reference in Eusebius (see also *PLRE* I, p. 692).
82 Seston (1946: p. 156) argues that Diocletian's primary concern was to eliminate the Manichaeans as agents of Persian influence, and thus the Edict ought to be dated to the time of the siege of Alexandria, when Rome and Persia were at war.
83 Lact. *de mort. pers.* 12.3.
84 *P. Oxy.* 2673, see Judge (1980), p. 2.
85 Eus., *HE* 7.5. 1–2.
86 *Ibid.,* 8.1.7.; see Trompf (1983), pp. 139–40.
87 Jerome, *Chron.* p. 227 (Helm). The actual marginal date is 299 (the sixteenth year of Diocletian), but it is placed chronologically between Galerius' two Persian campaigns, i.e. in the course of 297.
88 Lact. *de mort. pers.* 10.1–4.
89 *Ibid.,* 10.4.
90 Jerome, *Chron.* p. 227 (Helm); also *PLRE* I, p. 955.
91 *Acta Maximiliani,* 2.9 (Musurillo 1972: p. 246f.).
92 *AE* (1981) 777; Drew-Bear (1981).
93 Drew-Bear (1981), p. 113f.
94 As Tomlin (1998: p. 24) speculates.
95 Eus., *HE* 8.4.3.
96 Tert., *Apol.* 37.4–5.
97 For discussion here, see Helgeland (1979); Tomlin (1998), pp. 21–5.
98 On *protectores*, see Grosse (1975), pp. 13–15; Jürgen Deininger, *RE* S.band XI, 1115–17; Jones (1964), Vol. II, p. 636ff.
99 Constantine had probably served in the army of Galerius, perhaps as *protector* (see Barnes, 1976: p. 184). Barnes considers that Constantine served as a tribune. This is possible. Certainly another future emperor, Maximin Daza, saw service as a *protector* (Lact. *de mort. pers.* 19.6). By 305, Constantine was a *tribunus primi ordinis* (Lact. *de mort. pers.* 18.10). A number of third-century military martyrdoms of credible quality also attest Christians achieving military rank. In the *Acta Marini,* for example (Eus. *HE* 7.15; Musurillo, 1972: pp. 240–3), Marinus is denounced as a Christian by colleagues jealous of his nomination to the centurionate. The support of peers was evidently crucial for such a promotion (see here Speidel, 1992).
100 Eus. *HE* 8.1.4 (Dorotheus and Gorgonius); 8.6.1–5 (Dorotheus, Peter and Gorgonius).
101 *Ibid.,* 8.1.3.
102 Lact. *de mort. pers.* 10.1. Creed (1984: p. 91) argues on the basis of the known movements of the emperors and from the implied evidence of *Divine Institutes* 4. 27. 4–5, that both Diocletian and Galerius were present and that the momentous sacrifice took place

in 299/300. This cannot be the case since by that time Galerius had departed for the Danubian provinces (see Chapter 3).

103 Jer., *Chron.* p. 227 (Helm).

104 Lactantius claims that members of the emperor's household were also vetted at this time for religious affiliation (*de mort. pers.* 10.4 *universos qui erant in palatio*). Such a screening can only have been at the highest levels, since middle-ranking bureaucrats like Dorotheus were not affected. Dorotheus superintended the imperial dye-works at Tyre (Eus. *HE* 8.1.4), but he, along with Gorgonius and Peter were spared until 303, at which time the screening was so thorough that even imperial consorts were obliged to sacrifice (Lact. *de mort. pers.* 15.1).

105 Jerome (*Chron.*: p. 227) simply calls him *magister militiae*, an office otherwise unattested at this time. Eusebius calls him "a stratopedarck" (Eus. *HE* 8.4.3), the Latin equivalent of which, before Diocletian was *praefectus castrorum* and later, *magister militum* (see Mason, 1974: p. 13). It may also be used for the Latin *dux* (Eus. *de Mart. Pal.* (S), 13. 1–3). This vagueness surely results from uncertainty as to his actual title. Barnes (*NE*, p. 136 n. 62) considers that Veturius was Galerius' Praetorian Prefect, but, as has since been shown, Galerius did not have one.

106 Eus. *HE* 8.4.

107 On the potential autonomy of the Christians, see Digeser (2000), p. 51f., a point made clear by Galerius himself in the Edict of Toleration (Lact. *de mort. pers.* 34.2: "*ut non illa veterum instituta sequerentur, quae forsitan primum parentes eorundem constituerant, sed pro arbitrio suo atque ut isdem erat libitum, ita sibimet leges facerent quas oservarent, et per diversa varios populos congregarent*" ("so that they did not follow those principles of the ancients, which perhaps their very own ancestors had instituted, but were following their own judgement and desire, and were inventing for themselves the laws they were to keep, and were collecting together different groups of people in a number of locations"). See also *ibid.*, p. 55f.

108 Barnes (1973), pp. 29–46.

109 Lact. *de mort. pers.* 11.3.

110 Diocletian had prevailed upon Maximian to swear an oath in his presence in the Temple of Capitoline Jupiter that he would abdicate (*Pan. Lat.* 6.15.6). This surely means that he intended to abdicate before he went to Rome. On Maximian's oath, see Nixon (1981); Kolb (1987), pp. 143–50, *contra* Thomas (1973).

111 See Barnes, *NE*, p. 51f.

112 Culcianus was in office on 6 June 301 (*P. Oxy.* 3304). On Culcianus' hostility to Christianity, see Eus. *HE* 9.11.4. He was subsequently executed on the orders of Licinius.

113 Lact. *de mort. pers.* 16.4, describes him as *ex vicario.*

114 Lact. *Institutiones Divinae*, 5.2.12, notes an author of two books against the Christians who was *e numero iudicum et qui auctor in primis faciendae persecutionis fuit.* Elsewhere, he refers to Hierocles as *auctor et consiliarius* (*de mort. pers.* 16.4). On Hierocles, see Barnes (1976A). It is worth noting here that Hierocles evidently composed the *Philalethes* well in advance of the events of 302/3, since Eusebius had sufficient time to compose a rebuttal of it that contains no mention either of the Persecution or Hierocles' role as persecutor (*ibid.*, p. 242). Most recently on Hierocles, see Digeser (2000), pp. 3–9.

115 As surely demonstrated by the size and conspicuousness of its wooden cathedral in Nicomedia (Lact. *de mort. pers.* 12.3).

116 As, for example, Davies (1989: pp. 66–94) argues.

117 On this gathering, see Amarelli (1983), pp, 112–15; Corcoran (1996), pp. 260–2; on the *consilium* under Diocletian, see Crook (1955), pp. 96–103.

118 Lactantius mentions a second pagan philosopher active in Nicomedia in the winter of 302/3 (*Institutiones Divinae*, 5.2.3–4). He draws a pen portrait in such extravagant terms that some have been reluctant to identify this figure with Porphyry (see, for example,

Barnes (1973B: pp. 437–9), although he since seems to have conceded the point in Barnes (1991 p. 240). Nevertheless, the weight of scholarship and the terms of Lactantius' sneering reference to "the priest of philosophy" have led many, including the present writer, to put the Lactantian polemic aside and identify Porphyry as the man defamed in this passage. See Wilcken (1984), p. 134f.; Digeser (1998), pp. 130–1, and (2000), pp. 93–102.

119 Lactantius notes, *inter alia*, that his anonymous philosopher dined in the *palatium* (*Institutiones Divinae*, 5.2.3).
120 On the date of composition of *Philosophy from Oracles*, see Digeser (1998), p. 134ff.
121 Lact. *de mort. pers.* 11.7; Eusebius, *Vita Constantini*, 2.50; Fontenrose (1998), pp. 206–8. Fontenrose is sceptical of Henri Grégoire's restoration of an inscription as the oracular response (Grégoire, 1913 and 1939B; cf. Baynes, *CAH* XII, p. 665, n. 3.). Cameron and Hall (1999: p. 245) misidentify the oracle referred to in the text as that of Delphi.
122 Lact. *de mort. pers.* 35.4
123 Lact. *de mort. pers.* 12.1; Scullard (1981), pp. 79–80.
124 Scullard (1981), pp. 79–80.
125 *CIL* XI. 351.
126 Ste Croix (1954), p. 75f.; Corcoran (2000), pp. 179–81.
127 Lact. *de mort. pers.* 34.3.
128 *Ibid.*, 13. 2–3; Eus. *HE* 8.5
129 This included the imperial consorts Prisca and Valeria. Lactantius (*de mort. pers.* 15.1) states that Diocletian obliged both of them to incur pollution by performing an act of sacrifice. This should not be taken to mean, as some have concluded, that both women were Christians. Barnes (*CE*, p. 19), for example, considers that the imperial ladies were at least "sympathetic" to Christianity on the basis of this evidence. Grégoire (1964: p. 78) goes even further. The evidence does not say this. To Lactantius, the act of sacrifice was pollution and idolatry, honouring demons who aped the true godhead.
130 Lact. *de mort. pers.* 14. 2–7.
131 Eus. *HE* 8.6.6.
132 Constantine, *Oratio ad Sanctos* 25.
133 Tac. *Ann.* 15. 38–40.
134 As argued by J. Rougé (1964); see also Davies (1989), p. 80. Ogilvie (1978: pp. 41–4, esp. p. 43) argues that Lactantius was unaware of Tacitus since he made no direct reference to his work, but this in itself means little. Lactantius must have read and known the work of narrative historians, but he only ever directly refers to Livy and Sallust at any length. Moreover, in the *de mortibus persecutorum* he never refers to his sources at all.
135 Eus. *HE* 8.6.6.
136 *Ibid.*, 8.6. 2–5; Grégoire (1964), p. 78.
137 Eusebius refers obliquely to this revolt (*HE* 8.6.8). More detail is furnished by Libanius (*Or.* 20.17; 19.45 for the name of Eugenius).
138 Lib. *Or.* 19.45.
139 Libanius' own grandfather was executed as a consequence of this revolt (*Or.* 19.45). Grandsons are more inclined to interpret such actions as imperial savagery rather than family complicity.
140 Eus. *HE* 8.6.8.
141 Melitene is one of the more remote districts of the empire. The Edicts did not reach Caesarea Palestina until a week after their promulgation in Nicomedia on 23 February (Eus. *HE* 8.2.4). On the martyrs of Melitene, see Frend (1965), pp. 442, 526 n. 109.
142 Tiridates, the King of Armenia, was a convert to Christianity, perhaps as early as 270, during his exile (Frend 1965: p. 123).
143 For the date, see Ste Croix (1954), p. 76.

144 Baynes (1924), pp. 189–93; *CAH* XII, p. 667f.; cf. Ste Croix (1954), p. 108.
145 Eus. *de Mart. Pal.* (L) 1.5b.
146 Ste Croix (1954), p. 77.
147 This view has been criticized by Ste Croix (1954) and Davies (1989: p. 74f.), who both argue from the evidence of Diocletian's known activities in 304 that he was hale at the time of the issue of the Edict, Lact. *de mort. pers.* 17 3–4. It is worth noting two further points: the silence of the polemical Lactantius; and the fact that Diocletian's illness only became critical after he returned to Nicomedia in the second half of 304.
148 Such would be the implication of Lact. *de mort. pers.* 15.7.
149 E.g.: Altendorf, s.v. "Galerius" *RAC* 8.787; Ensslin, s.v. "Maximianus (Galerius)" *RE* XIV, 2523; Barnes, *CE*, p. 18f.; Frend (1965), p. 489; *CAH* XII, p. 338 (N.H. Baynes), p. 668 (H. Mattingly). Grégoire (1964: p. 78f.) is the most passionate, at points likening Galerius to Hitler, Diocletian to Hindenburg and the fire at Nicomedia is called a *Reichstagsbrand*.
150 A full summary of the testimony of antiquity is given by Kolb (1987), pp. 128–31. Lactantius' version can be found at *de mort. pers.* 18–19. Modern scholars who substantially accept the Lactantian version include Barnes (1981: *CE*, p. 25f.), Seeck (1897: pp. 35–41) and G.S.R. Thomas (1973: 229–47).
151 Constantine, *Oratio ad Sanctos*, 25.1; a tradition picked up by Zonaras (12.33) and ascribed by him to Eusebius.
152 Julian, *Caesares* 315 B; Eutropius 9.27.1.
153 Lact. *de mort. pers.* 16–17.
154 Eus., *H.E.* 8.13.11, although if he is going to choose anything, it will be illness.
155 Gibbon (1896), p. 389.
156 Burckhardt (1949), p. 259.
157 Baynes, *CAH* XII, p. 668; Baynes (1924), pp. 189–94.
158 Lietzmann (1953), p. 67; Jones (1948: pp. 56–7) flirts with Lactantius, but settles on a kind of scepticism.
159 Ensslin, s.v. 'Diocletianus' *RE* VIIa 2489f.; also Seston, s.v. 'Diocletianus', *RAC* 3, 1044; Mattingly, *CAH* XII, 340f., a view followed by Williams (1985: p. 189f.) who blames Diocletian's long and severe illness for his decision.
160 Grégoire (1964), pp. 78–80.
161 For the date, Lact. *de mort. pers.* 19.1; for the cabbages, *Ep. de Caes.* 39.6.
162 Lact. *de mort. pers.* 18.6.
163 *Ibid.*, 18.
164 Eus. *Vit. Const.* 1.18.
165 E.g., the unfocused narrative of the *Origo Constantini* 2.2–3.5.
166 Lact. *de mort. pers.*17.1; Eus. *Mart. Pal.* 1.5.
167 *ILS* 640 (= *CIL* VI. 1130).
168 *Pan. Lat.* 7. 15. 4–6; 6.9.2.
169 Lact. *de mort. pers.*17.4. He was only just healthy enough to dedicate a circus on 24 November 304.
170 *Ibid.*, 17.8.
171 *Ibid.*, 19.6.
172 *Ibid.*, 18.12; *Origo Constantini Imperatoris*, 3.5, 4.9; Eutr. 10.9.1; Aur. Vict. *de Caes.* 40.1; *Ep. de Caes.* 40.1; Zos. 2.8.1; on the location of Maximian's retirement, Eutr. 9.27.2, 10.2.3, although Lactantius suggests Campania (*de mort. pers.* 26.7).
173 See Barnes, *NE*, p. 46.
174 On the age of Nerva at his accession, see Dio. 68.4.2, Eutr. 8.1.2; for Pertinax, see Eutr. 8.16, *SHA, Vit. Pert.* 36; for Tacitus, see Zonaras 12.28.
175 Augustus was 75 when he died (Suet. *Div. Aug.* 100.1); Tiberius was even older (Suet. *Vit. Tib.* 73.1). Vespasian came to power at the age of 58 and died aged 69 (Suet. *Div.*

Vesp. 24). Antoninus Pius died at the age of 69 (*SHA, Vit. Ant.* 12.4) and Septimius Severus at 65 (Dio [Xiphilinus], 76.15.2–4).

176 *Pan Lat.,* 7.15.4–6; 6.9.2. The date is clearly November 303. Diocletian was in Ravenna in January 304 to commence his consulship (Lact. *de mort. pers.* 17.3) and fell ill some time later (*Ibid.,* 17. 4–9). For a summary of the historiography on the question of Maximian's oath, see Kolb (1987), pp. 128–31. Barnes (1996: pp. 544–6) suggests that all four met before the *vicennalia* while en route to Rome but Galerius was subsequently called away by a military emergency, and did not come to Rome for the celebrations.

177 Lact. *de mort. pers.* 17. 5–19 makes it clear that the crisis of Diocletian's illness occurred between November 304 and March 305. He must have definitely been on the mend to preside at a ceremony on 1 May 305, perhaps almost fully recovered.

178 Maximian thus added his contribution (the *Quinquegentiani*) to the tetrarchic formula of the *KG* (Aur. Vict. *de Caes.* 37.22; Eutr. 9.22). See also *Pan. Lat.* 5.5.2; *ILS* 645 (fragmentary); *RIC* VI 422–26; Pasqualini (1979), pp. 64–9.

179 Lact. *de mort. pers.* 8.4.

180 *Ibid.,* 18; see, for a full discussion, Kolb (1987), pp. 131–9.

181 Lact. *de mort. pers.* 20.3–5.

182 *Ibid.* 18.1. For an interesting interpretation of this meeting, see Baynes (1924).

183 Lact. *de mort. pers.* 20.2.

184 *Pan. Lat.* 7.7.1; *Origo Constantini Imperatoris* 4; Barnes, *NE,* p. 61.

185 *Origo Constantini Imperatoris,* 4.

186 See chapter on "Galerius Augustus", pp. 236–41.

187 Lact. *de mort. pers.* 20.4.

188 See Bulic and Karaman (1929); more recently Marasovic (1982); Wilkes (1986); McNally (1989); Marasovic and Marasovic (1994); McNally (1994); also Barnes (1996), p. 551f. A subsequent study also suggests that this was a working villa. See Belmaric (2004).

189 On the palaces in "tetrarchic capitals", see Millar (1992), pp. 41–53; on a tetrarchic *palatium* in Upper Egypt, see Wareth and Zignani (1992).

190 Lact. *de mort. pers.* 19.6.

191 On the mausoleum, see Wilkes (1986); McNally (1994), p. 109f.; Mannell (1995), p. 235f.; on the dome, see Niksic (2004).

192 See Kolb (1987), pp. 63–7. Kolb quite rightly points out that the motives for the use of the names were soon superseded by events. On the religious significance of the names, see Nock (1947), pp. 102–16; Seston (1946), pp. 211–30; *Pan. Lat.* 4.41; 9.8.3 (addressing Constantius as *Herculius Caesar*). For an idiosyncratic view on this question, see Mattingly (1952).

193 Baynes, *JRS,* 25 (1935), p. 84; *Pan. Lat.* 4.9.2; 2.11.6 (*Iove rectore caeli et Hercule pacatore terrarum*); Kolb (1987), pp. 88–114.

194 *Pan. Lat.* 6 (7) 15.4–6; Aur. Vict. *Caes.* 39.48; Eutr. 9.27; Barnes (1996), pp. 544–6.

195 Lact. *de mort. pers.* 11.3.

196 There is some suggestion (Mannell, 1995: p. 235) that construction of the palace at Split might have commenced as early as 295.

197 Lact. *de mort. pers.* 18. 12–15, a view echoed by Barnes (1996) and critiqued by Mackay (1999).

198 Julian, *Caesares* 315, A–C. The Maximian might not be Galerius, of course, but since Maximian Herculius was Julian's grandfather, the identification of this figure with Galerius is more probable.

199 Leadbetter (1998A), pp. 74–85.

200 Mackay (1999), pp. 198–209.

201 Galerius' daughter was married to the brother of Constantius' wife. This is hardly *propinquitas,* although doubtless *adfinitas.*

202 Severus' imperial nomenclature was "Flavius Valerius Severus" indicating his adoption by Constantius (Flavius Valerius Constantius). *PLRE* I, p. 837, no. 30; Kienast (1996), p. 290.
203 Lact. *de mort. pers.* 18. 12–15.
204 On the date of the birth of Valerius Romulus, see *ILS* 666/7 (= *CIL* XIV 2825, 2826, found near Rome on the *via Labicana*) which attests Maxentius as still *clarissimus* in the lifetime of his son. Maxentius had been eulogized as his father's successor when a boy (*Pan. Lat.* 2.14.1).
205 Lact. *de mort pers.* 18.10.
206 *ILS* 667, 671; See Chapter 6, pp. 177–179.
207 Lactantius speaks of Maximian's policies in this regard (*de mort pers.* 6.6). Even if this were put down to rhetorical exaggeration, there must have been many imperial estates in Italy, given centuries of confiscation. One could easily have been set aside as Maximian's retirement palace.
208 On Constantius' earlier career, see the summary in Barnes, *NE*, p. 41f.
209 Lact. *de mort pers.* 18.10. The rank is otherwise unknown, and the reality may be that he was a tribune of the *protectores*, as Maximinus was. See Mackay (1999).
210 *Pan. Lat.* 6.6.2; on the marriage (about which there has been some question), see Barnes, *NE*, p. 42f. Ancient writers are not unanimous. Some writers call Minervina a concubine (*Ep. de Caes.* 41.4; Zos. 2.20.2; both are following a tradition which is hostile to Constantine) and Zonaras 13.2. Barnes argues that the contemporary evidence of the panegyric is sufficiently decisive evidence. This is not necessarily so; the *stilus maior* of the panegyrists did not often permit a spade to be called by its proper name (see S. McCormack, 1975: pp. 159–66).
211 *Origo.*, 2.
212 Maxentius lived in Rome, well within reach of his father, but not of Diocletian or Galerius (*ILS* 666/7).
213 Eus. *VC* 1.19; see Barnes, *NE*, pp. 39–42; Baynes (1929), p. 7; Piganiol (1932), pp. 36–42; MacMullen (1969), p. 21f.; Leadbetter (1998), pp. 74–85.
214 Eus. *VC* 1.19.
215 *Origo* 2; *Oratio Constantini ad Sanctos*, 16.2; Barnes, *NE*, p. 41f.
216 *Origo* 3.
217 Lact. *de mort pers.* 18.10; 19.1.
218 As is clear from Lactantius' account (*de mort pers.* 17.4–9) at one point, Diocletian's death was rumoured. Clearly much of his work was in other hands. Galerius' presence from the end of the year makes it clear whose they were.
219 See Millar (1977), pp. 40–53; Corcoran (2004), p. 70.
220 *Origo* 2; *PLRE* I, p. 227 n.12. The *SHA*, *Vit. Car.* 17.6 dates his governorship (of Dalmatia) to the reign of Carinus. If so, his support (either active or passive) will have been critical in the civil war of 285 in which Diocletian emerged as victor.
221 On the best dating, that of Barnes (*NE*, p. 78), Maxentius was born *ca.* 284/5 and Constantine perhaps ten years earlier (*Ibid.*, p. 39ff.).
222 *Origo* 4.
223 Lact. *de mort pers.* 12.12.
224 *Ibid.*, 18.13–14; *Ep. de Caes.* 40.1, 40.19; Zos. 2.8.1; Mackay (1999).
225 Lact. *de mort pers.* 19.6.
226 Lactantius (*de mort pers.* 18.2) states that this was a *fait accompli* on the part of Galerius. If Lactantius' peculiar biases are set aside, it is clear nevertheless that the stage management involved in two identical ceremonies in geographically distant places implies the selection of Severus well before 1 May. The very complexity of this business is well illustrated by Lactantius' peculiar claim of Galerius' appointment of Severus without Diocletian's knowledge.

227 Lact. *de mort pers.* 9.8.
228 On the peace negotiations, see Pet. Patr., fr. 14. It is Diocletian who is remembered for celebrating the triumph over the Persians: Eutr. 9.27.2; Zonaras 12.32.15.
229 Lact. *de mort pers.* 18.1. Barnes (1994) now rejects this visit, preferring to insert a conference of all four emperors early in 303 in northern Italy.
230 Lact. *de mort pers.* 17.8.
231 On a possible campaign by Maximian in Spain, see *P. Argent.* 480.1 *verso.* 3; Barnes, *NE*, p. 59; *IGRR* I 1291.
232 Lact. *de mort pers.* 17.8.

5

CONSTANTIUS AUGUSTUS

The abdications of Diocletian and Maximian ended their formal tenure of power, but not their influence over events. Diocletian was determined and disciplined in his desire to make his abdication work and leave the empire in the hands of successors whom he had selected, promoted and trained for the task. By contrast, Maximian chafed at his retirement, perhaps resentful that the reward for his loyalty and service had not been promotion but relegation. There was also an unresolved dynastic problem. When Severus had been nominated as Constantius' Caesar, he had also been adopted into the Flavian/Herculian branch of the dynasty. When that occurred, he joined a large family: his bastard brother Constantine, and the six legitimate children of Constantius and Theodora. The challenge for both Constantius and Galerius was to sort through this clutter of imperial aspirants, including Galerius' own bastard, Candidianus, as well as his new son, Maximinus. It was precisely this challenge which they not only failed to meet, but actually declined to address. The source of that refusal lay in the relationship between Constantius and Galerius. Athough Diocletian had selected both of these men, neither of them had selected each another. That led to a quite different personal and political relationship between the new rulers of the empire from that which had pertained between Diocletian and Maximian. All of the sources – both laudatory and hostile – concur on the remarkable unity between Diocletian and Maximian. That quality was entirely lacking in the new imperial dynamic. While there is no substantive evidence of real hostility between the two new Augusti, there was certainly none of the warmth or depth of trust which had existed between their respective fathers.

Our image of Constantius as ruler is, moreover, largely shaped by a Christian hagiographical tradition which prefers to portray him as an invalid, whose principal historical mission was to survive long enough to proclaim Constantine as his successor. This can be found most clearly in the pages of Lactantius' *de mortibus persecutorum* in which it is claimed that, at the time of the abdications, Constantius was ill and not expected to live long.[1] This is an image which has been taken up by some contemporary scholars.

T.D.Barnes, who has long argued for Lactantius' essential reliability on matters both of fact and interpretation, notes in *Constantine and Eusebius*:

> Constantius received Spain to add to Gaul and Britain; Galerius added Asia Minor to the Balkans and Greece; Severus was assigned Italy and Africa, and perhaps a part of Pannonia; Maximinus got the large diocese of Oriens ... Beyond the Alps, Constantius was supreme for the present. But illness and age (he was fifty-five) rendered an immediate decease probable. Galerius then hoped to spread his authority over the entire empire.[2]

This statement or its type is not unusual.[3] It reflects a view of the succession to Diocletian which necessarily sees Galerius as largely in control both because of the dynastic dispositions and the feebleness of his colleague.[4] Such a view is both propagandistic and erroneous. It accepts the fact, embarrassing to Constantine, that his father had not insisted upon his nomination in 305. It also asserts, incorrectly, that Constantius was a mild man, hampered by poor health and intimidated by the success of his colleague into passively awaiting his inevitable demise.

There is something more than faintly incredible in Lactantius' picture of a moribund emperor surrendering power to a junior colleague. Given the nature of events as they turned out, it must be concluded that Constantius had a far more active role than has been supposed. While it might be difficult to draw a detailed picture of the rule of Constantius it is, nevertheless, clear that he was not afraid of asserting himself. To what extent, then, did he actually exercise executive power over the empire? At the time of his promotion to Augustus, he was still actively leading armies in the field.

In 305 he was apparently continuing measures to secure the pacification of trans-Rhenish German tribes.[5] There had evidently been instability on the Rhine frontier for some years and Constantius had taken on the task of returning a measure of security to the vulnerable Gallic provinces.[6] Every year between 300/01 and 304, he had taken the title *Germanicus Maximus*, in the same way that Galerius had taken the title *Carpicus Maximus*. Extant panegyrics celebrate the martial achievements of Constantius. Not only did he save Britain from the piratical Carausius, but he also achieved a series of less spectacular but more significant victories in Gaul. The panegyric to Constantine of 310 dwells considerably upon these achievements of Constantius.[7] According to the panegyrist there was no small danger to the Gallic provinces, and Constantius proved his mettle, not merely by his tenacious campaigning, but also by his style of personal bravery. In the campaign in the territory of the Lingones, Constantius was near enough to the forefront of the action to sustain a wound.[8] While there is always a certainty of hagiography when looking at source material dealing with Constantius, the campaigns of the early fourth century are well enough attested to take them firmly out of the realm of fantasy. A panegyrist could scarcely fabricate the story of a wound. Indeed, the panegyrist paints a picture of a vigorous and assertive warrior, summoned by the gods for one last campaign in Britain before his final journey to the gathering of the gods. While this image is in itself tainted by the panegyrist's task, it directly contradicts Lactantius' image of an enfeebled and moribund ruler.[9]

In 305, Constantius changed his focus from the Rhine theatre to a campaign in northern Britain. Significantly, Constantius did not entrust this task to his Caesar, Severus, but preferred to undertake it himself.[10] This is a particularly interesting observation since one might expect an emperor who was not in the best of health to leave such a matter to a deputy. This is precisely the approach which Diocletian had taken when he was ill. Rather than seek to lead the troops himself when the need had arisen for an urgent military response on the Danube, he had sent Galerius. Constantius also received his son Constantine, who had come to him from the court of Galerius. There is a great deal of mythology about this event since it was Constantine's translation from the court of Galerius to that of his father that enabled him to claim power upon Constantius' death. Sources hostile to Galerius paint a picture of Constantius repeatedly summoning his son only to meet a wall of refusal from Galerius. Instead, Galerius deliberately sends Constantine into situations of great danger, which he not only survives, but earns great distinction. Ultimately Galerius can stall no longer and gives his permission. Constantine leaves at once, before the order can be rescinded, and gallops furiously across the breadth of the empire, hindering pursuit by slaying the post-horses as he goes. He arrives either as his father is about to depart for Britain (*Origo Constantini Imperatoris*) or dying (Lactantius).[11] The reason for Constantine's journey is a matter for speculation. One reason can be discarded: that his father, anticipating imminent death, sent for him.[12] Constantius may well have preferred to keep Constantine at a distance: the elder son represented a threat to the dynastic expectations of his younger brothers. It is more likely that Constantine took action on his own behalf.[13] The stories about his flight appear in sources which, for various reasons, always seek a positive construction for Constantine's actions. His later propaganda might well have needed to find an explanation for the apparent desertion of his post. It will have been with mixed feelings that Constantius welcomed his eldest son, an able senior officer, but an ambitious one also.

The British campaign of 305/6 was not a departure from previous policy, but instead marked a continuation of Diocletian's renovation of the empire's frontiers. It was, perhaps, intended to be the final settlement of the British frontier — a seal of some years' feverish activity in the British provinces following the defeat of Allectus. Certainly the recovery of the island for Rome reversed some evident neglect of the defence infrastructure in the north. The fort at Birdoswald on Hadrian's Wall, for example, renovated at this time, had been in such a bad state of repair that the *praetorium* was covered with earth.[14] There is a great deal of circumstantial archaeological evidence of more violent activity elsewhere. It has been well suggested that this was the result of cross-border raids on a significant scale as a result of the stripping of garrison units in the north by Allectus.[15] This conclusion has drawn its critics, but the strength of the evidence is considerable.[16]

It seems plain that the frontier of Roman Britain underwent the same kind of renovation as other frontiers during the time of Diocletian. The evidence of both neglect and invasion demonstrates the need for such a renewal to have occurred and the archaeology reveals something of the actual occurrence. Most notably, Eboracum was extensively refortified, and there is evidence for a great deal of similar work elsewhere in the British provinces.[17] This work did not begin with the accession of Constantius Augustus. Building dedications indicate dates between 296 and 305, and therefore belong firmly to the policy of imperial renewal directed by Diocletian. Constantius nevertheless had something to do with it, perhaps indirectly overseeing the work on the infrastructure before crossing to Britain for the culminating campaign.[18]

The conclusion of this work of renovation was marked by Constantius' campaign beyond the Wall. While the extent of this campaign has already been remarked upon, the essential reasons for it have not. Roman Britain was, in a sense, the last frontier. All the other border areas of the empire had been secured by warfare. Britain's had not been. This fits into the policy of reconstruction and defence in depth established by Diocletian.[19] From Egypt to Syria, from Moesia to Germany, fortifications had been renewed, treaties revised and raiders neutralized. In the region of Moesia, for example, the Danube frontier had been secured through the refortification of such places as Transmarisca and Durostorum followed up by several years of war. Constantius' Pictish campaign, then, makes perfect sense in this context. The recovery of Britain from Allectus in 296 and the expulsion of raiding tribes which followed only marked the beginning of the process of recovery within its provinces. But once the infrastructure for an effective border force had been repaired, a campaign designed to impress and intimidate the Caledonian tribes was a logical and coherent follow-up.

Constantius' visit to Britain was more than a courtesy call. It was his own implementation of the will of Diocletian. The campaign itself was a major undertaking, penetrating far into the north of the island. Its material remains have been identified at old Severan forts deep in Scotland: Carpow on the Tay and Cramond near Edinburgh. This evidence suggests that a fleet was used in conjunction with a land force, indicating a complex and coordinated operation.[20] Likewise, a golden brooch commemorating the *vicennalia* of Diocletian and Maximian has been discovered in the region of Moffat in Dumfriesshire, thereby establishing another possible area of operation or perhaps route of march for this campaign.[21] The panegyrist of 310, who is our major narrative source for this war, praises Constantius, in customarily exaggerated terms, as active in penetrating the uttermost parts of the north.[22] His foe is identified as the Picts, perhaps the first occasion upon which they were of importance to the imperial province of Britain.[23] Their lands were far to the north, past the territory of the Votadini and across the isthmus straddled by the Antonine Wall.[24] It was therefore no easy march. It is also an error to assume that the Votadini were always on friendly terms with Rome, so progress to the Firth of Forth cannot be perceived necessarily as a simple line march through friendly territory.[25] And even when that was achieved Constantius still had Picts to face. His campaign probably penetrated as far into Scotland as those of Agricola and Septimius Severus. Indeed, Salway notes useful parallels between the campaigns of Severus and Constantius.[26] The campaign was complete by the end of 305. Constantius had taken the victory title *Britannicus Maximus* by or before 7 January 306.[27]

The campaign was a serious matter, but it also had its own political implications for Constantius. Some contemporary detractors asserted that he was out for cheap glory.[28] The fact of that assertion reveals something of the political dynamic of the time between the two Augusti. It is certainly clear that the *concordia* with which Diocletian had governed his colleagues had vanished. In its place was a more formal relationship. Orosius, in his account of the succession to Diocletian, makes a very curious observation:

> *Galerius et Constantius Augusti primi Romanum imperium in duas partes diviserunt.*[29]

(Galerius and Constantius as Augusti were the first to divide the Roman empire into two parts.)

Orosius is noted neither for his originality nor for his depth of analysis, but in this case he has made a significant departure from his source. Up until this point in his account of this period, Orosius has been slavishly paraphrasing the text of Eutropius. The *primi*, however, jars when the two texts are compared. Eutropius says:

> *Constantius et Galerius Augusti creati sunt divisosque inter eos ita Romanus orbis.*[30]

(Constantius and Galerius were raised to the rank of Augustus and divided the Roman world between them.)

It is possible that Orosius inferred the novelty of the division from this text, but unlikely. Orosius was a creature of his sources, a cutter and paster of prodigious mediocrity. It is most likely that Orosius derived this particular nugget of information from another written source. While that source cannot be identified with any certainty, it is likely that the author wrote in Latin.[31]

While the reliability of this testimony cannot be confidently assumed, it is consistent with what is otherwise known: Diocletian did not formally divide the empire; yet it was formally divided at some point. It is reasonable and consistent with the evidence to identify the accession of Constantius and Galerius as the point at which this division occurred.

This initial split of the empire was a most significant step. Not only does it represent the first actual negotiated division of the empire into eastern and western halves, but it also represents very precisely the nature of the political relationships within the imperial dynasty and between the new emperors. Diocletian's regime had operated by virtue of an imperial *concordia* which focused upon the person of Diocletian. The thing which the emperors had in common, their unifying factor, had been loyalty to him. Diocletian himself had sought to replicate that state of affairs after his abdication, with Galerius as the focus of loyalty. That focus, however, broke down when it came to Constantius. He could not and did not accept the political victory of Galerius. While he was *de iure* the senior emperor, *de facto* he had adopted as son and raised as Caesar a man to whom he was not close and, in all likelihood, did not trust. Further, it was clear that Severus remained loyal to Galerius, who in turn enjoyed the loyalty of the other Caesar, Maximinus, and the inheritance of Diocletian's machinery of government. Therefore, it became vital to define very precisely the limits of authority of each of the four emperors.

The necessary corollary to that definition of the jurisdiction of each of the emperors was an increase in the power of the Caesars. The Caesars had hitherto operated as the *imago Augustorum*, but Constantius could not trust his own Caesar's loyalty. Since loyalty and trust had been an implicit factor in the functioning of the First Tetrarchy, and since these factors no longer applied between the Augusti and between Constantius and his Caesar, a more formal definition of power became inevitable. Up until this point, the powers of the Caesars had never been spelled out, and so they remained effectively at the mercy of their Augusti. Once their powers had been defined, complete with distinct geographic areas of control (because only in this way could Constantius effectively isolate Severus), they took on a whole new role. They were no longer images and embryos of the Augusti. They were emperors in their own right.

This is not mere supposition. Both judicial and numismatic evidence exists which tends to confirm this theory. While there is still no attested praetorian prefect for either of the Caesars, it would seem from a law preserved in the *Codex Justinianus* that the Caesars took on law-making functions which only the Augusti had hitherto enjoyed. A rescript addressed to Verinus, the *praeses* of Syria, was issued from Apollinopolis in the Thebaid on 5 November 305.[32] This law cannot have derived from Galerius since at this time he was almost certainly in Europe, probably at Serdica. Only a short time before the issue of this law Constantine had departed from the court of Galerius to join Constantius near Bononia. Given the absence of any reference to ships, boats or ferries in the heroized narratives of Constantine's voyage to his father, it is clear that Galerius was nowhere near Egypt at the time.[33] It is most probable that the rescript was issued by Maximinus Daza.[34]

If so, then it is evident that the Caesars had taken on defined legislative functions within their own areas of control. Presumably the Augusti still retained the right to legislate for the empire as a whole, and prescribed limits for their subordinate colleagues. But in any case this represents a substantial change in the legal structure, and therefore the political, since, before May 305, the Caesars had no demonstrable legislative functions at all.[35] There might be even more to this than initially meets the eye. Verinus, the appellate judge to whom the rescript was directed, was a senator, following what amounted to a regular senatorial career in the late third century. At this point, Verinus held the post of *praeses Syriae*, and as such received a number of rescripts and edicts.[36] Other notable senators had held this office and then gone on to great things. Virius Lupus, who had shared a consulship with the Emperor Probus in 278, had served as *praeses* of Arabia and Syria-Coele and *iudex sacrarum cognitionum* for Egypt (probably) and the East (certainly) in the time of Aurelian, and had also held the influential priesthood of Sol. L. Aelius Helvius. Dionysius had also held the priesthood of Sol, been *corrector* in Italy, *praeses* of Syria-Coele and *iudex sacrarum cognitionum*, proconsul of Africa, and urban prefect. There is no evidence of his having held an ordinary consulship, but a suffect consulship is likely with this career. There are also two other *clarissimi* attested as governors of Syria at this time: Latinius Primosus, governor under Diocletian and Lartorius Pius Maximus, described as a *legatus Syriae Coeles* early in the reign of Diocletian.[37]

This was, it would seem, not merely a senatorial office held in the ordinary course of events, but one frequently graced by high flyers.[38] Verinus himself was one such. An epigram of the elder Symmachus celebrates a Verinus who, among other attainments, had been a successful commander in an Armenian war.[39] The only Verinus known to whom this could possibly refer is the governor of Syria who received Daza's rescript.[40] Daza fought two campaigns in the east, one in 310 and the other in 312.[41] Either would provide a context for Symmachus' reference to Verinus. But Symmachus' epigram also leads us in an important direction. It appears in a series in which the other four honorands had clearly served as urban prefect.[42] It follows that Verinus also did so and, indeed, there was a Verinus who served as urban prefect from 323 until 325. He is readily identifiable as Locrius Verinus, *vicarius* of Africa 318–321.[43] If, as is likely, the Syrian Verinus and the urban prefect are one and the same, a coherent and stellar career emerges very similar to the earlier cursus of Helvius Dionysius: *praeses* and judge in Syria, *vicarius* of Africa, and finally urban prefect.[44]

162

Verinus' status as senator, and his subsequent career, both point to the limitations of any division of powers and territory between the new emperors. Verinus' name is of Etruscan origin, and there are Verini in a cemetery at Clusium.[45] This means that, in 305, an Italian could be appointed to Syria, serve a long term as governor, including the carriage of wars in Armenia, and then return to the west where he could then hold further and higher office. Evidently the division of the empire was not a partition, as Eusebius' rhetorical description suggests, but something more complex and nuanced. While in later years, Verinus became a man most useful to Constantine, he seems to have been of considerable utility to Maximinus.[46]

The more independent status of the Caesars is confirmed by numismatic evidence. There were a number of mints operating throughout the empire in the late third and early fourth centuries. Each mint struck coins with its own distinctive mint-mark. This was unusually an abbreviation of the name of the city where the mint was located. Between 293 and 305, that abbreviation was augmented by the letters SM (*Sacra Moneta*) if an Augustus was resident in a minting city. The three mints which make this clear are the mints of Ticinum, Thessalonica and Antioch. The Ticinum mint struck with the SM mark when Maximian was resident in Milan in 294/5, when the emperors progressed through the area in 303/4, en route to and from the *vicennalia* celebrations in Rome, and then for Severus as Caesar during his brief residence in Milan. The mint of Thessalonica, which was active during Galerius' residence in the city between 299 and 303, and which serviced his building programme there, did not strike SM coinage at all until 308 when Galerius moved from Serdica. This would certainly confirm that mints did not strike with the SM mark for Caesars before 305. The mint of Antioch also displays this pattern. It struck SM coinage between 293 and 297, when Diocletian was in the east and based in Antioch. Then there was a hiatus of two years while Diocletian went to Egypt, and the mint begins its SM issues again in 299 and continues until 305, both for Diocletian's residence in the east and for the *vicennalia*. It then struck with the SM mark after 305 for Maximin Daza as Caesar.[47] The evidence of the coinage would therefore seem to indicate quite decisively that the Caesars had a new dignity and status. Symbols of empire which had hitherto applied only to the Augusti now applied to them also. This matter goes beyond the symbolic matter, goes beyond symbols. It is arguable that SM coinage was issued not only as a result of the imperial presence in a city, but also from the bullion store carried by the imperial *comitatus*. The implication of this is that Diocletian's Caesars did not carry around a bullion store with their courts, but their successors did.[48]

The evidence would seem clear, then, that the Caesars did obtain quite explicit formal authority and jurisdiction after the abdications of 305, although their autonomy must have been limited by the Augusti. This must certainly mean that the models of the succession to Diocletian which have been accepted hitherto need to be revised. Galerius' supposed domination is not as clear-cut as might appear from the pages of Lactantius, nor is the submission of Constantius quite so obvious from the actual course of events. The Caesars had greater deliberative and legislative power within the more explicit division of territories, along with the symbolic language which attended such responsibility, but the empire's internal borders were in other respects nominal and did not hinder the pursuit of careers in government or (probably) the military.

A good many disparate threads have been identified here which need to be brought together. Much occurred in the latter part of 305 which needs both recognition and interpretation. It is clear that Constantius himself was not an enfeebled figure. Rather, he was actively going about the business of ruling, first, by himself fighting an arduous but necessary war in Britain and, second, by imposing his will on Galerius. This latter can be seen in the division of the empire in 305, in the new powers of the Caesars, and in the reception of Constantine from the court of Galerius. The evidence itself is too fragmentary to be able to build up a coherent picture of the policy of Constantius. What can be perceived, however, is a series of actions designed to undermine the effective position of control which Galerius enjoyed as a result of the settlement of 305. Galerius' own position was particularly weakened by the definition of spheres of imperial control for the emperors. While this did not serve explicitly to strengthen Constantius, it did implicitly dilute Galerius' hold on universal authority. Diocletian's supremacy had depended upon an unspoken consensus. That consensus did not require a formal division of the empire, hence the boast of an "undivided inheritance" made by a panegyrist of Maximian.[49] The division of the empire after the abdication of Diocletian can only reflect the evaporation of that underlying unity, and the definition of imperial territories in a clear endeavour to avoid conflict and maintain an appearance of unity. Constantius must have been the driving force for this division. He had otherwise not done well out of the succession arrangements since he had been obliged to adopt a son he did not choose in order to augment a family already well stocked with males. He can only have agreed to this arrangement, which ran counter to his own interests and those of his children, through the assurance of the maintenance of his own authority. Such an assurance was best given by the transformation of the loose relationships of Diocletian's reign into much more tightly defined relationships.

There was little that Galerius could actually do about all this. This was the political price which he paid for his own dynastic victory in 305. Moreover, he may have hoped that Constantius, deprived of the apparatus of government and fearful of the destabilization of his own family through the reappearance of Constantine, would have contented himself with the status of senior Augustus and left the business of actually running the empire to Galerius. But both Diocletian and Galerius had misjudged Constantius' tenacity. He defused the threat of Constantine by receiving his son with apparent honour and keeping him close. He asserted himself in war and in politics. His approach negated and defeated the *concordia* upon which the new dynasty had been constructed. By refusing to accept a *de facto* subordinate status while in a *de iure* position of absolute authority, Constantius rejected Diocletian's arrangements for the succession. The choice which he offered Galerius was either to pick up the gauntlet and fight it out or to acquiesce. Galerius let it be, at least initially. Whether it was horror of civil war, fear of the consequences of action or simple indecision, Galerius did not seek at any stage to challenge the formal superiority of Constantius. But it must have been with some relief that he received the news of Constantius' sudden death at Eboracum in July 306.[50] The man who had refused to accept his political superiority was dead and now Galerius was senior Augustus in name as well as in fact. In theory at least he was now in a position to make whatever dispositions he chose. This should have been a stroke of good fortune for Galerius, but it was not to be. He was presented with a new dilemma.

The nature and circumstances of the coup which brought Constantine to power remain obscured by subsequent propaganda and myth making. Constantine clearly wanted people to believe that he had received the blessing of his father who, for this purpose, had secured his presence in defiance of Galerius' wishes. While Constantine had, without doubt, fled to his father, it is by no means certain that Constantius trusted his eldest son. He may well have welcomed Constantine's presence precisely because he could keep a better eye on him. One point which father and son had in common, however, was opposition to Galerius. Both were able and ambitious men with no desire to play second fiddle. Moreover, they were father and son, with a bond more profound than that between Constantius and his other adult son, the Caesar Severus. Severus had been forced on Constantius in 305, clearly as the nominee of Galerius. Severus had a son of his own, and clearly had little reason or incentive to guard and enhance the interests of the children of Constantius and grandchildren of Maximian.[51] A dying Constantius had every reason to turn to Constantine as protector of his young family. That family was not distant, if Eusebius is to be believed at this point, but attended the bedside of the dying emperor.[52]

Eusebius' account here emphasizes the dynastic links between father and son, and Constantius' right to nominate Constantine as his successor. In this respect, he is quite correct. Constantine did not usurp power, but received it in the same way as his colleagues and predecessors had: at the hands, and by the patronage, of a superior. Constantius' acclamation of his son as his successor ensured the dynastic continuity of Constantius' own family against that of Galerius. It ensured the continuity of the resistance to Galerius' complete political victory. A significant focus of that opposition to Galerius had gathered at Constantius' court. Among others, these almost certainly included Christian refugees, who found Constantius' policy of tolerance far more congenial than Galerius' hostility.[53] Apart from the Christians, an influential figure seems to have been an auxiliary general or allied king, Crocus, described by the *Epitome de Caesaribus* as a *rex Alamannorum*.[54] He appears to have had a part to play in arranging for Constantine's acclamation by the troops. Whatever the palace machinations, it is clear that Constantius had not long been dead when Constantine, claiming nomination by his dying father and supported by his generals, was hailed as emperor by the troops in York.[55] Immodestly, he claimed, as his father's successor in that office, the higher dignity of Augustus. He swiftly took steps to inform Galerius by sending him his laurelled portrait.[56] Once he had been acclaimed, Constantine felt sufficiently confident to cross the Channel and campaign against the Franks.[57]

Constantine's acclamation as Augustus presented Galerius with a political situation of some delicacy. Constantine claimed that his father had designated him Augustus.[58] It was a claim which Galerius was in no position to dispute, and may well have been true. There were clearly two rival legitimacies in conflict: the legitimacy of Diocletian's own arrangements; and the legitimacy which permitted a reigning Augustus to make his own provision for succession. It was in this that the weakness of Diocletian's arrangements for the succession became apparent. They depended for their survival upon the actuality of *concordia* between the Augusti, not its mere appearance. Division between the Augusti split the empire. Galerius' solution was astute. It was to effect a compromise. If Constantine had given Galerius the ultimatum either to accept or reject him as emperor, Galerius did neither. He recognized Constantine as Caesar, not Augustus. In so doing, he conceded Constantine's legitimacy, but on his own terms.[59] Constantine was offered a reward for audacity, but one in which he was obliged to accept a subordinate role. There were clear advantages for Constantine in accepting Galerius' offer. It also meant, however, that he accepted Galerius' rank and authority as senior Augustus. Constantine could have rejected Galerius, of course, but that was a way fraught with danger. It necessitated the certainty of a civil war in which Constantine would be perceived as the aggressor and would have to fight experienced generals with experienced troops. The choice which Galerius presented him was both wise and, in the circumstances, generous. Constantine was swift to accept.

Galerius did exercise one form of control upon his new colleague. He did not enrol Constantius among the the gods.[60] In 306, only one mint struck a memorial issue to "DIVO CONSTANTIO AVG", that of Lugdunum, controlled by Constantine.[61] No other mint in the empire struck an issue in commemoration of the divine Constantius until some years later.[62] The epigraphic evidence for Constantius' consecration is meagre and can be discounted.[63] Galerius' refusal to countenance divine status for Constantius was not revenge but policy. By keeping Constantius mortal, he denied the rhetorical status of divine descent both to Constantine and the other children of Constantius. The merits of being the son of a deified ruler were well known to Romans. Galerius had no intention of handing Constantine, or his brothers, any such advantage.[64]

In July 306, Constantine inherited the quarrel which his father had with Galerius. It was Galerius' hope that Constantine could be contained and tamed by being brought into the legitimate power structure, albeit at the most junior level. But the settlement was a delicate one, and easily upset. In fact, Galerius had not ruled three months as senior Augustus when it was upset by another ambitious son, his own son-in-law, Maxentius.

Notes

1 Lact. *de. mort. pers.* 20.1.
2 Barnes, *CE*, p. 26.
3 See Gibbon (1995: p. 400) for his reconstruction of events, which remained influential for many years; for a most fanciful reconstruction, given the paucity of the evidence upon which it is based, see J.H. Smith (1971), p. 58f.
4 Although see here more recently Lenski (2006), p. 60f.
5 Constantius was fighting the Germans in the winter of 304/5. See *Pan. Lat.* 7. 6.4; Barnes, *NE*, p. 61.
6 See Barnes, *NE*, p. 61; also Table 7, p. 257 for the incidence of victory titulature; also Barnes (1976), pp. 189–91.
7 *Pan. Lat.* 7. 5–8.
8 *Ibid.*, 6.3.
9 See also Barnes, *CE*, p. 26.
10 As first noted by Salway (1981), p. 318.
11 Lact. *de. mort. pers.* 24.3; *Origo.* 4; Zos. 2.8. 2–3.
12 A question posed by Burckhardt (1949: p. 251) and never answered.
13 Averil Cameron (2006), p. 19f.
14 Frere (1981), p. 384; Salway (1981), p. 314; S. Johnson (1980), p. 84f.; Todd (1981), p. 214; cf. Collingwood and Wright (1965).
15 Frere (1981), pp. 382, 400 n. 14.
16 Johnson (1980), pp. 83–5; Todd (1981), p. 214f. But see the reiterated and augmented arguments of Frere (1967), p. 341f. n. 4 (1981), p. 400 n. 14, and (1987), p. 332 n. 14.
17 Butler (1971). Butler assigns the Multangular Tower in York and the work associated with it to the reconstruction of the late third/early fourth centuries. See now Bidwell (2006). The Birdoswald fort has already been noted. Elsewhere on the Wall, a fragmentary inscription from Housesteads records a building dedication in the time of Diocletian (*RIB* I. 1613). See also Todd (1981), p. 215.
18 As suggested by Butler (1971).
19 See Luttwak (1976), chapter 3; also Brennan (1980).
20 Salway (1981), p. 319; also Frere (1981), p. 386.
21 Barnes, *NE*, p. 61, n. 69; Hassall (1979), p. 107f.
22 *Pan. Lat.* 7.7.2; the panegyrist speaks of Constantius' enjoyment of the phenomenon of the long days associated with the far north, contrasting this with the *lux aeterna* enjoyed by the gods.
23 *Pan. Lat.* 7.7.2.
24 See S. Johnson (1980), pp. 51–4.

25 *Ibid.*, pp. 58, 65–8. See also Alcock (1979), p. 135f. on the suggestion that the Traprain Law hoard was a late fourth-century bribe to the Votadini in order to maintain good behaviour.

26 Salway (1981), pp. 319, 322.

27 A military diploma from Tuscany, dated 7 January 306, records the emperors as BR. M. II (*AE*. 1961.240). This means that the British campaign must belong to the latter part of 305. See Barnes, *NE*, p. 20, no. 4.

28 *Pan. Lat.* 7.7.1.

29 Oros. 7.25.15.

30 Eutr. 10.1.1.

31 In all probability Orosius could not read Greek; see Brown (1967), p. 356.

32 *Cod. Just.* 3.12.1.

33 On Galerius' presence in the Balkans, see Barnes, *NE*, pp. 62, 64. But Galerius' Caesar, Maximinus, could well have been in southern Egypt. It was, after all, a part of his defined *Herrschaftsgebiet* (Eutr. 10.2.1).

34 Corcoran (2000), pp. 143, 271. Corcoran has also suggested that a second rescript addressed to Verinus (*CJ* 2.12.20), conventionally dated to 294 and issued from "Demessos", be reassigned to Maximinus and the "Demessos" emended to "Damascus". See Corcoran (1993), p. 118 n. 124.

35 *Pace* Corcoran (2000), pp. 268–70.

36 *CJ* 3. 12, 2. 13. 20; see Morris (1965), p. 363f.

37 For Virius Lupus, *PLRE* I, p. 522, no. 5; L.Aelius Helvius Dionysius, *PLRE* I, p. 260, no.12; Latinius Primosus, *PLRE* I, p. 275; L.Artorius Pius Maximus, *PLRE* I, p. 589, no. 43.

38 See Morris (1965); Arnheim (1972), p. 40.

39 Symm., *Ep.* 1.2.7.

40 We know of no other man named Verinus, let alone one who had a military command in the east. Thus, Morris (1965), p. 363f.; cf. Kuhoff (1983), p. 358, no. 4.

41 In 310, against the Persians: Barnes, *NE*, pp. 66, 256f. In 312, against Armenia: Eus., *HE* 9. 8.4; Barnes, *NE*, p. 66, p. 256. Chastagnol (1962: p. 76) places this campaign much later, after the defeat of Licinius. Given that Verinus was by that time a senior *clarissimus* and that Constantine was in possession of a highly competent army, this reconstruction seems rather unlikely. Perhaps, as Morris (1965: p. 364) suggests, the *res feliciter gestae* referred to in *CJ* 3. 12.1 are the happy outcome of a series of frontier skirmishes.

42 Aradius Rufinus (I.2.3), *praef. urb* 312–13, *cos.* 311; Amnius Anicius Iulianus (I.2), *praef. urb* 326–9, *cos.* 322; Petronius Probianus (I.2.6), *praef. urb* 329–31, *cos.* 322; L. Aradius Valerius Proculus (I. 2.4), *praef. urb* 337–8, *cos.* 340.

43 Chastagnol (1962), pp. 74–6, no. 30.

44 *PLRE* I, p. 951; Arnheim (1972), p. 64f.; Arnheim is unjust here in his comments on the *PLRE*. While it fails to make the identification of the two unambiguous, it does suggest it. A law addressed to Verinus and dated to 30 January 314 (*C.Th.* 12. 11.1 and not *CJ* 3. 12.1 as Arnheim avers in his footnote) has been redated by Seeck to 320, when Verinus was *vicarius Africae* (*Regesten*. p. 25). See also Chastagnol (1962), p. 75.

45 Morris (1965), p. 364, *PLRE* I, p. 951, no. 2. Ironically, Morris suggests that Verinus may have been of Christian family on the basis of the appearance in a Christian grave-yard at Clusium of a couple who may have been Verinus' parents (see also *PLRE* I, p. 951, no. 2).

46 Chastagnol (1962), p. 76.

47 *RIC* VI, pp. 90–3.

48 *RIC* VI, pp. 92f.

49 Leadbetter (2004).

50 Socrates, *HE* 1. 2.1; Barnes, *NE*, p. 61.
51 Lact. *de mort. pers.* 50.4.
52 Eus. *Vit. Const.* 1.21.2; Cameron and Hall (1999), pp. 198f.
53 Eusebius (*HE* 8.13.13) states that Constantius neither demolished churches nor harassed Christians, but rather saved those among his people from ill-treatment. His realm would have been a natural haven for Christians fleeing persecution. Barnes (1973: pp. 43–6, and consistently since) has argued that Constantine's first measure as emperor was a benefit to the Christians of his realm.
54 *Ep. de Caes.* 41.3; on Crocus, see the discussion by Wood (2006).
55 On Constantine's nomination as Augustus by Constantius, see Lact. *de mort. pers.* 24. 8–9, *Pan Lat.* 7.7.5 (see Creed's commentary on the *de mortibus*, p. 105); on his proclamation by the troops, Zos. 2 9.1, Eus. *HE* 8 13.14, Aur. Vict. *de Caes.* 40 3–4, *Origo* 2.4.
56 Lact. *de mort. pers.* 25.1.
57 See Barnes, *NE*, p. 69.
58 This is certainly the view reflected by the contemporary Lactantius (*de mort. pers.* 24.8–9), and in the propaganda of the panegyrics. See especially *Pan. Lat.* 7. 14. 3–7.
59 Lact. *de mort. pers.* 25 3–5; Barnes, *CE*, p. 26. Galerius' despatch of the purple was not immediate (Barnes *NE*, p. 25f.).
60 On the neglect of *consecratio* at this time, see S. MacCormack (1981), pp. 106–11.
61 *RIC* VI, p. 256, no. 202. The date of this issue is not definite, but the weight of the coin suggests late 306 (*Ibid.*, n. 2).
62 Issues commemorating Constantius' death and deification were used for propaganda purposes both by Constantine (*RIC* VI, p. 131, no. 110; p. 217, nos 789–90; pp. 260–3, nos 251, 264–9) and Maxentius (*RIC* VI, p. 294, nos 96–7; p. 326, no. 127; p. 404, nos 27–9).
63 Epigraphic references to *divus Constantius* derive entirely from the west, and most appear in dedications to Constantine or his family (*CIL* 2. 4910; 7. 1170, 1153; 8. 10178; 10. 6003; 12. 5560, 5881; 13. 3255, 8978, 9130; *AE.* 1901, 62). Those which do not appear in this context appear either later (*AE.* 69/70. 375, on a milestone with Licinius *iunior*); *in tandem* with a dedication to Galerius as *divus* (*CIL.* 8. 10376); or from Africa in a totally ambiguous and undatable context (*CIL.* 8. 4484, 10736, 22212).
64 On the continuing effectiveness of *consecratio* as a political weapon, see S. MacCormack (1981), p. 112f.

6

THE *IOVII* AND *HERCULII*

If the elevation of Constantine to the dignity of Caesar constituted a satisfactory, even clever response to the family conundrum posed by Constantius, it was also singular and unrepeatable. An analogous problem soon presented itself which could not be so readily resolved. The newly constituted dynastic arrangement of 306 ought to have represented the beginning of a new *concordia* centred upon Galerius, and his consequent unchallenged rule as Augustus. His nephew was a Caesar, his friend was an Augustus and Constantine had been acknowledged and brought within the imperial college in subordinate rank. Within this structure of relationships, Galerius stood at the head. He was senior Augustus and father of them all. Such a situation, however, only briefly pertained: the months from July to October 306 represent the zenith of his political power. This ended on 28 October 306. Maxentius, Galerius' son-in-law and the only son of the abdicated Maximian, took the purple in Rome, proclaiming himself, significantly, as *princeps*, rather than Augustus.[1] The circumstances of this proclamation seem to be clear enough. Three issues came together here: taxation reform; the proposed abolition of the Praetorian and Guard; and the frustrated ambitions of Maxentius, the relegated son of Maximian.

The tax policy of Diocletian and his successors is not particularly easy to discern clearly amid the generalities, banalities and bias of our sources. Taxation is a complex enough business without trying to make sense of fragmentary evidence from a variety of sources. Although scholarly consensus on late Roman taxation is elusive, it is clear that Diocletian effected major reform.[2] Diocletian's reign had seen a considerable expansion and regulation of the Roman public sector. Lactantius complained of its effects, depicting a brutal system in which there were more people in receipt of public salaries than taxpayers, of penurious farmers fleeing fields which were thus reverting to woodland.[3] The images which he conjures are neither surprising nor accurate. But they do reflect a considerable expansion of the public sector. Integral to Diocletian's policy for the recovery of the empire was a massive spending programme. The army was augmented and expanded, buildings rose in massive numbers, major wars were fought. The building programme still has the power to impress, with its vast and far-flung remnants mute testimony to and legacy of Diocletian's passion for architectural monuments. Arguably, this was a necessary response to the empire's problems of the third century, which had highlighted a number of economic inadequacies in the state, in particular the relatively small size of the public sector.[4]

In order to fund all of this, Diocletian had sought to regularize the tax base. It certainly desperately needed reform, since emperors had raised taxation in a largely unsystematic fashion for the past century. The levying of extraordinary indictions is a clear demonstration of this. Originally intended to be a measure invoked in emergencies only, they became a far more regular impost once price inflation and the collapse of the monetary system rendered it imperative to tax in kind.[5] Diocletian made the imposition and collection of the indiction an annual responsibility.[6] However, any annual indiction needed to be mindful of taxpayers' capacity to pay. Indictions were, in origin, occasional military requisitions. Applied in emergencies, there was no need to assess the capacity of taxpayers to provide the resources, since the circumstances were usually dire. When Diocletian determined upon an annual indiction, the necessity arose to ensure that taxpayers were assessed fairly since the impost was now annual. It is commonly held that Diocletian introduced a five-year cycle of censuses in order to assess the regions for taxation.[7] As a result of these regular reassessments, it became possible to establish a standard taxable unit, known in some provinces as the *iugum*.[8] There is a great deal of good sense in this. In times of economic and demographic stability, there is no real need to carry out a tax assessment. Financial stability means stability of tax levels. The third century, however, had seen inflation on a massive scale.[9] The coinage had been debased and Diocletian, despite a currency reform in the middle of the 290s, still considered it necessary to try and peg price rises artificially through the Edict on Maximal Prices. In this economic climate, regular reassessment for tax purposes became absolutely vital to the government. Diocletian began this process early: there is evidence of annual reassessment in Egypt from 287.[10]

By 306, then, the census was not a new phenomenon. If Diocletian had begun the process of instituting the census fairly early in his reign, by 306 it had been operating in some parts of the empire for some time and performed a fundamental role in the determination of tax levels. The conduct of the census had always been undertaken by state officials (*censitores*) in collaboration with the local towns as a municipal responsibility which the *censitores* merely had to supervise.[11] It was in the interests of local town councils to ensure an accurate tax assessment, since they were made legally liable for any shortfall.[12] Of course, it was possible for the curial class to achieve a reduction in their own tax liability by an understatement of their property. Nor is it impossible that many *censitores* were bribed into connivance.

Diocletian had sought to reform the tax base of the empire through published requisitions (indictions) based upon what was known about a region's capacity to pay. Whilst this sounds like an entirely sensible policy and, indeed, pertained thereafter, wealth assessment was based upon a regular and repeated census. This practice was not uniformly applied, but rolled out across the entire empire, region by region.[13] By the time the turn of the western provinces arrived, Diocletian had retired and Galerius made the decision to include the towns in the census, most particularly the city of Rome.

The accounts of Galerius' census present a quite different picture. Assessment is conducted solely by the *censitores*. Both Lactantius and Eusebius speak of public servants visiting communities in order to perform the necessary tax assessment.[14] There is little doubt that the result of this was that the 306 assessment was extremely severe. The taxpayers of Autun certainly complained of it. More to the point, both Maximin Daza and Licinius later both promised relief to communities from the level of taxation imposed as a consequence of the 306 census. There is little doubt that the tax assessment was a harsh one. It subsequently became a political rallying point of some power.[15] External assessors are less likely to have either been generous in their assessments towards the locals, or even to have assessed accurately, since it is quite improbable that they took into account any possible variations in local conditions. This may then explain the severity of the 306 census. Galerius involved the Roman civil service in the census process, making them directly responsible for the tax estimates. Thus Galerius took away from each individual city the right to make its own assessment and gave it to his own bureaucrats. The inherent danger in this was twofold. First, that assessors would be largely ignorant of local conditions, and second, that the needs of the treasury would dictate what people would pay to a far greater extent than their actual capacity. In 306, of course, the state needed funds. Diocletian's building projects were still under way and needed massive financial support.[16] Galerius also now had his own to support as well – in particular his retirement palace at Gamzigrad.[17] In addition, there were the usual necessities of funding the bureaucracy and paying for the army – indeed, precisely the factors which Lactantius laments.

This regulation of the census-collection procedure is only one aspect of altered procedures. Another is the imposition of the poll tax upon urban citizens, specifically upon Romans. Lactantius gives the impression that the events of October 306 were caused by a unique imposition upon the city of Rome. While this might be true, it might have been less surprising than it appeared. Diocletian had already imposed taxation liabilities upon a part of Italy.[18] This was the north, which became known as *Italia annonaria*. Here, the ancient tax immunity of Italians was bypassed by the simple loophole of requiring an indiction rather than a formal tax.[19] This meant that there was now a regular tax upon a part of Italy, dressed up as a military requisition, and assessed on the basis of the local standard unit, the *millena*.[20] The remainder of the peninsula, *Italia suburbicaria*, was merely obliged to provide revenues for the city of Rome.[21] The city, however, remained, as it had been for centuries, immune from taxation.

This was the situation which applied in Italy before the census of 306. During the course of that census, the innovation occurred of enforcing poll tax (*capitatio*) upon the cities as well as upon the rural areas. This extension of *capitatio* reflects, in all probability, the under-taxation of the cities. There were wide taxes on inheritance, manumission and trade, and the cities were left substantially to manage their own taxation arrangements. As time went on, in fact, the cities also tended to take over even this function of administering the imperial indirect taxes.[22] With respect to the *tributum*, the curial class were guarantors for the assessed taxable amount, and were responsible for arranging its collection. Where needed also, the empire could call upon large numbers of townsfolk to perform unpaid labour – *munera*. This was Caracalla's gift to the towns – by extending the privilege of Roman citizenship he had also extended its burdens.[23] A law of Diocletian's specifically exempted *rustici* from the tedious performance of *munera*. Their liability for the *annona* and the capitation was deemed sufficiently onerous.[24] This was all very unsystematic, however. Analogous towns could be liable for vastly differing amounts. The tax liability of a community depended more upon the honesty of its self-assessments than actual capacity to pay. In addition, the rural population which was the active producer of wealth was subject to the same indirect taxes, as well as taxes on their land holdings and their heads. If the principle of equity adumbrated in the Edict of Aristius Optatus were to be applied, then there needed to be reform in the ways that cities were taxed as well as the rural areas. This does not necessitate the introduction of *capitatio* in an urban context, and there was no suggestion of this in Diocletian's time.[25]

In 306, however, the approach to urban taxation was simply to regularize the assessment of the urban areas, entrusting the task to the *censitores*, officials attached to the staff of the provincial governor.[26] It was determined to organize this system in the same way that rural taxation had been regulated – by the application of a standard, the *caput*. By doing this, tax income could be maximized by the elimination cities as tax shelters, and spread the burden of taxation more equitably over the empire. By levying *capitatio* on the towns, the emperor thereby endeavoured to ensure that the tax liability of a locality was based upon the number of people economically sustained within it, and not on some arbitrary provincial official supervising the self-assessment of a town's curial class.

The taxation of the cities in this fashion was not the only innovation of the census of 306. Included in the list of cities to be taxed was the city of Rome itself. Rome had long been immune from taxation. *Tributum* was paid to it, not the other way around. The attempt to tax the city was, perhaps, the recognition of a reality. One view would see Rome as an idea; the city itself, a fossil of empire, retaining privileges rendered redundant by the historical momentum which took the focus of empire from it. The city was also a financial drain consuming resources and producing nothing in return. Rome's privileged status was a function of history, no more. The focus of power was no longer the city, but the person of the emperor himself. From well before the accession of Diocletian, Rome rarely saw an emperor. Even Maximian, who had dwelt in Italy, chose to live and centre his administration in Mediolanum.[27] Rome's senatorial class, which had long formed the core of the administrative and officer corps, was now reserved for highly regulated civilian careers. Even the Praetorian Prefect, whose functions were now more civil than military, rarely saw the guard of which he was nominal commander. If Rome had had its day as the capital city, it nevertheless retained a romantic aura. It was the mother city and the symbol of empire. But such a view is more rhetorical than real: even if Diocletian disliked the inhabitants of Rome themselves, he adorned their city with a vast baths complex and a new Senate House. It was here that Diocletian chose to celebrate his great triumph, the symbol of his political, military and economic success. He adorned the city with monuments of his victories, including a triumphal arch and a monument to celebrate the *decennalia* of the Caesars.[28] Diocletian clearly valued Rome's symbolic significance, and perhaps also venerated her. Rome had long since been imbued with a symbolic significance which transcended the political. She was not merely a teeming city; she was also a goddess to whom worship must be offered.[29] She featured heavily on coins as "ROMA AETERNA" or "DEA ROMA AETERNA".

Not only had there long been a cult of Rome, taken seriously in the city itself at least from the beginning of the second century AD, and endowed with its own body of priests, but that cult was also actively exploited by the emperors on their coins. If Rome was no longer the centre of power, it remained the symbol of that power, with its own cult, its own priests and, it seems, its own defenders. Diocletian's own capacity to be impressed by this was, perhaps, limited by the attitude of the Romans themselves. His time in the city in 303 was not happy. Lactantius says that Diocletian left Rome early, angered by the independence of the locals. They may have had cause: the triumphal celebration was marred by the disastrous collapse of a temporary stand at the Circus while largesse was being distributed. Thousands were killed.[30] Diocletian's unfortunate experience in the city of Rome did not lessen his commitment to its empire, but it did perhaps serve to cement in his mind the distinction to be made between the idea of Rome and the more corporeal inhabitants of the city.

It was this very dichotomy which was attacked in the application of the census in 306. Lactantius depicts Galerius' decision to impose tax on the cities, and the city of Rome in particular, as the act of a madman.[31] Nevertheless, the decision was backed by very good argument and was, quite probably, not his. Rome was a considerable cost to the state, both in terms of the food and entertainments which emperors customarily provided, and also because it was a tax haven. Taxation of the city of Rome would necessarily offset some of the vast cost of feeding, clothing and entertaining its inhabitants. Constantine himself recognized this in later years. While too clever to repeat the mistake of the imposition of a poll tax, Constantine hit upon another method to obtain revenue from the empire's cities. He imposed two new taxes designed to raise precious metal revenue from the cities, the *collatio lustralis* and the *collatio glebalis*. The first was a tax levied upon income derived from trade or the imposition of fees, and the second was specifically levied upon senators. The glebal tax permitted few exceptions and was assessed on the basis of property holdings.[32] These taxes were levied upon the very people in the cities who might be regarded as making money: urban professionals, and the curial class, with whom was concentrated much agricultural wealth. Another significant point here is the responsibility for the decision to tax Rome and the cities. Lactantius blames Galerius, yet by his own account the census was well in progress in 305, and in that account he states very clearly that the census was conducted both in provinces and cities.[33] That means, at the very least, that Constantius himself acceded to the extension of the census to the cities. It is more likely that the impetus came from Diocletian himself since the administrative arrangements would need to be made well in advance. In this respect both Constantius and Galerius might be best understood as continuing to apply policies worked out by Diocletian and rolled out over time.

The city of Rome represented a vast and untapped source of wealth. Moreover, extension of the poll tax to the city had a particular implication for its senatorial elite. The curial class in the provinces had always taken responsibility for the assessed tax liability of their cities. If the same principle were applied in Rome, then the Senate became the guarantor of the assessed capitation liability of the entire population of Rome. The senatorial class, now largely isolated from military careers, had little contribution to make to the smooth running of the state, other than ceremonial and financial.[34] The highest office to which a senator could aspire was that of Urban Prefect – the administrator of the city of Rome and chairman of the Senate.[35] Senators still featured on the *fasti* from time to time as ordinary consuls, but that was a post of more ceremonial than real value, dispensed by imperial favour.[36] Governorships such as those of Asia and Africa might still be held in the service of the state, but most posts reserved for senators were of minor importance and rarely involved command of soldiers.[37] Nevertheless, even if the senatorial aristocracy had become politically irrelevant, it still represented a significant concentration of wealth. A fundamental prerequisite for membership of the senatorial order was the possession of a great deal of money. The senatorial order was no longer the fixed and hereditary elite of the early empire. Much of the makeup of the Senate was different in each generation, with families tending to follow a pattern of either rising to power and suffering its consequence or, upon achieving senatorial status, regarding that as a sufficient end, remaining in obscurity and, at length, withdrawing from office. The sociological consequence of this was the widening of the pool of potential senators, until it took in the curial class of virtually every province in the empire.[38] The economic consequence was that large numbers of very wealthy people paid very little tax. Those who were in the Senate paid no ordinary taxes at all, while those whose fathers or grandfathers had been senators enjoyed varying degrees of tax immunity.[39] The very financial necessity of taxing senators can be perceived in Constantine's subsequent imposition of the *collatio glebalis*. Just as his introduction of the *collatio lustralis* abundantly illustrates the necessity for an ordered tax on urban populations, so does this tax on senators illustrate the continual and blatant inequity of their position of financial privilege. This is not to say that senators had had no public obligations. While they enjoyed the considerable advantage of immunity from *munera*, they were nevertheless obliged at some point in their careers to hold games for the Roman populace. In addition, the Roman Senate was liable for the payment of *aurum oblaticium*.[40] They do not appear to be onerous tasks within the context of senatorial wealth, and exemption from the performance of *munera* excluded them from the expense of public building. The emperor took care of that task.

One had to be very wealthy to be a senator. There were probably still only six hundred senators, and admission to the clarissimate was either by birth or adlection. Because of the requirement to hold games during the quaestorship (and therefore to gain direct membership of the Senate itself), there could be no poor senators.[41] There had always been a property qualification for membership of the Senate, although the financial threshold in the early fourth century, after a century of economic change, is uncertain. If illustrations of senatorial wealth are needed, however, the extensive and extravagant villa at Piazza Armerina – perhaps owned by the Aradii Rufini – or the elaborate and expensive monuments to the achievements of the Iunii Bassi should suffice.[42] The source of this wealth was agricultural: senators still owned *latifundia*, as they had in the days of the Gracchi; a poor senator was still a very rich man.[43] Because their tax burdens were comparatively insignificant, Rome had become a tax haven for as many as twelve hundred or so wealthy families.[44] What would be more natural than that an emperor, seeking to supplement his revenue, should seek to tap this rich vein? Constantine certainly did. While Diocletian's policy, as enforced by Constantius and Galerius, differed in its particulars, the principle was the same.

Up until 306, it is fair to say that the Roman Senate had been a most complaisant body. Eclipsed by the Danubian military, it had not provided emperors of any consequence for half a century. More recent emperors were military nominees who had worked their way through the ranks. Diocletian was of humble origin; Galerius of a peasant family; Maximian's family had kept a shop in Sirmium.[45] Not only did such men feel no necessary affinity with the senatorial order, but the senators themselves, reduced to political impotence, had not resisted their dominance. The Senate had continued to play a marginal role in affairs under Diocetian. He still called upon senators for certain governorships, most notably that of Syria.[46] Nevertheless, the extent to which senators were called upon to perform such tasks was very limited. This had led one scholar to label Diocletian, somewhat emotively, as "the hammer of the aristocracy".[47] While Arnheim's arguments here go too far in their concentration upon Diocletian, it is fair to say that the Senate under Diocletian had no real power. Diocletian nevertheless paid a certain amount of lip-service to senatorial pretension. A significant number of senators held ordinary consulships between 284 and 305, and a handsome new Curia, to replace that destroyed in the time of Carinus, was built in the Forum.[48]

Despite such concessions, the Senate remained impotent. The only revenge which members of the senatorial order could now take was literary: emperors whom they detested, for example, Gallienus and Carinus, suffered after their deaths from the malice of senatorial pens.[49] The same animus can be found against Diocletian and his colleagues. Lactantius' characterization of Maximian, for example, is a model of classical rhetorical polemic against a "bad" emperor.[50] Lactantius' account of the tax measures of 306 reflects the views of the same class. He is particularly vivid, describing savage *censitores*, the torture and suffering of innocent taxpayers, the empire as a subjugated land, Galerius as its savage conqueror; and the *censitores* as agents of his barbarian vengeance.[51] While this is good rhetorical stuff, it also reflects a kind of political chatter. In passages like this, Lactantius is at his most valuable, conveying the views and rhetoric of the political élite with which he identified.[52] Thus, the revolt of October 306, when it came, emerged from a disgruntled and alienated senatorial class which had tolerated more than enough impertinence from rough soldier-emperors.

The success of the revolt, however, required far more than senatorial discontent. It needed a figurehead and it needed troops. The figurehead was not difficult to identify. Maximian's son Maxentius, himself a senator, had resented his omission from the arrangements of 305 and now sought to ameliorate this. In many ways he was better positioned, in terms of dynastic relationships, than Constantine, whose success he evidently envied. Maxentius was the son of Maximian, the son-in-law of Galerius and the father of Diocletian's grandson.[53] He was also, as has been noted, a singularly difficult young man. Zosimus tells the story that, when he heard of Constantine's success, he:

> thought it intolerable that Constantine, the son of a harlot, should realize his ambition while the son of so great an emperor should stand idly by and possess the power rightly his by inheritance.[54]

Zosimus' account derives, in all likelihood, from his principal source, Eunapius. While neither had any love for Constantine, there is something curiously authentic about the anecdote. Even that such a story might be told illustrates that the dichotomy had occurred to someone in Rome in the fourth century – if not to Maxentius himself. Maxentius had good reason to expect succession to the purple. We first hear of him in 289, when he is still a child, standing beside his father in the palace at Trier to listen to a panegyric from the orator Mamertinus. In the peroration to the speech, the orator turns his attention to the boy, commending his father to him as the *exemplum* of an ideal ruler.[55] By 304 he had married Valeria Maximilla, the daughter of Galerius and Valeria, who was in turn the granddaughter of Diocletian. The marriage had taken place by 304 and it bore the fruit of a child in late 305 or early 306.[56] But Maxentius wore his status proudly, making clear his disdain for Galerius. In other circumstances, he might have served a key role for the dynasty since his marriage to Maximilla and production of a male heir bound an adoptive family with ties of blood. Perhaps it was his consciouness of this and desire to exploit it that induced Diocletian and Galerius to pass him over in the first place.[57]

In passing him over, however, Galerius eliminated Maximian's immediate blood family from imperial office. The intent may have been to nullify any power base which the Herculean house had managed to build up and ultimately to supersede it completely. The appointment of Severus can be seen in the context of this design, particularly since he had a son of his own.[58] Curiously, however, there was no attempt to rearrange the imperial families. Galerius did not compel his daughter to divorce Maxentius in order to provide a wife for either Severus or Constantine, an observation which strengthens the argument that the alleged divorces and remarriages of 293 did not occur.[59] Maxentius was, however, in no immediate position to assert his pretensions and the claims of his house. He was no soldier, but had been directed upon a political path as a member of that very body which, according to Lactantius, his father had despoiled so shamelessly.[60]

These accusations of Maximian cannot be taken too seriously. They represent a pattern of polemical rhetoric which serve more to identify the prejudices of a narrow class than inform about their object. In fact Maximian had good reason to ensure that there was an effective link with the Senate. While the Senate had been reduced to a minor role in politics, its symbolic importance remained enormous. It was still the Senate which formally nominated the emperor, a fact of which Diocletian was well aware when he nominated his very first consul, the senator L. Caesonius Ovinius Manlius Rufinianus Bassus.[61] Bassus had performed the important task of representing Diocletian to his colleagues and died, proud of his status, as a friend of emperors.[62] An informal representation of an imperial viewpoint in the *curia* will have gone some way to convincing the senators that they were still sufficiently important for their loyalty to be worthwhile.

This makes good sense of Maxentius' presence in Rome and a civil, rather than military, career. Other imperial males were put to the service of the regime as officers in the army.[63] Maxentius' task was different. He was its newest representative in the Senate. Diocletian and Maximian had always required such a service. Bassus was the first in an honourable line. Another predecessor can be identified: Afranius Hannibalianus, a soldier of great distinction and a relative of Maximian.[64] Hannibalianus had also been a successful commander. His exploits as a general were sufficiently noteworthy for him to be included in a list of commanders – some real, and the others, fictional – which appears in the *Vita Probi*.[65] He had served as Praetorian Prefect along with Julius Asclepiodotus and both men were ordinary consuls in 292.[66] He must have entered the Senate either during his prefecture or upon his assumption of the consulship, although it has been argued that he was a member of the body from much earlier.[67] While Asclepiodotus became Praetorian Prefect a second time, perhaps recalled specifically to aid Constantius in the recovery of Britain, Hannibalianus went on to become Prefect of the City, thus achieving the summit of senatorial ambition.[68]

All things, however, come to an end. It is reasonable to expect that at some stage even Hannibalianus might die or retire. He would therefore require a successor in his role, and this is the role for which the young Maxentius was earmarked. He was closely related to both branches of the imperial dynasty. As such, he was uniquely placed to determine exactly what level of discontent existed within the city of Rome. If his task was to defuse it, he was in an excellent situation to turn it to his own advantage. By 306, with the recognition of Constantine's succession, Maxentius had good reason to feel slighted and passed over by his father-in-law. It is hardly surprising to find him turning away from his family and looking to his own direct interests.

If a ringleader was to hand in the person of the relegated Maxentius, an army of sorts could be found in the tattered remnants of the Praetorian Guard and urban cohorts. The mutiny of these troops and the murder of a number of officials who remained loyal, including Abellius, the *vicarius* of the urban prefect, marked the beginning of the revolt.[69] Just as Rome's urban populace had good reason to be dissatisfied, so too did the city's garrison fear for its future. By 306, the Praetorian Guard was another fossil of imperial grandeur. In 41 it had been the arbiter of empire, handing the principate to the surprised Claudius. Its support had secured Nero his throne and, in periods of instability, was a major player in the imperial power game. The Praetorians had murdered and enthroned emperors for two centuries, on one celebrated occasion even auctioning the empire.[70] But power had passed decisively from them to the frontier armies. Their opportunity seriously to influence events passed once emperors no longer resided customarily at Rome. Their last real nominee had been Gordian III.[71]

Between the time of Domitian and Diocletian, the Praetorian Guard had ten cohorts. Unlike legionary units, the Guard cohort stood at double strength (around 1,000 men), giving the Guard at any time a membership of

10,000 troops.[72] These soldiers, apart from receiving regular and generous donatives, were the best paid in the Roman army.[73] Most were quartered in the city of Rome, in the large *Castra Praetoria* in the north-east.[74] Although their traditional function was to protect the emperor, they nevertheless did do some fighting from time to time. There were Praetorian cohorts in Aurelian's campaign against Zenobia and Maximian evidently took some Praetorians to Africa in his campaigns against the Quinquegentiani.[75] But these are brief interruptions of a long trajectory of decline.

Aurelius Victor states that Diocletian reduced the number of Praetorian cohorts.[76] The last inscription attesting ten cohorts is dated to 298.[77] The diminution of the Guard happened after that, and perhaps a suitable context can be found in Diocletian's visit to Rome in 303. Diocletian reportedly disliked the larrikin spirit of the Roman populace. He can hardly, then, have been impressed with a corps of 10,000 highly paid and privileged soldiers whose ostensible function was to guard a person who mostly wasn't there. If Diocletian had begun the process of dismantling the Guard in 303, its completion was left to his successors. According to Lactantius, there were only a handful of soldiers left (*milites pauci*) when Galerius finally gave the order to abolish the Guard.[78] This estimate may reflect anything from a few hundred to a few thousand soldiers. Whatever the number, their own long history of political activism demanded that they not go quietly. They refused to accept the order to disband and mutinied. At this point, the discontent within the Roman Senate bore its fruit. C. Annius Anullinus, the *praefectus urbi*, who ought to have quelled the mutiny, joined it.[79] The urban cohorts likewise added their numbers to the rebellion, as did at least one of their officers, Lucianus, who was also tribune of the pork supply (*tribunus fori suarii*).[80]

Maxentius' successful seizure of power in 306 must be seen therefore as a complex interplay of factors, each of which by themselves might have come to nothing. The discontent in the city over taxation could have been silenced by a judicious show of strength; the readiness to mutiny among the Praetorian Guard could have been obviated by either a more vigorous phasing out of the Guard (Constantine disbanded it unilaterally)[81] or, again, a timely display of legionary power; Maxentius' frustration might have continued where the populace and troops had been either coerced or cajoled into loyalty towards another. But this was not to be. These three factors combined inexorably to destroy the settlement of August 306 and fatally disrupt the new dynastic arrangements.

Ultimately, the responsibility for all this must be ascribed to Diocletian and Galerius. It had been Diocletian's policies which had created both the initial resentment amongst urban taxpayers, and the sense of unease amongst Praetorians. His preference for Galerius in 305, moreover, had resulted in the alienation of Maxentius. Galerius, for his part, acted as the enforcer of policies and processes which were not his own. He could act with prudence; he had defused a potential civil war with Constantine. But when the issue went beyond mere politics and into policy, he (and perhaps Constantius also) adhered rigorously to the models devised and enacted by Diocletian. Certainly Galerius' approach in this matter is consistent with that of Diocletian. Both were insensitive, determined and brutal. Galerius' miscalculation in relation to Rome is as explicable as Diocletian's problems in Egypt. Both pursued a series of policies heedless of their implications and possible consequences. Both incited civil war. Both men also failed abjectly in their judgement of Maxentius. The sources make it clear enough that Galerius disliked Maxentius.[82] Yet Galerius still trusted him enough to permit him to remain in Rome, perhaps clinging to the tenuous authority of dynastic propinquity. Maxentius, after all, had not been dealt out of the game completely. He was the father of Galerius' grandson and of Diocletian's great-grandson. Such blood ties promised some power, some role and some relevance. But Maxentius did not merely desire relevance; he saw power as his birthright. Neither Diocletian nor Galerius perceived this in time. This was an error – a misjudgement of the city of Rome, its people and its most imperial resident.

Although Maxentius took the purple in October 306, his intentions at that time remain unclear. Lactantius seems to have believed that he was attempting to graft himself on to the imperial college as a fifth emperor, and his political judgement as a contemporary ought not to be dismissed cavalierly.[83] Certainly his view has merit and has been accepted by careful and critical scholars.[84] It is obvious that Maxentius had no desire to wreck the dynasty, since his own legitimacy derived from within it. In his own propaganda he was initially content to be proclaimed as *princeps iuventutis* and *princeps invictus*. He did not take the title of Augustus, although he might have done since the ragged remnants of the Praetorian Guard had, presumably, used this title in proclaiming him emperor.[85]

In all likelihood, he followed Constantine's lead in immediately sending a courier to Galerius bearing a laurelled portrait.[86] His tentative use of nomenclature indicates a negotiating tactic. Like Constantine, he sought recognition from Galerius. Unlike Constantine, he had no claim to the formal succession to an imperial vacancy. There was none. Instead, Maxentius possessed his name, the city of Rome and a small army. In leaving the question of his status open, he also offered Galerius a neat solution. Neither need be embarrassed by resultant compromise – in his case, that of demotion to the rank of Caesar; in that of Galerius, the recognition of a *fait accompli*. Maxentius thus sought to combine his seizure of the purple with the legitimation of his act through the support of the ruling Augustus, who also happened to be his father-in-law.

That does not mean that Maxentius was not beyond dropping a few hints as to what he thought Galerius ought to do. Up until October 306, the mint of Rome had mostly been striking *folles* bearing the titles and image of Galerius and Severus as Augusti, and Constantine and Maximin Daza as Caesars. After Maxentius' coup, the mint ceased to strike for Severus and

Daza, but continued for Galerius and Constantine. The new precious metal issues did not feature Galerius, however. He was replaced by Maxentius' father, hailed as *Maximianus Senior*, in order to differentiate him from Galerius.[87] From this it should be clear that Maxentius recognized neither Severus nor Daza. This is clearly an implicit statement that he wished to replace one of them. He had left Galerius with the choice: he could strip the purple from either Severus or Daza and Maxentius could take their place. Where Constantine had enjoyed a ready-made vacancy through the demise of his father, Maxentius needed to manufacture his own by threatening Galerius with schism in the empire. Maxentius can only have seen this as his birthright. In a regime which leaned heavily upon the language of dynasty and family affinity, he had been passed over despite his clear dynastic qualifications. He affected not to be particular about the role that he took, or whose place he assumed. That means, at the very least, that he sought recognition at the expense of either of Galerius' nominees or neither of them (if Lactanius is correct). The task of determining the nature of that recognition and crafting a role for Maxentius in the new state was left to Galerius. In this respect, Maxentius appeared diplomatic and conciliatory. He was not seeking anything unreasonable, only what was due to him.

Maxentius' stance was not completely passive. He asserted himself later in the year with his nomination of consuls for 307. These provided a very clear hint as to how Galerius might respond to Maxentius' claim to power. The nomination of consuls was a prerogative of the Augusti, and generally worked out well in advance. For the most part, since 290, they had been the emperors themselves. In 305 Constantius and Galerius had taken up their consulships as Caesar. In the following year, they also held ordinary consulships, but as Augusti. Given that pattern of office-holding it is likely that the consuls for 307 were long known to be Severus and Daza, nominated as Caesars in 305.[88] Maxentius rejected this arrangement, nominating instead Galerius himself in the place of Severus.[89] This must be seen in the same context of Maxentius' deployment of titulature. It was an offer to Galerius to avoid conflict by recognizing Maxentius' legitimacy, and to give a broad hint to his father-in-law as to how to do it – the removal of the interloper Severus from office and acknowledgement that one closer in blood (if more distant in spirit) had a greater claim to the purple. In setting his cap at Severus' place, he sought directly to inherit all that had been his father's: the palace at Milan, to which Severus now had the keys; command of Maximian's old troops and control of Maximian's old treasury.[90] Maxentius had thus set himself a more difficult task than Constantine had. Where Constantine wished to succeed an emperor, Maxentius wished to displace one. It all depended upon Galerius' reaction.

Galerius received the laurelled portrait at a busy time. Distracted by duty, he was in the midst of a war. Diocletian had commenced the policy of the settlement of the Danubian frontier along its length. Galerius had taken that over in his latter years as Caesar, and was now continuing it as Augustus.[91] While he had done great work in earlier years in subduing and resettling the Carpi in the Lower Danubian provinces, the problem of Sarmatian tribes on the middle and upper Danube remained. Both Diocletian and Galerius had already made war on them on a number of occasions, but the matter was not yet settled.[92] At least two campaigns against them were conducted by Galerius in the early years of the fourth century, probably in 302 and 306/7.[93] A third campaign can also be inserted late in 305, from the evidence of an anecdote in the *Origo Constantini Imperatoris* which records Galerius' vain attempt to have Constantine killed in battle against the Sarmatians.[94]

Galerius, therefore, spent much of 305 and 306 on the middle Danube, based at Sirmium and campaigning, probably, in the area around Margum.[95] He would have received the news of Maxentius' coup late in the campaigning season in Pannonia. Galerius had some leisure to consider Maxentius' offer, and a number of good reasons to accept it, but he rejected the proposal out of hand. Galerius had a powerful precedent to work from. In the late 280s Carausius had sought to graft himself into the imperial college through the proclamation on coinage that he had been adopted into the imperial fraternity. Coins struck in his mints showed imperial profiles of Carausius, Diocletian and Maximian with the legend "Carausius and his brothers". Diocletian refused to reciprocate and Carausius was consistently regarded as a piratical usurper.[96]

The precedent was a powerful one, particularly since it had commenced some years of rebellion in Britain. Galerius' reasons for rejecting Maxentius' offer must have been equally powerful. They were grounded, surely, in the ideology of *concordia* that had laid at the base of the edifice of power constructed by Diocletian. From Diocletian's accession, power had been bestowed as a gift. If the new dynasty functioned through *concordia*, that *concordia* was in turn guaranteed by the patronage of the Augustus. Even Constantine had seen the merit in this, preferring to accept the patronage of a living Augustus to the blessings of a dead one. If that patronage were negated by either the defeat or humiliation of the patron, then the dynastic structure would fall apart since the whole new structure was predicated upon a strict family hierarchy dominated by powerful men bound by blood and personal loyalty. Diocletian's appointment of Severus and Daza to the purple had been designed to ensure that Galerius would succeed to the charismatic authority which Diocletian had exercised in his time and, through it, guarantee the dominance of the Jovian line. If Galerius had dismissed Severus from office in order to accommodate Maxentius, it would mean that he had bowed to pressure from outside the college. This carried with it the clear implication that he was thereby abdicating his own rank. Thus, in reality, Maxentius left him no choice. Moreover, personal loyalty also plays a part. There was a clear bond of comradeship between Galerius and Severus. One source sees it as a sign of discredit:

Severus Caesar ignobilis et moribus et natalibus, ebriosus et hoc Galerio amicus.[97]

(Severus Caesar, low of birth and morals, was a drunkard and therefore a friend of Galerius.)

Friendship was one of the cementing bonds of the dynasty. Maxentius' own claim originated in his father's nomination to power by Diocletian, his trusted and trusting friend. The *concordia* brought by amity and fraternity was advertised on coins and monuments.[98] Such a basis was both powerful and fragile: it was powerful in that it implied four men, all committed to the same task, mutually supporting each other and watching each other's backs. It was fragile because, if one factor disrupted that harmony between the imperial brothers, unity of purpose would be lost, rivalry would take over and civil war result. Thus Galerius was loyal to Severus with a loyalty that possibly transcended Severus' eventual failure and death. Severus had a son, Severianus, who probably served in Galerius' household, and was certainly present at the court of Maximin Daza and *capax imperii* in 313. He may even have held office as *praeses* of Isauria in 308/9 after his father's failure.[99] If that is the case, it bespeaks a personal loyalty on the part of Galerius well beyond the necessities of imperial politics. It is not then hard to understand Galerius' outright rejection of Maxentius' offered compromise. The protocol which had been established by Diocletian and implemented by him had left him no option. Its flexibility had been tested by Constantine and shattered by Maxentius. Instead Galerius immediately summoned Severus from Mediolanum to Sirmium, where the two conferred on the course of action for the following year.[100]

By the end of the year the situation had acquired further urgency. Valerius Alexander, the equestrian *vicarius* of the African provinces, declared his loyalty to Maxentius. The mint of Carthage began to strike issues proclaiming Maxentius as *nobilissimus Caesar*.[101] This suggests that Alexander did not formally collaborate with Maxentius, and that the defection of the African provinces occurred soon after receipt of the news of Maxentius' own revolt. The African provinces were crucial to Maxentius since they continued to be a major source of grain. Their loyalty to him probably emerged from affection within the provinces for his father. Maximian had campaigned there against marauding tribes (the so-called *Quinquegentiani*) in 297/8 with great success, and seems to have commanded considerable residual loyalty from his troops as Severus' subsequent misadventure suggests.[102] Zosimus adds a curious point of detail that bears this out. In his account of the later secession of Africa from Maxentius' control, he gives the substantial reason for it as the garrison's loyalty to Galerius.[103] Since this is a patent error, it needs to be explained. The simplest explanation is that Zosimus or his source (presumably Eunapius) confused Galerius Valerius Maximianus with Aurelius Valerius Maximianus, that is, Galerius with Maximian. Therefore, what Zosimus is actually saying is that the African troops revolted out of loyalty to Maximian. This makes perfect sense, since the revolt occurred at a time when Maximian had been humiliated and exiled by his son.[104]

For Galerius, the loss of Africa was a major blow. The African grain, which might have been held back to starve Maxentius into submission, was now guaranteed for Rome. For centuries the stability of the sprawling, and largely unpoliced, metropolis had been guaranteed by the steady supply of free grain. That grain derived principally from Africa and Egypt. While Galerius could prevent the Alexandrian grain fleet from sailing to Rome, the loss of Africa to Maxentius meant that this could be made good with wheat from there.[105] Without such wheat, the revolt would have withered swiftly, since Rome had too many mouths to feed to withstand a siege unsupplied. With Africa loyal to him, on the other hand, Maxentius could sit more securely, since his grain supply was guaranteed.

Maxentius was still not totally secure. He had no army to speak of. The Praetorians in Rome and the distant African garrison were too insubstantial and scattered to provide an effective field army.[106] His bid for power had been a bold gamble, but, once Galerius had refused to acknowledge him, Maxentius' fortunes became extremely precarious. War was only a matter of time, and Maxentius had sparse resources to fight one. It was this, rather than any sense of filial duty, that drove Maxentius to his next act. He invited Maximian, his father, to Rome to resume the purple that had been so reluctantly resigned in 305.[107] At first glance the sources seem to offer little unanimity of testimony. The *Origo Constantini* dates Maximian's resumption of office to the period following the defeat of Severus. This is clearly wrong since it both contradicts and makes no sense of other narratives. Zosimus, drawing upon Eunapius, tells another story. He also suggests that Maximian's return to power was after the repulse of Severus, but all his own work, and owed nothing to an invitation from Maxentius. Following the tradition of the *Kaisergeschichte*, Eutropius suggests that Maximian's coup was not inspired by Maxentius.[108]

This tangle of literary sources can be resolved through a careful analysis of the coinage, specifically that of the mint of Carthage. Africa declared quickly for Maxentius. This can be seen in the coin issues and the inscription which erroneously ascribe to him the title of *nobilissimus Caesar*. Coins struck for Maximian as a regnant Augustus ("P.F. AVG") also appear within the same series of issues, as do coins struck in the names of Constantine and Daza.[109] These early issues can be put down to confusion at the mint as to the actual events in Rome.[110] Despatches from Rome cleared this up. Soon after these coins were struck, they were replaced by a second issue. This issue has a distinct mint-mark, and hailed Maxentius as *princeps invictus*. Daza was dropped from the series, but the elder Maximian remained, now with the title of Augustus Senior, clarifying his status as a retired emperor. When

Maxentius took the title Augustus, the title of *princeps invictus* was dropped from the coinage, with a new mint-mark to accompany the new titulature.[111] The evidence of the Carthage mint is important in disentangling the early months of Maxentius' rule. Clearly there were provincials who thought that Maximian had returned to power, with Maxentius as his Caesar. While they were swiftly disabused of this by more accurate information from the capital, it is clear that a return to power by Maximian would not be unexpected nor, necessarily, unwelcome.

If the mint of Carthage provides an insight into how loyal but ill-informed partisans sought to interpret the coup, the mint of Rome provides a more authoritative guide. The first group of Maxentian coins which it struck included an issue in the name of Maximian as Augustus Senior, with the epithets *pius* and *felix*.[112] Significantly, the title of *imperator* is missing. Maximian is not, then, regarded here as regnant but dormant. What was being celebrated was the dynastic link with a retired emperor, and not collegiality with a ruling one. This differs from Lactantius' account, although not his chronology:

> *patri suo post depositum imperium in Campania morenti purpuram mittit et bis Augustum nominat.*[113]

(He sent the purple to his father, who had been dwelling in Campania since his abdication, and nominated him as Augustus a second time.)

This is an interesting version of events but not compelling. Lactantius makes the claim that Maxentius nominated Maximian as Augustus for the second time. Not only was such an act without precedent, but any claim by Maxentius to conduct it could only be based upon his own ambiguous and invented status as *princeps invictus*. He could not offer the purple to another while his own position was so vague, and hope for recognition by Galerius still remained. Nor was it in Maxentius' interests so to do. Maxentius had sought by his coup to gain power for himself, not for his father. If Maxentius had done the legally impossible and, in the midst of his own vague, if hopeful, usurpation, declared his father Augustus, what was the consequence? Who was the senior, and who junior? All Maxentius would have done would have been to invite his father to return from unwilling retirement and frustrate the designs of Diocletian and Galerius by reclaiming the lordship of the West. Maxentius did not become involved in a coup because he coveted second place.

If we take the evidence of the coinage and Lactantius together, however, a resolution can be achieved. Towards the end of 306, Maxentius was in a tenuous position. Support from Africa must have given him some heart, but he knew that if negotiations with Galerius failed he would necessarily need to defend himself. He was untried as a general, his military experience per-haps even non-existent.[114] Furthermore, he had few soldiers with whom to challenge the western Augustus. His only weapon was nevertheless strong – dynastic legitimacy. Maximian was both a skilled general and the source of such legitimacy. In that context, it makes perfect sense that Maxentius invited his father to return to Rome – not as ruling Augustus, but as valued adviser and symbol of Maxentius' claim to the purple – Augustus *senior,* but not Augustus *imperator.* Maximian's return to the city was celebrated in a coin issue proclaiming "FELIX INGRESSVS SENIORIS AVGVSTI". On the same coin, perhaps by a pious fiction, Maximian was accorded a second celebration of his *vicennalia* with the legend "VOT. XXX".[115]

Early in 307, this policy was vindicated. After a conference between Galerius and Severus in Sirmium, Severus returned to Milan.[116] The north-ern Italian diocese was still loyal, since the mints of Ticinum and Aquileia continued to strike for Galerius and Severus.[117] Galerius, campaigning against the Sarmatians, could not send his own troops, so Severus was con-strained to use the troops bequeathed him by Maximian.[118] It was a gamble, although the emperors, accustomed to decades of freedom from mutiny (the last against an emperor in command had been in 281 against Probus), might not have seen it as such. If so, they miscalculated. They overestimated the loyalty of their soldiers to a previous commander. There is no doubt that the soldiers who formed Severus' army were composed in a large part of Max-imian's veterans. Zosimus calls them "Moorish legions" – a gratuitous detail which therefore inspires some trust. Maximian had been successful in Africa, and doubtless some, or all, of these troops had served under him there.[119] It was with this army, lately commanded by his rival, that Severus was obliged to settle the revolt of Maxentius. Lactantius notes the irony:

mittit eum cum exercitu Maximiani ad expugnandi Maximiani filium.[120]

(he sent him with the army of Maximian to achieve the removal of Maximian's son.)

There has been some confusion over the chronology of the conflict. Two dates are certain: April 307, when Maxentius ceased to recognize the con-sulships of Galerius and Daza; and 25 July, when Constantine still styled himself as a Caesar.[121] April is the more probable month for the invasion. It sent a very clear message that Galerius had no intention of coming to terms with Maxentius. Severus' march on Rome made the conflict unambiguous and inevitable. It was the point at which Maxentius abandoned the appear-ance of loyalty, took the title of Augustus and dropped the names of Galerius and Daza from his consular formulae.[122] It was a bold gamble: Maxentius lacked sufficient forces to assert it. When Severus commenced his march on Rome from Milan there was no force to impede his progress. He was also able to invest the city of Rome itself. But the walls were strong and it was there that things went wrong. While it should have been easy enough to wait out a siege, the magic of Maximian's name proved a stronger offensive tactic than Severus could withstand. His soldiers deserted and Severus was left marooned, an emperor without an army. The old commander, the old loyalty, the old fidelity, triumphed over any pretension of succession.[123]

Severus weighed up discretion and valour, and fled. He made for Ravenna. Maximian pursued him swiftly and, as he pushed towards Ravenna, northern Italy, with its mints of Ticinum and Aquileia, fell to him without any apparent conflict.[124] In Ravenna, Severus perhaps hoped to obtain a ship and flee to Galerius. He still had some troops, but not enough to withstand a siege. No doubt he purposed to retreat, gather an army loyal to him and fight it out in a second invasion of Italy. He did not, however, escape. Maximian pursued him relentlessly, evidently determined to secure his capture. Severus' death or enforced abdication would create a vacancy in the imperial college that Maxentius could claim to fill. Perhaps, however, Maximian already had ideas of his own designs. With Ravenna invested, Maximian opened negotiations with Severus.[125] The fugitive emperor might have hoped to buy time, secure behind marshland and walls, to make an escape by sea. He neglected the views of the townsfolk, however, who can scarcely have welcomed a man for whom they had no natural affection, and whose presence might brand them traitors. Severus was trapped and had little choice but surrender to Maximian upon the promise of his life. Severus now returned the purple that he had once received from Maximian less than two years previously.[126] Galerius' designs had failed and the necessary vacancy had been generated.

If Severus had saved his life by surrender to Maximian, he did not keep it long. Lactantius implies that he committed suicide soon after his capture.[127] There is some merit in this view, and it certainly has the virtue of simplicity. Like many simple views, however, it is wrong. The papyrological evidence provides a different story. Severus was still regarded as Augustus in Egypt as late as 29 September 307.[128] One way in which Galerius continued to oppose Maxentius' bid for power was through the assertion in titulary of his deposed and humiliated colleague's right to rule. Once Severus was dead, this was no longer a possibility. Accepting the evidence of the papyri means that Severus was imprisoned after his surrender and held as hostage for Galerius' good conduct. It was a considerable disincentive to invasion. Galerius' own personal loyalty to Severus and the deep bond of friendship between them is unquestioned. As powerfully as the personal, the political imperative here was also to preserve Severus, since it was his right to rule that Galerius was asserting, and he could hardly do so if Severus were dead.

Maxentius and Maximian now waited. Galerius was not too far distant in Illyricum.[129] Galerius had a difficult choice. He could act by force, but then the life of Severus was forfeit. Since his objective was to defeat Maxentius in order to vindicate Severus, invasion was self-defeating. On the other hand, he could submit and acknowledge Maxentius, thereby compromising his own rule, possibly fatally. A swift response was necessary. Constantine had so far held aloof from the contest either from necessity or policy. When Severus was marching on Rome, Constantine was warring on the Franks and visiting Britain.[130] His consular nominations indicate his crafted and deliberate independence: Galerius and himself. This has the appearance of studious loyalty, but Galerius himself recognized Severus and Daza.[131] Constantine was waiting to be wooed and, no doubt, recognized by Galerius as legitimate Augustus of the West. This was a station to which Constantine could reasonably expect nomination from Galerius. The Augustus had abdicated. He was the Caesar. The place should be his.

Galerius could not do this. Severus' defeat had been a dangerous political reverse, seriously exacerbated by the twin humiliations of his surrender and abdication. Galerius' response was simply not to admit to either. Severus' abdication had been under patent duress, giving Galerius sufficient grounds to ignore it. Hence we find Severus recognized as both Augustus and consul in the documents of the eastern empire up until his death in September 307.[132] This also maintained Diocletian's dynastic symmetry of two Augusti and two Caesars, but at the cost of one nominal Augustus and two claimants in rebellion. As far as Galerius was concerned, there was no imperial vacancy at the top, no office for Constantine legitimately to succeed to. Maxentius, however, was emboldened by his success.

Constantine was now being openly courted by Maximian. Galerius' refusal to improvise a solution left Constantine little option but to drift into disloyalty. Galerius' inflexibility was Maximian's opportunity. Not long after Severus' abdication, Maximian travelled to Gaul to meet with Constantine. He arrived some time in September, probably to Trier, an imperial city and Constantine's base.[133] He brought the immense prestige he had acquired through two decades of successful rule; he brought the potent authority that had reclaimed the army from Severus; he brought his daughter. It is perhaps a matter of sentiment rather than history that the new relationship between Constantine and Maximian was proclaimed in the vast apsidal hall which still stands in Trier. It was a great occasion, marked by a great speech. A panegyrist marked the day in an oration that proclaimed the price of Constantine's benevolent neutrality: marriage to Maximian's daughter Fausta, and the rank of Augustus.[134] The speech marks a significant moment and the atmosphere of uncertainty in which it occurred. It is as important for what it does not say as for what it does. One commentator has noted:

> Although the speech names neither Galerius nor Maxentius, even by a periphrasis, all knew that the two were about to confront each other beyond the Alps.[135]

189

The panegyrist opens with a familiar theme – that of the unity generated by dynastic ties. As such, it is immediately political: Maximian is hailed as Augustus *aeternus*, whether he wants to be or not (*velis nolis*); Constantine is more obliquely saluted as "rising emperor" (*oriens imperator*). These two are to be joined by the family bond of Constantine's marriage to Fausta. In his praise of marriage, the panegyrist is unambiguously dynastic. He looks forward to the prospect of children born, rather than called, to the purple. He eagerly anticipates a future dominated for ages to come by the Herculean dynasty.[136] The orator then neatly expands upon his dynastic theme through his praise of Constantine. Constantine's multiple relationships with Maximian ("grandson through adoption; son by ranking; soon to be son-in-law") are clearly enunciated. The orator then elides to the more familiar theme of praise of Constantine's father. This marks an extended comparison between the two men, the point of which is less to establish that Constantine and his father shared particular rhetorical virtues than it is to stress the theme of dynastic continuity.[137]

This brings the orator to a significant point in the speech. Hitherto, he has referred to Constantine as *imperator*. Suddenly he leaps from comparison to list. Constantine is wise, brave, fortunate, youthful, yet impressive and, finally, mature. It is a strange point upon which to end the list, but all is made clear in the next sentence. It is a maturity that has led him to accept the title of Caesar until such time as Maximian could declare him Augustus. The orator then makes it plain that Maximian's own right to do so is asserted through a newly assumed status of senior emperor (*summo imperatore*).[138] There follows some polite fiction about the portents of love between Constantine and Fausta before it returns to the theme of Maximian's eternal rule. The panegyrist begins with some conventional praise for Maximian's achievements before his abdication but then describes the events afterwards as the kinds of things which occur when the gods no longer pay attention to what is happening in the world. He speaks of natural disasters in an allegory of the political earthquakes which had torn the Roman world asunder after the death of Constantius I. At that point the panegyrist uses imagery rather than narrative to describe the problems faced by the Roman world, but is most specific in his claim that Maximian had no right to abdicate.[139] He praises Maximian's loyalty to an old and sick friend as the motive for his abdication and, in so saying, accepts Diocletian's right to retire from power but denies Maximian's:

Sed tamen utcumque fas fuerit eum principem, quem anni cogerent aut vali-tudo deficeret, receptui canere, te vero, in quo adhuc istae sunt integrae soli-daeque vires, hic totius corporis vigor, hic imperatorius ardor oculorum, immaturum otium sperasse miramur.[140]

(But nonetheless, however right it might have been for that prince, whom his years constrained or whose health failed, to sound the retreat, we wonder that you yearned for an untimely leisure, you

whose strength is even now unimpaired, whose entire body is yet
vigorous, whose fiery glance is till that of an emperor.)

The panegyrist has strayed on to dangerous ground here. He must walk the
tightrope between asserting the legitimacy of Diocletian's retirement, but
not that of Maximian. He was not alone. The Roman world had never before
beheld an emperor collecting his superannuation. How did one refer to a
retired ruler? Some attempt had been made to clarify their status. A new title
had been invented, that of "senior Augustus". This was not intended to mean
that they outranked those who were merely "Augusti", that is, Constantius
and Galerius. The coins struck for Diocletian and Maximian as August*i seniores*
were not intended to advertise their rule, but to add prestige to those who did.
It was thus that Maxentius had initially invoked his father. It was thus that
Galerius subsequently called upon Diocletian. The title was never entirely
credible and, for Maximian, the Panegyrist immediately abandons it, claiming
instead that the reason that Diocletian really retired was so that Maximian
could take over completely and unite the rule of two emperors in himself.[141]

In making this grandiose and absurd claim, the orator does two things: he
asserts Maximian's eternal authority as emperor, and he denies the legitimacy
of Galerius. This position has a particular implication. If Maximian had
succeeded to the station of Diocletian, as well as retained his own, then
Galerius was the usurper. Both images almost plead to be plausible in their
denial of the recent past. The real point here is not the casuistry of the
orator. After all, the situation was not of his making. He was merely trying
to put a decent face on it. The significance is in the political reality which it
represents. Diocletian's regime had been predicated upon *concordia*, not
merely between the four emperors, but also between their two families. This
panegyric conspicuously ignores or denies the Jovian line, and exalts the
Herculian.[142] In so doing, the panegyrist fractures the unified extended
family of Diocletian into two competing dynasties. This was the political
cost of Constantine's ambition. Galerius was legitimate Augustus but Constantine could not look to him for the promotion he desired. Maximian was
illegitimate but credible, and offered him the patronage that raised Constantine from the rank of Caesar to that of Augustus. This is expressed by the
panegyrist as he moves, through his speech, from the phrase *oriens imperator*
to the more formal and precise "Constantine Augustus".

In accepting Maximian's patronage, Constantine was explicitly abandon-
ing any hope or expectation that he would receive promotion from Galerius.
Galerius had made it clear that he did not recognize Severus' enforced abdication. His name did not disappear from official documents in the east until
after his death and so, until that time, Galerius did not consider there to be a
vacancy to be filled.[143] Nor did Constantine necessarily expect further promotion from Galerius. Recognition as Caesar had been grudging; Galerius
had his own family to promote.

The panegyrist's task is not profound political analysis. It is to express the political arrangement between Maximian and Constantine. Maximian is *aeternus* Augustus, ruling in lofty majesty, deciding policy, determining peace and war. Constantine is *novus* Augustus, the mighty servant: making war, seeking advice, heeding the directions of the senior man.[144] In short, the relationship between the senior Augustus and the Augustus in the new arrangement is identical to that between the Augustus and Caesar in the old. No other could be trusted to reign supreme but Maximian. Diocletian was aged and ill, Severus was incompetent, a Phaëthon thrown from the sun's chariot, a chariot returned to its course by Maximian.[145]

Throughout the whole panegyric, Galerius is ignored. The reason is not merely that the conflict with Maxentius had yet to be settled. It is that Maximian coveted a newly identified status – that of senior Augustus. Diocletian had ruled as the *paterfamilias* of an imperial dynasty. His authority had been universal, patriarchal and charismatic. A diluted version of this role had been inherited by Constantius and then by Galerius. Constantine owed his own legitimacy to that inherited authority since, through it, Galerius had recognized his elevation as Caesar. At that point Constantine recognized Galerius as holding a superior and legitimate authority that entitled him to dictate the affairs of the entire empire, not merely those assigned to him. Now Maximian was claiming that role, attempting to wrest supreme legal authority from Galerius. The panegyrist ignores Galerius because to mention him in any context would necessarily raise questions about Maximian's own legitimacy. Galerius was no usurper: he was the son and son-in-law of Diocletian.

This view is borne out by the coinage of the Lugdunum mint. Its issues are idiosyncratic, at variance certainly with those of the Trier mint. From Lugdunum, we find a series of coins struck for Maxentius with standard reverse types, but we also find two unique issues: one in the name of Diocletian with the title of "AETERNVS AVGVSTVS", and another for Galerius as "MAXIMIANVS IVNIOR AVGVSTVS".[146] Sutherland has discussed the *Aeternus* type in some depth and the possible motive for the mint in striking it.[147] What does need to be noted is the subtle but important distinction between Diocletian as the *Aeternus* Augustus of the coinage and Maximian as the *semper* Augustus of the panegyrist. This distinction sets out a new protocol of power. Diocletian's authority is depicted as existing on a plane far removed from the mere mortal. The word *aeternitas* is numinous, whereas the word *semper* infers a more mundane endurance. Maximian, in this sense, will live and die an Augustus whether he wants to or not (the *velis nolis* of the panegyrist).[148] The Galerius coin is ambiguous – perhaps intentionally so. Tetrarchic coin portraiture is so stylized as to give little clue as to whom it refers and, since the whole phrase is in the nominative, there is no indication other than the word order as to whether the coin is celebrating Maximianus Junior, Augustus or Maximianus, Junior Augustus. There are no commas on coins, so which is it? Surely if the coiner had intended the former, then the simple expedient would have been to omit the IVN and substitute the initial of Galerius (C) to distinguish him from Maximian (M). However, the coiner ignored this and used instead the ambiguity which we find. Since this obvious mode of distinction was avoided, the ambiguity must be deliberate. Thus, the Lugdunum mint proudly proclaims the eternity of the only inactive retired emperor, and implied a status for Galerius inferior to that of Maximian. It is as if the abdications had not occurred. Sutherland suggests that the mint felt itself walking a political tightrope.[149] Both issues discussed here tend to confirm this view. But the master of the mint was still Constantine and he must, at the very least, have acceded to both coin types.

For Galerius, although these constitutional challenges to his authority were of some importance, the immediate issue was Maxentius. Severus' failure had been more than a loss of face for Galerius. It also represented a major challenge to his authority since imperial rule was predicated upon success. Galerius might recover from a defeat, as he had in Persia, but he could not lose the war. Victory over Maxentius would transform Constantine's opportunistic alliance with Maximian into folly. These considerations seem to have tempted Galerius into a premature, and unsuccessful, invasion of Italy.

Our narrative sources do not provide a clear picture of this campaign. The more detailed accounts, those of Lactantius and the *Origo*, suggest that Galerius began to suffer desertions from his force as he neared Rome and, having made an attempt at negotiation, beat a hasty retreat along the *via Flaminia*, plundering the towns as he went.[150] While there is no reason to doubt the substantive truth of the events themselves, these authors are Constantine's partisans, and so an element of distortion is to be expected.[151] The *Origo* does make it clear that Galerius did not invade Italy immediately upon the debacle of Severus' defeat. This document links Galerius' invasion with Severus' death, a most reasonable proposition given Severus' position as a hostage.[152] The *Chronicle of 354* conveniently gives the precise date of Severus' demise as 16 September.[153] This has been rejected by one scholar as impossibly late, but the papyrological and numismatic evidence tends to confirm it.[154] Nor ought so unequivocal a date be rejected merely because it does not fit a theory. That means that Galerius' march on Rome occurred in the late summer and autumn of 307. This is very late in the year, carrying its own inherent risks for campaigning.

Galerius, however, had not been free to act upon Severus' failure. He was tied down by his own war. A campaign against the Sarmatians was conducted at about this time and one against the Carpi soon afterwards.[155] Galerius was still engaged in the work which had occupied him since his Persian victory, that of pacifying Rome's longest river frontier. Since he was engaged in this long and arduous pacification, it would have been foolhardy in the extreme to break off a necessary foreign war in order to pursue domestic political objectives. He therefore put an end to his Danubian campaign as swiftly as he responsibly could, gathered his court and army together and marched on Rome.

As he had done once before in Persia, Galerius invited defeat by a rash move. Severus himself did not survive it since his value as a hostage was now expended. He was slain as Galerius' forces marched south. This invasion could only be a swift affair since it was so late in the year. His invasion route was the most direct possible – the *via Flaminia*. This is evident not merely because it was the route of his retreat, but also from his encampment at Interamna, which lies squarely on this road.[156] Thus Galerius' campaign was far from a methodical isolation of his enemy. He spent no time in securing northern Italy or the Alpine passes, but instead planned a lightning raid on Rome. Maximian, however, had already allowed for such a contingency since the city was strongly fortified, provisioned and held. Furthermore, Maxentius was not sufficiently unwise to risk battle. Galerius may well have hoped that he would venture out from behind the secure walls of Rome and hazard the purple in a contest, but such a hope was vain – Maxentius did not budge.

So Galerius attempted negotiation. He sent trusted and senior men – his *contubernalis* Licinius who was, perhaps, his closest adviser, and Pompeius Probus, later *consul ordinarius* and Praetorian Prefect.[157] The *Origo* is terse in its account of the negotiations:

> *Tunc legatos ad urbem misit Licinium et Probum, per colloquium petens ut gener apud socerum, id est Maxentius apud Galerium,precibus magis quam armis optata mercaretur.*[158]

(So he sent Licinius and Probus as ambassadors to the city requesting that the son-in-law [that is, Maxentius] seek to obtain his wishes from that father-in-law [that is, Galerius] through negotiation rather than force of arms.)

The expression rings true. Galerius was making a concession to Maxentius here, reminding him that legitimate power came through negotiation within the family. The two may have counselled patience. Galerius was nearing retirement; another member of the family would need to take his place. Maxentius was the father of Galerius' grandson, Diocletian's great-grandson. He was well placed to be a powerful and influential man far into the future. Any such assurances were no doubt thoroughly insincere and designed only to persuade Maxentius to divest himself of his corner of the purple. No matter how hard Probus and Licinius may have attempted to convince Maxentius otherwise, however, the blood of Severus remained ineradicably on his hands, as well as the sundering of the dynasty. The attempt to negotiate a solution was therefore rightly scorned by Maxentius, who no doubt foresaw death hard upon any renunciation of the purple on his part.

Lactantius states that Galerius' army was of insufficient number to mount a siege of Rome because the Augustus in his provincial simplicity had vastly underestimated the size of the city.[159] In fact, Galerius cannot have had any serious intention of besieging Rome when he invaded Italy. It was late in the year; Rome was well provisioned; Galerius had no way of cutting off Rome from Ostia.[160] Nevertheless, he seems to have considered the option when negotiations failed. This makes sense of the mutinies which broke out among his troops.[161] They had been campaigning all year and no doubt looked forward to winter quarters. All Galerius could offer them were the considerable hardships of a winter siege. And Maxentius had placed his agents in the camp of the Augustus – a not uncommon practice in a civil war, and one which had worked for him in the past. Certainly, this is the view of Aurelius Victor:

ibi cum obsidione distineretur, militibus eadem qua superiores, via attentatis, metu ne desereretur, Italia decessit.[162]

(When he [Galerius] was being delayed by the siege, and his soldiers being tempted in the same ways as their predecessors, he forsook Italy, fearing that he would be left abandoned.)

According to Lactantius, Galerius humbled himself before his army, begging them not to desert him, and bribed them to stay loyal.[163] Although Lactantius is the only writer to mention this, it is a likelihood. Galerius was obliged to abandon the siege. He had to announce it. This must have been done in a military assembly so as to end the damaging desertions. The terms of the speech can only be speculated upon, but Lactantius' account excites some suspicion, describing Galerius' condition as "pride broken and spirit gone" (*fracta superbia dismissisque animis*).[164] Further events show that this is hardly true. More likely, Galerius reminded them of the potential cost of their desertions to themselves and to him, appealed to their loyalty and agreed to lift the siege. Maxentius had escaped again. This was not an escape without hurt, however. Perhaps to placate his troops, certainly to give them something for their trouble, Galerius ordered the plundering of towns along the *via Flaminia*.[165]

Lactantius paints a picture of a frightened Galerius hastening northwards with a handful of troops, and plundering the countryside to please them.[166] The author of the *Origo* offers a more balanced and credible view, suggesting that Galerius' abandonment of a siege, for which he was ill-prepared, had a bitter and natural consequence for those dwelling on his line of march:

et ut militi suo praedam quamcunque conferret. Flaminiam iussit auferri.[167]

(and so that he might bestow booty of some kind upon his soldiers, he ordered that the Flaminia be looted.)

In reporting that Galerius ordered the *via Flaminia* to be plundered in order to furnish the troops with booty, the *Origo* belies the polemical image painted by Lactantius. Lactantius' image of Galerius barely leading a fragmenting rabble is inconsistent with his order to conduct a scorched-earth operation, with its implication of a wide dispersal and invitation to desert. Neither sees the retreat as a tactic, which it clearly was. While the pillage rewarded the troops for a hard year's campaigning, it also put significant pressure on Maxentius to emerge from the fastness of Rome's walls and give battle to protect the territory that he claimed as his. Maxentius was not to be drawn, but the strategy undermined, to some degree, the popular support that he enjoyed in Italy.

Even so, as Galerius retreated northwards to the security of his own Pannonian lands, he had to acknowledge failure. At best, he had undermined Maxentius' popularity by the ravaging of central Italy. In so doing, however, he had not endeared himself to people over whom he claimed legal authority, nor had he defeated Maxentius. Severus was dead. Constantine claimed the rank of Augustus. Maximian, malicious and grasping at the purple, was permitting himself to be regarded as the symbol of legitimacy by those in revolt. Nor had Galerius yet settled the Danubian frontier. But all was far from lost. He retained the obedience of Daza, his nephew and colleague. Because of his own previous success, and that secure and dutiful loyalty, Galerius still ruled two-thirds of the Roman world. It was a world, too, that was largely at peace. Nevertheless, Galerius' failure in Italy gave Constantine the encouragement he needed to persevere in his alliance with Maximian. That alliance confirmed Galerius' own view that, by the end of that year, the empire possessed only two legitimate rulers. The others were usurpers.[168]

Constantine seems to have taught Galerius a lesson about legitimacy. Maximian had (for his own purposes) consented to be the vehicle of Constantine's irregular promotion, but Maximian's own claim to the purple stemmed from the patronage of and propinquity with the one man who had as yet played no direct part in any of the manoeuvrings – Diocletian. Diocletian himself had done his best to ensure Galerius' supremacy; much of his work depended upon a stable and united imperial college. That had collapsed with the death of Constantius and the dynasty had split apart with the usurpation of Maxentius and Constantine's marriage to Fausta. This might have been remedied had Galerius taken Rome. This failure required a more drastic measure. The nature of that measure had already been discerned by Constantine when he had looked to Maximian to assert his legitimacy. Galerius could go one better. Messengers were sent to the capitals of the empire to announce that the consuls for the following year were to be himself and Diocletian.[169]

It was a considerable coup. Constantine, regarded by Galerius as being in revolt since the September wedding, recognized the consulships. Maxentius was hostile to the arrangement but did not nominate consuls of his own.[170]

This move by Galerius was only a foretaste. He still intended to settle the matter, but was prevented from giving it his full attention early in 308 by a campaign against the Carpi.[171] While he was thus engaged, two events occurred which complicated affairs even further.

The ideology expressed in the panegyric of 307 invested senior authority in Maximian. According to the panegyrist, Maximian ruled and the other Augusti ran his errands. Maximian's titulature reflects this change. The formula of Augustus Senior was progressively neglected in favour of the more activist *imperator Caesar Pius Felix* Augustus. It was as such that Maximian returned to Rome late in 307 or early in 308.[172] An ambiguity nevertheless remained. Constantine had driven a hard bargain but he was shrewd enough to stick to it. Maximian was, at least to his own mind, successor to Diocletian as senior emperor. His arrangements were far less tidy, however, being borne from political necessity rather than policy. His claimed authority extended to about one-third of the empire and, within that third, he was compelled to manage two Augusti — one his son; the other his son-in-law — neither of whom was especially compliant. The arrangement was fragile but could have been made to work if both had deferred to their *paterfamilias*. Constantine seems, at least superficially, to have done so (his legitimacy as Augustus, after all, depended upon it) and went off to make war in Germany.[173] Maxentius was a different matter.

Lactantius' account reflects both the new status of Maximian and its inherent ambiguity:

> *post huius fugam cum se Maximianus alter a Gallia recepisset habebat imperium commune cum filio.*[174]

(After his [Galerius'] flight, the other Maximian came back from Gaul and held power together with his son.)

The two in fact could not rule together. Maxentius had no intention of accepting the newly asserted authority of the father whom he had summoned from retirement. The Romans themselves evidently accepted Maxentius as emperor and if so it was Maxentius, not his father, who transacted policy and did the business of ruling. Such an arrangement was both inconsistent with Maximian's high view of himself, as expressed in the panegyric of 307, and intolerable to him in practice since it meant taking direction from his son.[175] The tension between father and son may well be reflected in the nomination of consuls for 308. Later events indicate that Maximian clearly respected the authority of Diocletian. One can hardly therefore conceive of him failing to recognize his former colleague's consulship. Maxentius had no such scruples. Diocletian's name, after all, was paired with that of Galerius whom Maxentius had just sent packing from Italy. In such circumstances, the failure of Rome to have any consuls at all in the early part of 308 may well reflect a compromise between the two Roman Augusti: one of whom desired the proclamation of Diocletian, at least, and, perhaps also Galerius; while the other was equally firmly opposed.[176] Certainly as soon as father and son parted company, consuls were nominated: Maxentius himself, and his son, Valerius Romulus.[177]

Maximian precipitated the decisive confrontation with his son in the April of 308.[178] Begrudging his son's independent power base, Maximian sought to destroy it through the army. He called an assembly of soldiers and citizens and, before the assembled throng, Maximian mounted the platform and discoursed upon the evils of the times. The blame, he said, belonged to Maxentius. Turning to his son, Maximian attempted to tear the purple from Maxentius' shoulders and so depose him.[179] The father had miscalculated. The son called upon his Praetorians for support and they rallied around him; Maximian fled Rome.[180] Maximian's attempt to displace his son may seem in retrospect to have been foolhardy, but it did not seem so to him. Maxentius had been the stumbling-block in Maximian's grand vision of a west reunited under his overall command. Maxentius was self-made, proud and independent. He had his own place in the dynasty as the father of Diocletian's great-grandson and Galerius' grandson. He needed either to be brought into obedience, as piety demanded, or eliminated, as necessity required. Moreover, Maximian might reasonably have expected that the Romans would take his side since he had twice saved them from occupation by hostile troops, and the great new baths in the city bore his name. As it was, their loyalty belonged far more to Maxentius.[181]

Maximian's expulsion from Rome tore from Maxentius whatever vague claim to legitimacy he had and seriously weakened his position. He was not only now irrevocably in revolt against Galerius, whose terms he had rejected, but also against the father whom he had both returned to power and then driven from it. Further, he had alienated Constantine by his rejection of Maximian. This is made abundantly clear by the fact that the first place that Maximian went upon leaving Rome was to his new son-in-law in Trier.[182] The isolation of Maxentius did render him vulnerable. With no friends as allies amongst his brother emperors, and in a relatively weak military position, his rule invited overthrow and his lands, annexation. Maxentius' weakness was highlighted by the defection of the African provinces. The sources do not provide us with an especially clear picture here but what is apparent is that the Domitius Alexander, *vicarius* of Africa, mounted a revolt. The date of his rebellion was probably about June 308, although the literary sources are not very precise here.[183] This has led to equivalent controversy among modern scholars. Most recently, Chastagnol and Andreotti have dated the usurpation to late in 308 or early in 309 as a consequence of Maxentius' failure to gain legitimate recognition at Carnuntum.[184] This is an unnecessary connection to make. Maxentius was as much a usurper before Carnuntum as after it.

Zosimus preserves a garbled version of events that helps make sense of the reasons for the revolt itself and its timing. According to his narrative, Maxentius was refused recognition as Augustus by the troops in Africa because of their residual loyalty to Galerius. Upon the advice of his augurs, Maxentius did not seek to enforce his authority by invasion but the troops fled Africa nevertheless. Arriving in Egypt, they were refused asylum in Alexandria, and so, reluctantly, returned to their posts in Africa. Upon their return, Maxentius sought to secure the loyalty of the diocese by demanding the son of the *vicarius* as hostage. This *vicarius*, identified by Zosimus as Alexander, refused to surrender his son, whereupon Maxentius sent agents to murder him. They were discovered and, with the aid of the suspect soldiery, Alexander was proclaimed Augustus.[185]

There are undoubted difficulties in this account. To begin with, Zosimus has plainly confused Galerius and Maximian. This is quite credible given that they both bore the name. Indeed, Lactantius invariably calls Galerius "Maximian". This confusion is borne out by the internal logic of the tale. Troops loyal to Galerius would not have failed to find refuge in Alexandria. Furthermore, there is excellent reason for African troops to recall Maximian with affection. It had been the personal intervention of Maximian which had saved Africa from the ravages of the Moorish tribes. The author of the *Kaisergeschichte* seems to have ranked this as Maximian's proudest achievement and the mint of Carthage was always effusive in his praise.[186] It would be scarcely surprising to find numerous troops still under the eagles in Africa who served under him in that campaign. So the affection of the African garrison for Maximian is certainly explicable. Maxentius' anxiety (as implied by Zosimus) to secure Africa by whatever means, is equally explicable. Africa remained a major source for Rome's grain. One privilege that the city had retained over the centuries was the free grain ration. Control of the city of Rome necessitated the assumption of the responsibility for that supply. Rome's annual demand for free corn at this time may well have run as high as 27 million *modii* every year.[187] Egypt's surplus grain was clearly unavailable to Maxentius, as was that of Spain. He was therefore obliged to depend upon the resources of Africa, Sicily, Sardinia and the depleted fields of Italy itself.[188] Of these sources, African production was the greatest, perhaps sufficient to meet the needs of the capital on its own.[189] This factor alone explains the urgency of Maxentius' desire to retain control of the African provinces.

An inscription helps to make further sense of Zosimus' account. Maxentius' authority was still recognized in Africa after the end of April 308. This is clear from an inscription that labels him both Augustus and consul.[190] It is perhaps to the following month that the events of Alexander's usurpation ought to belong. If so, Zosimus' account makes some sense. It suggests that a significant number of troops from the African garrison had been unwilling to accept the disgrace of Maximian, but, since their commander had remained loyal to Rome, they had little choice but to acquiesce. Maxentius, perhaps concerned by reports of discontent among the troops in Africa, demanded the son of the *vicarius* as a tangible guarantee of support. Alexander was alienated, and, in that alienation, the troops found the leader they had sought and declared their governor Augustus. Soldiers as far away as Sardinia joined in the mutiny and recognized Alexander's authority, thus further restricting Maxentius' possible sources of grain.[191] Maxentius' freedom from his father's interference was thus won at great cost – half his realm and a vital source of corn for Rome.

Alexander failed to find allies among his new peers, nor did any of them recognize his authority as legitimate. There is no suggestion in the sources that he sought recognition through the dispatch of laurelled portraits, as Constantine and Maxentius had done. Unlike them, he was a complete outsider to the imperial family. Rather than seeking to graft himself on to the dynasty, Alexander more likely held out hopes of exploiting its manifest divisions to his own advantage. There is some suggestion, moreover, that he sought to form an alliance with Constantine.[192] Alexander's successful coup in Africa meant that the empire had now fragmented even further: Maxentius ruled in Italy and Alexander in Africa, estranged from one another and without allies elsewhere; Constantine ruled the rest of the West, but was no longer recognized by Galerius; Maximian wore a purple robe, called himself emperor, but controlled no territory; and Galerius, the senior Augustus, ruled the East and Danubian provinces, aided by his Caesar, Maximin Daza, who remained unshakeably loyal throughout the breakup of the imperial college in the West.

If Diocletian's consulship had been intended to provide a catalyst for unity and the resolution of conflict, it failed. It might not have done so but for the conflict between Maximian and Maxentius. A more assertive measure was needed that addressed the divisions in the imperial family without warfare. Diocletian still exercised enormous prestige that could be brought to bear on the older members of the family, particularly Galerius and Maximian, but also Constantine who still clearly expressed public respect for Diocletian.[193] Galerius therefore called together a gathering of the imperial family at Carnuntum in Rhaetia. This conference had its precedents in those imperial meetings convened by Diocletian, and was designed to bring together all of those who legitimately had held or still held the office of Augustus so as to reorder the dynasty, re-establish its basic unity and provide an authoritative settlement for the affairs of the divided empire. The location was chosen for convenience. Carnuntum was in Pannonia, relatively close both to Diocletian's vast fortified palace at Split and the location of Galerius' final campaign against the Carpi on the middle Danube.[194]

Lactantius downplays the fact and significance of this conference. He depicts it merely as a series of incidents in which Maximian participated solely for the purpose of assassinating Galerius:

rediens rursus in Gallias et ibi aliquantum moratus {est} profectus < est >
ad hostem filii sui Maximianum, quasi ut de componendo rei publicae statu
et cum eo disputaret, re autem vera, ut illum per occasionem reconciliationis
occideret ac regnum eius teneret, exclusus a suo.[195]

(Returning then to Gaul, and having remained there for some time,
departed to Maximian [Galerius], the enemy of his son, supposedly
to discuss the resolution of the state of the empire, but really to use
this opportunity for reconciliation to murder him [Galerius] and
seize his lands, since he had been barred from his own.)

Lactantius' tortuous and speculative rationale for Maximian's attendance at
Carnuntum is more from puzzlement than malice. In retrospect, Maximian
had little to gain from attendance and much to lose. Diocletian and Galerius
had long been close, especially in the years leading up to Diocletian's abdication. On the other hand, the newly assertive Diocletian raised the significant prospect of a legitimate return to power for the senior men.
Whatever the outcome of the conference, Maximian must have realized that
failure to attend necessitated his future exclusion from any claim to the
legitimate exercise of imperial power. The summons from Diocletian, then,
not merely carried the great prestige of the senior man, but also the hope
that participation in this conference would lead to an equally important role
in the future counsels of the empire. Moreover, Maximian had his own long
friendship and brotherhood with Diocletian to exploit. It was precisely this
friendship which had made Maximian an emperor in the first place, and
perhaps may even have assisted Diocletian in his own seizure of power.[196]

This is not mere speculation. Zosimus' account — less jaundiced than that
of Lactantius and useful in matters of circumstantial detail — provides some
insight into Maximian's conduct at Carnuntum. In particular, Zosimus notes
that Maximian importuned Diocletian to resume the purple.[197] The implication of this request is that Maximian's own resumption of imperial status
would thus be legitimized. If this was his intention, he failed. Maximian
misjudged Diocletian. Events had moved faster than any recollection of the
good old days could restore. Diocletian came down squarely on the side of
Galerius as his son and chosen heir.

Diocletian's own motives for this decision are not difficult to discern even
in hindsight. The twin resumption of the purple by the retired emperors
would not have simplified the situation, but complicated it. While Galerius
and Daza might possibly have acquiesced, and perhaps even Constantine,
Maxentius and Alexander would have remained disloyal. The civil war that
would undoubtedly have resulted would have fractured the newly restored
empire forever, and decisively opened the frontiers to those whom the
emperors had worked hitherto so assiduously to repel. Diocletian's patient
work of reconstruction would have been for nothing. Moreover, it would

have been an admission of the failure of abdication as an instrument of succession and the inadequacy of the contrived imperial dynasty as a mechanism for state power.

Galerius' own objectives at Carnuntum are as easily identified. There was a vacancy in the imperial college which needed to be filled. The logical candidate for this ought to have been Constantine, legal Caesar in the west, but he had proven himself far from reliable. Galerius did not trust him, nor had Constantine given any reason for Galerius to do so. Constantine's alliance with Maximian, while opportunistic, fatally injured his chances of recognition as Augustus by Galerius. If Constantine were not to be the new Augustus, then inevitably the offence to his dignity would, at the very least, prejudice his loyalty to the new appointee. Therefore it was necessary to invest the new Augustus with as much charismatic authority as possible. So it was necessary for Galerius to gain the *imprimatur* of both Diocletian and Maximian for the new arrangements in order to maximize loyalty to the regime amongst troops who had recently been less than reliable and undermine any basis for Constantine to reject the new order. Galerius had learned from Maximian's recent activities. The army still remembered the old emperors with affection, and, at Carnuntum, Galerius sought to exploit that lingering bond.

The implication of Zosimus' account is that Maximian was the chief actor, petitioning Diocletian to resume his power. Lactantius' account, by contrast, asserts that the elevation of Licinius was Galerius' fait accompli, acceded to by Diocletian, and for which the presence of Maximian was quite incidental.[198] Both accounts largely overlook the conscious role of Diocletian, yet the retired emperor was there to do far more than add lustre to Licinius' appointment. His primary aim was surely the survival of the dynasty which he had forged at so much cost in the furnace of civil war. But that cannot be all. He had made a conscious decision at the time of his abdication to entrust his empire to Galerius, and so he also had the wisdom of that choice to defend. Diocletian was the only man with sufficient innate authority to have been able successfully to transcend his own abdication. He may even have entertained the possibility of resuming power, as Maximian had urged him, but he ultimately disdained it, submitted himself to his own new legality, and so gave his full support to Galerius.

One cardinal principle of the Diocletian's regime had been *concordia*, that is, the unity of the imperial college within the will of Diocletian. Julian's picture of the tetrarchs in his *Caesares* ought not to be forgotten. Julian had a sufficiently profound understanding of imperial ideologies to endeavour to craft one of his own, and this lends his perception some weight. His image is of Diocletian surrounded by the three others as "a kind of chorus", each holding the other's hand.[199] Underpinning this *concordia* of the imperial college, and therefore fundamental to the unity of the family, was patronage. Each new emperor received the purple from the hands of his predecessor by adoption and nomination rather than force. It was precisely this principle which had been assailed by the ambitions of Constantine and Maxentius. To be sure, in the case of Constantine, Galerius had reaffirmed it by an adroit political manoeuvre to which Constantine had submitted in order to gain time to strengthen his position. Maxentius, however, had been offered nothing by Galerius save perhaps a fatal demotion, which he had wisely refused.

Having rejected the option of a return to power, Diocletian's primary task became, together with Galerius and Diocletian, to re-establish the authority of the patronage of the senior emperor. In order to do so, they needed to fill the imperial vacancy by appointing a man with sufficient capacity to vindicate their choice and thereby restore to the college and the empire a unanimity of commitment to the dynasty of Diocletian. The vision itself is not difficult to discern – an empire united by a religio-political ideology of service to heaven by service to the state, governed by peripatetic soldier-emperors who functioned in an imperial college tightly knit by kinship, loyalty, friendship and the certainty of promotion regulated by periodical abdication. Galerius himself was fiercely committed to this ideology. It could be assumed that his nominees were also.[200] What Diocletian and Galerius therefore both needed was someone who was another Galerius.

The choice fell upon Licinianus Licinius, a soldier of Dacian origin who had served Galerius well in the past and whom Lactantius describes as particularly close to the emperor:

> *veteris contubernii amicum et a prima militia familiarem, cuius consiliis ad omnia regenda utebatur.*[201]

(a friend and, of old, tent-mate, on close terms from the beginning of his [Galerius'] service as a soldier, and whose counsel, as emperor, he had always sought.)

Licinius and Galerius had much in common. Both were Dacians from rural families and had risen through the ranks, perhaps, as Lactantius implies, together.[202] Their ages were similar and Eutropius notes that the two had served together in the Persian War. Notably, Licinius was one of the two negotiators sent by Galerius to Maxentius in Rome.[203] Indeed, Licinius was so much the logical candidate that Lactantius suggests that it had been Galerius' intention to elevate him to the purple upon the death of Constantius, a promotion prevented by Constantine's coup.[204] Furthermore, Licinius was a talented man, experienced in war, diplomacy and counsel. His subsequent career demonstrates him as an astute and ruthless politician. The event was celebrated by the restoration of an altar to Mithras as the unconquered sun and patron of the Roman state. The inscriptional dedication reinforced the unity and the piety of the dynasty: "The most religious Iovian and Herculian Augusti and Caesares restored this shrine to the Unconquered Sun God, Mithras, patron of their empire."[205]

Licinius' initial and most urgent task was the suppression of Maxentius.[206] Italy had been allocated to him as a territory over which he had jurisdiction and, so, removal of the usurper was a task he was thus obliged to undertake at some point, just as Constantius had once been awarded the task of removing Carausius some years earlier. The removal of Maxentius was, however, largely incidental to Licinius' broader task of reimposing imperial unity under the Jovian line. Licinius was adopted by Galerius and received the appellation *Iovius*.[207] Adoption into the Jovian line might seem problematic if the imperial vacancy is conceived of as somehow "belonging" to Herculian emperors. This is to mistake imprecise religious terminology with profound religious implications for a precise political office. The appellations were initially employed to clarify the relationship between Diocletian and Maximian.[208] After the abdication of Diocletian, the distinction between *Iovius* and *Herculius* had become redundant. Constantius, notional senior Augustus with his name appearing first in imperial titles, was *Herculius*. The adjectives no longer reflected the protocol of power and came instead to identify the two branches of the imperial dynasty, as can be clearly seen in the panegyric of 307. At Carnuntum, Galerius had a different purpose in reviving a nomenclature which had been rendered obsolete by events. He fully intended to retire after the celebration of his *vicennalia* and required a strong successor.[209]

In November 308, therefore, he had less than four and a half years remaining to him as Augustus. He needed a man experienced in war and diplomacy to take up his work. Daza had his own responsibilities in the east to fulfil. Moreover, his appointment belonged to days when the empire was untroubled by the ambitions of Constantine or Maxentius. Their activities meant that whoever succeeded Galerius had to possess the strength and authority to suppress Maxentius and ensure Constantine's acquiescence. Galerius then hoped that, upon his abdication, Licinius would become senior Augustus and Constantine would receive the status which he had long sought – as legitimate Augustus of the West. Daza would remain as Caesar while a candidate for the vacant western Caesarship would have to be found. Galerius may have had his own son in mind for this. Candidianus, his child by a concubine, would have been about seventeen in 312 – young, but old enough.[210] Thus, in time, the Jovians would come to rule, and the Herculians be eclipsed.

This is not mere speculation. Some evidence can be adduced to support this interpretation of Galerius' plans. In his account of the abdications of 305, Lactantius states that his ambition even then was to retire, leaving Severus and Licinius as Augusti and Daza and Candidianus as Caesars.[211] Lactantius is not averse to reading later events into former events, as his account of the death of Galerius illustrates. Coarse hindsight on Lactantius' part may well relate to this particular observation, so that Galerius' later motivation is also assumed to be his former one. If so, then, by simply substituting the name of Constantine for that of Severus, we have an excellent summary of Galerius' intentions at Carnuntum.

Furthermore, Galerius' supremacy in the new arrangement was made perfectly clear by the elevation of his wife Galeria Valeria to the rank of Augusta.[212] Diocletian had disdained to bestow the title upon his wife Prisca, Valeria's mother. Presumably, he never felt the need to, especially since it would negate the impression of coeval Augusti, which impression he was careful to cultivate. Galerius not only did not perceive such a need, but required in fact to convey the reverse. The proclamation of Valeria as Augusta not only did honour to an extraordinary woman, as she clearly was, but also set the stamp upon Galerius' formal supremacy within the college, establishing him firmly as senior Augustus.

Thus it was that on 11 November 308, Licinius was adopted by Diocletian into the imperial Valerian *gens*, taking the name Valerius Licinianus Licinius.[213] He was likewise *Iovius*, the anointed successor of Galerius. He did not marry an imperial princess. None was available except Daza's infant daughter, hardly a match for a man approaching fifty, or the daughters of Constantius, with whom any match was, at this point, politically impossible.[214] But, if Galerius hoped that this appointment would serve to settle the turbulence in the imperial college in the longer term, all he had done was to exacerbate it in the immediate term. He had offended his hitherto loyal nephew and yet again frustrated the ambitions of Constantine. By attempting to play the statesman, Galerius forgot to be a politician.

This chapter began with Galerius' diplomatic success in the containment of Constantine. It concludes with his boldest – and least successful – diplomatic venture at Carnuntum. What remained consistent throughout, with the disastrous crumbling of dynastic unity, was Galerius' determination to implement the policies constructed by Diocletian. Galerius' unshakeable belief in Diocletian and the dynasty he had crafted combined with his personal qualities of obstinacy, valour, loyalty and inflexibility made poor politics. He fully expected others to bend to his will as they had to Diocletian's and never really took account of the fact that they might fail to do so. This was his greatest failure, as was made pitilessly clear to him in his final years.

Notes

1 On the date, *Pan. Lat.* 9.16; Lact. *de mort. pers.* 44.4; Barnes *NE*, p. 12f. On the titulature, *Ibid.*; *RIC* VI, pp. 338, 367. It is worth noting that, at this juncture, the reverse of the issue upon which Maxentius proclaims himself *princeps invictus* bears the legend "CONSERVATOR VRBIS SVAE". See also Cullhed (1994), p. 33f.; Kienast (1996), p. 291.

2 Walter Goffart (1974), p. 47. Goffart's overall conclusions, however, remain highly controversial. See, for example, Duncan-Jones (1977), pp. 202–4.

3 Lact. *de mort. pers.* 6.3–4.

4 See, for example, the comments of Heather (2006), pp. 64–7f.
5 Jones (1964) I, p. 411; Goffart (1974), p. 31.
6 Jones (1964), p. 61; on the institution of the quinquennial indiction cycle, cf. J.D. Thomas (1978), pp. 133–45, dating this reform in Egypt at least to 287. His conclusions are accepted by Bagnall and Worp (1978), p. 2.
7 See J.D. Thomas (1978); Jones (1964), p. 61f.; Barnes *NE*, p. 228 n.9, for a brief history of the consensus. Barnes, however, argues for a longer history of a quinquennial census.
8 Jones (1957), pp. 88–94, esp. 94; Goffart (1974), p. 34f.; for a rationale for the reform, see the Edict of Aristius Optatus (*P. Cair. Isidor.* I).
9 The degree of the inflation is clearly reflected in the debasement of the coinage. This was at its most extreme in the early 270s. See here Cope (1969), pp. 145–61.
10 J.D. Thomas (1978).
11 See Jones (1940), pp. 138–9; Rostovzeff (1957), p. 520; Goffart (1974), p. 34f.
12 Cities rather than individuals were assessed for taxation. The council of the relevant town was responsible for payment. See Rostovzeff (1957), p. 520; Brunt (1981), p. 168f.; also Jones (1974), pp. 16–17 and Jones (1940), pp. 152–5 for evidence for the fourth century and later. On attempts to evade curial liability, *C. Th.* 13.10.1.
13 Jones (1964), pp. 64–6; Goffart (1974: p. 44f.) ascribes this policy, erroneously, to Galerius. Galerius' apparent innovation was to extend the census to the towns for the application of a poll tax (*capitatio*). See also Nixon and Rodgers (1994), p. 272f., Rees (2004), p. 38f.
14 Lact. *de mort. pers.* 23.1–4; Eus. *de mart. Pal.*, 4.8 (L); *Pan. Lat.* 8.5.4–6.
15 See Goffart (1974), pp. 44–6. The measure was nowhere popular. Constantine relieved the burden at least of Autun (*Pan. Lat.* 8.5.1; 6.1; 10.5; 11.1; 13.1). Maximin Daza cancelled the census of Bithynia in order to court popularity (Lact. *de mort. pers.* 36.2), and subsequently those of the province of Lycia and Pamphylia, and the whole diocese of Oriens (*C. Th.* 13.10.2). See also Mitchell (1988), pp. 122–4.
16 The Thessalonica palace was still under construction at least (see Vickers, 1972). For other major projects, see chapter "Galerius Augustus", pp. 232–241.
17 At Gamzigrad, Galerius' elevation had perhaps necessitated a restructuring of the project, with a new palace, a second temple complex and a vaster, more elaborate fortification (see Srejovic *et al.*, 1978: pp. 54–63; also Srejovic *et al.*, 1983: pp. 226f.).
18 See Déléage (1945), pp. 219–26; Thomsen (1966), p. 219.
19 Jones (1964), p. 64f.
20 Déléage (1945), pp. 220–4.
21 Thomsen (1966), p. 219.
22 Rostovzeff (1957), p. 520. Not all taxes, nevertheless, fell to the administration of municipal officials.
23 A point made by Dio Cassius. After 212 most of the inhabitants of the empire (with the exceptions noted by Jones (1968), pp. 129–40) were liable to manumission and inheritance taxes (Dio Cassius 77.9).
24 *CJ* 11.55.1.
25 Four poll tax receipts from Egypt might cast doubt upon this view since they are dated 301, 305, 308 and 314. But these are unique both to one place and, more significantly, to one person, and in the absence of further corroborative documentation must be seen as localized and peculiar rather than empire- or even province-wide. See Jones (1964), I, p. 63; III, p. 7f. (n. 47).
26 Lact. *de mort. pers.* 23.1.
27 See Barnes *NE*, pp 56–60.
28 See *MGH* I, 148; Curran (2000), pp. 43–6.
29 Temples to Rome had been constructed as early as 195BC. Coupled with either a Republican general, Augustus or the ruling emperor, its temples and priests were found

in most centres of the Roman world (for a detailed study see Fayer 1976; also, Ferguson (1970), p. 89f.). In general, see Ferguson (1970), p. 89f.; Price (1984), p. 41f. Hadrian built a temple in the city itself (*SHA, Vita Hadriani* 19.6; Dio Cassius 79.4), and a cult of the city was maintained there until at least the end of the fourth century (Prudentius, *contra Symm.* 1.121ff.). Maxentius carried out a major reconstruction and restoration after a fire in 307 (*Chron. Min.* I, p. 148; *Ep. de Caes.* 40.26).

30 *MGH* I, 148. Curran (2000) argues that Diocletian's unpopularity in the city stemmed from his secondary treatment of it. This is unlikely, given the amount of building and largesse devoted to the city, not to mention the splendour of the triumph. It is more likely that his unpopularity in the city had a more proximate cause – the thousands of deaths occasioned by the collapse of these temporary bleachers. On the significance of the circus as an extended audience chamber in the palaces of late antiquity, see Frazer (1966), pp. 385–92; S. MacCormack (1981), pp. 42f.

31 Lact. *de mort. pers.* 26.2.

32 See Jones (1964), I, pp. 110, 430–2.

33 Lact. *de mort. pers.* 23.2.

34 The Senate acknowledged the emperor, and thus was a source of imperial legitimacy (Talbert 1984: p. 354; Millar 1977: p. 351f.). Certain provincial governorships were still a senatorial prerogative, although Jones (1974A: pp. 263–76, esp. 275) claimed this function largely atrophied under Diocletian. This view is echoed by Arnheim (1972), Chapter II. Jones (1964: Vol. II, p. 525), however, notes the continuing prestige of the body. This is despite the decline in their importance after Gallienus had prohibited senators from military careers (Aur. Vict. *de Caes.* 33. 12). While there has been considerable disagreement about this (see the summary in Bird 1994: p. 145 n. 31) the continued attenuation of the power of the Senate cannot be denied (Arnheim 1972: pp. 32–4).

35 See Jones (1964), I, p. 386f.; Sinnigen (1957), p.4f.

36 Between 284 and 303, there were seventeen non-imperial ordinary consuls. Since the time of Tiberius all consuls had been nominated by the emperor. They had retained their judicial functions, but not their legislative or military ones. A consul might nevertheless expect to receive a governorship, perhaps of Africa, Syria or Achaea, although such offices did not follow automatically.

37 Jones (1964), I, p. 525.

38 Hopkins and Burton (1983), pp. 184–93. Cf. Talbert (1984), pp.29–38.

39 Senators were understood to have their *origo* in Rome, and thus enjoyed the general immunity from taxation common to all Italians (Rostovtzeff, 1957: p. 575); on particular senatorial privileges in this respect, see Hopkins and Burton (1983), p. 190f. Senatorial status had been heritable down to the third generation from the time of Augustus (*Dig.* 23.2.44, pr.).

40 On immunity from curial *munera*, see Jones (1964), I, p. 539; Hopkins and Burton (1983), p. 191; Talbert (1984), p. 40; on the requirement to provide games, see below.

41 Jones (1964), II, pp. 525, 537. The provision of games remained a senator's most onerous compulsory burden (Talbert 1984: pp. 56–63; Jones 1964: II, pp. 537–40). Nevertheless, as Jones points out, their financial obligations were not fixed in this regard, and their outlays, consequently, were, within limits, discretionary. Furthermore, as a general point, the holding of games was associated with the tenure of magisterial office. Ambition, thus, largely determined the number of times an individual senator paid for, or contributed towards, the cost of games. This also means that the obligation was not ongoing, but peculiar to a particular phase in a senator's career.

42 See Carandini *et al.* (1982), pp. 31–44. Ragona (1962) has also argued that the owner was Claudius Mamertinus, while Wilson (1983) has preferred to leave the question of ownership unsettled, although he does argue against the idea of an imperial owner and

THE *IOVII* AND *HERCULII*

in favour of a private, if extremely wealthy, proprietor. See also Whittaker (1983). Iunius Bassus, ordinary consul in 331, constructed a basilica on the Esquiline Hill (*CIL* VI. 1737). Also, an inscription discovered in the basement of Santa Croce in Gerusalemme records a list of senators of the time of Diocletian, each of whom seems to have made a contribution in excess of HS 400,000 for the construction of a public building (*CIL* VI 37118). Included in the list are Annius Anullinus, cos. 295; Cassius Dio, cos. 291; Acilius Glabrio; Iunius Tiberianus, cos. II 291; Virius Nepotianus, cos. 301. On senatorial wealth in the later Roman Empire in general, see Jones (1964), II, pp. 554–7.

43 Jones (1964), II, pp. 554–7.
44 Hopkins and Burton (1983: p. 136) have estimated that 65 per cent of consuls in the first three centuries of the empire "are not known to have had a consular or senatorial direct descendant for three generations after they held the consulship". While not every senator became consul, the estimate of 1,200 is based on Hopkins and Burton's figures, and the assumption that the membership of the Senate remained more or less constant at 600 (Jones 1964, II: p. 525).
45 *Ep. de Caes.* 40.15–16; Lact. *de mort. pers.* 9.2.
46 This is notwithstanding Diocletian's earlier policy of seeking rather than demanding the support of the Senate, notably in the person of T. Claudius Aurelius Aristobulus (*PLRE* I, p. 106). On the governorship of Syria, see Arnheim (1972), p. 42f.
47 Arnheim (1972), Chapter II.
48 Diocletian nominated seventeen senatorial ordinary consuls (including Bassus in 284 and Aristobulus in 285) out of a possible total of forty-six. This means that 37 per cent of ordinary consulships were held by senators as distinct from members of the imperial college. The percentage total as a whole for senators holding the ordinary consulship between 250 and 337 is 44.5 per cent. It is also worth noting that Diocletian nominated no senators to ordinary consulships after 301, which might well indicate a change in policy on his part. Certainly, before this observed change, Diocletian did not hammer the aristocracy by denying consulships. On the rebuilding of the curia by Diocletian after the fire of 283, see *MGH* I, p. 148.
49 Each is reported to have been a lecher, a drunk and a money-grubber, with a predeliction for preying upon the nobility. These are common enough *topoi* of polemical rhetoric, usually applied to emperors who fall foul of senatorial historians. For Gallienus: *SHA, Gallieni duo,* 9.3–5; 12.6; 16.1–18.5; *Ep. de Caes.* 33. 1–2; Eutr. 9. 8.1; for Carinus: *SHA, vit. Car* 16.1–18.2 (see Meloni 1948: pp. 159–64).
50 Lact. *de mort. pers.* 8.1–6.
51 *Ibid.,* 23; Barnes, *NE,* p. 227f.
52 Corsaro (1978), pp. 25–55.
53 Lact. *de mort. pers.* 26. 1–2. On Maxentius' expectation that he would succeed his father, see *Ibid.,*18.9 and *Ep. de Caes.* 40.14. noting his refusal to perform *adoratio* to either Diocletian or Galerius. One with a spirit both *superbus* and *contumax*, whose father was a ruling Augustus, could hardly not believe himself either *capax imperii* or in fact deserving of the purple.
54 Zos. 2.9.2 (R. Ridley, trans.).
55 *Pan. Lat.* 2. 14.1, 2. Maxentius may have been as young as six at the time (Barnes *NE,* p. 34).
56 Lact. *de mort. pers.* 18.9. The date is indicated by an inscriptional dedication to Valerius Romulus (*CIL* XIV 2825 = ILS 666) which attests Maxentius as *clarissimus vir*, but does not mention his own Maximian. This should indicate a date after Maximian's abdication, but before Maxentius' usurpation.
57 Lact. *de mort. pers.* 18.9. Lactantius must here be seen as reporting a current view to the discredit of the subject of his polemic.

58 Named Severianus, the young man is described by Lactantius as *aetate robustum* in 313 (*de mort. pers.* 50.4) and certainly *capax imperii*. He must have been in his teens in 305 if that is the case. He may have even been older if he is the Fl. Valerius Severianus who was *praeses Isauriae* under Galerius (*AE.* 1972, 652).

59 See, for example, Leadbetter (1998A), pp. 71–85.

60 Lact. *de mort. pers.* 8.4–5.

61 Barnes, *NE*, p. 97.

62 *AE* 1964, 223.

63 Notably Galerius' nephew, Maximin Daza (Lact. *de mort. pers.* 19.6), and Constantine (Barnes *NE*, p. 42f.). It is worth noting that the later adoptees, Severus and Licinius, had both had military careers: Lact. *de mort. pers.* 18.12 (Severus); Lact. *de mort. pers.* 20.3, Eutr. 10.4.1 (Licinius).

64 Barnes (*NE*, p. 33f.) suggests he was father of Maximian's unknown first wife, although he could equally have been her brother. In any case, he was a blood relative of Maximian's daughter Theodora, who was married to Constantius, and thus related by marriage to both members of the Herculian house.

65 *SHA*; *Vit. Prob.* 22.3.

66 On the Praetorian Prefecture, *ILS*. 8929. The date must be before 292 when Hannibalianus was consul along with Asclepiodotus (*PLRE*. I, p. 407, no. 3).

67 Chastagnol (1962), p. 28f. The terminal dates cited by Chastagnol are 282 and 286.

68 Eutr. 9.22; Aur. Vict. *de Caes.* 39.42; for discussion of Asclepiodotus' tenure as Praetorian Prefect, see "Iovius and Herculius", pp. 71–72. On Hannibalianus, see Chastagnol (1962), pp. 27–9.

69 Zos. 2. 9.3. His rank is given in *PLRE* I as a *vicarius* of the *praefectus urbi*.

70 Eutr. 9.2.2; Herodian 8.3–7. See Durry (1938), pp. 389–91.

71 Even their murder of Philip *Iunior* was no more than a mopping-up operation – his father was already dead (Aur.Vict. *de Caes.* 28.11).

72 The size of the guard cohorts stood at 1,000 men each after the time of Septimius Severus (Durry, 1938: p. 87), giving a total of 10,000 guardsmen at any given time.

73 Augustus fixed Praetorian pay at double that of a legionary (Dio 53.11.5). They also received a greater proportion of imperial legacies and gratuities (Suet. *Div. Aug.* 101; Dio 55.23.1). By the time of Caracalla, Praetorians were paid 2,500 denarii annually, compared with a legionary's pay of 750 denarii (Durry, 1938: p. 265f.). Praetorians also received higher donatives than the legionary troops (Herodian 4.4.7; Durry, 1938: p. 268f.).

74 This camp was built by Tiberius when he centred the camp in the city (Suet. *Tib.* 37; Tac. *Ann.* 4.2; Cass. Dio. 57.9.6). The area enclosed by the walls comprised 16.72 hectares or 41.2 acres (Richmond, 1927: p. 12). Richmond identifies no fewer than three refurbishments of the camp between the times of Tiberius and Aurelian. This great camp, situated on a height and facing towards the Palatine Hill, all but dominated Rome.

75 Zos. 1.50–3, *CIL* VIII. 21021; Durry (1938) p. 392.

76 Aur.Vict. *de Caes.* 39.47.

77 Cited by Durry (1938), p. 81. The date is between 298 and 305 (*Ibid.*, p. 392).

78 Lact. *de mort. pers.* 26.3.

79 Zos. 2.10.1; on Annulinus, see Potter (2004), pp. 346, 664 n. 63, *contra* Barnes, *NE*, p. 117.

80 Zos. 2.9.3. Zosimus names two other officers, Marcellus and Marcellianus, both of whom held the rank of military tribune and therefore commanded either Praetorian or Urban cohorts (*PLRE* I. p. 550; p. 543.).

81 Lact. *de mort. pers.* 44.6; Aur. Vict. *de Caes.* 40.24–5; for discussion, see Durry (1938), p. 373f.

82 Lact. *de mort. pers.* 18.9–11.

83 This would seem to be the implication of Lact. *de mort. pers.* 26.4.

84 Jones (1948), p. 59f.; Barnes, *CE*, p. 30. Moreau (1954: Vol II, p. 346f.) points out that this is a subtle irony on the part of Lactantius, since he depicts the imperial system as the creation of Galerius, fashioned out of his struggle to persuade Diocletian to abdicate. Now Galerius was the prisoner of the system which was his only claim to legitimate power.

85 Moreau (1954), p. 347; *RIC* VI, pp. 367–71; on this question, see Cullhed (1989). Cullhed's argument that Maxentius did not take the title out of respect for his father is difficult to sustain when it is considered, first, that Maximian was only summoned back to power by his son as a response to Severus' invasion; and, second, that Maxentius never intended his father to be a ruling emperor, but rather to fill a symbolic role and thereby lend his own usurpation legitimacy.

86 Cf. Lact. *de mort. pers.* 25.1.

87 *RIC* VI, pp. 337–8f. For Maximian, the legend "MAXIMIANVS SEN P F AVG" occurs immediately with an *adventus* reverse (*RIC* VI, p. 367, no. 136).

88 *PLRE* I, p. 1042, on the nomination of consuls, see Bagnall *et al.* (1987), pp. 13–18.

89 On the consuls for 307, see *Ibid.*, p. 148f.; Barnes, *NE*, pp. 93–4.

90 On Milan as Maximian's capital, see Barnes, *NE*, p.56f. n. 46. For building in Milan, see Krautheimer (1984), pp. 69–93.

91 Barnes, *NE*, p. 64, p. 255; also Barnes (1976), 174–93.

92 See chapter 3 on "Augustus and Caesar ", pp. 97–101.

93 The wars could not as yet have been regarded as finished. Barnes (*NE*, pp. 255–7) lists one "CARPICVS MAXIMVS" and two "SARMATICVS MAXIMVS" titles taken between 306 and 310.

94 *Origo* 3. See *Ibid.*, p. 41f.

95 Brennan (1980), p. 564f.; also Kolendo (1969), p. 381f.; Barnes, *NE*, p. 64; Barnes (1976), p. 192.

96 Casey (1994), p. 65. As if the point was not clear enough, the reverse of the coin depicted a figure of Pax holding an olive branch, with the legend "PAX AVGGG" (the Peace of the three Augusti). *RIC* V2, pp. 442, 550, no. 1; see p. 58.

97 *Origo* 9; also Lact. *de mort. pers.* 18.12. Severus must have had a reputation as a party-goer since Lactantius repeats the same accusation, and also adds dancing to Severus' list of character flaws.

98 *Concordia* is a frequent theme. CONCORDIA types were struck on both precious metal and *aes* types, primarily in western mints during the period of both Diocletian and his immediate successors (*RIC* VI, p. 671, no. 61 from Alexandria; p. 279, no. 1, p. 287, nos 49a, b, 50 from Ticinum; p. 472, no. 148, p. 465, nos. 91a, b 92 a, b, p. 475. nos, 172–5 from Siscia; p. 203 no. 624 from Trier; p. 310, nos. 2 a,b, p. 317, nos 41a, b, 42 from Aquileia; p. 355, 47a, b, p. 358, 68a, b, 69,70a, b from Rome; p. 260, nos 246–8 from Lugdunum). The figure of *homonia* appears on the Arch of Galerius, see Kinch (1890), p. 36; Laubscher (1975), p. 56. On the iconography of *concordia*, see L'Orange (1985), p. 183ff. See also Kolb (2001), pp. 32–4.

99 Lact. *de mort. pers.* 50.1; *PLRE* I. p. 828, no.1. On the Severianus who was governor of Isauria, see *AE* 1972, 652; published initially by Bean and Mitford (1970), p. 196, no. 217.

100 Lact. *de mort. pers.* 26.5.

101 Aur. Vict. *de Caes.* 40.17; Zos. 2.12.2; see Barnes, *NE*, p. 14 on Domitius Alexander. On the coinage, see *RIC* VI, p. 43, no. 48a (*aureus*), with *aurei* also struck for Maximin Daza and Constantine as *nobilissimi Caesares*; p. 431, no. 51a (*aes*) with *aes* struck as for the *aurei*.

102 *Pan. Lat.* 5.5.2; *RIC* VI, 422–6 (Carthage) 1, 2, 10–28; *Pan. Lat.*, 4.21.2. [Corippus, *Joh.* 1. 478ff.]. Barnes, *NE*, p. 59. Curiously no victory title was ever taken for these campaigns.

103 Zos. 2.12.1.
104 Maximian was forced to flee from Rome by Maxentius (Zos. 2.12; Lact. *de mort. pers.* 28. 1–4) in April 308. The date is made clear by Maxentius' assumption of the consulship with his son Valerius Romulus on 20 April (*Chron. Min.* I. 66.). Domitius Alexander was proclaimed Augustus later in that year, probably in June (see Maurice, 1902). An alternative date after the Carnuntum conference has been argued by Andreotti (1969).
105 On the importance of Africa to the grain supply of Rome, see Rickman (1980), pp. 108–13. On the mechanism of grain collection in this period, Tengström (1974), pp. 14–15, 256f.
106 Lact. *de mort. pers.* 26.3 speaks of "a few soldiers" (*milites pauci*). Even if one added the urban cohorts to the already attenuated Praetorians (see Frank, 1969: p. 47), the *vigiles*, which were still in existence (see Reynolds, 1926: pp. 122–8) and the II Parthica, created by Septimius Severus and stationed at Alba, the sum total of troops cannot have been great compared with the armies available to the legitimate emperors. The number of battle-trained soldiers must likewise have been commensurately less.
107 Lact. *de mort. pers.* 26. 6–7.
108 *Origo* 4.10; Zosimus 2.10.2; Eutropius 10.2. For discussion, see Creed (1984), p. 107 n. 7.
109 See n. 101 above.
110 King (1959), p. 59f.
111 *RIC* VI, p. 432, no. 53.
112 *RIC* VI, p. 367, no. 137 ("HERCVLI COMITI AVGG ET CAESS NN"); p. 369, no. 145 ("FEL INGRESSVS SEN AVG"); pp. 370, 156–7 ("VIRTVS MILITVM").
113 Lact. *de mort. pers.* 26.7.
114 There is no tradition at all of Maxentius having served the same military apprenticeship as Constantine. The only evidence of Maxentius' life before October 306 is the inscription entitling him *vir clarissimus* (*ILS* 666). If his birth is to be dated to the early 280s, as Barnes (*NE*, p. 34) argues, then it is more than likely that Maxentius was brought up as an imperial prince rather than as an officer cadet.
115 *RIC* VI, p. 367, no. 136. *RIC* VI, pp. 290–2; p. 293, no. 81 for Severus Augustus is the key here; NB pp. 271–4; King (1959), p. 49f.
116 Zos. 2.10.1.
117 *RIC* VI, pp. 290–2.
118 The soldiers whom Severus used in this context can only have been his *comitatus*, originally Maximian's. On the *comitatus*, see Jones (1964), p. 52ff.
119 Zos. 2.10.1. The *cohortes Mauri* and *equites Mauri* existed as distinct field units from the early third century (see Speidel, 1975: pp. 208–21; their service in the sacred *comitatus* was apparently well-known, see Jones, 1964: p. 52f.).
120 Lact. *de mort. pers.* 26.8.
121 Bagnall *et al.* (1987), p. 148f.; Barnes, *NE*, p. 69f. n. 103; *contra* Seston (1937); Lafaurie (1966); Paschoud (1971), p. 109; Galletier (1952), p. 3f.
122 Maxentius took the title of Augustus before May 307 (Cullhed, 1994: p. 40f.), and the date of the change in consular salutations is fixed in April by the Chronographer of 354 (Bagnall *et al.*, 1987: p. 148f.).
123 Origo 3.6; Zos. 2.10.1; Lact. *de mort. pers.* 26. 8–9; Pasqualini (1979), p. 85.
124 King (1959), pp. 52f. (Ticinum), 56f. (Aquileia); although see Sutherland, *RIC* VI, p. 272f.
125 Lact. *de mort. pers.*, 26.8; Eutr. 10.2.4; Zos. 2.10.1.
126 Lact. *de mort. pers.* 26, 9–10.
127 Lact. *de mort. pers.* 26, 11; Hanson (1974).
128 *P. Mil.* 55; see Creed (1984), p. 107f.
129 Barnes, *NE*, p. 64.
130 *Ibid.*, p. 69; NB *RIC* VI, p. 129, no. 82.

131 Bagnall *et al.* (1987), p. 148f.
132 Bagnall and Worp (1979), p. 31.
133 Lact. *de mort. pers.* 27, 1–2; Barnes, *NE*, p. 69; It is simply improbable to argue, as Seston (1937: pp. 197–218) does, that the meeting took place on 31 March, first, because Maximian was preoccupied with the invasion of Severus at that time, and second, because Constantine was still content to call himself Caesar in July 307. See Nixon, in Nixon and Rodgers (1994), pp. 179–85.
134 The two are clearly simultaneous. See Barnes (*NE*, p. 69), against the host of French scholars listed in n. 121.
135 Barnes, *CE*, p. 31.
136 *Pan. Lat.* 6.1.1–2.5; for discussions of the import of this panegyric, see Nixon (1993); Rees (2002), pp. 153–84.
137 *Pan. Lat.* 6.3.3–5.2.
138 *Ibid.*, 5.3.
139 *Ibid.*, 6.9.1–10.5; although see S. MacCormack (1981: pp. 22–33) on the importance of the emperor as *deus praesens*; *Pan. Lat.* 6.11. 5–6. On the theological import of her term *deus praesens*, see Kolb (2004), pp. 27–37.
140 *Pan. Lat.* 6.9.5 (Nixon translation).
141 *Pan. Lat.* 6.9.6.
142 Rees (2002), p. 173.
143 *P. Mil.* 55.1, dated 29 September 307 includes Severus' regnal year in its dating formula. See also Barnes, *NE*, p. 5 n. 13. The mints, however, ceased striking in the name of Severus.
144 *Pan. Lat.* 6.14.1–2.
145 On the panegyrist's view of Severus, see *Pan. Lat.* 6.12.3. This is taken by both Grünewald (1990: p. 33) and Nixon (1993: p. 239) to be a reference to Maxentius. This identification has problems. Maximian had not yet broken with his son, to whom he returned after his visit to Trier. Likewise, Constantine was still striking coins for Maxentius at both Lugdunum and Trier (*RIC* VI, p. 237). As Nixon himself has argued, the panegyrists were not so much adumbrating an official stance as responding to one. More likely the maladroit driver of the chariot of heaven was intended to represent Severus, now defeated and languishing in prison, not Maxentius, who was not only Maximian's son, but also in firm control of Italy and Africa, scarcely a fall from heaven. Another and later panegyrist offers a less periphrastic view (*Pan. Lat.* 9.3.4).
146 *RIC* VI, p. 260ff., nos 258, 290 ("D.N. DIOCLETIANO AETERN AVG"); p. 260ff., nos 247, 254, 272, 277, 282 ("MAXIMIANVS IVNIOR AVGVSTVS"); see also Gautier (1985).
147 Sutherland, *RIC* VI, p. 237f. (*Maximianus iunior*), 238f.
148 *Pan. Lat.* 6.1.1.
149 Sutherland, *RIC* VI, p. 238 n. 78.
150 Lact. *de mort. pers.* 27.2–8; *Origo* 3.8–7.
151 The *Kaisergeschichte* apparently had little to say about this either. Victor's chronology is confused, although it makes the same point about desertions (Aur. Vict. *de Caes.* 40.9) while Eutropius omits the episode altogether. See also *Pan. Lat.* 9.3.4 for a very brief account.
152 *Origo* 4.10.
153 The Chronicler states that Severus reigned for three years, four months and fifteen days (*Chron. Min.* I, p. 148), therefore dating his death to 16 September 307. This makes good sense of the papyrological evidence. The last papyrus using Severus in a dating formula is dated 29 September (*P. Mil.* 55.1). By 24 December, his name was gone from the dating formulae (*P. Merton* 31; *P. Col.* 138).
154 Hanson (1974); for a summary and discussion, see Barnes, *NE*, p. 5 n. 13.

155 Barnes, *NE*, p. 64; Corcoran (2006A), p. 233.
156 *Origo* 3.6 (Interamna), 8 (Via Flaminia).
157 *PLRE* I, p. 740. It is tempting to identify Pompeius Probus with Sicorius Probus (*FGH* IV. 189), but no evidence really suggests, let alone compels, such a view.
158 *Origo* 3.7.
159 Lact. *de mort. pers.* 27.2.
160 *Ibid.*, 27.3–4; *Origo* 3.7; Aur. Vict. *de Caes.* 40.9; *Pan. Lat.* 9.34.
161 Lact. *de mort. pers.* 27.2–4; *Origo* 3.7.
162 Aur. Vict. *de Caes.* 40.9.
163 Lact. *de mort. pers.* 27.4–5.
164 *Ibid.*, 27.4.
165 *Ibid.*, 27.5; *Origo* 3.7.
166 Lact. *de mort. pers.* 27.6–8. Creed's (1984: p. 108 n. 5) suggestion that Lactantius is here implicitly identifying Galerius with the precursor to the Antichrist goes too far. Lactantius' own view of history would preclude such a view.
167 *Origo* 3.7.
168 Corcoran (2006A), p. 239f.
169 Bagnall *et al.* (1987), p. 150f.
170 *Ibid.* See also Barnes (1981), *CE*, p. 32.
171 Barnes (1982), *NE*, p. 64.
172 A silver issue from the Trier mint which evidently marked the marriage of Constantine and Fausta was struck in the name of Maximian as "IMP MAXIMIANVS P F S AVG". Later *aes* coinage from the same mint gave him the nomenclature "IMP C VAL MAXIMIANVS PF AVG" (*RIC* VI, p. 216f.). The Lugdunum mint, further from the centre of power, called Maximian "D N MAXIMIANVS P F S AVG" (*RIC* VI, p. 256f.). This is a clear change from the post-abdication issues in which Maximian received the bare epithets *beatissimus* or *felicissimus* (*RIC* VI, p. 206, Trier; p. 255, Lugdunum; p. 291, Ticinum; p. 318, Aquileia). Maxentius, at least initially, found it politic to humour his father's ambition in a similar series of issues from the Rome and Carthage mints (*RIC* VI, pp. 367–73, 430). See also Pasqualini (1979), p. 88f.
173 Barnes, *NE*, p. 70.
174 Lact. *de mort. pers.* 28.1.
175 *Ibid.*
176 Barnes, *CE*, p. 31. Barnes argues that Maxentius was adopting a "more conciliatory" attitude to Galerius. The editors of *Consuls of the Later Roman Empire* prefer to argue that Maxentius was adopting a "wait and see" attitude. Maxentius was not really likely to be conciliatory to the man who had just invaded his realm twice, and devastated part of it upon his retreat. Bagnall *et al.* (1987) are less plausible, in what are essentially arguments from terminology rather than circumstance, in their conclusion that Maxentius was fence-sitting. His victory over Galerius and his execution of Severus had ensured that negotiation with the senior emperor was impossible. Better to see here the tension between father and son attested by Lactantius, and resolved by Maximian's abrupt departure from Rome.
177 Bagnall *et al.* (1987), p. 150.
178 The date of Maxentius' assumption of the consulship is given by the Chronicle of 354 as *xii kal. Mai.* See *Ibid.*, pp. 150–2; Creed (1984), p. 109; Pasqualini (1979), p. 90.
179 Lact. *de mort. pers.* 28. 2–4; Eutr. 10.3.2.
180 *Ibid.*
181 See Cullhed (1994), pp. 42–4.
182 Lactantius (*de mort. pers.* 29.1) states that Maximian returned to Gaul; the panegyrist of 310 states that he was received into Constantine's *palatium* (*Pan. Lat.* 7.14.6). Given that, at this stage, Constantine was campaigning on the Rhine (Barnes: *NE*, p. 70),

Trier emerges as Constantine's most likely headquarters at this time. It had the added benefit of being a place where Maximian was already well known. Maximian's relinquishment of imperial regalia at this time (Lact. *de mort. pers.* 29.1) no doubt made it possible for him to attend the Conference at Carnuntum.

183 Zosimus places the revolt after Galerius' retreat from Italy (Zos. 2.12.1), as does Aurelius Victor (*de Caes.* 40.12). The Epitome states that Alexander was suppressed by Constantine (40.2). The revolt must have taken place after May 308 since an inscription from Numidia (*ILS* 668 = *CIL* 8. 10382) calls Maxentius consul. For a summary of the scholarship with respect to this revolt, see Barnes, *NE*, p. 14f.

184 Andreotti (1969), p. 158ff.; Chastagnol (1982), p. 113; see also Pflaum (1962/5), pp. 159–61.

185 Zos. 2.12.2. One added piece of evidence may be adduced here. Barnes (*NE*, p. 14) identifies Domitius Alexander with the Alexander who was *vicarius Africae* in office in 303. As an appointee of Diocletian and Maximian, Alexander's loyalties can easily be understood to lie with Maximian rather than with Maxentius. This makes sense of Maxentius' initial mistrust of him and the demand for hostages (Zos. 2.12.2).

186 Eutropius (9.22.1) and Aurelius Victor (39.24) both rank Maximian's resolution of the problem with Galerius' victory over Narses, Diocletian's suppression of the Egyptian revolt, and Constantius' recovery of Britain. On the individualism apparent in the policy of the Carthage mint, see *RIC* VI, p. 411.

187 Rickman (1980), p. 198.

188 On the different corn-producing areas, see *Ibid.*, pp. 101–19. The Italian corn harvest was usually used to feed the Italian cities (*Ibid.*, p. 103) and may in any case have been somewhat depleted after two invasions in 307, of which one involved the use of scorched-earth tactics. Sicily could provide Rome with about 12 million modii of grain annually (*Ibid.*, p. 105), and was still a basic source of grain for Rome in the middle of the fourth century (*Exp. tot. mund.* § 65).

189 Africa was Rome's major source of grain (*Ibid.*, p. 112).

190 *ILS* 668; Barnes, *NE*, p. 14 n. 17.

191 *AE* (1966), 169; Sotgiu (1964). The milestone in question records the names of Domitius Alexander and also Papius Pacatianus, the *praeses* of the province, later *vicarius* in Britain, ordinary consul in 332 and Praetorian Prefect of Constantine (*PLRE* I, p. 656; Pflaum 1962/5).

192 *ILS* 8936 is evidence of the recognition of Constantine by Alexander. As Barnes (*NE*, p. 14) points out, there is no evidence of reciprocal recognition by Constantine of Alexander. The later career of Papius Pacatianus (Pflaum 1962/5) only goes so far as to show that at least one of Alexander's adherents enjoyed promotion under Constantine. This does not presume alliance, however. Senators who held office under Maxentius continued to do so under Constantine, notably Annius Anullinus, Maxentius' Praetorian Prefect and twice praefectus urbi, later proconsul of Africa under Constantine (*PLRE* I, p. 79). Pacatianus had ample reason later to desert to Constantine in any case. The defeat of Alexander by Maxentius had led to a brutal purge of the rebels in Africa and the looting of Carthage (Zos. 2.14. 3–4; Aur. Vict. *de Caes.* 40.19).

193 Constantine recognized the consulship of Diocletian (Bagnall *et al.*, 1987: p. 150) and his mint at Trier issued coins in the name of Diocletian ("D N DIOCLETIANO P F S AVG" [*RIC* VI, p. 210f.]). Maximian's continued respect for Diocletian can be perceived in his behaviour at Carnuntum (Lact. *de mort. pers.* 29.2; Pasqualini, 1979: p. 91).

194 On Galerius' campaigns in 308, see Barnes, *NE*, p. 64. According to Barnes, Galerius was at Serdica in October, and then proceeded to Carnuntum, presumably after the campaigning season had ended.

195 Lact. *de mort. pers.* 29.1.

196 On the friendship between the two, see *Pan. Lat.* 3. 5–6; Aur. Vict. *de Caes.* 39.17. The deliberate mention of the Euphrates in *Pan. Lat.* 2.2.6 makes it most likely that Maximian was with Carus in Persia. It can be reasonably concluded from this that he played some part in the accession of Diocletian (see also Barnes, *NE*, p. 33; on the bond of fraternity, see Leadbetter, 2006).

197 Zos. 2.10.4.

198 Lact. *de mort. pers.* 29.2.

199 Julian, *Caesares* 315, A.

200 Lact. *de mort. pers.* 20.4; further on Galerius' intention to abdicate, see *infra*, "Galerius Augustus", pp. 240–291.

201 Lact. *de mort. pers.* 20.3; see also Eutr. 10.4.1.

202 Lact. *de mort. pers.* 20.3. The *Origo* states that Licinius came from Dacia Nova (*Origo* 13), and was of humble origin. In this he also had much in common with Galerius. See also Barnes, *NE*, p. 43f.

203 Eutr. 10.4.1.

204 Lact. *de mort. pers.* 20.3.

205 *ILS* 659.

206 *Origo* 13; "Licinius ... was made emperor by Galerius in order to make war upon Maxentius" (*Licinius ... a Galerio factus imperator, velut adversum Maxentium pugnaturus*).

207 *ILS* 676 (= *CIL* IX, 6026). The Siscian mint issued "IOVI CONSERVATORI" types on the reverse of coins of Licinius (*RIC* VI, pp. 451, 477–8).

208 Leadbetter (2006).

209 Lact. *de mort. pers.* 20.4.

210 *Ibid.*; see Barnes *NE*, p. 38.

211 Lact. *de mort. pers.* 20.4.

212 *ILS* 8932 (= *CIL* III 13661); *IGR* IV 1562; *RIC* VI, pp. 477–9 (Siscia), 513–14 (Thessalonica), 559–63 (Nicomedia), 625–40 (Antioch), 671–80 (Alexandria). Valeria seems to have been raised to the rank of Augusta prior to the Carnuntum conference. Issues from both Serdica and Nicomedia which predate the conference (there are no coins in these series struck for Licinius) already hail her as Augusta (*RIC* VI, pp. 489, 548).

213 *ILS* 678 (= *CIL* V 330); *ILS* 679 (= *CIL* VIII 1357) for his full name. The name "Valerius" should indicate formal adoption by either Diocletian or Galerius, thereby making good sense of his Iovius titulature.

214 Daza's daughter was seven in 313 (Lact. *de mort. pers.* 50.2), hardly a fitting betrothal for a mature man in 308. She may, in any case, already have been promised to Candidianus (*Ibid.*).

7

GALERIUS AUGUSTUS

Tiberius Galeriusque subiecti aliis egregia pleraque, suo autem ductu atque auspicio minus paria experti sint.[1]

(In the service of others, both Tiberius and Galerius achieved many outstanding things, but under their own authority and leadership, their efforts were inferior by comparison.)

What kind of an emperor was Galerius? Discussions of Galerius' achievements and policies tend to be overshadowed by the failure to keep his political inheritance intact, and his reputation as a resolute foe of Christianity. The hostility of Christian tradition has certainly led to many summary dismissals of whatever talent for power Galerius possessed. Instead, many accounts prefer to represent him as a skilled warrior, but otherwise brutish and brutal.[2] On the rare occasion that Galerius' reign as Augustus is discussed, his five years of rule over most of the empire tend to be ignored in favour of a focus upon his disastrous relationships with Maxentius and Constantine, and his evident hostility to the Christian communities under his authority. Something of his character and the nature of his other policies can be discerned, nevertheless.

Victor's bracketing of Galerius with Tiberius is a useful corrective to bilious caricatures from Christian polemicists. In offering us the perilous insight of historical comparison, it draws some powerful parallels. Tiberius was, very deliberately and very explicitly, not an innovator. He possessed a conservative's mistrust of novelty and expressed a studious reverence for his predecessor.[3] An unhappy emperor, he finally tired of the hypocrisy inherent in the structure of the Augustan principate and withdrew to Capri where he endeavoured to live the life of refined luxury enjoyed by a senior statesman, and died pursued by the treachery of subordinates, the intrigues of his family and salacious rumour prompted by his reclusive lifestyle.[4] Galerius was likewise reluctant to be innovative. This is clear enough from the inflexibility of his effort to retain the imperial settlement bequeathed him by

Diocletian. The parallel is not pure, however. He pursued some legal and economic reforms – most disastrously, the extension of capitation to the cities, and more positively (but obscurely) his reform of the corps of *Caesariani*.

Galerius and his colleagues

The question of the identification and assessment of Galerius' achievements as Augustus is complicated by the division of the empire. While under Diocletian, there was no formal division of the empire; mistrust between Galerius and Constantius necessitated the formal division between east and west in 305.[5] Galerius may have imagined this as a temporary arrangement made more palatable by the appointment of Severus. Constantine's swift coup in York, upon the death of Constantius, diminished whatever hopes may have existed in that direction, and Severus' failure and death in Italy certainly buried them. Thereafter, Galerius ruled the provinces east of Italy. The remainder was divided between Constantine, recognized by Galerius as legitimate Caesar, and Maxentius and Alexander, both regarded as usurpers. Maxentius, in turn, did not acknowledge the authority of Galerius, once his overtures had been rejected. The coinage of Constantine demonstrates a grudging recognition of Galerius' authority up until Carnuntum, and none after that.[6] Galerius may have intended one day to assert his authority in the west, but after his failure in Italy he seems to have left that task to Licinius.

Galerius sought to preserve Diocletian's arrangements where he could. He despatched Maximinus Daza to guard the eastern frontier and ensure internal peace. This is indicated by his imperial residences, and evident presence, at Antioch and Caesarea.[7] Similarly, Licinius was resident in Sirmium from whence he conducted his campaigns.[8] This was a most convenient base for his twin tasks: the protection of the Danube frontier, and the recovery of Italy from Maxentius. Despite the presence of an Augustus, the mint at Sirmium was not reopened, but the mint at Siscia continued to supply coinage for the region.[9] The mint at Siscia displayed no policy which might be described as "independent". Rather, its types tended to mirror those of Thessalonika, Nicomedia and other eastern mints.[10]

This arrangement might have become complicated after Daza's elevation to the rank of Augustus in 310 if Daza had sought an active breach with his uncle. He did not, preferring to recognize Galerius' seniority and superior status. When Daza took the title of *Persicus Maximus* in 310, perhaps as a result of an opportunistic campaign against the Persians during the minority of Shapur II, Galerius shared it, demonstrating his approval of the act, and implying that he had ordered it.[11] Daza's policy towards the Christians also reflects Galerius' approach rather than his own. After 311, however, the policy towards the Christians in the east took a more subtle turn. Daza not only attacked the Church in the ancient way (arrest, torture and exile), but he also sought to turn the inchoate Hellenistic paganism of the east into a

217

popular movement by both soliciting requests from the cities of his realm petitioning him to persecute Christians and organizing traditional religion into a coherent structure, mimicking that of the Church in order to create an infrastructure for charitable works.[12] He also sought to attack the apologetic and intellectual base of Christianity by the issuing of forged *Acta* of Pilate.[13] These techniques, while identical in intent, reflect a tactical difference to those of Galerius.[14] They do not emerge, however, until after Galerius' death, and so it seems that Daza, however much he may have chafed under either Galerius' lack of imagination or interest, felt bound to follow his policies. Galerius' imperial rank and status, then, remained supreme over the authority of both Licinius and Daza. The essential unity of the empire was retained in those provinces in which Galerius and his colleagues exercised rule. As Diocletian had done, Galerius preferred to leave the patrol of the frontiers to his subordinate colleagues. He went, instead, to dwell in the great and rambling imperial palace at Thessalonika, which was perhaps by now largely complete.[15] The tasks of securing the Danube frontier and recovering Italy from Maxentius now devolved upon Licinius.[16]

In 309, Licinius proceeded to commence a far more cautious campaign against Maxentius than either Severus or Galerius had undertaken. Maxentius himself was coming under increasing pressure. He had sacrificed his popularity with the Senate in order to raise money for an extensive building pro- gramme,[17] the vast extent of which can still be seen in Rome: the renovation of Hadrian's Temple of Venus and Rome; an imperial villa along the *via Appia* with the customary circus attached; and the largest basilica constructed in Rome.[18] The costs of these projects must have been both ongoing and very high, given their scale. The basilica and temples were not completed by October 312 and so must have been a continual drain on the Treasury.[19] Furthermore, his army, considerably augmented by desertions from the field forced of both Severus and Galerius, had to be maintained and the normal demands of government provided for. To pay for this, Maxentius had only the resources of Italy, long unused to the exactions of the tax collectors. Second, Maxentius' loss of Africa to Alexander meant famine in Rome. Grain was short. So was money. Maxentius was now compelled to tax his people in order to raise money. There is some suggestion of riots, mercilessly suppressed by the Praetorians.[20] Maxentius' popularity in Rome, which had been the essential base for his oppositional regime, had now collapsed. Faced with the realities of government, Maxentius abandoned populism for brute force.

This gave Licinius an advantage that neither Severus nor Galerius had enjoyed. Maxentius could no longer depend upon the walls of Rome as a secure barrier. Licinius did not exploit this to the full. He preferred instead to build towards a more durable victory by eroding Maxentius' control of his more distant lands. In 309, his forces took control of the Istrian peninsula and the head of the Adriatic.[21] Maxentius closed and never reopened the northern mints at Aquileia and Ticinum.[22]

Licinius' strategy was cautious and prudent, but ultimately overtaken by other events. By sniping at Maxentius, and inflicting a series of minor defeats, Licinius was able to accentuate the decline in Maxentius' standing in Rome. These piecemeal victories attacked the morale of Maxentius' hitherto successful soldiery, now the principal base for Maxentius' authority. By the time Licinius came to invade in force, he no doubt thought that Maxentius' army would become vulnerable to desertion and unable to sustain a siege of the city. A final confrontation was, however, delayed by the necessary business of empire. The Danubian frontier was still not completely secure, so Licinius was compelled to turn his attention to it. In 310, he won a victory as *Sarmaticus Maximus*.[23] This might suggest that Galerius was already ill, since he might have undertaken the campaign, either himself or through his Praetorian Prefect Tatius Andronicus, leaving Licinius free to continue his campaign against Maxentius.[24]

The Sarmatian campaign came as a providential reprieve for Maxentius. He could now take action against Alexander, and sent his Praetorian Prefect Rufius Volusianus, who had governed Africa and owned estates there, with the few troops he could spare.[25] Perhaps the generals in his entourage, rather than the aristocratic Volusianus, worked something of a miracle because Alexander was defeated.[26] His troops were incorporated into Maxentius' army, and the failing treasury was augmented by the sack of several cities, including Carthage.[27] By this victory, Maxentius was able to strengthen his domestic position. It arrested the decline in his troops' morale, restored the grain supply from Africa, and alleviated the need to raise funds. Maxentius demonstrated his gratitude to Volusianus by making him Urban Prefect, and, following that, consul.[28] The victories were celebrated in a series of coin issues featuring Mars, Victoria and Virtus.[29] Things did not all go Maxentius' way. Valerius Romulus, his son and talisman of legitimacy, died during 309.[30] Romulus was Galerius' grandson, Maximian's grandson and Diocletian's great-grandson. As in life he had tied both branches of the imperial dynasty together, his death sundered them again. Maxentius turned a personal tragedy into a propaganda advantage. He deified his dead son, built him a mausoleum adjacent to the imperial villa and circus on the Appian Way, and perhaps also a small temple to him in the Forum. Maxentius was now the father of a *divus*, whose consecration was proclaimed on the coinage.[31] Frustrated by his own imperial priorities, Galerius could only look on.

Galerius also had a closer relationship to manage. Daza had been passed over at Carnuntum and was evidently much aggrieved by the appointment of Licinius as Augustus. Daza had held office the longest of all Galerius' colleagues, had been steadfastly loyal, and was clearly competent. He could claim, with justice, to be senior to both Licinius and Constantine. Sometime in 309, Daza wrote to Galerius asking for promotion. Our principal source here is Lactantius, and his account is characteristically jaundiced.[32] He suggests that Galerius sent a number of envoys to Maximinus, begging him to respect Licinius' seniority on the basis of his age and experience. The details of this depiction are anomalous and inconsistent with known events. While there was clearly an issue between uncle and nephew, negotiations were conducted carefully, and with respect. Daza was not pre-emptive, contenting himself throughout the negotiating period with the title of *nobilissimus Caesar* on coins and such dating formulae as survive.[33] A compromise was sought. The new title of *Filius Augustorum* was invented and conferred.[34] Daza was not satisfied, but played for time. He struck coins for Constantine as *Filius Augustorum*, but not for himself.[35] He asserted his status in November 309 by nuancing the religious policy of enforcing sacrifice upon which Diocletian had embarked in early 304 and which was still operative. There is some suggestion that this was through an Edict independently issued by Daza, but the evidence does not compel this view. The principal source, Eusebius' *Martyrs of Palestine*, speaks of an Edict (*grammata*), leading to an intensification of anti-Christian policies. Examined more carefully, the practices instituted under the emperor's instructions are not specifically anti-Christian but directed at supporting traditional urban cults. Eusebius himself makes it clear that, under Daza's new directions, ruined temples were to be restored, there was to be an act of universal sacrifice, and food for sale in marketplaces, and entrants to bathhouses be sprinkled with sacrificial water and blood.[36] These instructions do not depart from the policy announced in the Edict of 306, but can be seen to have been issued under the policy parameters set long before by Diocletian, although tinged in application by Maximinus' own views. This was an individual policy, not an independent one.

Galerius' obstinacy in refusing to accord his nephew full promotion is represented by Lactantius as an attempt to assert Licinius' seniority. While this is a superficially plausible public line, it does not stand much scrutiny. The reality is that, if Galerius had promoted Daza to the rank of Augustus, then he would have been compelled to do the same for Constantine. He was more than reluctant to do this, both because of the mutual antipathy between the two men, and because he had gone to some trouble to reassert Diocletian's imperial model of two Augusti and two Caesars, and would not easily let it go. That was the structure which Diocletian had bequeathed him and therefore the structure which he sought to maintain. After Carnuntum, this was a structure founded upon pretence and false hope. In order to sustain it, Galerius had to ignore Constantine's assertive ambition, the meddling of Maximian, and the usurpation of Maxentius. Any promotion conceded to Daza would have thrust a torch into the dry twigs of this settlement and destroyed it. The reality of these considerations overrode any personal loyalty or connection that Galerius felt for his nephew. The title *filius Augustorum* was intended to reassure Daza of his dynastic role: that he had not been passed over or forgotten; that his day would come. Daza's refusal to accept it was respectful, but maintained a breach, of a sort, between the two men.

Maximian, aware of the conflict, may well have journeyed to the east in order to attempt to effect what Galerius would not.[37] If so, Daza was not tempted by him but persisted in his request for promotion from his uncle. At length, frustrated by Galerius' refusal to bend any further than an unsatisfactory compromise, Daza permitted his elevation through acclamation by his own soldiery.[38] Only when Galerius had received the laureate portrait and no doubt heard the reports of his agents did he reluctantly concede Daza the rank and title of Augustus. He could do little else. Maximinus was simply too important to him and to his own dynastic hopes to have alienated him further. In recognizing Daza's self-promotion, Galerius quietly abandoned the Diocletianic symmetry reimposed by Carnuntum. Any pretence of an ordered dynasty bound by *concordia* and *pietas* was now abandoned. The weaknesses of Diocletian's attempt to invent a dynasty were now apparent. The bonds of kinship forged through adoption and intermarriage had proved insufficiently strong to hold the fractured imperial family together. Daza himself was certainly aware of this. Once his promotion was achieved, he reverted to his role as loyal and trusted deputy. Daza's only known piece of self-assertion in terms of policy was an order that Christians be no longer executed, but mutilated instead. This order was issued in June or July of 310, only a few weeks after his acclamation as Augustus.[39]

This is consistent with Daza's apparent preoccupation with the suppression of Christianity. While this policy had been inherited from Diocletian, and Galerius had been its diligent executor (see below), Daza evidently had a much more urgent and vigorous approach to its implementation. The evident absence of major conflict in the eastern provinces following Galerius' victory over the Persians, together with the demographic fact of large concentrations of Christians, provided a clear context for the continuation of Diocletian's ideological war against the Christians. This was a war which had ended in the western portion of the empire after 303, a reflection both of the distaste felt by Maximian and Constantius for the policy, and of subsequent political change. In the eastern provinces, Galerius had dutifully enforced Diocletian's policy. He had retained Clodius Culcianus, a thoughtful and energetic intellectual appointed by Diocletian as Prefect of Egypt, in office for some years.[40] In 306 he sought to make use of the census to enforce Diocletian's 304 Edict requiring universal sacrifice.[41]

Galerius and the Christians

Galerius' own policy towards the Christians essentially continued that of Diocletian, but he made it far more systematic and therefore less open to abuse. In linking the census with the order for universal sacrifice, he established a clear and straightforward way of enforcing a difficult policy, placing the onus, as it had been in the time of Decius and Valerian, upon municipal authorities to enforce.[42] It should not be thought, simply because Diocletian inaugurated and set the tone for the Great Persecution by the issuing of the four Edicts of 303/4, that Galerius was out of sympathy with it. On the contrary, he was a deeply pious man as were most people of his time. Alternatives to that piety were largely unimaginable. To say that he was a "fanatical pagan", as some have, is to misunderstand the nature of classical civic religion.[43] Strictly speaking, and as Garth Fowden has noted, "paganism" did not exist as a discrete phenomenon.[44] It was a term invented by Christian polemicists in order to depict all of their opponents (Jews and heretics excepted), irrespective of standpoint, as primitive and ignorant. Galerius believed and trusted in his gods, and the blessings which they brought both to the individuals and to the communities who properly performed their religious duties. His private villa at Gamzigrad encloses temples to Jupiter and Cybele.[45] These were intended evidently both for the soldiers and servants who staffed the villa and for the private devotions of the emperor himself and his family. In the public sphere, Galerius was a beneficiary of, and sincere participant in, the theology of power that had initially impelled Diocletian's order to suppress the empire's Christians.

In linking the order to sacrifice issued by Diocletian as the fourth Edict of persecution in 304, Galerius provided a simple mechanism for the enforcement of his predecessor's will.[46] It was, as Eusebius ruefully notes, more notable for its successes than its failures.[47] Elsewhere, in the provinces where his authority was more directly experienced, the persecution was pursued with apparent vigour but relatively few casualties. The Christian communities of the Danubian provinces, in particular, experienced a number of assaults, but the level seems commensurate with the small number of Danubian towns possessing Christian communities of any significance. There were martyrdoms in Sirmium and Durostorum, but these are more notable as exceptions than the norm.[48] For the most part, the peoples of this region seem to have clung to their traditional gods more tenaciously than in Egypt, Anatolia or Palestine and so been less exposed to the religious conflict being waged by their rulers. Galerius' policy, then, was a continuation and a refinement of that of Diocletian. It was neither particularly savage, nor particularly pacific, but rather dutiful and sincere. This is particularly important to note, since the policy had initially emerged from the theology of power articulated by and under Diocletian, and in which Galerius himself shared.

While Galerius was happy to share in complicity for the persecution, others of his colleagues and rivals were less enthusiastic. Maxentius, keen to differentiate himself from the policies and practices of his father-in-law, provided the large Christian community of Rome with both toleration and even encouragement. Constantine, equally eager to demonstrate his independence, both extended a benevolent toleration over those few Christians who dwelt in his realm and provided a safe haven for refugee Christians in his demesne. It may well be at this point that Lactantius came to his court, and was rewarded with the task of tutoring the young prince, Crispus.[49]

His imperial rivals may well have been either luckier or better informed than Galerius. Much of the initial impetus and support for the policy of persecution had come from a section of the urban intellectual elite. That support was not apparently widespread either amongst the curial class as a whole, or the general urban population. There is evidence of sympathetic pagans hiding Christians who were on the run from the authorities.[50] Lactantius points out that even some governors were unwilling to enforce the persecution.[51] It has, moreover, long been accepted that the actual number of martyrs from the entire persecution is comparatively small.[52] This highlights the widespread indifference to it. In using the municipal structures and the mechanism of the census, Galerius had hoped to ensure some kind of system to make the policy work. While there were some notable successes, it is evident that denunciations of Christians were comparatively rare. Estimates vary as to the size of the Christian population in the east from the relatively large (Barnes) to about 5 per cent (Lane Fox).[53] Even 5 per cent is a considerable proportion of the population, and so one might expect, on this basis, a much greater quantum of suffering: more trials; more condemnations to the mines; more executions. Given the polemically Christian nature of most of our sources here, the reason that we do not hear of this can only be because it did not happen. And the simple reason that it did not happen was because denunciations were rare rather than common and many of those were self-inflicted.[54] The *municipia*, perhaps out of sorts with the emperor because of the imposition of taxation upon them, may well have been content to turn a blind eye to those who failed to sacrifice according to the decree of 304. This argument is given further weight by Daza's actions after the death of Galerius. Conscious both of the lack of enthusiasm for the persecution in the *municipia* and also of the importance of their assistance, Daza offered material inducements to those towns which petitioned him to persecute. It has been shown that the principal inducement that Daza offered the towns was a return to Diocletian's taxation arrangements and the consequent abolition of urban capitation in those towns which made the request, a move which was clearly well received by some towns.[55]

If, despite Galerius' best efforts, the persecution was administered in a desultory and haphazard way, the climate that it created was oppressive. Christians could only meet in secret, if at all. They were kept safe by their pagan neighbours' indifference to the persecution, but that safety was tenuous. Secrecy, of course, was anathema to the emperors, since it bred suspicions of disloyalty and atrocity. Thus, on these counts alone, the Persecution was failing in its objective to recall all those who had wandered from the truth to the true worship of the gods. Instead, it was unpopular and drove the untrustworthy underground where their disloyal malice (to the mind of Galerius) could flourish in secret.

A failure more subtle, but also more urgent, was in Galerius' own health. During the course of 310, he contracted a painful and enduring malady. The nature of the disease cannot be clearly discerned from the strident polemics of the Christian writers. Less tainted sources offer suggestions. Zosimus calls it an infected wound. Aurelius Victor agrees.[56] In stark contrast to these bare statements, Lactantius offers an account of an illness which many have recognized as having considerable similarity to the narrative, in II Maccabees, of the death of Antiochus Epiphanes.[57] The polemical nature of the sources, and their lack of medical precision, mean that any attempt to determine the nature of the disease is futile. What can be said with certainty is that it was unpleasant, protracted and agonizing. Nevertheless, its effect on Galerius himself can be surmised. It must have shocked Galerius, hitherto a man of action and a warrior, into introspection. Galerius may have rejected the uniqueness of the God of the Christians, but he nevertheless believed that such a God both could and did exist.[58] Such was the nature of the syncretistic religion of the time that what both he and Diocletian saw themselves fighting was not Christianity as such, but its exclusivity, its novelty and its adherents' stern refusal to sacrifice to the Gods of the empire for its safety.

Galerius was not an intellectual and had no pretensions to be one. Lactantius attacked him for his ignorance and neglect of learning and culture, and his preference for military judges over aristocratic jurists.[59] But he was a devout man who sincerely believed in the power of the divine, both to reward and to punish. He was also a man who was dying a slow and relatively early death. Galerius' illness, both protracted and agonizing, gave him leisure for introspection and a serious question to address. It would not have been difficult for him, then, to connect his illness with the God whose existence he accepted, but whose devotees he rejected. Once that connection was made, it would be a matter of simple reasoning to link his catalogue of failures – Constantine's proclamation; Maxentius' usurpation; Severus' failure and death; the Sarmatian invasion of 310 which prevented Licinius' destruction of Maxentius; Daza's successful insistence upon the rank of Augustus – with the vengeance of the Christian God. Others certainly made that link, most notably Lactantius himself.

Seen in this kind of intensely personal context, the Edict of Toleration of 311 scarcely comes as a surprise. It was Galerius' last political act. He did not live long enough to draft the instructions to provincial governors to set the machinery of the Edict of Toleration in motion.[60] Unlike Diocletian, who had ordered universal sacrifice but given no instructions for its administration, Galerius was unwilling to enact a decree and leave no instructions as to how it was to be effected. Death, nevertheless, intervened. Galerius' Edict of Toleration is an important document. It provides both an elaborate rationale for the persecution and also for its cessation.[61] In his text, Galerius justifies the instigation of the Persecution by the claim that Christians had abandoned ancestral practices and the traditional rules of community (*"publicam disciplinam"*) and were instead inventing laws for themselves (*"ita sibimet leges facerent et quas observarent"*). He reflects upon the course of the persecution, admitting that many had suffered and died (*"multi periculo subiugati; multi etiam deturbati sunt"*), but to no purpose since, rather than returning to the temples and time-honoured practices, Christians had ceased to worship at all (*"ac videremus nec diis eosem cultum ac religionem debitam exhibere nec Christianorum deum observare"*). This observation may well have been the decisive factor for Galerius. Constantine and Maxentius, who had both exercised a policy of open toleration, had prospered.[62] And according to traditional ways of thinking, all of the gods had to be placated to ensure the continual well-being of the empire. This new god clearly was not content, since the requisite worship was not being performed. The conclusion of the Edict has long gone unmarked, although Galerius here does far more than simply order a cessation of the Persecution. Galerius now orders the restoration of places of worship so that Christians might again gather (*"ut denuo sint Christiani conventicula sua componant"*), and the Edict concludes with a clear injunction to Christians to pray to their God on his behalf, and for that of the empire (*"deum suum orare pro salute nostra et rei publicae ac sua, ut undique versum res publica praestetur incolumis et securi vivere in sedibus suis possint"*).[63]

Thus, Galerius admitted defeat. Struck down by political failures and by infirmity, he acknowledged that this new religion had a part to play in the continual well-being of the state. He may even have intended to restore confiscated property.[64] Lactantius certainly says so and such an intention is not out of keeping with the sentiments or tone of the Edict. Such an order may have been intended for the instruction promised in the Edict (34.5). Those instructions were, however, never issued. In the regions ruled by Daza there was no restoration of property, which remained in the hands of the state until Licinius' conquest of Daza's territories enabled the enforcement of the terms of the Edict of Milan across the entire empire.

These twin failures of Galerius – to retain both the political structure and the religious policy bequeathed him by Diocletian – are reflections upon the limits of Diocletian's success. Diocletian's new dynasty was only as strong as the loyalty between those adopted into kinship. This loyalty was celebrated as *concordia* in imperial propaganda, and Diocletian believed that it was cemented and maintained by kinship. This was his mistake. The ordered consensus of his reign was, in the first instance, maintained by loyalty to him as the father, elder brother and senior of the new dynasty. After his retirement, both Constantius and Galerius proved inadequate replacements. Despite his political success in securing his choices as the next generation of Caesars, Galerius had neither the strength of personality nor the skill to hold the dynasty together. In plain political terms, he should have confronted and removed Constantine in 306, whatever the cost to the borders or to the stability of the empire. This he was unwilling to do, confident that

Constantine could either be brought to heel by Severus or be marginalized within the family as a difficult cousin. This policy might have prospered, especially if Severus had been successful against Maxentius. The revolt of Maxentius and the successive failures, of both Severus and Galerius himself, to suppress it allowed Constantine's rule in Britain, Gaul, Germany and Spain to flourish unchallenged. The Carnuntum conference was an attempt to regain the initiative, and the extent of Galerius' predicament can be gauged by the necessity to recall Diocletian in order to lend his prestige and dignity to the decisions of the gathering. Diocletian's readiness to assist is important. While he had no desire to resume the authority he had laid down, he did see the necessity to support the man he had chosen as his son and successor. The selection of Licinius as Augustus was clearly Galerius' decision. What was also Galerius' decision was an attempt to maintain the dynastic model of two regnant Augusti supported by two Caesars that Diocletian had devised to meet his own needs. This necessitated Constantine remaining with the dignity of Caesar only and implied that he was unworthy to succeed to the station of Augustus, since he had been passed over for Licinius. This was a consequence of the uneasy personal relationship, and complete lack of trust, between Galerius and Constantine. As a gesture, it was predictable (Constantine was absent from the conference for good reason) and, as a measure to limit his power, it was futile. It was already too late. Constantine was too strong, already effectively exercising the powers of an Augustus; Maxentius had stolen the imperial army that might otherwise have confronted him. Even Daza, loyal as he was, felt snubbed. Galerius' essential unwillingness to depart from the structure created by Diocletian led to its destruction. In the same way, Galerius had pursued Diocletian's religious policy with dutiful diligence, even devising a means to impose it more rigorously. Only at the last minute, and as a result of the collapse of his own health, did he abandon it.

Galerius Augustus

These failures, highlighted by largely hostile sources, must be set against some qualified successes in warfare, law and administration. The *Epitome de Caesaribus* described Galerius as "an excellent and fortuneful warrior" (*eximius et felix bellator*); Eutropius as "outstanding in military affairs" (*re militari egregius*).[65] War was the medium in which Galerius excelled. Politics was not his forté. It is significant that of Galerius' two great reverses in war, that in Persia was made good by a stunning victory which enabled Rome to recover all of the territory which it had lost during the third century; while that in Italy was brought about by lack of readiness and the unsuitability of the season, and was never regarded as finished.

After Carnuntum, Galerius felt the lower Danube to be secure enough to withdraw from his residence at Serdica further south to Thessalonica, since annual campaigns in the region had made its provinces safe.[66] The benefits of this can be seen in the evident prosperity of the Danubian provinces at this time. Victor adds a useful detail. He states that Galerius ordered Lake Pelso to be canalized and partially drained in order to develop new farming land.[67] In this, Galerius was following the example of Probus who had ordered the draining of the region around Sirmium and had fostered the development of viticulure around Sirmium and in Moesia.[68] Likewise, according to Victor, Galerius pursued a policy of deforestation – again, in order to foster agriculture, the economic base of the empire.[69] These achievements cannot be dated specifically. If Galerius took a personal interest, as Victor implies, then they are most likely to have been encompassed between 303 and 308, the five years in which Galerius was based in Sirmium, although an earlier date has been suggested.[70] Galerius thought highly of the achievement. The province was renamed Valeria in honour of his wife, the Augusta.[71] Elsewhere, in Moesia, the inhabitants of the town of Heraclea Sintica were pleased to receive an imperial letter raising the status of their community to that of a city.[72]

The Danubian provinces were not the only beneficiaries of his desire to revitalize the economic base of the empire. A series of inscriptions from Pisidian Antioch refer to Galerius with particular effusion. While this effusion may mark no more than Galerius' primacy in the imperial college, it is clear that these texts mark the completion of a number of significant building projects in the city, perhaps as a result of its elevation to the status of the metropolis of the newly created province of Pisidia. One of these projects is clearly a new theatre, since one inscription was placed over the entrance to the tunnel through the *cavea* of the theatre. Another was from the architrave of a major public building; a third is a statue base which was clearly one of a series of all four regnant emperors. The principal study of these texts also notes the considerable scale of the building and the critical role of the governor, M. Valerius Diogenes, later to become prominent as a vigorous promoter of Daza's anti-Christian policies.[73] Pisidian Antioch may not have been the only beneficiary. An inscription from this period also records the promotion of Tymandus in Pisidia to the status of a city.[74]

Other communities are more explicitly attested to have enjoyed Galerius' benevolence. No fewer than five towns east of the Adriatic were graced with the new name of Maximianopolis. Most notable of these is the town of Maximianopolis in the Thebaid discussed in an earlier chapter. This town was perhaps a refoundation of Coptos and dates from Galerius' defeat of the revolt in the Thebaid early in his career as Caesar. Two other towns bearing the name of Maximianopolis would seem to belong to the same period inasmuch as they can be linked to Galerius' reorganization of the *limes Palestinae* in 295. The larger of them would seem to have been the Maximianopolis in Palestine which had been the legionary camp of the VI Fretensis.[75] The smaller, in Arabia, is identified by A.H.M. Jones as the village of Saccaea raised to municipal status.[76] No doubt Galerius was the emperor on the spot for these decisions but those decisions were accepted by Diocletian. Moreover, these are not the only towns to receive his name. A poorly attested Maximianopolis in Pamphylia sent a bishop to the Council of Nicaea in 325.[77] Ramsay considers this town to have been renamed from Tymbrianassus, although this identification lacks absolute certainty.[78] Even so, it can probably be put into the same category as the Maximianopolis of Thrace, mentioned in the *Itinerarium Burdigalense* and by Ammianus in his description of Thrace.[79] This has been identified as the more ancient town of Porsule, modern Komotini, and this identification has been accepted by modern cartographers of the late Roman world.[80] None of these towns were new foundations, but old towns with new names. The honour done to Galerius marked either his benevolence in granting municipal status, or some other example of imperial patronage. Such a policy was so completely consistent with the policy of Diocletian that it is difficult to distinguish a distinct urban policy for Galerius. Rather, he continued the work of Diocletian in promoting urban life, funding public works where necessary or desired, upgrading the status of villages, and continuing in the work of restoration and reconstruction.

The benefits which both this specific policy brought, and the maintenance of the peace of the provinces in general, must be stressed. Despite what our sources lament as a heavy burden of taxation, and the bleak pictures painted by Eusebius and Lactantius, the maintenance of armed peace promoted prosperity, assisted recovery and encouraged development. In 312, Daza could speak without irony of *felicitas temporum*: the fields bearing rich produce and the security of a life without war.[81] Such a statement was equally true in Pannonia, Greece and Gaul as it was in Asia. Given that at least one purpose of the empire, if not its actual justification, was the provision and maintenance of peace and security, and bearing in mind the bloody history of the third century, this was an achievement in itself. Galerius continued the process begun by Diocletian of a vigorous and assertive frontier policy that took battle to the peoples and confederacies that menaced the border provinces, rather than wait for them to attack. Like Diocletian, Galerius also sought to revitalize the flagging economies of regional centres through major programmes of public works. Moreover, and as Diocletian had also done, Galerius was keen to ensure the development of agriculture in border lands. He provided land and, perhaps too, the people to farm it.

Another aspect of the administration of Galerius seems to have been a concern about corruption. Diocletian had been a foe of corruption, taking the considerable step of the wholesale abolition of the *frumentarii*, the imperial secret police, because of evident complaints about the activities of agents, particularly in the more distant parts of the empire. This corps was later found indispensable by Constantine and reconstituted as the *agentes in rebus*, later to be loathed by Ammianus Marcellinus and complained of by Aurelius

Victor.[82] Galerius continued this policy by an attempt to eliminate abuses within the imperial administration. Within a few months of his elevation to the dignity of an Augustus, in 306, Galerius had issued the first of his edicts on the behaviour of the *Caesariani*. A collection of inscriptions, from a variety of provenances, have been identified as a dossier of related edicts and ascribed to Galerius.[83] The earliest of these, preserved in fragmentary inscriptional texts from Athens, Ephesus and Tlos in Lycia, can be dated before 19 September 305.[84] This Edict seeks to provide a remedy for taxpayers being exploited by unscrupulous officials, in this case, the *Caesariani*. These were members of the imperial administration employed as treasury officials within the office of the *rationalis*. The name is, in all likelihood, a relic of an earlier time when imperial administration was leaner, and staffed principally by the emperor's freedmen.[85] The *Caesariani* did not have a good reputation. Diocletian already had cause to issue a rescript to one of his officials, perhaps the *rationalis*, ensuring that the *Caesariani* required clear imperial instructions to seize the property of debtors to the Treasury. Without that clear authority, alleged debtors were authorized to resist them, by force if necessary.[86] Galerius' Edict repeated the common belief that they were corrupt, in this case forging or falsifying treasury claims (*adnotationes*) upon citizens. These false claims were designed either to extort or to provide a more direct private benefit. Galerius ordered that those who had suffered adverse judgements on the basis of dubious documents would have their convictions overturned. Applicants under this provision had to lodge their claims by 19 September 305. Where the matter was still before a provincial court, it would be immediately referred to the emperor's court for resolution. The Edict provided a means of redress to those who had suffered at the hands of the *Caesariani*, and any future actions required the *adnotationes* on which they were based to be authenticated at the imperial court.

This document is, however, only one of three.[87] The connection between the three edicts has been made as a result of painstaking epigraphic work. The second document of the dossier is an edict on accusations (*de accusationibus*), which is preserved in a number of copies, including a shorter version in the Theodosian Code, and is more usually ascribed to either Licinius or Constantine.[88] The law, in its complete version, seeks to discourage frivolous or fraudulent accusations brought to a court by imposing a punishment upon any failed accuser. In cases of *maiestas*, where torture is an authorized legal instrument, a failed accuser will himself become subject to torture in order to identify any confederates in a failed charge. The law applies both to the accusers in a criminal case (*accusatores*) and in a fiscal case (*delatores*), and restricts the right to bring charges related to taxation and treasury claims to officials of the fisc, in other words, *Caesariani*. Slaves and freedmen are barred from acting either as accusers or *delatores* of their masters/patrons on pain of crucifixion.[89] Anonymous letters containing accusations (*libelli*) are to be ignored and destroyed and their authors identified and punished. The third decree also relates to the *Caesariani*. Known principally through an inscription from Lyttus in Crete, this text was found in close association with a fragment of the Edict on Accusations.[90] While the text of the third Edict has proven difficult to discern in its details, it is clear in its essential thrust. The Edict orders the restoration of particular properties that had been confiscated to the Treasury by *Caesariani* and others. Treasury claims still in dispute are summarily dismissed. The responsible treasury officials (*procuratores* and *Caesariani*) are condemned, not for their corruption, but for their officiousness (*temeritas*) and greed (*avaritia*).[91]

It is clear from the contexts that these three laws, together with a preamble condemning the Caesariani for the slanderous accusations (*calumnias*) they had confected, belong to a single collection of related decrees which was widely published in cities in the eastern provinces of the empire. Their provisions are entirely consistent with the legislative language and style of Diocletian, providing a rationale for the measure, thereby explicitly emphasizing the care exercised by the emperors for their subjects (*providentia*).[92] Taken together, they represent a firm stance by the emperor(s) against the overbearing, excessive and often self-serving measures taken by their own subordinates. It has been argued, and with great plausibility, that the dossier belongs to the beginning of Galerius' reign when the new Augustus was seeking to establish himself as a clear and populist champion for the rights and expectations of the ordinary citizens of the empire. The broad publication of these edicts through the breadth of the eastern provinces provided for Galerius a clear medium within which he might both establish his political credentials to succeed Diocletian and also enact a policy that was both merciful and generous. In publishing the dossier so broadly, Galerius was also following the model established by Diocletian himself. When the Prices Edict was issued, it was widely published throughout the empire. Its grandiose language of self-justification provided a complex expression of imperial benevolence that provided an exemplar to the legal author(s) of the documents comprising the Caesariani dossier. It was a useful example to set, since imperial lawmaking was turned from a simple function of the imperial office into a tool for the projection of the imperial image. In following this model, Galerius made the most of it, asserting his own benevolence and concern that citizens of his empire were governed well and honestly.[93]

Galerius' view of himself quite naturally stands at considerable variance with the image projected of him in this context by the splenetic Lactantius, who characterizes Galerius' legal practices as vicious and inhumane. According to Lactantius, Galerius virtually made torture compulsory, regardless of rank; imposed the death penalty in preference to any other; decreed such savage executions that death by the sword was seen as a mark of favour; enjoyed seeing condemned criminals fed piecemeal to his pet bears; exiled litterateurs; and failed to appoint legal advisers to assist his soldier-governors. This is rhetorical grotesquery and the credibility of the

claims is justly compromised by the extent of the caricature. Yet below
this lies a kernel of truth: first, the misuse or overuse of the courts by
government officials to impose apparently burdensome punishments upon
taxpayers, and, second, a preference for policy results over judicial processes.
Lactantius complains:

> *Iam illa huic levia fuerant: eloquentia extincta, causidici sublati, iure consulti aut relegati aut necati, litterae autem inter malas artes habitae, et qui eas noverant, pro inimicis hostibusque protriti et execrati.*[94]

(For it was a trifle to him that eloquence was eliminated; advocates
removed; jurists banished or slain; even literature was numbered
amongst the wicked arts and those who professed it were vilified and
condemned as personal and public enemies.)

At the very least, this passage provides us with the source of Lactantius'
animus. Lactatius was a lawyer, a rhetorician and a student of literature. He
was also an exile, who had fled the court of Diocletian and spent the years of
Galerius' reign unable to practise his profession.[95] Others were more fortunate, since Galerius was not the crude thug of Lactantius' portrayal. The
voice of literature was not stilled, nor were the liberal arts silenced. Literary
figures like Sossianus Hierocles, Andromachus and Paul of Lycopolis prospered.[96] Moreover, Galerius' own legislation with respect to the practices of
the *Caesariani* implies an impatience of, and mistrust for, judicial process.
Galerius evidently preferred summary and simple military-style justice.
Lactantius complains of the appointment of unsupervised military judges to
serve in the provinces. The nature of his complaint was not that they were
ignorant of the law, but that they were men without culture or refinement
(*iudices militares humanitatis litterarum rudes*).[97]

There is a danger of reading too much into meagre evidence but it seems
plain from Lactantius' criticisms that the courts were applying torture as a
means of ascertaining evidence rather too readily. The wealthy classes had
never been totally immune from torture. They had been customarily subject
to it in *maiestas* cases for a long time.[98] It does not seem likely that there was
a sudden increase in *maiestas* cases at this time, or Lactantius would have
made a point of it. Rather, Lactantius is suggesting that judges increasingly
used torture as a first rather than a last resort. This is not a new observation.
Diocletian himself complained of the practice and legislated against it.[99]
Clearly these abuses of process took place, but, as Diocletian's rescript clearly
shows, that does not mean that they were policy. It is easy to mistake Lactantius' polemic for a sober narrative and conclude that the courts had been
debased through the emperor's own brutishness and contempt for privilege.
It is true that Galerius mistrusted the courts and their processes, but the
objective evidence suggests that his response was the appointment of men

231

whom he understood and trusted to oversee the judicial work. While this may have had results that Lactantius disliked, amongst non-Christian writers it earned Galerius a reputation as a man of energy and ability.[100]

One interesting oddity in Lactantius' cantankerous portrait of Galerius is his accusation that Galerius wished to turn the Roman state into a Persian-style despotism.[101] Significantly, this is the first charge he makes in his list of complaints, and it is a familiar one, but more frequently made of Diocletian.[102] For Lactantius, this desire is consistent with Galerius' essential otherness, his barbarism. Since he had not been imbued by Roman tradition, he had no respect for it, trampled upon it and preferred to emulate foreign practices.[103] More consistent, if less rhetorical, is the likelihood that he simply followed Diocletian's policy and, on formal occasions, clad himself in tiara, jewelled robe and pearl-encrusted sandals, and required a carefully choreographed ceremonial.

Galerius was also careful to maintain Diocletian's grandiose programme of public works. Lactantius had mocked this vast expenditure of public money on civic amenity in Nicomedia in the following terms:

> *Hic basilicae, hic circus, hic moneta, hic armorum fabrica, hic uxori domus, hic filiae. Repente magna pars civitatis exciditur.*[104]

(Here a basilica, there a circus, a mint, an arms factory; here a palace for his wife, for his daughter. Before long, the greater part of the city had been destroyed.)

Aurelius Victor, by contrast, celebrated this acceleration of imperial building:

> *Veterrimae religiones castissime curatae, ac mirum in modum novis adhuc cultisque pulchre moenibus Romana culmina et ceterae urbes ornatae, maxime Carthago, Mediolanum, Nicomedia.*[105]

(The most antique religious practices were cared for with the greatest propriety, and the hills of Rome as well as other cities – particularly Carthage, Milan and Nicomedia – were adorned with wonderful, innovative and beautifully elegant structures.)

This was a policy that proudly proclaimed the confidence of the new empire as civil and imperial amenities rose on a monumental scale from Eboracum to Alexandria. It also provided a vast injection of money into the depressed economy of the empire and ended the dragging recession of the late third century. The urban renewal in Rome alone, with a baths complex of lavish dimensions, a new Senate House, a Triumphal Arch and various monuments, was considerable.[106] To add to that, the number of building projects speak for a mighty concentration of resources in construction: the palace complexes of Milan, Trier, Thessalonica, Carthage, Sirmium, Antioch and perhaps Eboracum; the renovation of Ephesus; the eastern fortifications of the *strata Diocletiana*; the continuation of the construction of the forts of the Saxon Shore; and the many municipal buildings.

It is not possible, in most cases, to distinguish between Galerius' building projects and those of Diocletian. Although many structures are attributed to Diocletian, their construction continued after his abdication. Galerius did add some of his own, however. The most obvious of these is the imperial palace at Thessalonica. This is the place most obviously connected to Galerius as it was his residence for two distinct periods: as Caesar from 299 until 303, and as Augustus from 308 until shortly before his death.[107] His intermediate residence at Serdica has not been excavated, nor can it be, since it lies beneath the modern city of Sofia.[108] Unfortunately this means that the two palaces cannot be compared, and one can only infer into them archaeological conclusions available from Thessalonica.

Any emperor had a duty to develop amenities in any city in which he was resident for any length of time. Even Sirmium, long possessed of an imperial palace, received the benefit of a new baths complex whilst Licinius was resident there.[109] Galerius' residence in Thessalonica likewise indicates his general responsibility for the palace there. While it was built under his authority, and might therefore be expected to reflect something of his wishes, it is also part of a much wider context of palace building in the Diocletianic era. As such, it is a consistent exemplar of the ideology that both Diocletian and Galerius professed. Much of the palace lies under the modern city, although a significant amount has now been exposed. It is clear from the size of the complex and the rotunda, its sole surviving complete building, that it was typical of the monumentality of contemporary architecture.[110] Clear evidence of the scale of that architecture can be seen in its surviving examples: the *aula* at Trier; the remains of the Baths of Diocletian which today house a museum and a church, both on a scale large by modern standards and abutting the spacious Piazza della Repubblica, which follows the lines of the ancient exedra of the Baths.

Construction of the palace must have begun when Galerius took up residence in the city. Two details make this clear. First, the design of the complex is such that its focal point is the Arch of Galerius.[111] This was probably not a triumphal arch in the strict sense, but an octopyle gate marking both the northern end of the palace and the southern entrance of the rotunda, and also serving as a thoroughfare for east–west traffic on the *via Egnatia*.[112] The extant pylons of the Arch display an ideology which is characteristic of the reign of Diocletian. In one famous scene, Diocletian and Galerius are portrayed as sacrificing together at the Altar of Jupiter. In another, the four emperors are shown taking their places amongst the gods.[113] Although there is no evidence to suggest that Galerius altered this ideological perspective when he became Augustus, it can still be reasonably concluded that the commencement of the Arch and palace belongs to the earlier period of his residence in the city. This is made clear by the nature of the only extant building of the palace – the rotunda (see Figure 7). The function of this building has occasioned some discussion amongst modern scholars. Some consider it to have been Galerius' intended mausoleum, others are less certain.[114] This question should surely be regarded as settled by the presence of six sepulchral niches in the walls of the rotunda.[115] If the rotunda's original intention indeed was as a mausoleum, it is significant that it was never used as such. At least one other Diocletianic capital – Mediolanum – possessed a mausoleum attached to the palace complex,[116] as did Maxentius' villa on the outskirts of Rome.[117] Now the fact that Galerius was buried elsewhere – at Romuliana – yet was probably resident in Thessalonica for most of his final illness seems to indicate a change of mind on his part. The fact that the rotunda was completed would indicate that, like the Arch of which it was an architectural piece, it was a part of the earlier phase of construction of the palace.

It would seem, therefore, that the palace complex which now bears Galerius' name was commenced, and its major structural features completed, while Galerius was Caesar. It follows the pattern of similar constructions within the empire and work on it continued during Galerius' second

Figure 7 Galerius' original mausoleum subsequently converted into the church of St George (photo: the author).

residency in the city. Such work does not seem to have been hurried. While the small arch, now in the Thessaloniki Museum, that bears a tondo portrait of young Galerius originally stood over the approach to the octagonal ceremonial chamber, it is likely that construction of this room was still in progress at the time of Galerius' death.[118] The Thessalonica palace is much of a piece with other imperial residences built during this period. More were constructed than were needed at any given time in order to suit the essentially peripatetic nature of the imperial court. There is evidence, either written or archaeological, of imperial palaces built at this time at Antioch, Nicomedia, Sirmium, Serdica, Aquileia, Mediolanum and Trier.[119] There must also have been residences of some kind at Eboracum, Massilia, Carthage, Arelate and Londinium.[120] The function of these palaces was not merely to provide shelter for roving emperors or their officials. They were also the noticeboards for imperial propaganda. The famous porphyry group of Diocletian and his colleagues, now in Venice, had its counterparts elsewhere in the empire.[121] The Arch of Galerius was not the only triumphal monument of the age. Fragments of an equivalent monument survive in the remains of fourth-century Nicaea.[122] In Antioch, the emperor Julian gave his public reading of the *Misopogon* at the Tetrapylon of the Elephants, perhaps another celebration in stone of Galerius' victory over the Persians.[123] Certainly Ammianus attests the existence in that city of a great bronze statue of Galerius holding an orb.[124] A triumphal arch was built for Diocletian's triumph in Rome, a victory column was constructed in Alexandria, and other similar monuments adorned the cities of the Roman east, including the ancient Temple of Luxor, now renovated into an imperial fortress.[125] One can imagine from the words of an enraged local who tore down the first Edict announcing the Great Persecution in Nicomedia that that city was similarly adorned.[126]

It would be a danger to read too much of Galerius into the Thessalonica palace complex. The place did have a function in imperial propaganda, but this was far less to glorify Galerius than to proclaim the success of Diocletian's new dynasty. Nevertheless, Galerius chose it as his home for two major periods of his reign: first as Caesar, than as Augustus, and there are now clear personal associations between him and the city. It is his face that stares down from the tondo in the small arch recovered in the excavations, twinned with a matching medallion of the *tyche* of the city. The link between the two is unambiguous enough and these personal touches ought not to surprise.[127] Portraits of Galerius are also found elsewhere, as should not be surprising, inasmuch as Galerius was a serious power in the Roman world for nearly two decades.[128] In the same way, the presence of an apparent triumphal arch that has traditionally borne his name ought not mislead one into the consideration that this was a unique reflection of his success. The Arch is not a complete artefact and, while representations of Galerius on the extant portions of the Arch certainly emphasize his achievement in destroying the Persians, it would be peculiar if this were not the case. Nevertheless, the ideological summary of the victory can be seen expressed in two scenes from the Arch reliefs and within these statements Galerius' victories are represented as of a piece with imperial victories everywhere. First, the so-called "sacrifice" scene shows Galerius in military uniform standing to the left of Diocletian, in civilian dress. Galerius offers sacrifice upon an altar upon which the figures of both Jupiter and Hercules are carved, whilst Diocletian looks on, together with a crowd of figures, three of which have been identified as *Aion*, *Eirene* and *Oikoumene*.[129] Whilst Galerius' individual achievement is commemorated, it is thus clearly placed in an overall context of subordination to Diocletian and to Heaven. A second panel, adjacent to the sacrifice relief, adds further emphasis to this picture. It depicts the Augusti enthroned between the Caesars. Beside Diocletian stands Constantius; beside Maximian, Galerius. The emperors are shown in the act of raising up personifications of the provinces of Syria and Britain. Around them can be discerned the figures of Isis, Virtus, the Dioscuri, Sarapis, Jupiter, Honos, Fortuna, Oceanus, Tellus and others.[130] The success of the dynasty is proclaimed in no uncertain terms with the company of Heaven gathered to witness the restoration of threatened provinces. There is no special attention paid to Galerius here. It is the dynasty itself which is the focus of the celebration; it is the dynasty which has triumphed; it is the dynasty which is blessed by the gods. Indeed, the remainder of the Arch may not have featured Galerius at all. Four pillars are missing and fragments of an analogous victory monument at Nicaea celebrate the achievements of Constantius in Germany.[131] Surely then, the Arch of Galerius must be seen in this overall context. An accident of preservation has given us the piers of the Arch which concentrate upon Galerius, but lost to us are the western piers which may well have featured the celebration of a quite different series of imperial victories in which Galerius played no part.[132]

However, if no distinctively Galerian building policy can be discerned in the palace complex of Thessalonica, nor in the triumphal Arch which is its architectonic focus, one construction belonging to this period can be credited to Galerius, and this is the most important of all. The *Epitome de Caesaribus* gives the place of Galerius' burial as Romulianum, named for Galerius' mother, in Dacia Ripensis, the province of his birth (see Figure 8).[133] The site has been identified as a villa, provided with strong walls near the confluence of the two branches of the Timacus River, and close to sulphur baths. The modern name is Gamzigrad. The ancient name was long uncertain but has now been firmly identified as Romuliana.[134] It was the place where Galerius was born and the place where he was buried.[135] The villa itself was fortified and, like Split, it attracted a later settlement, including a Christian basilica built over Galerius' *aula*.[136] It was refortified under Justinian and much of the monumental fortification still visible on the site dates from this period.[137]

Figure 8 Archivolt from Gamzigrad, bearing the name 'Romuliana' (photo: courtesy the National Archaeological Museum, Zajecar).

This was the place of Galerius' birth. The imperial buildings overlie a farm complex dating from the middle of the third century. Beneath that, there is no evidence of habitation after the neolithic period.[138] Lactantius states that Galerius' family had fled across the Danube and settled in New Dacia.[139] This, then, was the land of Galerius' birth, the rural landscape where he earned the nickname of *Armentarius* and where sheep still graze. The villa itself is in fact a large complex of buildings which appears to have been constructed in two stages.[140] Although the excavation of the site is ongoing, what has emerged hitherto is that during the first phase of construction a villa was built, near to but not replacing the earlier farmhouse, as well as a temple, both being surrounded by a defensive curtain wall punctuated by rectangular bastion towers.[141] The temple may give an important clue as to the purpose of this earlier phase inasmuch as it possesses a ditch which has been identified as a *fossa sanguinis*. Thus, it can be clearly associated with the worship of Cybele in whose honour *taurobolia* were celebrated.[142] To the second phase of construction belongs a second and more magnificent palace, a longer and more elaborate curtain wall and a monumental Temple of Jupiter with a double crypt.[143] Mosaics from this period include geometric designs, a hunting scene and a figure of Dionysus riding a tiger.[144] Further buildings are still being excavated.

Fragments of sculpture retrieved from the second phase include a 1.5 times life-size porphyry hand holding an orb – probably a fragment of a statue of Galerius himself.[145] The laurelled head from this statue has also been recovered from the fill of a rubbish pit on the site (see Figure 9). The portrait is well preserved, and is recognizably the same person as in the Venice portrait, the Athribis bust and the Thessalonica tondo, but now advanced from robust youth to rubicund middle age.[146] The original statue

Figure 9 Porphyry portrait of Galerius from Gamzigrad (photo: courtesy the National Archaeological Museum, Zajecar).

probably depicted the emperor being crowned by Victoria. The crown itself is shown as bejewelled and adorned with the miniature busts of four, quite different, figures. One is heroically naked; another wears scale armour; another wears a civilian cloak and the fourth, a *paludamentum*. Individual identification is not possible on the basis of the portraiture, since the faces no longer survive, but since the portrait is of an older Galerius, the figures probably represent, respectively, Diocletian, Maximinus, Galerius and Licinius: the emperors of the Jovian line.

The two stages of construction can be dated with approximation rather than exactitude. Coins, which function only to give a *terminus post quem*, give an indication. The earlier phase of construction seems to belong to the last decade of the third century or early into the fourth; while the second part, to which the mosaics belong, must have been completed after 309. A coin datable to between 308 and 311 was found in the foundations of one of the polygonal fortification towers (see Figure 10), while another, of Licinius, has been found in the substructure of a mosaic in Hall D of Palace I.[147] Since the laying of mosaic should mark the completion stage of any construction, and Palace I belongs to the second stage of the building project, it is permissible to conclude that this structure was completed in about 310. The palace itself was not the product of civilian engineers and builders, but was constructed by a detachment of the V Macedonica. *Vexillations* from this legion had served Galerius in Egypt and the east, and he might well have felt some personal affection for it.[148]

Figure 10 The Gamzigrad site from the air (photo: courtesy the National Archaeological Museum, Zajecar).

239

The Gamzigrad palace is far more than a remote imperial hunting lodge. It marks the place of Galerius' childhood and presumably the residence of his mother. The first stage of the construction was built for her during Galerius' period as Caesar in order to provide himself and his family with the sort of rural retreat appropriate to his new station, and reflects his mother's exotic religious tastes so scorned by Lactantius (see Figure 11).[149] What then was the purpose of the second stage? If Galerius already possessed a country mansion, why embellish it further? It is Lactantius who provides an answer since he clearly refers to Galerius' intention to abdicate.[150] The second stage, far more elaborate and impressive than the first, was intended then as Galerius' retirement palace, his version of Split. It was to the green hills and fields of his birth that Galerius intended to return after he had laid down his power.

Nothing in Galerius' building policy can therefore be seen to have been substantially different from that of Diocletian. He continued, it would seem, the process of urbanization and embellished at least one seat of his government, Thessalonica, with a palace that stood as a powerful and solid statement of the dynasty's achievement. The apparent glorification of his own victories must be seen in that context. His only identifiable piece of construction, his fortified villa at Romuliana, mirrored Diocletian's villa at Split. Unlike Diocletian, however, he was fated never to enjoy the *otium* which he had envisaged for himself amid the rolling hills of the land of his birth.

Figure 11 The Gamzigrad palace from the air (photo: courtesy the National Archaeological Museum, Zajecar).

As the Gamzigrad palace drew near to completion, the plans for Galerius' *vicennalia* began to be laid. These seem to have commenced in 309 and the *vicennalia* itself was due to commence in March 312. Lactantius complains that tax-gatherers were already raising the necessary funds.[151] He also adds an important detail with respect to Galerius' *vicennalia*. The emperor intended, at the conclusion of the celebration, to abdicate and hand over the reins of government to Licinius. He also adds that Galerius intended to raise his son Candidianus to the rank of Caesar.[152] It has been suggested that Galerius actually did make Candidianus Caesar, but this lacks substantial evidence.[153] Little is known of Candidianus, other than that he was Galerius' natural son, who had been adopted by Valeria so that, to all intents and purposes, he was their legitimate son. The intention, however, is consistent with the dynastic strategy already pursued by Galerius through the promotion of Maximinus in 305.

It was certainly Galerius' intention to leave Licinius the dignity of ranking Augustus. Even after the recognition of Daza and Constantine as Augusti, the regnal formula was not altered and so Licinius retained second place – the emperor clearly anointed to replace Galerius.[154] This evidence would suggest that Galerius intended to be succeeded by an imperial college consisting of Licinius supreme and ruling in the West as senior Augustus with Constantine and Daza as subordinate Augusti and Candidianus, who would have been about sixteen in 313, joining the college as its most junior member.

Galerius' intention to retire is indubitable and highly significant. There is no reason for Lactantius to have embellished a rumour to that effect since that would reflect no discredit upon Galerius; and it is given further support by the discovery of his retirement palace at Gamzigrad. The repetition of Diocletian's policy is apparent, although fortunately Galerius had no coeval who had to be induced to join him in retirement. He could simply divest himself of the purple at the close of his *vicennalia*, give Licinius his blessing, name a Caesar, and retire to a life of farming, hunting and feeding his bears.[155] Nature had other plans. In 310, as the preparations for the *vicennalia* were gathering pace, Galerius was stricken by a severe disease.[156] Lactantius' bitter and lascivious account – in Finley's words "complacent", in those of Gibbon one of "singular accuracy and apparent pleasure" – accords with other accounts of Galerius' death in the central element, that of some kind of infection associated with the genital area.[157] While its precise nature is obscured by tendentious piety, a general description can be drawn from sources with no polemical intent. These agree that it was an infection of some kind, either of a wound or of some kind of genital ulcer.[158]

Galerius' illness was protracted, and the location of his suffering difficult to determine. There is a considerable confusion in our sources, which has long led to the assumption that Galerius died at Serdica.[159] It receives implicit support from Lactantius' account in which a city is mentioned as filled with the stench of Galerius' decaying body.[160] Unfortunately,

Lactantius is more specific about the smell than the city. This is a product of Lactantius' rhetorical conceit, a clear doublet of II Maccabees 9.9 on the matter of the odour of Antiochus IV's worm-ridden body, which the author of that document states "sickened the whole army".[161] The *Origo Constantini Imperatoris* is more specific:

> *ipse ad Serdicam regressus, morbo ingenti occupatus sic distabuit, ut aperto et putrescenti viscere moreretur.*[162]

(he came back to Serdica, where he was taken ill with a disgusting disease, wasting away such that he perished with his insides exposed and in a state of putrefaction.)

At this point, however, the *Origo* is compressing events severely. Galerius' illness is placed hard upon his return from Carnuntum or, rather, Pannonia (the *Origo* is rather vague on this point). Furthermore, the evidence of the mints makes it clear that Galerius did not return to Serdica at all, but moved his court to Thessalonica.[163] So, while the account in the *Origo* is quite specific, it is also misleading. What do the other sources offer? The Chronicle of 334 gives the place of Galerius' death as "in Dardania".[164] The *Epitome de Caesaribus* states that Galerius was buried at Romulianum, the place named for his mother.[165] Felix Romuliana does not lie in Dardania (neither did Serdica) but in the province of Dacia Ripensis. If the Chronicler is correct, it cannot have been at Romuliana that Galerius breathed his last. The road from Thessalonica via Naissus to Romuliana did run through Dardania and is the most direct route between the two places.[166] The very vagueness of the Chronicler therefore suggests a solution: that Galerius, sick and dying in Thessalonica, rejected the notion of interment in the mausoleum built for him in that city, but instead ordered that he be taken to Romuliana to die and there receive burial.

Accordingly, sometime in April 311, perhaps having already issued the Edict of Toleration, he began his final journey. Licinius evidently came to meet him at some point along the way, since he was present at Galerius' deathbed, whence he proceeded to Serdica where he issued a law on 9 June 311.[167] Perhaps weakened by his journey, Galerius died en route. His last act was to entrust the welfare of his family – Valeria the Augusta and Candidianus the young heir – to the hands of Licinius.[168] The cortege then moved on to Romuliana. It may well have been Licinius, as was appropriate under the circumstances, who oversaw Galerius' funeral rites and interment in the mausoleum there.[169]

Maxentius, upon receiving the news of the death of Galerius, persuaded the Senate to enrol him among the gods.[170] It was an act of hypocrisy, performed out of simple political expediency. When his vexatious father, in 310, had plotted against Constantine once too often and paid with his life, he too had been deified so that Maxentius could proclaim himself the son of a god.[171] Now, he could proclaim himself the son-in-law of another.[172] More genuine expressions of regret can be found in the dedications of Galerius' old soldiers. Inscriptions from Pannonia and Africa commemorate the divine *"Iovius Maximianus"*.[173]

Galerius' family did not long survive him. In entrusting them to the *patria potestas* of Licinius, Galerius had chosen ill. Licinius was to be a far more able and, indeed, more ruthless politician. Unmarried, he proposed a marriage alliance with the Augusta so that he might be, in all things, Galerius' successor. Licinius' proposal of marriage to Valeria is nowhere explicitly attested by the sources, but Lactantius gives two clues. He states that Valeria went to live at the court of Daza, accounting it safer than elsewhere because he was married.[174] When Daza, for the same reasons, proved equally as ardent as Licinius in courtship, despite the existence of a wife, Valeria refused him out of loyalty to her dead husband and respect for Daza's wife.[175] Lactantius states:

> *Qui omnes Licinium iam pridem quasi malum metuentes, cum Maximino esse maluerant praeter Valeriam, quae veluti Licinio < omnes > Maximiani hereditates iure < se > cedere idem Maximino negaverat.*[176]

(They had all long feared Licinius as a wicked man, and had all [Valeria excepted] preferred to remain with Maximian, and she gave the same answer to Maximian as she had to Licinius: that it would not be just for her to cede to him her inheritance from Maximianus [Galerius].)

Daza's response was vindictive. Long relegated to subordinate rank by Galerius, he no doubt resented similar treatment by Valeria and so he relegated both her and her mother Prisca.[177] Diocletian sued for their return to him at Split. Daza refused his envoys, and the old man, with his portraits destroyed by Constantine and his family in exile, perhaps even regretting his decision to abdicate, decided that he had lived too long. The greatest of the Jovian line and the longest lived died on 3 December 311.[178] Candidianus remained at Daza's court where he had been betrothed to the emperor's daughter.[179] Upon Daza's defeat by Licinius, mother, son and grandmother were all put to death as well as Severianus, the son of Galerius' friend and ephemeral emperor Severus. Thus, the Jovian line, the families of both Diocletian and Galerius, were wiped out. But Licinius did not profit from it. Constantine did.

Notes

1 Aur. Vict. *de Caes.* 42.17.
2 See, for example, Jones (1948), p. 28; Barnes, *CE*, p. 23; Odahl (2004), pp. 75–6.
3 See Levick (1976), p. 224f.; R. Seager (1972), *Tiberius*, London, pp. 187–202.

4 For example, Suetonius, *v. Tib.* 42–5. Levick (1976: p. 167), by contrast, prefers to label him "an elderly amateur of scholarship who enjoyed passing the port".

5 Eutropius 10.1.1–2.

6 *RIC* VI, pp. 119f., 158, 238. No coinage at all was struck for Galerius after Carnuntum at Londinium, Trier or Lugdunum. It was personal rather than political. The same mints struck for Licinius and Daza.

7 On Daza's residences, see Barnes, *NE*, p. 65, citing Downey (1961), p. 331f., although Downey only conjectures that at this point Antioch was Daza's residence. Although he visited Caesarea on a number of occasions (Barnes, *NE*, p.66), Antioch is his logical permanent residence, given its possession of a palace and a mint which continued all through this period to strike both *aes* and precious metal issues (*RIC* VI, pp. 603–11).

8 Barnes, *NE*, p. 80; *CIL* III, 10107. Barnes' alternative suggestion of Naissus is based upon the identification of the Gamzigrad site with Licinius' palace. That identification has now been rendered impossible by an inscription from the site confirming its ancient name as Romuliana (*AE* 1986, 625; NB Duval (1987) concedes the identification).

9 *RIC* VI, pp. 447–52, 477–81.

10 *RIC* VI, pp. 450–2; 477–81. This is made particularly clear by the introduction of the GENIUS types at Siscia (*RIC* VI, p. 452). There are exceptions in the gold issues, where Siscia issued a number of reverse types unique to it ("ORIENS AVGG"; "SALVS AVGG NN"; "SECVRITAS AVGG"; "VIRTVS AVGG"; and "SECVRITAS AVGG"). However, it also issued types common at other eastern mints ("IOVI CON-SERVATORI"; "VENERI VICTRI") as well as the *Genius* type on its *aes* coinage (*Ibid.*).

11 Barnes; *NE*, p. 257; 1976, p. 189.

12 Eus. *HE*, 8.14.9; 9.42; Lact. *de mort. pers.* 36.4–5; on the priesthoods themselves, see R. Grant (1975).

13 Eus. *HE*, 9.5.1.

14 See Grant (1975).

15 The inference is from the closing of the Serdica mint and the reopening of the Thessalonica mint, which now struck both precious metals and *aes* with the S(acra) M(oneta) mint-mark. See Barnes, *NE*, p. 61f. On the Thessaloniki palace, see Speiser (1984), pp. 97–9.

16 He took the title *Sarmaticus Maximus* (Barnes, *NE*, p. 81; *ILS* 664 for the date), which indicates that he took over from Galerius on the upper Danube (Barnes, *NE*, p. 64).

17 Eus. *HE*, 8.14.1–4 expatiates upon Maxentius' cruelty. Aurelius Victor (*de Caes.* 40.24) is more precise: *uti ... primusque instituto pessimo munerum specie patres aratoresque pecuniam conferre prodigenti sibi cogeret*, NB Stein, s.v. "Maxentius", *RE* XIV 2, 2454. A list exists of uncertain date (but from approximately this period) of senators who made donations on a huge scale for some unknown project (*CIL* VI 37118).

18 *MGH* I, p.148; Stein, *RE* XIV 2, 2459–64.

19 Aur. Vict. *de Caes.* 40.26 makes it plain that Constantine dedicated these monuments.

20 The Chronicle of 354 refers to a tax on gold imposed at this time, and famine and violence, giving the figure of 6,000 citizens massacred by the soldiery. Aurelius Victor (*de Caes.* 40.24) and Eusebius (*HE*, 8.14.4) refer to Maxentius' soldiers massacring large numbers of Romans. Curran also makes the link to the failure of the African grain supply. See here Curran (2000), p. 66 and Cullhed (1994), p. 71f.

21 *ILS* 675, a milestone from Aquileia, records Licinius as Augustus. Aquileia later passed into the hands of Constantine, although Calderini (1930) dates the evidence for this to 314, but see more recently Picozzi (1976), which argues a campaign (or at the very least, the fear of one) in 310 on the basis of a coin hoard at Centur. A single coin hoard is in itself insufficient evidence, but taken with the inscriptional material, is a useful indicator of Licinius' activities at this time. See also Barnes, *CE*, pp. 33, 300 n. 51.

A unique issue from Aquileia celebrating Maxentius' impending *quinquennalia* might indicate that the mint had reopened by the winter of 310 (*RIC* VI, p. 326, no. 128). See also King (1959), p.57f.

22 *RIC* VI, pp. 277, 308. The absence of any AETERNAE MEMORIAE types indicates that the mints were closed in the first part of 309, before the death of Romulus in the course of that year (Barnes, *NE*, p. 99). See also King (1959), p 54f. (Ticinum); p. 57f. (Aquileia).

23 For the date (27 June 310), see *ILS* 664; also Barnes, *NE*, p. 81.

24 Galerius' Praetorian Prefect was Tatius Andronicus, consul in 310 (Bagnall *et al.*, 1987: *CLRE*, p. 155; Barnes, *NE*, p. 126).

25 Aur. Vict. *de Caes*. 40.18.

26 Victor (*Ibid.*) refers to *militares duces* accompanying the force, although local contacts might have helped, since Volusianus had governed Africa (*ILS* 1213) and owned estates there (*ILS* 6025).

27 Aur. Vict. *de Caes*. 40.18–19; Zos. 2.14.

28 *PLRE* I, p. 976ff.; Chastagnol (1962), pp. 52–8. Volusianus was Urban Prefect from 28 October 310 until 28 October 311. His tenure of this office briefly overlapped with his first consulship which he held from September until December 311 (*Chron. Min.* I. 76; I. 231); see Bagnall *et al.* (1987), *CLRE*, p. 156.

29 *RIC* VI, p. 379, nos 218–25; p. 380, nos 227–37; p. 383, nos 265–9; p. 384, nos 272–7; p. 400, no. 3; p. 401, no.6; p. 402, no. 13; p. 403, nos 21, 22; p. 405, nos 48–50, 52; p. 406, no 57, 60–4. See also King (1959), pp. 64–5 (Ostia); pp. 71–2 (Rome).

30 Barnes, *NE*, p. 99.

31 *RIC* VI, p. 377, no. 207; p. 379, no. 226; p. 381, nos 239–40; p. 382, nos 249, 256, 257; p. 400, no. 1; p. 404, nos 32–4; p. 406, nos 58, 59. On the buildings, see Stein *RE* XIV, 2, 2454; Bertolitti *et al.* (1988); Cullhed (1994), pp. 49–60; Curran (2000), pp. 55–63; Oenbrink (2004), pp. 189–92.

32 Lact. *de mort. pers*. 32.3; 43.2.

33 *RIC* VI, pp. 606–9. For dating formulae, see Bagnall and Worp (1979), pp. 33–5. It is worth noting that the latest dated papyrus with a regnal formula is *P. Oxy*, XLVI 3270, bearing the date 15 October 309. After that point, the extant papyri date by numerals only and avoid regnal formulae altogether.

34 Lact. *de mort. pers*. 32.5.

35 For the issues: *RIC* VI, pp 630–4, nos 100, 103, 109, 117, 118a, 120, 124, 125 (Maximian); cf. pp. 630–4, nos 104, 105, 111, 118b (Constantine).

36 Eus. *de Mart. Pal.* (L) 9.2–3; (S) 9.2. For a discussion of the nature of the imperial direction, see Corcoran (2000), p. 185f.

37 Sydenham (1934). Sutherland and Carson doubt this (*RIC* VI, p. 607); Pasqualini and Barnes ignore it.

38 Lact. *de mort. pers*. 32.5.

39 On the date of Maximinus' elevation to the rank of Augustus, see Barnes, *NE*, p. 6 n. 21; Sutherland *RIC* VI, p. 15. On the question of Maximinus' religious policy, see Grant (1975); although Grant dates the decree forbidding the death penalty to Christians (Eus. *HE*, 8.12.8–9) to 308, it belongs properly to 310 (as is clear from Daza's letter to Sabinus; Eus. *HE*, 9.9a.2–3), since it was issued a year before Daza arrived in Nicomedia (Eus. 9.9a.5), which was in June or July 311 (Barnes, *NE*, p. 66). On the whole matter of Daza and the Christians, see Mitchell (1988), pp. 103–24.

40 *PLRE* I, p. 23f., appointed in 301 (*P.Oxy* 3304 is dated 6 June 301). The latest dated document of his prefecture is *P. Bodmer* XX (4 February 307). His zeal as a persecutor, or perhaps his ability as a pagan intellectual, commended him to Daza (Eus. *HE*, 9.11.4). He was followed in Egypt by a number of governors who may have been Lactantius' *iudices militares* (Lact. *de mort.* pers. 22.5). Only when Daza became Augustus did

an intellectual again rule Egypt – Sossianus Hierocles (Barnes, 1976A: pp. 243–5). The author of the *Epitome de Caesaribus* (40.18) noted that Daza (in contrast to his uncle) was an enthusiastic patron of the arts and literature.

41 Eus. *Mart. Pal.* 4.8. reports that an imperial Edict ordered that all persons should sacrifice and that the responsibility for this was with the town councils. The Edict differs in no way from the Edict of 304 except in that it dictates the administrative arrangements. Given the date reported by Eusebius (late 305/early 306), I have succumbed to temptation and linked it to the 306 census (but see Ste Croix, 1954: p. 113). While Eusebius blamed Daza for this innovation, he did so from the parochial standpoint of an inhabitant of Caesarea recording the progress of the persecution in Palestine.

42 Knipfing (1923), esp. p. 343f.

43 For example, see Barnes, *CE*, p. 19.

44 Mitchell (1988), p. 176; Macmullen (1981) in his preface speaks of "the endless variety of cults" (p. xii).

45 For the identification, see Srejovic *et al.* (1980).

46 Ste Croix (1954), p. 98.

47 Eus. *Mart Pal.* 4. 8–10.

48 A detailed study of the traditions of martyrdom in the Danubian provinces has been conducted by Bratoz (2005). He notes that, of the known martyrs, none were of senatorial rank, two were of equestrian rank, one member of the curial class, one member of the imperial bureaucracy, and no peasants or slaves (*Ibid.*, p. 137).

49 Jerome, *de vir. ill.* 80.

50 Athanasius, *Hist. Arian. ad Monach.* 64.

51 Lact. *D.I.* 5. 11.13.

52 Ste Croix (1954), p. 104f.; Lane Fox (1986), p. 597.

53 Barnes, *CE*, p. 175; but see Lane Fox (1986), p. 592.

54 Ste Croix (1954), p. 102f. Frend (1965: p. 520f.) seems too preoccupied with Christianity's triumph to notice, but see Lane Fox (1986), p. 597.

55 Mitchell (1988).

56 Zos. 2.11; Aur. Vict. *de Caes.* 40.9.

57 Noticed by Gelzer (1937), p. 381f.; NB, Moreau (1954), I, pp. 61–4; see also Africa (1982). Davies (1989: p. 87) deals with this matter only briefly in his discussion of Lactantius' account of origin of the Great Persecution.

58 As long ago recognized by Pichon (1901), p. 378; and more recently by Moreau (1954), II, p. 395.

59 Lact. *de mort. pers.* 22.4–5.

60 The Edict was posted in Nicomedia on 30 April 311 (Lact. *de mort. pers.* 35.1); *post dies paucos* (a few days later), Galerius was dead. If Grégoire (1938) is correct in filling the lacuna in the text at 35.4 with *medio* (*Ibid.*, p. 551), then Galerius probably died about ten days after he issued the Edict. He may have given instructions to Licinius in that period as to what form his instructions would take, but after Galerius' death Daza was successful in his bid to be recognized as senior Augustus, and therefore interpreter of the Edict. It is tempting to assert that these instructions were finally issued by Constantine and Licinius as "the most perfect law on behalf of the Christians" (Eus. *HE* 9.9.12; Lact. *de mort. pers.* 44.11; Barnes, *NE*, p. 67) after Constantine's proclamation as Augustus Maximus by the Roman Senate (Lact. *de mort. pers.* 44.11).

61 See here Creed (1984), p. 113 n. 7.

62 On Constantine, see Lact. *de mort. pers.* 24. 8–9; on Maxentius, see Eus. *HE* 8.14.1; Decker (1968).

63 Lact. *de mort. pers.* 34.

64 *Ibid.*, 33.11 ("*exclamat se restituturum dei templum satisque pro scelere facturum*").

65 *Ep. de Caes.* 40.15; Eutr. 10.2.1.

66 On the Danubian provinces and their growing prosperity, see Mócsy (1974), pp. 297–338; for Thrace, see Velkov (1980), p. 266; for Noricum, see G. Alföldi (1974), pp. 205–8.
67 Aur. Vict. *de Caes.* 40.9.
68 *Ibid.*, 36.4; Mócsy (1974), p. 266, although on p. 272 he dates the work to the mid-290s when Galerius was in the east.
69 Aur. Vict. *de Caes.* 40.9.
70 Perhaps as farmland upon which to settle the tribesmen relocated upon Roman soil in about 303 by Galerius (Lact. *de mort. pers.* 38.6).
71 Aur. Vict. *de Caes.* 40.10; *Lat. Ver.*, fo. 255, verso 16.
72 *AE* (2002) 1293; Mitrev (2003); Lepelley (2004).
73 Christol and Drew-Bear (1999); *AE* (1999) 1613–20.
74 *ILS* 6090; *MAMA* IV 236; Jones (1937: p. 142) ascribes the inscription to the period of Diocletian; Corcoran (2007: p. 244 n. 226) prefers Galerius.
75 *It. Burd.* 19.19; see Jones (1940), p. 87; Jones (1971), p. 279f.; Millar (1993) p. 543f.
76 Jones (1971), p. 289; Millar (1993) p. 184f.
77 *RE*, XIV ii, *s.v.* "Maximianopolis", no. 3.
78 Ramsay (1895), p. 323f.; Ramsay (1890), p.173. Tymbrianassus was located quite close to Pisidian Antioch, which was certainly a beneficiary of imperial generosity.
79 Amm. Marc. 27.4.13.
80 Velkov (1977), p. 125; Cornell and Matthews (1982), p. 141.
81 Eus. *HE* 9.7.
82 Aur. Vict. *de Caes.* 39.45.
83 Corcoran (2007). I am particularly indebted to Simon Corcoran for his advice and frequent offprints on the matter of these texts.
84 *CIL* III 12134 = *CIG* 356, reprinted and translated in Johnson *et al.* (1961), p. 237f., no. 300. Now see Feissel (1995), pp. 51–3; Feissel (1996), pp. 274–7, 278, 282; Corcoran (2007), p. 224f.
85 Jones (1964), p. 564f., Corcoran (2007), p. 236f.
86 *CJ* 10.1.5; on the identity of the recipient of the rescript, see *PLRE* I, p. 342.
87 For this point, and the epigraphic detail that supports it, see Corcoran (2007).
88 *C. Th.* 9.5.1; on Licinius, see Barnes (1976B), followed by Corcoran (1993), pp. 115–17 (Corcoran has now revised his view and prefers an earlier date and allocation to Galerius). On Constantine, see Seeck (1919), p. 169. Seeck prefers the later date of 320 on the basis of the text of the Theodosian Code in which the summary rescript is addressed to an Urban Prefect named Maximus. There was an Urban Prefect, Valerius Maximus Basilius, who held office at this time (Chastagnol, 1962: pp. 72–4, no. 29). Matthews (2000: p. 269) was the first to suggest the earlier dating followed here.
89 This provision alone makes it doubtful that the law belongs to Constantine since he forbade the imposition of crucifixion as a criminal punishment (Aur. Vict. *de Caes.* 41.4; Barnes, *CE*, p. 51).
90 Corcoran (2007), p. 234f.
91 *Ibid.*
92 Corcoran (2004), (2006).
93 In a number of publications (2002, 2004, 2006, 2007) Simon Corcoran has argued that this was an expression of Galerius' own legal policy rather than an innovation of Diocletian's. This view, while attractive, is not necessary, and a simpler view is that Galerius was following Diocletian's lead rather than imposing a legal policy upon him.
94 Lact. *de mort. pers.* 22.4.
95 Corcoran (2000: p. 20) suggests that Lactantius fled from the court of Galerius and not that of Diocletian.
96 *Ibid.*, p. 92f.; Eunapius, *Vit. Soph.* 457.
97 Lact. *de mort. pers.* 22.5.

98 Justinian, *Digest*, 48.10.1.
99 *CJ* 9.41.8, 11.
100 Aur. Vict. *de Caes.* 40.10; also *Ep. de Caes.* 40.15, Eutr. 10.2.1.
101 Lact. *de mort. pers.* 21.2.
102 Note the comments of Moreau (1954: p. 325) and his list of authors who ascribe this innovation to Diocletian.
103 Corsaro (1978), pp. 34–6; Leadbetter (1998), p. 248.
104 Lact. *de mort. pers.* 7.9.
105 Aur. Vict. *de Caes.* 39.45.
106 *MGH* 1. 148 (Chron. of 354); see Dudley (1967), p. 24; Krautheimer (1980), p. 7; Curran (2000), pp. 41–6; on the decennial monument in the Forum, see Kähler (1964); on other renovatory works, *CIL* VI, 773, 1130.
107 Barnes, *NE*, pp. 61–2.
108 See Hoddinott (1975), pp. 169–78.
109 *ILS* 3458; Mócsy (1974), p. 312.
110 For a thorough discussion of the Palace of Galerius, and a summary of scholarship, see Speiser (1984), pp. 97–9, 109–11.
111 Pond Rothmann (1977), p. 429; H. Meyer (1980), p. 434. Meyer argues that in fact the Arch was not an orthodox triumphal arch, but the monumental gateway to the palace complex.
112 Pond Rothmann (1977); although see Velenis (1979) for the argument that the Arch was north of the roadway rather than over it. The evidence for this, however, is far from compelling.
113 For the purpose of identification, the Arch reliefs will be cited according to the formula used by Rothman (1977), p. 433 n. 101. In this case the relevant reliefs are Pier B 1.17; Pier B II.21.
114 Suggested by Grégoire (1939), followed by Dyggve (1954), p. 361f., and Laubscher (1975), p. 10; but note the caution sounded by Speiser (1984: p. 117). Passuello and Dissegna (1979) argue that the architectural style of the rotunda is consonant with the architectural tradition both for temples and mausolea.
115 Dyggve (1954), p. 361f. uncovered porphyry footings which might have been intended for a sarcophagus or a throne. If for the former, then the parallel between the Thessalonica rotunda and that of Sta. Costanza in Rome, the mausoleum of Constantine's sister, is inevitable.
116 Krautheimer (1984), p. 69f.
117 See Frazer (1966), pp. 386, 389; Bertolitti *et al.* (1988), pp. 33–45.
118 Vickers' (1972) view that a brick design incorporated in the wall of the apse represented a cross and palms is implausible. More likely is the earlier assertion that the figure is a representation of the sun. The function of this room remains uncertain (Speiser, 1984: pp. 113–23); although it is tempting to identify it as an audience chamber. On the tondo portrait, see Cagiano de Azevedo (1979), p. 17.
119 On Antioch, see Downey (1961), pp. 318–23; on Nicomedia, Lact. *de mort. pers.* 7.10; on Sirmium, see Popovic (1971), pp. 125–6, Popovic and Ochsenschlager (1976), A. Mócsy (1974) n. 99; on Serdica, see Hoddinott (1975), pp. 169–78, where it is possible that the remaining complex of buildings attached to the Church of St George are a part of the old imperial palace; on Aquileia, see *Pan. Lat.* 6.6.2; on Mediolanum, see Ausonius, *de Clar. Urb* V, Krautheimer (1974), pp. 69ff.; on Trier, see Wightman (1971), pp. 103–10.
120 Diocletian and his colleagues spent considerable time in each of these cities without them actually being considered imperial "residences". Constantius and Constantine both resided for a time at Eboracum, where they may have been content with the old Severan palace, although there is evidence of building at this time (see Wacher 1974: p. 156ff.;

Salway 1984: p. 324f.); Maximian led his evanescent revolt against Constantine in Massilia, where he was later put to death (Lact. *de mort. pers.* 29.7); he had also spent time in Carthage, where he was better remembered (Barnes, *NE*, p. 59); the Arras medallion famously records Constantius' "liberation" of Londinium after the defeat of Allectus.

121 See Bandinelli (1971), p. 281; Kleiner (1992), p. 401f. There is a porphyry fragment of an emperor's head, perhaps from Niš, preserved in Frankfurt (*Spätantike und frühes Christentum: 16 Dezember 1983 bis 11 März 1984*, Liebeghaus Museum für alter Plastik, Frankfurt-am-Main, 1984), not to mention the famous, if caricaturist, Vatican group of sculptures (see L'Orange, 1965: pp. 47–53; Kleiner, 1992: p. 403). Other than these, there are a large number of instances of groups of imperial statues, notably in Rome on the decennial monument (Kähler, 1964), or elsewhere, for example, in the east (Vermeule 1968: p. 329f.). On sculpture from this period in general, see Kleiner (1992), pp. 399–428.

122 Vermeule (1968), p. 350f., Laubscher (1971), p. 105f.

123 See Downey (1961), pp. 322, 393f. n. 88.

124 Amm. Marc. 25.10.2.120. Vermeule (1968), pp. 329–34.

125 Malalas, 12.41.2; see Bowman (1986), p. 205f., Thiel (2006). On the Luxor temple, see Vandorpe (1995).

126 Lact. *de mort. pers.* 13.2.

127 There is a danger of making too close an association, however. Dontas (1975) has argued for the identification of an otherwise unidentified portrait of an emperor as Galerius largely on the basis of its probable Thessalonian provenance. But see now Riccardi (2000) identifying the portrait more plausibly as an aged Trajan.

128 There is a silver portrait head of Galerius in the Mainz Museum, probably originally from a military standard. See Künzl (1983). On portraits from the Argolid, Antioch, Gortyn in Crete, and Ephesus see Vermeule (1968), pp. 329–34; on the Athribis bust in the Cairo Museum, see L'Orange (1965), who suggests that it might be Licinius. Bandinelli (1971) argues that it is Galerius. The emperor represented is clearly young, and so the portrait ought properly to belong to either Galerius or Maximinus, more probably Galerius.

129 Pond Rothman (1977), Pier B I. 17, p. 440f.

130 *Ibid.*, Pier B II. 21, p. 444. See also Pond Rothman (1975).

131 Vermeule (1968), pp. 329–34; Laubscher (1971), p. 105f.; Hanfmann (1975), p. 77f.

132 On the subjects of the missing piers, Laubscher (1971) has been judiciously indecisive (p. 105f.). Pond Rothman (1977), on the other hand, concedes the likelihood that the lost piers were "based on the military history of the Tetrarchy ... another of Galerius' campaigns, the exploits of Diocletian, or events in the western territories of the Empire" (p. 453 n. 63).

133 *Ep. de Caes.* 40.16.

134 *AE.* 1986, 625.

135 On the location of Galerius' death, see *Ep. de Caes.* 40.16. On the evidence for his funeral rites, see Srejovic and Vasic (1994A), pp. 152–5.

136 On the fortifications, see Canak-Medic (1978), pp. 221–6 (French abstract); also Mócsy (1974), p. 303f.; Duval (1971). On the later stages of habitation, see Srejovic *et al.* (1983), p. 199f. (English abstract). On the Christian basilica, see Canak-Medic (1978), p. 230f.

137 On the refortifications, see Procopius, *Buildings*, 4.4.

138 See Srejovic *et al.* (1983), p. 194.

139 Lact. *de mort. pers.* 9.1.

140 Canak-Medic (1978), pp. 222–4; Srejovic *et al.* (1983), p. 194f.

141 The mid-third-century villa is in the southern area of the site, and the later villa, known as Palace II, together with the temple, are both north of the *decumanus* (Srejovic *et al.*, 1983: p. 195).

142 On the temple, see Srejovic *et al.* (1980), p. 77f. (French abstract) and Srejovic *et al.*, (1983), p. 196. On Cybele and *taurobolia*, see Ferguson (1970), pp. 29–31; Vermaseren (1977), pp. 101–6.

143 Srejovic *et al.* (1980), p. 196; Srejovic *et al.* (1983), p. 194f.

144 Srejovic *et al.* (1983: p. 75), from the *triclinium* of Palace I.

145 *Ibid.*, p. 87 n. 138 (Catalogue nos. 26 and 27). On the significance of the use of porphyry for tetrarchic statuary, see Bandinelli (1971), p. 281.

146 Srejovic (1992/3).

147 Canak-Medic (1978), p. 229f., Christodoulou (2002), p. 275f.

148 Christodoulou (2002); *P. Oxy.* 2953; a detachment of the V Macedonica is listed in the *Notitia Dignitatum* as serving under the *Magister Militum per Orientem* (*ND.* Or 7.39), and may well have relocated to the East under Galerius. It is tempting to locate the link between Galerius and the legion within Galerius' unknown personal history, since the legion had been one of the two permanent garrison units of the Roman province of Dacia, the origin of Galerius' family.

149 *Pace* Srejovic (1983), p. 198; Lact. *de mort. pers.* 11.1–2.

150 Lact. *de mort. pers.* 20.4–5.

151 *Ibid.*, 31.2–6.

152 *Ibid.*, 20.4–5.

153 Chastagnol (1976), p. 228f.; but see Barnes, *NE*, p. 38 n. 18. Chastagnol does not seem to have pressed the idea. There is no mention of it in his subsequent treatment of the period (e.g. Chastagnol, 1982: pp. 110–14).

154 See Bagnall and Worp (1979), p. 33.

155 Lact. *de mort. pers.* 20.4–5; on Galerius' bears, see Lact. *de mort. pers.* 21.5–6. On Galerius' rural origins, see Aur. Vict. *de Caes.* 39.24 who thenceforth calls Galerius "Armentarius", *Ep. de Caes.* 40. 15.

156 Lact. *de mort. pers.* 33. 1 dates it to the eighteenth year of Galerius' reign, i.e. between 1 March 310 and 1 March 311.

157 Gibbon (1995), p. 573f.; Finley (1977), p. 137.

158 Zos. 2.11.1; Aur. Vict. *de Caes.* 40.9 (an infected wound); *Origo* 8, Eus. *HE* 8.16–17 (for variations on Lactantius' account). The *Ep. de Caes.* (40.4) says neutrally *consumptis genitalibus*. For a cautionary note here, see Africa (1982), pp. 1–18.

159 This belief can be found in the work of scholars as distant in time as Seeck and Millar. See, for example, Millar (1977), pp. 52, 578; W. Ensslin, *RE* XIV, 2528, citing Seeck (1919), p. 159.

160 Lact. *de mort. pers.* 33.7: *"odor it autem non modo per palatium sed totam civitatem pervadit"*.

161 Observed by Gelzer (1937), p. 381f. Africa (1982) p. 12f. draws the parallel more closely.

162 *Origo* 8.

163 Barnes (*NE*, p. 64) follows the *Origo* in putting Galerius in Serdica from 308 until his death, but see *RIC* VI, p. 486, p. 505f. The mint at Serdica was closed after Carnuntum, and that of Thessalonica reopened, striking precious metal issues with a S(acra) M(oneta) mint-mark. The conclusion is inescapable that, just as the mint had followed Galerius from Thessalonica to Serdica, its return to that city indicates Galerius' return there also.

164 *Chron. Min.* I, p. 148.

165 *Ep. de Caes.* 40.16.

166 Cornell and Matthews (1982), p. 141.

167 *RIC* VI, p. 506. Licinius was in Serdica on 9 June 311 (*FIRA2* 1.93; Barnes 1982: *NE*, p. 81).

168 Lact. *de mort. pers.* 35.3 states that Galerius put his family into the hands of Licinius *in manum* (i.e. under his legal power as *paterfamilias*). Probably true, it also serves the author's purpose in highlighting the subsequent *impietas* of Licinius' subsequent execution of them both (see Creed, 1984: p. 113f.; Moreau, 1954: p. 396).

169 On the Mausoleum of Galerius at Gamzigrad, see Srejovic and Vasic (1994), pp. 82–107.

170 See *RIC* VI, p. 346f.; King (1959), p. 73. Of all of Galerius' imperial colleagues, only Constantine did not strike "DIVO MAXIMIANO" issues (Ensslin, *RE* XIV, 2528).

171 See *RIC* VI, p. 381, obverse legends 2a, 2b (laying it on thick), 2c.

172 *Ibid.*, 5c, 5d.

173 *ILS* 661 (from Styria); also 662 (from Mauretania) to *divo Galerio Maximiano*.

174 Lact. *de mort. pers.* 39.1–2, 4.

175 *Ibid.*, 50.5.

176 *Ibid.* The bracketed words are Creed's additions and accepted here.

177 *Ibid.* 41.2–42.3.

178 Lact. *de mort. pers.* 50.6; on the date of Diocletian's death, see Barnes (1982), *NE*, p. 32.

179 Lact. *de mort. pers.* 50.4.

APPENDIX: *STEMMA* OF THE *IOVII* AND *HERCULII*

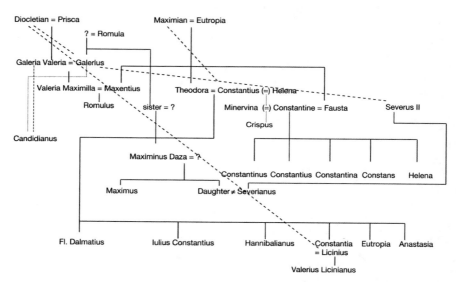

Key: Unbroken line indicates direct blood relationship. Broken line indicates adoption.

BIBLIOGRAPHY

Africa, Thomas N. (1982), Worms and the Death of Kings, *Class. Ant.* 1, 1–17

Alban, B. (1943), The Conscious Role of Lactantius, *CW*, 37, 78–9

Alcock, Leslie (1979), The North Britons, the Picts and the Scots, in P.J. Casey (ed.) *The End of Roman Britain* (*BAR*. Ser. 71)

Alföldi, A. (1939), The Sources for the Gothic Invasion of the Years 260–270, *CAH*, XII, 721–3

—— (1948), *The Conversion of Constantine and Pagan Rome*, Oxford

—— (1974), *Noricum*, (A.Birley, trans.), London

Amarelli, Francesco (1983), *Consilia Principum*, Pubblicazioni della Facoltá Giuridica dell' Università di Napoli, Napoli

Amélineau, E. (1893), *Géographie de l'Egypte à l'Époque Copte*, Paris

Anderson, J.G.C. (1932), The Genesis of Diocletian's Provincial Re-organisation, *JRS*, 22, 24–32

Ando, Clifford (2000), *Imperial Ideology and Provincial Loyalty in the Roman Empire*, Berkeley, CA

Andreotti, R. (1969), Problemi di eprigrafica constantiana I: La presunta alleanza con l' usurpatore Lucio Domizio Allesandro, *Epigrafica*, I, 144–80

Arnaldi, A. (1972), La successione dei cognomina gentium e le loro iterazione nella titolatura dei primi tetrarchi, *Reconditi dell' Istituto Lombardo, Classe di Lettre, Scienze e Storiche*, 106, 28–50

Arnheim, M.T.W. (1972), *The Senatorial Aristocracy in the Later Roman Empire*, Oxford

Astarita, M.L. (1983), *Avidio Cassio*, Rome

Austin, N. and B. Rankov (1995), *Exploratio: Military and Political Intelligence in the Roman World from the Second Punic War to the Battle of Adrianople*, London

Avi-Yonah, M. (1976), *Gazetteer of Roman Palestine*, Jerusalem

Bagnall, Roger S. (1993), *Egypt in Late Antiquity*, Princeton, NJ

Bagnall, R. and K. Worp (1978), *The Chronological Systems of Byzantine Egypt*, Zutphen

—— (1979), *Regnal Formulas in Byzantine Egypt*, *BASP*, Supp. 2, Missoula

Bagnall, R.S., Alan Cameron, Seth R. Schwartz and K.I. Worp (1987), *Consuls of the Later Roman Empire*, Atlanta

Bandinelli, R.B. (1971), *Rome: The Late Empire. Roman Art AD 200–400* (P. Green, trans.), London

Barnes, T.D. (1970), The lost *Kaisergeschichte* and the Latin Historical Tradition, *BHAC*, 7, pp. 13–43

—— (1972), Some Persons in the Historia Augusta, *Phoenix*, 26, pp. 140–82

—— (1973A), Porphyry Against the Christians: date and attribution of the fragments, *JTS*, 24, pp. 424–42

—— (1973B), Lactantius and Constantine, *JRS*, 63, 29–46;

—— (1976), Imperial Campaigns AD 285–311, *Phoenix*, 30, 174–93

—— (1976A), Sossianus Hierocles and the Antecedents of the Great Persecution, *HSCP*, 80, 243–5;

—— (1976B), Three Imperial Edicts, *ZPE*, 21, 275–81

—— (1978), *The Sources of the Historia Augusta*, Brussels

—— (1980), The Editions of Eusebius' Ecclesiastical History, *GRBS*, 21, 191–201;

—— (1981), *Constantine and Eusebius*, Cambridge, MA

—— (1982), *The New Empire of Diocletian and Constantine*, Cambridge, MA

—— (1991), Pagan Perceptions of Christianity, in I. Hazlitt (ed.) *Early Christianity: Origins and Evolution to* AD *600*, London, pp. 231–43

—— (1996), Emperors, Panegyrics, Prefects, Provinces and Palaces, *JRA*, 9, 532–52

—— (1998), *Ammianus Marcellinus and the Representation of Historical Reality*, Ithaca, NY

Bastien, P. (1972), *Le monnayage de l'atelier de Lyon: Dioclétien et ses coregents avant le réforme monétaire (285–294)*, Wetteren

Baynes, N.H. (1924), Two Notes on the Great Persecution, *CQ*, 18, 189–194

—— (1929), *Constantine and the Christian Church*, London

—— (1948), Review of W. Seston, *Dioclétien et la Tétrarchie*, *JRS*, 38, 109–13

—— (1955), Eusebius and the Christian Empire, in idem, *Byzantine Studies and Other Essays*, London, pp. 168–73

Bean, G.E. and T.B. Mitford (1970), *Journeys in Rough Cilicia 1964–1968*, Vienna

Begley, Vimala (1993), New investigations at the port of Arikamedu, *JRA*, 6, 93–108

Belmaric, Josko (2004), Gynacaeum Iovense Dalmatiae–Aspalatho in A. Demant, A. Goltz, H. Schlange-Schöningen (eds) *Diokletian Und Die Tetrarchie: Aspekte Einer Zeitenwende*, (*Millenium-Studien zu Kultur und Geschichte des ersten Jahrtausends n. Chr*, edited by W. Brandes, A. Demandt, H. Leppin and P. von Möllendorf, Band I), Berlin and New York, pp. 141–62

van Berchem, Denis (1952), *L'armée de Dioclétien et la reforme constantinienne*, Beirut

Bernard, André (1984), *Les Portes du désert: receuil des inscriptions grecques d'Antinooupolis, Koptos, Tentyris, Apollinopolis Parva et Apollinopolis Magna*, Paris

Bertolitti, Romana de Angelis, Giovanni Ioppolo and Giusseppina Pisani Sartorio (1988), *La Residenza Imperiale di Massenzio: villa, mausoleo e circo*, Rome

Bichir, Gh. (1976), *The Archaeology and History of the Carpi*, (N. Hupartumian trans.) BAR Supplementary series 16 (ii). Oxford

Bidwell, Paul (2006), Constantius and Constantine at York, in E. Hartley, Jane Hawkes, Martin Henig and Frances Mee (eds) *Constantine the Great: York's Roman Emperor*, York, pp. 31–9

Bird, H.W. (1976), Diocletian and the deaths of Carus, Carinus and Numerian, *Latomus*, 35, pp. 123–132

—— (1993), *Eutropius: Breviarium: Translated with an Introduction and Commentary*, Translated Texts for Historians, vol. 14, Liverpool

—— (1994), *Aurelius Victor: de Caesaribus: Translated with an Introduction and Commentary*, Translated Texts for Historians, vol. 17, Liverpool

Birley, A. (1987), *Marcus Aurelius: A Biography*, rev. edn, London

—— (1988), *The African Emperor: Septimius Severus*, rev. edn, London

Birley, E. (1978), The Religion of the Roman Army, *ANRW* II. 16 (2), pp. 1506–41

Blockley, R.C. (1972), Constantius Gallus and Julian as Caesars of Constantius II, *Latomus* 31. 433–68

—— (1981), *The Fragmentary Classicising Historians of the Later Roman Empire*, Vol. I, Liverpool

—— (1983), *The Fragmentary Classicising Historians of the Later Roman Empire*, Vol. II, Liverpool

de Blois, Lukas (1976), *The Policy of the Emperor Gallienus*, Leiden

den Boer, W. (1972), *Some Minor Roman Historians*, Leiden

Bowen, Anthony and Peter Garnsey (2003), *Lactantius: Divine Institutes, translated with an introduction and notes*, Translated Texts for Historians 40, Liverpool

Bowersock, G.W. (1983), *Roman Arabia*, Cambridge, MA

Bowman, A.K. (1978), The Military Occupation of Upper Egypt Under Diocletian, *BASP*, 15, 25–38

—— (1984), Two Notes, *BASP*, 21, 33–8

—— (1986), *Egypt After the Pharaohs*, London

Brandt, Hartwin (2006), Die Tetrarchie in der Literatur des 4 Jhs. D. Chr., in Dietrich Bosching and Werner Eck (eds) *Die Tetrarchie: Ein neues Regierungssystem und seine mediale Präsentation*, Wiesbaden, pp. 401–19

Brandt, Samuel (1897), *Berliner Philologische Wochenschrift*, 1903, no. 39, Vienna

Bratoz, Rajko (2005), Die diokletianische Christenverfolgung in den Donau- und Balkanprovinzen, in Demandt, Alexander, Goltz, Andreas and Schlange-Schöningen, Heinrich, *Diokletian und die Tetrarchie: Aspekte einer Zeitenwende*, Berlin, pp. 115–40

Brenk, B. (1968), Der Datierung des Reliefs am Hadrianstempel in Ephesos, *Ist. Mitt.* 18, 238–58

Brennan, P. (1980), Combined legionary detachments in late Roman Danubian bridgehead dispositions, *Chiron* 10, 554–67

—— (1984), Diocletian and the Goths, *Phoenix*, 37, 142–6

Brown, Peter (1967), *Augustine of Hippo*, London

—— (1969), The Diffusion of Manichaeism in the Roman Empire, *JRS*, 59, 92–103

—— (1978A), *The Making of Late Antiquity*, Cambridge, MA

—— (1978B), A Debate on the Holy, in Peter Brown, *The Making of Late Antiquity*, Cambridge, MA, pp. 1–27

Brunt, P.A. (1981), The Revenues of Rome, *JRS*, 71, 161–72

Bulic, F. and L. Karaman (1929), *Kaiser Diokletians Palast in Split*, Zagreb

Burckhardt, Jakob (1949), *The Age of Constantine the Great*, (M. Hadas trans.), New York

Bury, J.B. (1923), The Provincial List of Verona, *JRS*, 13, 127–151

Butler, R.M. (1971), The defences of the fourth century fortress at York, in R.M. Butler (ed.), *Soldier and Civilian in Roman Yorkshire*, Leicester, 97–106

Cagiano de Azevedo, M. (1979), Il Palazzo Imperiale di Salonicco, *Felix Ravenna*, 117, 7–28

Calderini (1930), *Aquileia Romana: Richerche di Storia a di Epigrafia*, Milan, 1930

Callu, J.-P. (1969), *La Politique Monétaire des Empereurs Romains de 238 à 311*, Paris

Cameron, Alan (1967), The date of Porphyry's KATA KRISTIANON *CQ*, 17, pp. 382–4

Cameron, Averil (2006), Constantius and Constantine: An Exercise in Publicity, in Elizabeth Hartley, Jane Hawkes Martin Henig and Frances Mee, *Constantine the Great: York's Roman Emperor*, York, pp. 18–30

Cameron, Averil and Stuart G. Hall (1999), *Eusebius: Life of Constantine*, Oxford

Canak-Medic, M. (1978), *Gamzigrad*, Belgrade

di Carandini, Andrea, Andreina Ricci and Mariette De Vos (1982), *Filosofiana: the villa of Piazza Armerina*, Palermo, 1982

Casey, P.J. (1977), Carausius and Allectus: rulers in Gaul?, *Britannia* 8, 283–301

—— (1994), *Carausius and Allectus: The British Usurpers*, New Haven, CT, and London

Chastagnol, André (1962), *Les Fastes de la Préfecture de Rome au Bas-Empire*, Paris
—— (1967), Les années regnales de Maximien Hercule en Egypte et les fêtes vicennales du 20 Novembre 303, *Rev. Num.*, 9, 54–81
—— (1976), La datation par années régnales égyptiennes à l'époque constantinienne, *Aiôn: Le Temps chez les Romains: Caesarodunum*, 10bis, Paris, pp. 221–38
—— (1982), *L' évolution politique, sociale et économique du monde romain de Dioclétien à Julien*, Paris
—— (1989), Un nouveau préfet du prétoire de Dioclétien: Aurelius Hermogenianus, *ZPE*, 78, 165–8
Chaumont, M.-L. (1969), *Histoire d'Arménie de l'avénement des Sassanides à la conversion du royaume*, Paris
Chesnut, Glen F. (1977), *The First Christian Histories: Eusebius, Socrates, Sozomen and Evagrius*, Macon
Christensen, A.E. (1939), Sassanid Persia, *CAH1* XII, Cambridge, pp. 109–37
—— (1944), *L' Iran sous les Sassanides*, Copenhagen
Christensen, Arne Søby (1980), *Lactantius the Historian*, Copenhagen
Christodoulou, Demetrios N. (2002), Galerius, Gamzigrad and the Fifth Macedonian Legion, *JRA* 15, 275–81
Christol, Michel and Thomas Drew-Bear (1999), Antioche de Pisidie capitale provinciale et l'ocuvre de M. Valerius Diogenes, *L'Antiquité Tardive*, 9, pp. 39–71
Christol, Michel and Maurice Lenoir (2001), Qasr el-Azraq et le reconquête de 1 Orient par Aurélien, *Syria* 78, pp.163–78
Clarke, G.W. (1969), Some Observations on the Persecution of Decius, *Antichthon* 3, pp. 63–76
Collingwood, R.G. and R.P. Wright (1965), *Roman Inscriptions from Britain I*, (*RIB*,) Oxford
Conybeare, F.C. (1912), "Contra Hieroclem", in *Philostratus: The Life of Apollonius of Tyana*, Cambridge, MA, pp. 484–605
Cook, S.A., F.E. Adcock, M.P. Charlesworth and N.H. Baynes (eds) (1939), *The Cambridge Ancient History*, XII, Cambridge
Cope, Lawrence H. (1969), The Nadir of the Imperial Antoninianus in the Reign of Claudius II Gothicus, AD 268–270, *NC*, 7th ser. 9, 145–61
Corcoran, Simon (1993), Hidden from History: the legislation of Licinius in J. Harries and I. Wood, *The Theodosian Code: Studies in the Imperial Law of Late Antiquity*, London, pp. 97–119
—— (1996), *The Empire of the Tetrarchs: Imperial Pronouncements and Government* AD, 284–324, Oxford
—— (2000), The *Empire of the Tetrarchs: Imperial Pronouncements and Government* AD 284–324, 2nd edn, Oxford
—— (2004), The publication of law in the era of the tetrarchs, in Demant, A., Goltz, A., Schlange-Schöningen, H. (eds) *Diokletian und die Tetrarchie: Aspekte einer Zeitenwende (Millenium-Studien zu Kultur und Geschichte des ersten Jahrtausends n. Chr)*, Berlin and New York, 56–73
—— (2006), The tetrarchy: policy and image as reflected in imperial pronouncements, in Boschung, Dietrich und Eck, Werner (eds) *Die tetrarchie: ein neues Regierungssystem und seine mediale Präsentation*, Wiesbaden, 31–61
—— (2006A), Galerius, Maximinus and the titulature of the Third Tetrarchy, *BICS*, 49, 231–40
—— (2007), Galerius's jigsaw puzzle: the *Caesariani* dossier, *L' Antiquité Tardive*, 15, 221–50
Cornell, T. and J.F. Matthews (1982), *Atlas of the Roman World*, Oxford

Corsaro, F. (1978), Le mos maiorum dans la vision éthique et politique du de mortibus persecutorum, in J. Fontaine and M. Perrin (eds) *Lactance et son temps: Récherches Actuelles. Actes du VIe Colloque d' études Historiques et Patristiques Chantilly, 21–23 Septembre, 1976*, Chantilly, pp. 25–55

Costa, G. (1926), Diocletianus, *Dizionario Epigrafico di Antichitá Romaine* II.3, Roma, 1793–1908

Coxe, A. Cleveland (1979), *The Ante-Nicene Fathers,* Vol VII: *Lactantius, Venantius, Asterius, Victorinus, Dionysius, Apostolic Teaching and Constitutions, Homily and Liturgies,* rep. 1979, Grand Rapids, MI

Cranz, F.E. (1952), Kingdom and Polity in Eusebius of Caesarea, *HTR*, 45, 47–66;

Creed, J. (1984), *Lactantius: de mortibus persecutorum*, Oxford Early Christian Texts, Oxford

Croke, Brian (1984), The Era of Porphyry's Anti-Christian Polemic, *JRH*, 13, 1–14

Crook, J.A. (1955), *Consilium Principis*, Cambridge

Cullhed, M. (1989), Maxentius as *princeps*, *Opuscula Romana*, 17, 9–19

—— (1994), *Conservator Urbis Suae: Studies in the Policy and Propaganda of the Emperor Maxentius*, Stockholm

Cumont, F. (1911), *The Oriental Religions in Roman Paganism*, Chicago, IL

Curran, John (2000), *Pagan City and Christian Capital: Rome in the Fourth Century*, Oxford

Dam, Raymond van (1985), *Leadership and Community in Late Antique Gaul*, Berkeley, CA

Daniels, C.M. (1975), The Roman army and the spread of Mithraism, in J. Hinnells (ed.), *Mithraic Studies: Proceedings of the First International Congress of Mithraic Studies*, Vol. III, Manchester, pp. 249–75

Davies, P.S. (1989), The Origin and Purpose of the Great Persecution, *JTS*, 40, 66–94

Decker, D. de (1968), La Politique religieuse de Maxence, *Byzantion*, 38, 474–562

Déléage, André (1945), *La Capitation du bas-empire*, Macon

Delehaye, H. (1897), *de Martyribus Palestinae: longionis libelli fragmenta*, Brussels

Demougeot, E. (1969), *La Formation de l' Europe et les invasions barbares*, Paris

Dessau, H. (1892), *Inscriptiones Latinae Selectae*, 5 vols, Berlin

Digeser, Elizabeth DePalma (1998), Lactantius, Porphyry and the Debate over Religious Toleration, *JRS*, 88, 129–46

—— (2000), *Lactantius and Rome: The Making of a Christian Empire*, Ithaca and London

Dignas, Beate and Engelbert Winter (2007), *Rome and Persia in Late Antiquity: Neighbours and Rivals*, Cambridge

Dodgeon, M. and S.N.C. Lieu (1991), *The Roman Eastern Frontier and the Persian Wars* AD *226–363: A Documentary History*, London

Domaszewski, A. von (1895), *Die Religion des Römischen Heeres*, Trier

Dontas, G. (1975), Portrait de Galére, *BCH*, 97 521–33

Downey, Glanville (1961), *A History of Antioch in Syria*, Princeton, NJ

Drake, H.A. (1975), *In Praise of Constantine: A Historical Study and New Translation of Eusebius' Trecennial Orations*, Berkeley and Los Angeles, CA

—— (2000), *Constantine and the Bishops: The Politics of Intolerance*, Baltimore, MD

Drew-Bear, Thomas (1981), Les voyages d'Aurelius Gaius, soldat de Dioclétien, in *La géographie administrative et politique d'Alexandre à Mahomet: Actes du Colloque de Strasbourg 14–16 Juin, 1979*, Université des sciences humaines de Strasbourg, Travaux du Centre de recherche sur le Proche-Orient et la Grèce antique, Strasbourg, pp. 93–141

Drinkwater, J.F. (1984), Peasants and Bagaudae in Roman Gaul, *Classical Views* N.S. 3, 349–71

—— (1987), The Gallic Empire: separatism and community in the north-western provinces of the Roman Empire AD 260–274, *Historia Einzelschrift* 52, Stuttgart, pp. 31–4

—— (1989), Patronage in Roman Gaul and the Problem of the Bagaudae, in Andrew Wallace-Hadrill (ed.) *Patronage in Ancient Society*, London, pp. 189–203

—— (1996), The Germanic Threat on the Rhine Frontier : a Romano-Gallic Artefact?, in Ralph W. Mathisen and Hagith Sivan (eds) *Shifting Frontiers in Late Antiquity*, Aldershot, pp. 20–30

Dudley, D. (1967), *Urbs Roma*, Aberdeen

Duff, J. Wight, and Arnold M. Duff (trans.) (1934), *Minor Latin Poets*, Cambridge, MA

Duncan-Jones, R.P (1977), Review of *Caput and Colonate, JRS*, 67, pp.202–4

Durry, M. (1938), *Les cohortes prétoriennes*, Paris

Duthoy, R. (1969), *The Taurobolium: its evolution and terminology*, Leiden

Duval, N. (1971), Palais et forteresses en Yougoslavie: recherches nouvelles, *BSNAF*, 115–22

—— (1987), Gamzigrad: un palais de Galére?, *BSNAF*, 61–84

Dyggve, E. (1954), La Région Palatiale de Thessalonique, *Acta Congressus Madvigiani*, Copenhagen, pp. 353–65

Eadie, J.W. (1967), *The Breviarium of Festus: A Critical Edition with Historical Commentary*, London

Enmann, A. (1884), Eine verlorene Geschichte der römischen Kaiser, *Philologus Sband* 4, 335–502

Ensslin, Wilhelm (1928), Maximianus Herculius, *PWRE*, XIV, 2486–516;

—— (1928A), Maximianus Galerius, *PWRE*, XIV, 2516–28;

—— (1942), *Zur Östpolitik des Kaisers Diokletian*, Sitzungsberichte der Bayerischen Akademie der Wissenschaft, München

—— (1948), Valerius Diocletianus, *PWRE*, 7.3 2419–95

—— (1952), Zu Pap. Oxyrhynchus I 43, Recto, *Aegyptus* 32, 163–78

Erim, K.T., and T.Reynolds (1971), The Copy of Diocletian's Edict on Maximum Prices from Aphrodisias in Caria, *JRS*, 61, 99–100

Fayer, Carla (1976), *Il culto della dea Roma : origine e diffusione nell Impero*, Pescara

Feissel, Denis (1995), Les constitutions des Tétrarques connues par l'epigraphie: inventaire et notes critiques *L' Antiquité Tardive*, 3, 33–53;

—— (1996), Deux constitutions tétrarchiques inscrites à *Éphèse, L'Antiquité Tardive*, 4, 273–289

Ferguson, J. (1970), *Religions of the Roman Empire*, London

Fink, R.O., A.S. Hoey and W.F. Snyder (1940), The Feriale Duranum, *YCS*, 7, 1–223

Finley, M.I. (1977), The Emperor Diocletian, in M.I. Finley (ed.), *Aspects of Antiquity: Discoveries and Controversies*, 2nd edn., Harmondsworth, pp. 137–45

Fitz, J. (1966), *Ingenuus et Regalien*, Coll. Lat. 81, Brussels

—— (1976), *La Pannonie sous Gallien*, Coll. Lat. 148, Brussels

Fontenrose, J. (1982), *The Delphic Oracle: Its Responses and Operations with a Catalogue of Responses*, London and California

—— (1998), *Didyma: Apollo's Oracle, Cult, and Companions*, Berkeley, CA

Fowden, G. (1988), Between Pagans and Christians, *JRS*, 78, pp. 173–182

—— (1993), *Empire to Commonwealth: Consequences of Monotheism in Late Antiquity*, Princeton, NJ

Frank, R.I. (1969), *Scholae Palatinae: Palace Guards in the Later Roman Empire*, Papers and Monographs of the American Academy in Rome XXIII

Frankfurter, David N. (1993), *Elijah in Upper Egypt: The Apocalypse of Elijah and Early Egyptian Christianity*, Minneapolis

Frazer, Alfred (1966), The Iconography of the Emperor Maxentius' Buildings in the Via Appia, *Art Bulletin*, 48, 383–92

Freeman, P., J. Bennett, Z.T. Fiema and B. Hoffman (eds) (2002), *Limes XVIII: Proceedings of the XVIIIth International Congress of International Roman Frontiers Studies held in Amman, Jordan* (September 2000), Vol. I, British Archaeological Reports 1084 (I), Oxford, pp. 91–101

Frend, W.H.C. (1965A), *The Early Church*, London

—— (1965B), *Martyrdom and Persecution in the Early Church*, Oxford

Frere, Sheppard (1967), *Britannia: A History of Roman Britain*, 1st edn, London

—— (1981), *Britannia: A History of Roman Britain*, 2nd edn, London

—— (1987), *Britannia: A History of Roman Britain*, 3rd edn, London

Frye, Richard N. (1950), Notes on the Early Sassanid State and Church, *Studi orientalistici in onore di Giorgio Lava della Vida I*, Rome, 314–15

—— (1983), The political history of Iran under the Sassanids, in E. Yarshater (ed.) *The Cambridge History of Iran* (3 vols), Vol. I, Cambridge

—— (1984), *The History of Ancient Iran*, Munich

Galletier, E. (1952), *Panégyriques Latins*, 3 vols, Paris

Garsoian, Nina G. (1989), *The Epic Histories Attributed to P'awstos Buzand (Buzandaran Patmut iwnk): Translation and Commentary*, Cambridge, MA

Gautier, G. (1985), Un nummus inédit de Diocletien Aeternus Augustus frappé à Lyon, *BSFN*, 90, 593 ff.

Gelzer, Matthias (1937 [1963]), Der Urheber der Christenverfolgung von 303, *Kleine Schriften II*, 378–86

Gibbon, E. (1995), *The Decline and Fall of the Roman Empire*, (ed. David Womersley), Vol. I, Harmondsworth

Goffart, Walter (1974),, *Caput and Colonate*, Toronto

Golvin, Jean-Claude and Michel Reddé (1986), Quelques recherches récentes sur l'archéologie militaire Romaine en égypte, *CRAI*, 12, 169–96

Goyau, G. (1893), La 'Numidia Militiana' de la Liste de Vérone, *Mél. D'Arch.*, 13, 251–79

—— (1912), La tétrarchie: sommaire d'une étude d'ensemble, *Études d'histoire juridique offertes à Paul Frederic Girard par ses élèves*, I, Paris, 68–85

Grant, Michael (1974), *The Army of the Caesars*, London

Grant, R.M., (1975), The Religion of Maximin Daia, J. Neusner (ed.) *Christianity, Judaism and other Graeco-Roman Cults: Studies for Morton Smith at Sixty*, Leiden, Vol IV, pp. 157–60

Grégoire, H. (1913), Les chrétiens et l'oracle de Didymes, *Mélanges Holleaux*, Paris, 81–91

—— (1938), About Licinius Fiscal and Religious Policy, *Byzantion*,13, 551–60

—— (1939), La Rotonde de S. Georges à Thessalonique est la Mausolée de Galère, *Byzantion*, 9, 323–4

—— (1939B), Les pierres qui crient, *Byzantion*, 14, 320–21

—— (1964), *Les Persécutions dans l'Empire Romain*, Brussels

Groag, E. (1907), Notizien zur Geschichte kleinasiatischer Familien, *JÖAI*, 10, 282–99

Grosse, Robert (1975), *Römische Militärgeschichte von Gallienus bis zum Beginn der Byzantinischen Themenverfassung*, (reprinted), Arno

Grünewald, T. (1990), *Constantinus Maximus Augustus: Herrschaftspropaganda in der zeitgenössischen überlieferung*, Stuttgart

Gudea, N. (1974), Befestigungen am Banater Donau-Limes aus der Zeit der Tetrarchie, *Actes de IXe Congrès International d'Études sur les Frontières Romains*, Bucharest, Cologne and Vienna, pp. 173–81

Halsberghe, Gaston H. (1972), *The Cult of Sol Invictus*, Leiden

Hammond, Mason (1957), Imperial Elements in the Formula of the Roman Emperors During the First Two and a Half Centuries, *Mem. Am. Acad. Rom.* 25, 19–64

Hanfmann, E. (1975), *From Croesus to Constantine: The Cities of Asia Minor and their Arts in Greek and Roman Times*, Ann Arbor, MI

Hanson, R.P.C. (1974), The Circumstances Attending the Death of the Emperor Flavius Valerius Severus in 306 or 307, *Hermathena* 118, pp. 59–68

Hassall, M.W. (1979), Britain in the *Notitia* in P. Bartholomew and R.A. Goodburn (eds), *Aspects of the Notitia Dignitatum* (*BAR*. Supp. 15)

Heather, Peter (2006), *The Fall of the Roman Empire: A New History of Rome and the Barbarians*, Oxford

Heck, E. (1987), *ME THEOMACHEIN oder: Die Bestrafung des Gottesverächters: Untersuchungen zu Bekampfung und Aneignung römischer religio bei Tertullian, Cyprian und Lantanz*, Frankfurt

Helgeland, John (1978), Roman Army Religion, *ANRW* II, 16.2, 1472–505

—— (1979), Christians and the Roman Army, *ANRW* II, 23.1, 722–834

Helm R. (1956), *Die Chronik des Hieronymus*, Berlin

Hendy, M. (1972), Mint and Fiscal Administration under Diocletian, His Colleagues and His Sucessors AD 305–24, *JRS*, 62, pp. 75–82

Higham, N.J. (1992), *Rome, Britain and the Anglo-Saxons,* London

Hoddinott, R.F. (1975), *Bulgaria in Antiquity*, London

Hopkins, Keith (1983), *Death and Renewal: Sociological Studies in Roman History Vol. 2*, Cambridge

Hopkins, Keith, and Graham Burton (1983), Ambition and Withdrawal: the senatorial aristocracy under the emperors, in Keith Hopkins (ed.) *Death and Renewal: Sociological Studies in Roman History 2*, Cambridge, pp. 120–200

Howe, L.L. (1942), *The Pretorian Prefect from Commodus to Diocletian*, Chicago, IL

Humbach, Helmut, and Prods O. Skjaervø (1983), *The Sassanian Inscription of Paikuli*, 3.1, Wiesbaden

Isaac, B. (1992), *The Limits of Empire: The Roman Army in the East*, (rev. edn), Oxford

—— (1998), *The Near East Under Roman Rule : Selected Papers*, New York

Jacoby, Felix (1923–), *Die Fragmente der greichishen Historiker*, Berlin, and London

Jackson, Robert B. (2002), *At Empire's Edge: Exploring Rome's Egyptian Frontier*, New Haven, CT

Jeffreys, E., M. Jeffreys, R. Scott *et al.* (1986), *The Chronicle of John Malalas: A Translation*, Byzantina Australiensa 4, Melbourne

Johnson, A.C. (1963), *An Economic Survey of Ancient Rome II*, (Roman Egypt), Baltimore, MD

Johnson, A.C., P.R. Coleman-Norton and F.C. Bourne (1961), *Ancient Roman Statutes*, Austin, TX

Johnson, Anne (1983), *Roman Forts of the 1st and 2nd Centuries AD in Britain and the German Provinces*, London

Johnson, Stephen (1976), *The Roman Forts of the Saxon Shore*, London

—— (1980), *Later Roman Britain*, London

Jones, A.H.M. (1937), *The Cities of the Eastern Roman Empire*, Oxford

—— (1940), *The Greek City: From Alexander To Justinian*, Oxford

—— (1948), *Constantine and the Conversion of Europe*, London

—— (1957), Capitatio and Iugatio, *JRS*, 47, 88–94

—— (1964), *The Later Roman Empire 284–602: A Social, Economic and Administrative Survey*, Oxford

—— (1968), *Studies in Roman Government and Law*, Oxford

—— (1971), *The Cities of the Eastern Roman Provinces*, 2nd edn., Oxford

—— (1974), The Cities of the Roman Empire in P.A. Brunt (ed.), *The Roman Economy*, Oxford

—— (1974A), The Date and Value of the Verona List, in P.A. Brunt (ed.), *The Roman Economy*, Oxford, 263–76

Jones, A.H.M., J.R. Martindale and J. Morris (1971), *The Prosopography of the Later Roman Empire*, Vol. I, Cambridge, MA

Judge, E.A. (1980), *The Conversion of Ancient Rome: Ancient Sources of Modern Social Tensions*, Sydney

—— (1983), Christian Innovation and it Contemporary Observers, *History and Historians in Late Antiquity* (B. Croke and A. Emmett, eds.) Sydney, 18–19

Kähler, Heinz (1964), *Das Fünfsäulendenkmal für die Tetrarchen auf dem Forum Romanum*, Cologne

Kaiser, Otto (1975), *Introduction to the Old Testament*, (J. Sturdy, trans.), Oxford

Kalavrezou-Maxeiner, Ioli (1975), The Imperial Chamber at Luxor, *DOP*, 29, 227–51

Kannengiesser, Charles H. (1992), Eusebius of Caesarea, Origenist, in Harold W. Attridge and Gohei Hata (eds.) *Eusebius, Christianity and Judaism*, Leiden, Köln and New York, pp. 435–66

Kennedy, David (2004), *The Roman Army in Jordan*, rev. edn, London

Kennedy, David and H. Falahat (2008), *Castra Legionis VI Ferratae*: a building inscription for the legionary fortress at Udruh near Petra, *JRA*, 21 pp. 150–69

Kennedy, David and Abdul Gader al-Husan (1996), New Milestones from Northern Jordan, *ZPE*, 113, pp. 257–62

Kennedy, D. and H. MacAdam (1985), Latin Inscriptions from the Azraq Oasis, Jordan, *ZPE*, 60, 97–107

Kennedy, M.L. (1952), The Reign of the Emperor Probus, Diss. Mich

Keresztes, P. (1975), The Decian *libelli* and Contemporary Literature, *Latomus* 34, pp. 761–81

Kienast, Dietmar (1996), *Römische Kaisertabelle: Grunzüge einer römischen Kaiserchronologie*, rev. edn, Darmstadt

Kinch, K.-F. (1890), *L' Arc de Triomphe de Salonique*, Paris

King, C.E. (1959), The Maxentian Mints, *NC*, 19, 47–77

Kleiner, Diana E.E. (1992), *Roman Sculpture*, New Haven, CT

Knipfing, J.R. (1923), The Libelli of the Decian Persecution, *HTR*, 16, 345–90

Kolb, Frank (1987), *Diocletian und die erste Tetrarchie: Improvisation oder Experiment in der Organisation monarchischer Herrschaft*, Berlin

—— (1988), L'ideologia tetrarchica e la politica religiosa di Diocleziano, in Giorgio Bonamente and Aldo Nestori (eds) *I Cristiani a l' Impero nel IV Secolo: colloquio sul Cristianesmo nel mondo antico*, Macerata, pp. 17–44

—— (2001), *Herrscherideologie in der Spätantike*, Berlin

—— (2004), *Praesens Deus*: Kaiser und Gott unter der Tetrarchie in Wolfram Brandes, Alexander Demandt, Helmut Leppin, Peter von Möllendorf (eds) *Diokletian und die Tetrarchie: Aspekte einer Zeitenwende*, (Millenium-Studien zu Kultur und Geschichte des ersten Jahrtausends n. Chr, Band I). Berlin and New York, pp. 27–37

Kolendo, J. (1969), Les guerres contre les Carpes pendant les dernières années de la tétrarchie, *Hommages à Marcel Renard* (J. Bibeuw, (ed.)), vol II, Bruxelles, 378–85

König, Ingemar (1974), Die Berufing des Constantius Chlorus und Galerius zu Caesaren: Gedanken zur Entstehung der Ersten Tetrarchie, *Chiron* 4, pp. 567–76

Kornemann, Ernst (1930), *Doppelprinzipat und Reichsteilung in Imperium Romanum*, Leipzig and Berlin

Krautheimer, R. (1980), *Rome: Profile of a City*, Princeton, NJ
—— (1984), *Three Christian Capitals*, Berkeley, CA
Kuhoff, Wolfgang (1983), *Studien zur zivilen senatorschen Laufbahn im 4 Jahrhundert n. Chr.*, Frankfurt-am-Main
Künzl, E. (1983), Zwei silberne Tetrarchenporträts in RGZM und die römischen Kaiserbildnisse, *Jahrbuch des Römisch-Germanischen Zentralmuseums*, Mainz, 30, pp. 381–403
de Labriolle, Pierre (1962), *La Réaction Païenne*, Paris
Lacau, P. (1934), Inscriptions latines du temple de Luxor, *Annales du Service des Antiquités de l'Egypte* 34, 17–46
Lafaurie, J. (1966), Dies Imperii Constantini Augusti: 25 Decembre 307, *Mélanges Piganiol* 2, Paris, 795–806
Lake, Kirsopp (1926), *Eusebius: Ecclesiastical History*, Vol. I (Books 1–5), Cambridge, MA
Lander, James (1984), *Roman Stone Fortifications: Variation and Change from the First Century* AD *to the Fourth*, BAR International Series 206, Oxford
Langyel, A. and G.T.B. Radan (eds) (1980), *The Archaeology of Roman Pannonia*, Budapest and Kentucky
Lallemand, J. (1964), *L'administration civile de l'Egypte 284–382*, Brussels
Lane Fox, Robin (1986), *Pagans and Christians*, London
Laubscher, H.P. (1975), *Der Reliefschmuck des Galeriusbogens in Thessaloniki*, Archaeologische Forschungen I, Berlin
Leadbetter, Bill (1982), A *libellus* of the Decian Persecution, in G.H.R. Horsley (ed.), *New Documents Illustrating Early Christianity*, 2, Sydney, pp. 180–85
—— (1994), Another Emperor Julian and the Accession of Diocletian, *Ancient History Bulletin* 8.2, 54–9
—— (1998), Lactantius and Classical Paideia, in T.W. Hillard, R.A. Kearsley, C.E.V. Nixon and A.M. Nobbs (eds) *Ancient History in a Modern University, Vol. II: Early Christianity, Late Antiquity and Beyond*, Grand Rapids, MI, 245–52
—— (1998A), The Illegitimacy of Constantine and the Birth of the Tetrarchy, in S.N.C. Lieu and Dominic Montserrat (eds) *Constantine: History, Historiography and Legend*, London, pp. 74–85
—— (1998B), Patrimonium Indivisum? The Empire of Diocletian and Maximian, 284–89, *Chiron*, 28 pp. 213–28
—— (2000), From Constantine, to Theodosius, in Philip. Esler (ed.) *The Early Christian World*, London, 2000, pp. 258–92;
—— (2000A), Constantine, in Philip. Esler (ed.) *The Early Christian World*, London, 2000, pp. 1069–85;
—— (2000B), Galerius and the Revolt of the Thebaid, 293/4, *Antichthon* 34, 82–94
—— (2002), Constantine and the Bishop: the Roman Church in the Early Fourth Century, *Journal of Religious History* 26.1, pp. 1–14
—— (2002A), Galerius and the Eastern Frontier, *Limes XVIII. Proceedings of the XVIIIth International Congress of International Roman Frontiers Studies held in Amman, Jordan* (September 2000) Vol. I, edited by P. Freeman, J. Bennett, Z.T. Fiema and B. Hoffman. British Archaeological Reports 1084 (I), Oxford, pp. 85–90
—— (2003), Diocletian and the Purple Mile of Aperlae, *Epigraphica Anatolica* 36, pp. 127–36
—— (2004), Best of Brothers: fraternal imagery in panegyrics on Maximian Herculius, *Classical Philology* 99, pp. 257–66
—— (2004A), Trade, Frontiers and the *Limes Palestinae*, *Studies in the History and Archaeology of Jordan* 8, Amman, pp. 253–6

Lee, A.D. (2000), *Pagans and Christians in Late Antiquity: A Sourcebook*, London

Lenski, Noel (2006), The Reign of Constantine, in Noel Lenski (ed.) *The Cambridge Companion to the Age of Constantine*, Cambridge, pp. 59–90

Lepelley, C. (2004), Une inscription d'*Heraclea Sintica* (Macédoine) récemment découverte, révélant un rescrit de l'empereur Galère restituant ses droits à la cité, *ZPE*, 146, 221–31

Levick, B. (1976), *Tiberius the Politician*, London

Lewin, Ariel (1990), Dall' Eufrate al Mare Rosso: Diocleziano l'esercito e I confini tardoantichi, *Athenaeum*, 68, 141–65

—— (2002), Diocletian, Politics and *Limites* in the Near East, *Limes XVIII. Proceedings of the XVIIIth International Congress of International Roman Frontiers Studies held in Amman, Jordan* (September 2000) Vol I. P. Freeman, J. Bennett, Z.T. Fiema and B. Hoffman (eds) British Archaeological Reports 1084 (I). Oxford, pp. 91–101

Liebeschuetz, J.H.W.G. (1979), *Continuity and Change in Roman Religion*, Oxford

—— (1981), Religion in the Panegyrici Latini, in F. Paschke (ed.) Überlieferungsgeschichtliche Untersuchungen, Texte u. Untersuchungen 125, Berlin, 389–98

Lietzmann, H. (1953), *From Constantine to Julian: A History of the Church, Vol. III* (B.T. Woolf, trans.), 2nd edn, London

Lightfoot, C.S. (1981), The Eastern Frontier of the Roman Empire with Special Reference to the Reign of Constantius II, Oxford D. Phil. Thesis

Littmann, E., D. Magie and D.R.Stuart (1921–2), *Syria III: Greek and Latin Inscriptions, Publications of the Princeton University Archaeological Expedition to Syria in 1904–5 and 1909: III: Greek and Latin Inscriptions*, Leiden

Loi, V. (1965), I valori etici e politici della romanità negli scrini di Lattanzio, Opposti attegiamenti di polemica e di adesione, *Salesianum* 27, 65–133

Luttwak, Edward N. (1976), *The Grand Strategy of the Roman Empire*, Baltimore, MD

MacAdam, H.I. (1989), Epigraphy and the Notitia Dignitatum (Oriens 37), in D. French and C.S. Lightfoot (eds) *The Eastern Frontier of the Roman Empire*, BAR International Series 553, Oxford, pp. 295–309

MacCormack, Sabine (1975), Latin Prose Panegyrics, in T.A. Dorey (ed.) *Empire and Aftermath: Silver Latin II*, London and Boston, MA, pp. 143–205

—— (1981), *Art and Ceremony in Late Antiquity*, Berkeley, CA

MacDermot, B.C. (1954), Roman Emperors in Sassanian Reliefs, *JRS*, 44, 76–80

Mackay, Christopher S. (1999), Lactantius and the Succession to Diocletian, *Classical Philology* 94, pp. 198–209

MacMullen, Ramsay (1966), *Enemies of the Roman Order: Treason, Unrest and Alienation in the Empire*, Cambridge, MA

—— (1969), *Constantine*, London

—— (1981), *Paganism in the Roman Empire*, New Haven, CT

McNally, Sheila (1989), Introduction: The State of Scholarship, in Sheila McNally, Jerko Marasovic and Tomislav Marasovic (eds) *Diocletian's Palace: American–Yugoslav Joint Excavations*, Minneapolis, MN, pp. 3–43

—— (1994), Joint American–Croatian Excavations in Split, 1965–1974, *L' Antiquité Tardive* 2, 107–22

Magie, D. (1921), *The Scriptores Historiae Augustae: With an English Translation*, 3 vols, Cambridge, MA

Malaise, Michel (1972), *Les conditions de pénétration et de diffusion des cultes Égyptiennes en Italie*, Leiden

Mannell, Joanne (1995), The monopteroi in the west precinct of Diocletian's palace at Split, *JRA*, 8, pp. 235–44

Marasovic, J. and T. Marasovic (1994), Le ricerche nel Palazzo di Diocletiano a Split negli ultimi 30 anni (1964–1994), *L'Antiquité Tardive* 2, 89–106;

Marasovic, T. (1982), *Diocletian's Palace* (S. Wild-Bicanic, trans.), Belgrade

Mariq, A. (1958), Res Gestae Divi Saporis, *Syria* 35, pp. 295–360

Mason, Hugh J. (1974), *Greek Terms for Roman Institutions*, Toronto

Maspero, Gaston (1885), Fouilles de Copte, *Bulletin de l'Institut Egyptien*, 2nd ser. VI

Matthews, J.F. (1984), Tax Law of Palmyra: evidence for economic history in a city of the Roman east, *JRS* 74, 157–80

—— (2000), *Laying Down the Law: A Study of the Theodosian Code*, New Haven, CT

Mattingly, Harold (1939), The Imperial Recovery, in S.A. Cook, F.E. Adcock, M.P. Charlesworth and N.H. Baynes (eds) *The Cambridge Ancient History Vol XII: Imperial Crisis and Recovery, AD 193–324*, Cambridge, Chapter IX, 297–351

—— (1952), Iovius and Herculius, *HTR* 45, 131–4

Mattingly, Harold and Edward A. Sydenham (1933), *Roman Imperial Coinage*, Vol. II, London

Maurice, J. (1902), Mémoire sur la révolte d'Alexandre en Afrique, *MSNAF*, 61, 1–22

—— (1908), *Numismatique Constantinienne: iconographie et chronologie description historique des émissions monétaires*, Paris

Mazzini, G. (1956), *Monete Imperiali Romane*, IV Milan

Meloni, Piero (1948), *Il Regno di Caro Numeriano e Carino*, Cagliari

Mendelssohn, L. (1887), *Zosimus: Historia Nova*, Leipzig

Meredith, David (1952), The Roman Remains in the Eastern Desert of Egypt, *JEA* 38, 94–111

—— (1953), Eastern Desert of Egypt: notes on inscriptions, *Chron. d'Egypte* 28, 126–141

Meyer, Carol (1991), *Glass from Quseir al-Qadim and the Indian Ocean Trade*, Oriental Institute of the University of Chicago Studies in Ancient Oriental Civilization no. 53, 1991

Meyer, H. (1980), Die Frieszyklen am sogennanten Triumphbogen des Galerius in Thessaloniki, *JDAI*, 95, 374–444

Mierow, C.C. (1915), *The Gothic History of Jordanes in English Version: With an Introduction and Commentary*, Princeton, NJ

Milburn, R.A. (1952), *Early Christian Interpretations of History*, London

Millar, F. (1969), P. Herennius Dexippus: the Greek World and the Third Century Invasions, *JRS*, 59, 12–29

—— (1977), *The Emperor in the Roman World*, London

—— (1992), *The Emperor in the Roman World*, 2nd edn, London,

—— (1993), *The Roman Near East 31 BC – AD 337*, Cambridge, MA

Miller, Harry David (1996), Frontier Societies and the Transition Between Late Antiquity and the Middle Ages, in Ralph W. Mathiesen and Hagith Sivan (eds) *Shifting Frontiers in Late Antiquity*, Aldershot, pp. 158–74

Millett, Martin (1990), *The Romanization of Britain: An Essay in Interpretation*, Cambridge

Mirkovic, Miroslava (1971), Sirmium: its History from the First Century AD to 582 AD in V. Popovic (ed.), *Sirmium: Archaeological Investigations in Syrmian Pannonia I*, Belgrade, pp. 19–32

Mispoulet, J.B. (1908), Chronologie de Maximien Hercule, *CRAI*, 431–65

Mitchell, S.N. (1988), Maximinus and the Christians in 312: a new Latin Inscription, *JRS*, 78, 103–24

Mitrev, G. (2003), Civitas Heracleotarum: Heraclea Sintica or the Ancient City at the Village of Rupite (Bulgaria), *ZPE*, 145, 263–72

Mócsy, A. (1974), *Pannonia and Upper Moesia* (S. Frere, trans.), London

—— (1974A), Ein spätantiker Festungstyp am linken Donauer, *Roman Frontier Studies: Eighth International Conference of Limesforschung*, Cardiff, pp. 191–96

Molthagen, J. (1975), *Der Römische Staat und die Christen im zweiten und dritten Jahrhundert*, 2nd edn, Göttingen

Mommsen, T. (ed.) (1892), *Chronica Minora, Monumenta Germaniae Historicae: Auctores Antiquissimi*, Vols IX, XI, XIII, Berlin

Monéeaux, Paul (1905), Études critiques sur Lactance, *R. Ph.*, 29, pp. 104–39

Moreau, J. (1954), *Lactance: de la Mort des Persécuteurs*, 2 vols Sources Chrétiennes, 39, Paris

—— (1968), *Excerpta Valesiana* (rev. V. Velkov), Berlin

Morris, John (1965), Prosopography of the Later Roman Empire, *Klio* 46, 361–365

Mosshammer, Alden A. (1979), *The Chronicle of Eusebius and Greek Chronographic Tradition*, London and Princeton, NJ

Müller, C. (1849 [1975]), *Fragmenta Historicorum Graecorum*, Vol III, Frankfurt-am-Main

Musurillo, H. (1972), *Acts of the Christian Martyrs*, Oxford

Mynors, R.A.B. (1964), *Panegyrici Latini*, Oxford

Nicholson, O.P. (1981), Lactantius: Power and Politics in the Age of Constantine the Great, Oxford D. Phil. diss

—— (1984), The Wild Man of the Tetrarchy: a divine companion for the Emperor Galerius, *Byzantion* 54, 253–75

—— (1984B), Hercules at the Milvian Bridge: Lactantius, *Divine Institutes*, I, 21, 6–9, *Latomus* 53, 133–42

Niksic, Goran (2004), The Restoration of Diocletian's palace – Mausoleum, Temple and Porta Aurea (with the analysis of the original architectural design), in Demant, A., Goltz, A., Schlange-Schüningen, H. (eds) *Diokletian und die Tetrarchie: Aspekte einer Zeitenwende*, (*Millenium-Studien zu Kultur und Geschichte des ersten Jahrtausends n. Chr*) Berlin and New York, pp. 163–5

Nixon, C.E.V. (1981), The Panegyric of 307 and Maximian's visits to Rome, *Phoenix* 35, 70–76

—— (1987), *Pacatus: Panegyric to the Emperor Theodosius*, Liverpool

—— (1990), The Use of the Past by the Gallic Panegyrists in G.W. Clarke *et al.* (eds) *Reading the Past in Late Antiquity*, Canberra, pp. 1–36

—— (1993), *Constantinus Oriens Imperator*: propaganda and panegyric. On reading Panegyric 7 (307), *Historia* 42, 229–42

Nixon, C.E.V., and Barbara Saylor Rodgers (1994), *In Praise of Later Roman Emperors: The Panegyrici Latini: Introduction, Translation and Historical Commentary*, Berkeley, Los Angeles and Oxford

Nock, A.D. (1933), *Conversion*, Oxford

—— (1947), The Emperor's divine *Comes*, *JRS*, 37, pp. 102–16

Odahl, Charles Matson (2004), *Constantine and the Christian Empire*, London

Oenbrink, Walter (2004), Maxentius als *conservator urbis suae*, in Boschung, Dietrich and Eck, Werner, *Die Tetrarchie ein neues Regierungssystem und seine mediale Präsentation*, Wiesbaden, pp. 169–204

Ogilvie, R.M. (1978), *The Library of Lactantius*, Oxford

L'Orange, H.P. (1938), Ein tetrarchisches Ehrendenkmal auf dem Forum Romanum, *MDAI Röm. Ab.* 53, 1–34

—— (1965), *Art Forms and Civic Life in the Later Roman Empire*, Princeton

—— (1985), *The Roman Empire: Art Forms and Civic Life*, New York

Oulton, J.E.L. (1932), *Eusebius: Ecclesiastical History*, Vol. II (Books 6–10), Cambridge, MA

Palanque, J.-R. (1933), *Essai sur la Préfecture du Prétoire du bas-Empire*, Paris

—— (1938), Chronologie Constantinienne, *REA*, 40, 241–50

—— (1966), Sur la date du *de mortibus persecutorum*, *Mélanges offerts à Jerome Carcopino*, Paris, 711–16

Parker, H.M.D. (1933), The Legions of Diocletian and Constantine, *JRS*, 23, 175–90

—— (1935), *A History of the Roman World*, (1st edn) London, Methuen

Parker, S. Thomas (1986), *Romans and Saracens: A History of the Arabian Frontier*, American Schools of Oriental Research dissertation series, Winona Lake

—— (1986A), A tetrarchic milestone from Roman Arabia, *ZPE*, 62, pp. 256–8

—— (2002), The Roman Frontier in Jordan: an overview, in P. Freeman, J. Bennett, Z.T. Fiema and B. Hoffman (eds) *Limes XVIII. Proceedings of the XVIIIth International Congress of International Roman Frontiers Studies held in Amman, Jordan* (September 2000) Vol I. BAR International Series 1084, Oxford, pp. 77–84

Paschoud, F. (1971), *Zosime: Histoire Nouvelle*, Vol. I, Paris

—— (1994), Nicomaque Flavien et la Connexion Byzantine (Pierre le Patrice et Zonaras): à propos du livre récent de Bruno Bleckmann, *L'Antiquité Tardive*, 2, pp. 71–82

Pasqualini, A. (1979), *Massimiano Herculius: per un interpretazione della figura e dell' opera*, Rome

Passuello, F. and M.G. Dissegna (1979), *I Mausolei Imperiali Romani Templi del Sole. La Rotunda di Thessaloniki*, Firenze

Peachin, Michael (1990), *Roman Imperial Titulature and Chronology AD 235–285*, Amsterdam

Peacock, D.P.S. (1992), *Rome in the Desert: A Symbol of Power*, Southampton

Petrie, Sir Flinders (1896), *Coptos*, London

Pflaum, H.G. (1962/5), L'alliance entre Constantin et L. Domitius Alexander, *Bulletin d'archéologie Algérienne*, I, 159–61

—— (1966/7), P. Licinius Gallienus Nobilissimus Caesar et M. Aurelius Numerianus Nobilissimus Caesar Aug.: à la lumiére de deux nouveaux milliares d'Oum el Bouaghi, *BAA*, 2, pp. 175–85

Pharr, C. (1951), *The Theodosian Code and Novels and the Sirmondian Constitutions: A Translation with Commentary, Glossary and Bibliography*, Princeton, NJ

Pichlmayr, Fr. (1970), *Sexti Aurelii Victoris Liber de Caesaribus*, Leipzig

Pichon, R. (1901), *Lactance: Étude sur le mouvement philosophique et religieux sous la règne de Constantin*, Paris

—— (1906), *Les derniers écrivains profanes*, Paris

Picozzi, V., (1976), Una compagna di Licinio contra Massenzio nel 310 non attesta dalle fonte litteraria, *NAC*, 5, 267–75

Piganiol, Henri (1932), *L'Empereur Constantin*, Paris

Pinder, M. (1841), *Ioannis Zonarae: Annales*, 2 vols, CSHB, Bonn

Platner, Samuel Ball, and Thomas Ashby (1926), *A Topographical Dictionary of Ancient Rome*, Oxford

Pond, E.A. (1970), Inscriptional Evidence for the Illyrian Emperors: Claudius Gothicus through Carinus, AD 268–284, Diss. Mich

Pond Rothmann, M. (1975), The panel of the emperors enthroned on the Arch of Galerius, *Études Byzantines*, 21, 19–40

—— (1977), The thematic organisation of the panel reliefs on the Arch of Galerius, *AJA*, 81, 427–455

Poole, R.S. (1892), *Greek Coins in the British Museum*, London

Popovic, V. (1971), *Sirmium I*, Belgrade

Popovic, V. and E.L. Ochsenschlager (1976), Der spätkaiserliche Hippodrom in Sirmium, *Germania*, 54, 156–181

Portmann, Werner (1990), Zu den Motiven der diokletianischen Christenverfolgung, *Historia*, 39, 212–248

Potter, David (1990), *Prophecy and History in the Crisis of the Roman Empire: A Historical Commentary on the Thirteenth Sibylline Oracle*, Oxford

—— (2004), *The Roman Empire at Bay: AD 180–395*, London and New York

Preuss, Theodor (1869), *Kaiser Diocletian und seine Zeit*, Leipzig

Price, Simon (1984), *Rituals and Power: the Roman Imperial Cult in Asia Minor*, Cambridge

Ragona, Antonio (1962), *Il Proprietario della Villa Romana di Piazza Armerina*, Caltagirone, 1962

Ramsay, W. (1890), *The Historical Geography of Asia Minor*, London

—— (1895), *The Cities and Bishoprics of Phrygia, Vol. I*, Oxford

Raschke, Manfred G. (1978), New Studies in Roman Commerce with the East, *ANRW* II, 9.2., Berlin and New York, 604–1361

Rea, J., R.P. Salomon and K.A. Worp (1985), A Ration Warrant for an *adiutor memoriae*, *YCS*, 28, 101–15

Rees, Roger (1993), Images and Image: a Re-Examination of Tetrarchic Iconography, *Greece and Rome* 40, 181–99

—— (2002), *Layers of Loyalty in Latin Panegyric AD 289–307*, Oxford

—— (2003), Talking to the Tetrarchs: the dynamics of vocative address, in Carl Deroux (ed.) *Studies in Roman Literature and History XI*, Coll. Lat. 272, Bruxelles, pp. 447–92

—— (2004), *Diocletian and the Tetrarchy*, Edinburgh

—— (2005), The Emperors' New Names: Diocletian Iovius and Maximian Herculius, in L. Rawlings and H. Bowden (eds) *Herakles/Hercules in the Ancient World*, Swansea and London

Reinach, A. (1911), *Catalogue des Antiquités Égyptiennes de Koptos*, Paris

Reynolds, P.K.B. (1926), *The Vigiles of Imperial Rome*, Oxford

Riccardi, Lee Ann (2000), Uncanonical Imperial Portraits in the Eastern Roman Provinces: The Case of the Kanellopoulos Emperor *Hesperia*, Vol. 69, pp. 105–32

Richardson, E.C. (1890), The Life of Constantine by Eusebius, together with the Oration of Constantine to the Assembly of the Saints and the Oration of Eusebius in Praise of Constantine, in P. Schaff and H. Wace (eds), *A Select Library of the Nicene and Post-Nicene Fathers of the Christian Church*, Vol. I, Grand Rapids, rep. 1979, pp. 473–610

Richmond, I.A. (1927), The Relation of the Praetorian Camp to Aurelian's Walls of Rome, *PBSR*, 10

Rickman, G. (1980), *The Corn Supply of Ancient Rome*, Oxford

Ridley, R.T. (1982), *Zosimus*, Byzantina Australiensia 2, Melbourne

Ritter, Moriz (1862), *de Diocletiano novarum in re publica institutionum auctore*, Bonn

Rohrbacher, David (2002), *The Historians of Late Antiquity*, London and New York

Rolfe J.C. (1950), *Ammianus Marcellinus with an English Translation*, 3 vols, rev. edn, Cambridge, MA

Roll, Israel (1989), A Latin Inscription from Yotvata, *IEJ*, 39. 239–99

Roller, Karl (1927), *Die Kaisergeschichte in Laktanz "De mortibus persecutorum"*, Leipzig

Rostovzeff, M. (1957), *A Social and Economic History of the Roman Empire*, 2nd edn, Oxford

Rougé, J. (1964), L'incendie de Rome en 64 et l'incendie de Nicomédie en 303, *Mélanges d'histoire ancienne offerts à William Seston*, Paris, 433–41

Rousselle, A. (1976), La chronologie de Maximien Hercule et le mythe de la Tétrarchie, *Dial. d'Hist. Anc.*, 2, 445–467

Rubin, Ze'ev (1995), Mass Movements in Late Antiquity, in I. Malkin and Z. W. Rubinsohn (eds.) *Leaders and Masses in the Roman World: Studies in Honour of Zvi Yavetz*, Leiden, 129–88

de Ste Croix, G.E.M. (1954), Aspects of the Great Persecution, *HTR*, 47, pp. 75–109

—— (1982), *The Class Struggle in the Ancient Greek World from the Archaic Age to the Arab Conquests*, 2nd edn, London

Salway, Peter (1981), *Roman Britain*, 2nd edn, Oxford

Saunders, Randall T. (1992), Aurelian's Two Iuthungian Wars, *Historia* 41, 311–27

Schiller, Hermann (1887), *Geschichte der Römischen Kaiserzeit*, zweiter Band, Gotha von Schönebeck, H. (1937), Die zyklische Ordnung der Triumphalreliefs am Galeriusbogen in Saloniki, *BZ*, 3, 361–71

Schwartz, J. (1974), Autour de l'humiliation de Galére *Mélanges d'histoire ancienne offerts à William Seston*, Paris, 463–6

—— (1975), *L. Domitius Domitianus: Étude numismatique et papyrologique*, Brussels

Scott, S.P. (1932), *Corpus Iuris Civilis*, Vols. 12–17, Cincinnati, OH

Scullard, H.H. (1981), *Festivals and Ceremonies of the Roman Republic*, London

Seager, R. (1972), *Tiberius*, London

Seeck, Otto (1897), *Geschichte des Untergangs der Antiken Welt erster Band*, Berlin

—— (1898), *Geschichte des Untergangs der Antiken Welt Band I Anhang*, Berlin

—— (1919), *Regesten der Kaiser und Päpste für die Jahre 311 bis 476 n. Chr.: Vorarbeit zu einer Prosopographie der christlichen Kaiserzeit*, Stuttgart

Seston, William (1937), Recherches sur la chronologie du règne de Constantin le Grand, *REA* 39, 197–218

—— (1940), L'humiliation de Galére *REA* 42, 515–19

—— (1946), *Dioclétien et la Tétrarchie*, Paris

Shaw, I., J. Bunbury and R. Jameson (1999), Emerald mining in Roman and Byzantine Egypt, *JRA*, 12, 203–15

Shiel, N. (1978), *The Episode of Carausius and Allectus*, BAR, Oxford

Sidebotham, S.E. (1989), Ports of the Red Sea and the Arabia–India Trade, in D.H. French and C.S. Lightfoot (eds.) *The Eastern Frontier of the Roman Empire: Proceedings of a Colloquium held at Ankara in September 1988*, British Institute of Archaeology at Ankara Monograph No. 11, BAR International Series 553 (ii), Part ii, pp. 385–513

—— (1991), A *limes* in the eastern desert of Egypt: myth or reality?, in Valerie A. Maxfield and Michael J. Dobson (eds) *Roman Frontier Studies 1989: Proceedings of the XVth International Congress of Roman Frontier Studies*, Exeter, 494–8

Sidebotham, Steven and Willeke Wendrich (1996), *Berenike 95: Preliminary Report of the Excavations at Berenike (Egyptian Red Sea Coast) and the Survey of the Eastern Desert*, Leiden

Sidebotham, Steven E., Martin Hense and Henrik M. Nouwens (2008), *The Red Land: the Illustrated Archaeology of Egypt's Eastern Desert*, Cairo and New York

Sidebotham, Steven E., John A. Riley, Hany A. Hamroush and Hala Barakat (1989), Fieldwork on the Red Sea Coast: the 1987 Season, *JARCE*, 26, 127–66, pp. 133–46

Sidebotham, Steven E., Ronald E. Zitterkopf and John A. Riley (1991), Survey of the Abu Sha'ar–Nile Road, *AJA*, 95, 571–622

Sinnigen, W.G. (1957), *The Officium of the Urban Prefecture During the Later Roman Empire*, Papers and Monographs of the American Academy in Rome, XII

Skeat, T.C. (1964), *Papyri from Panopolis*, Michigan

Smith, John Holland (1971), *Constantine the Great*, London

—— (1976), *The Death of Classical Paganism*, London

Smith, R.E. (1972), The Regnal and Tribunician Dates of Maximian Herculius, *Latomus* 31, 1058–71

Smith, R.R.R. (1997), The Public Image of Licinius I: Portrait Sculpture and Imperial Ideology in the Early Fourth Century, *JRS*, 87, pp. 170–202

Sordi, Marta (1986), *The Christians and the Roman Empire* (A. Bedini, trans.), London

Sotgiu, G. (1964), Un millario sardo di L. Domitius Alexander e l'ampiezza della sua rivolta, *Archivo Storico Sardo*, 39, 149–58

Speidel, Michael (1975), The Rise of Ethnic Units in the Roman Imperial Army, *ANRW* II. 3, 202–31

—— (1978), *The Religion of Jupiter Dolichenus in the Roman Army*, Leiden

—— (1978b), The Roman Army in Arabia, *ANRW* II.8, p. 699

—— (1987), The Roman Road to Dumata (Jawf in Saudi Arabia) and the Roman Frontier Strategy of *Praetensione Colligare*, *Historia* 36, pp. 213–21

—— (1992) Becoming a Centurion in Africa: brave deeds and the support of the troops as promotion criteria in *Roman Army Studies II*, Stuttgart, pp. 124–8

Speiser, J.-M. (1984), *Thessalonique et ses monuments du IVe au VIe siècle: contribution à l'étude d'une ville paléochrétienne*, Paris

Sprengling, M. (1953), *Third-Century Iran*, Chicago, IL

Srejovic, Dragoslav (1983), *Gamzigrad: an Imperial Palace of Late Classical Times*, Belgrade

——, (1992/3), A Porphyry Head of a Tetrarch from Romuliana, (Gamzigrad) (V. Kostic, trans.), *Starinar*, 43/44, p. 41–7

Srejovic, Dragoslav and Cedomir Vasic (1994), Emperor Galerius's buildings in Romuliana (Gamzigrad, eastern Serbia) *L'Antiquité Tardive*, 2, pp. 123–41

—— (1994A), *Imperial Mausolea and Consecration Memorials in Felix Romuliana* (Gamzigrad, East Serbia), Belgrade

Srejovic, Dragoslav, A. Lalovic and D. Jankovic (1978), Two late Roman Temples at Gamzigrad, *Archaeologica Iugoslavica*, 19, 54–63

Srejovic, D., A. Lalovic and D. Jankovic (1980), Gamzigrad, *Starinar*, 31, 65–70, 78–9

Srejovic, D., D. Jankovic, A. Lalovic and V. Jovic (1983), *Gamzigrad: An Imperial Palace of the Late Classical Times*, Belgrade

Stade, Kurt (1926), *Der Politiker Diokletian und die letzte groёe Christenverfolgung*, Frankfurt-am-Main

Stein, A. (1925), Zu Lukans Alexandros, *Strena Buliciana. Commentationes gratulatoriae in honore F. Bulic,* Zagreb

Stein, Ernst (1928), *Vom Römischen zum Byzantinischen Staate (284–476 n.Chr.)*, Wien

—— (1957), *Histoire du bas-Empire*, J.R. Palanque (French trans.), Paris,

Stevenson, J. (1957), The Life and Literary Activity of Lactantius *Stud. Pat.* I (= *Texte und Untersuchungen* 63), pp. 661–77

Stoneman, Richard (1992), *Palmyra and its Empire: Zenobia's revolt against Rome*, Ann Arbor, MI

Straub, J. (1939), *Vom Herrscherideal in der Spätantike*, Stuttgart

Sutherland, C.H.V. and R.A.G. Carson (1967), *Roman Imperial Coinage*, Vol. VI, London

Sydenham, E. A. (1934), The Vicissitudes of Maximian after his Abdication, *NC* 14, 141–165

Syme, Ronald (1939), *The Roman Revolution*, Oxford

—— (1958), *Tacitus* 2 vols, Oxford

—— (1971), *Emperors and Biography: Studies in the Historia Augusta*, Oxford

—— (1971A), The Ancestry of Constantine, *BHAC*, 11, pp. 237–53

Talbert, R.J.A. (1984), *The Senate of Imperial Rome*, Princeton, NJ

Temporini, H. (ed.) (1972), *Aufstieg und Niedergang der Romischen Welt*, Stuttgart

Tengström, Emin (1974), *Bread for the People: Studies of the Corn Supply of Rome during the Late Empire*, Acta Instituti Romani Svecias XII, Stockholm

Tepper, Yoram (2002), Lajjun-Legio in Israel: Results of a survey in and around the military camp area, in *Limes XVIII. Proceedings of the XVIIIth International Congress of International Roman Frontiers Studies held in Amman, Jordan.* (September 2000) Vol. I. P. Freeman, J. Bennett, Z.T. Fiema and B. Hoffman (eds), British Archaeological Reports 1084 (I), Oxford, pp. 231–42

Thiel, Wolfgang (2006), Die Pompeius-Säule in Alexandria und die Vier-Saulen-Monumente ägyptens. Überlegung zur tetrarchischen Repräsentationskultur in Nordafrika in Boschung and Eck, pp. 249–322

Thomas, G.S.R. (1969), La solution persane et le lutte entre Galère et Dioclétien, *Latomus*, 28, pp. 658–60

—— (1973), L'Abdication de Dioclétien, *Byzantion* 43, 229–47

Thomas, J.D. (1971), On dating by the regnal years of Diocletian, Maximian and the Caesars, *Chron. d'Egypte* 46, 173–9

—— (1976), The date of the Revolt of Domitius Domitianus, *ZPE*, 22, 253–79

—— (1978), Dekaprotoi and Epigraphai, *BASP*, 15, 1978, 133–45

Thompson, E.A. (1982), *Romans and Barbarians: the Decline of the Western Empire*, Madison, WI

—— (1974), Peasant Revolts in Gaul in M.I. Finley (ed.), *Studies in Ancient Society*, London and Boston, MA, 304–21

Thomsen, R. (1966), *The Italic Regions*, Rome, 1966

Todd, Malcolm (1978), Villas and Romano-British Society, in Malcolm Todd (ed.), *Studies in the Romano-British Villa*, Leicester, 1978, 197–208

—— (1978b), *The Walls of Rome*, London

—— (1981), *Roman Britain 55 BC – AD 400*, London

Tomlin, Roger (1998), Christianity and the Late Roman Army in Samuel N.C. Lieu and Dominic Montserrat (eds), *Constantine: History, Historiography and Legend*, London, pp. 21–51

Trompf, G.W. (1983), The Logic of Retribution in Eusebius of Caesarea, in B. Croke and A.M. Emmett (eds), *History and Historians in Late Antiquity*, Sydney, pp. 132–46

—— (2000), *Early Christian Historiography: Narratives of Retributive Justice*. London and New York

Vandorpe, K. (1995), City of many a gate: harbour for many a rebel. Historical and topographical outline of Greco-Roman Thebes in S.P. Vleeming (ed.) *Hundred-Gated Thebes: Acts of a Colloquium on Thebes and the Theban Area in the Greco-Roman Period*, Leiden, pp. 203–39

Velenis, G., (1979), Architektonische Probleme des Galeriusbogens in Thessaloniki, *AA*, 249–63

Velkov, V. (1977), *Cities in Thrace and Dacia in Late Antiquity*, Amsterdam

—— (1980), La construction en Thrace à l'époque du bas-Empire, in idem (ed.), *Roman Cities in Bulgaria: Collected Studies*, Amsterdam, 263–77

Vermaseren, M.J. (1960), *Corpus Inscriptionum et Monumentorum Religionis Mithraicae* (2 vols), The Hague

—— (1963), *Mithras: the Secret God* (Therese and Vincent Megaw trans.), London

—— (1977), *Cybele and Atthis: the Myth and the Cult* (M.H. Lammers, trans.), London

Vermeule, C.C. (1968), *Roman Imperial Art in Greece and Asia Minor*, Cambridge, MA

Vickers, M. (1972), Observations on the Octagon at Thessaloniki, *JRS*, 62, 25–32

Vidman, Ladislav (1969), *Sylloge Inscriptionum Religionis Isiacae et Sarapiacae*, Berlin

—— (1970), *Isis und Serapis bei den Greichen und Römern*, Berlin

Vollmer, Dankward (1991), Tetrarchie: Bemerkungen zum Gebrauch eines antiken und modernen Begriffes, *Hermes* 119, 435–449

Wacher, John (1974), *The Towns of Roman Britain*, London

Walker, D.R. (1978), *The Metrology of the Roman Silver Coinage* Vol. III, BAR Supp. Ser. 40, Oxford

Wareth, U. and Pierre Zignani (1992), Nag al-Hagar. A Fortress with a Palace of the Late Roman Empire. Second Preliminary Report, *BIFAO*, 92, 185–210

Warmington, B.H. (1974), Aspects of Constantinian Propaganda in the *Panegyrici Latini*, *TAPA*, 104, pp. 371–384

Warmington, E.H. (1974), *The Commerce between the Roman Empire and India*, 2nd edn, Oxford

Watson, Alaric (1999), *Aurelian and the Third Century*, London

Webb, P.H. (1907), The Reign and Coinage of Carausius, *NC* 7, 1–88

—— (1927), *Roman Imperial Coinage*, Vol. V, Part I, London

—— (1933), *Roman Imperial Coinage*, Vol. V, Part II, London

Weill, M.R. (1911), Koptos, *Annales du Service* XI, 97–141

Wheeler, Everett L. (1993), Methodological Limits and the Mirage of Roman Strategy, *Journal of Military History*, 57, pp. 7–41, 215–240

Whittaker, C.R. (1983), Filosofiana: the villa of Piazza Armerina reconsidered, *Opus* 2, 1983, 553–7

Wightman, E.M. (1971), *Roman Trier and the Treviri*, New York

—— (1978), Peasants and Potentates in Roman Gaul, *American Journal of Archaeology*, 3, 97–112

—— (1985), *Gallia Belgica*, London

Wilcken, Robert L. (1984), *The Christians as the Romans Saw Them*, New Haven, CT

Wilkes, J.J. (1986), *Diocletian's Palace, Split: Residence of a Retired Roman Emperor*, Dept. of Ancient History and Archaeology Occasional Publications No. 2, University of Sheffield

Williams, Stephen (1985), *Diocletian and the Roman Recovery*, London

Wilson, R.J.A. (1983), *Piazza Armerina*, London

Winter, E. (1989), On the Regulation of the Eastern Frontier of the Roman Empire in 298, in D.H. French and C.S. Lightfoot (eds), *The Eastern Frontier of the Roman Empire: Proceedings of a Colloquium held in Ankara in September 1988, Part ii*, BAR International Series 553 ii, Oxford, 1989, pp. 555–89

Wlosok, Antonie (1989), L. Caecilius Firmianus: Das Werk, 5. De mortibus persecutorum, in Reinhart Herzog *et. al.* (eds), *Handbuch der lateinischen Literatur der Antike*, Vol. V, Munich, 1989, I 570, 375–404

Wolfram, H. (1988), *History of the Goths* (Thomas J. Dunlap, trans.), Berkeley CA

Wood, Ian (2006), The Crocus Conundrum, in Elizabeth Hartley, Jane Hawkes Martin Henig and Frances Mee, *Constantine the Great: York's Roman Emperor*, York, pp. 77–84

Wright, W.C. (1921), *Philostratus and Eunapius: The Lives of the Sophists*, Cambridge, MA

Zitterkopf, R. and S. Sidebotham (1989), Stations and Towers on the Quseir–Nile Road, *JEA*, 75, 155–89

INDEX